MW01000954

Power Pressure Cooker XL Top

500 Recipes

Written by: Jamie Stewart

Copyright © 2017

Warning-Disclaimer

The purpose of this book is to educate and entertain. The author or publisher does not guarantee that anyone following the techniques, directions, tips, ideas, or strategies will achieve the same results. The author and publisher shall have neither liability or responsibility to anyone with respect to any loss or damage caused, or alleged to be caused, directly or indirectly by the information contained in this book.

CONTENTS

INTRODUCTION

If you're thinking about making the leap from good to great, consider trying the Power Pressure Cooker XL. This revolutionary kitchen gadget is a highly efficient, modern-day invention that performs various cooking functions such as steaming, rice cooking, slow cooking, sautéing, and so forth. The Power Pressure Cooker XL utilizes the pressure of super-heated steam to cook your favorite meals.

The growing global awareness of healthy eating encourages manufacturers to produce more efficient kitchen devices. We are the generation that is constantly on the hunt for new ideas and intelligent solutions to improve our health, save time and energy. The secret lies in a simple approach – we should connect two major points: a healthy food and the right cooking method. In addition to providing an extremely tasty food, pressure cooking can greatly improve your health. So, grab your Power pressure cooker XL and get ready to explore the magnificent world of quick, easy and healthy cooking!

Before You Buy that Power Pressure Cooker XL

The pressure cooker is a fairly simple kitchen tool. Really! It looks like any other modernly designed stove pot, except its lid and a digital display that make it even easier to use. The liquid inside the cooker rapidly creates steam, and consequently, the pressure increases because it's trapped inside. It takes about 20 minutes for your cooker to come to pressure. These higher temperatures help your food to cook faster than conventional stovetop methods, so you can prepare your favorite recipes 10 times as fast!

How does it work in practice? Simply throw your ingredients into the inner pot; lock the lid and set the time! The power pressure cooker XL actually uses electrical power to create its heat and pressure so it can cook your food efficiently and perfectly. It really is as simple as that!

This programmable kitchen device has eight built-in programs, an automatic KEEP/WARM/CANCEL mode, COOK TIME SELECTOR and DELAY TIME KEY which allows you to set your cooker to start cooking later. The Power Pressure Cooker XL preset buttons:

SOUP/STEW – a function specifically for cooking budget-friendly meals like stews, soups, chowders, sauces, etc.
SLOW COOK – an excellent choice for everyone who wants a meal ready when they arrive home.
RICE/RISOTTO – this program is designed to boil or steam your rice and grains.
BEANS/LENTILS – this key is for making your favorite lentils, chilis and beans.
FISH/VEGETABLES/STEAM – it is the fully automated function for cooking and steaming delicate ingredients like vegetables, fish and seafood.
CHICKEN/MEAT – even the toughest of the cuts are made easy with this program.

All these buttons cook the same, except the canning button, but they offer different cook times. You can change the default cook time by using either the TIME ADJUSTMENT button or COOK TIME SELECTOR.

You can leave your device without supervision because when the time elapses the KEEP WARM mode is automatically activated. It will keep your food warm for up to four hours. You can sear and brown the meat as well as to sweat the onions and vegetables without an additional cookware. Simply press any of the pre-set buttons with the lid off and add the ingredients. In this way, you will be able to brown your food to enhance its flavors and aromas.

Long story short, the Power pressure cooker XL offers choices for the most common cooking tasks.

Here are a few major points to remember:

Always use enough cooking liquid (water or stock) so the pressure can build inside the inner pot.

There must be enough room for the pressure to build so don't fill the inner pot more than one-half to two-thirds full. Keep in mind that certain food will expand during the cooking process, so don't pack the ingredients tightly into the inner pot. For all these reasons, it is important to choose the right size of the cooker.

Cut the ingredients in even-sized chunks so they will cook at the same amount of time.

If you tend to adapt traditional recipes to your Power pressure cooker XL, it can be tricky but it can be done. The same goes for this recipe collection – you can use any of these 350 recipes and adjust it according to your taste.

Before this adventure, you should familiarize yourself with the Power pressure cooker XL but there are a few handy tricks. The best recipes to convert into a pressure cooker recipes include soups, stews, chilies, lentils and grains. Additionally, choose tougher, and even fattier, inexpensive pieces of meat. It's a great idea to adapt the recipes that call for root vegetables and dry beans. When it comes to the cook time, use a reliable chart and follow the specified cooking time for the longest cooking ingredient.

5. And last but not least, always follow the manual concerning amount of cooking liquid (water, broth, etc.)

How You'll Benefit from
the Power Pressure Cooker XL

The Power Pressure Cooker XL is known for its efficiency, ease of use, high standards and hygiene. Once you master the basics, cooking in your Power Pressure Cooker XL becomes a cinch. Here are just a few benefits of this programmable multi-cooker.

The Power Pressure Cooker XL can significantly cut cooking time and save energy.
You will be able to cook the complete meals to perfection in no time – 70% faster than traditional cooking methods like stovetop pots or a conventional oven. In addition, you can brown, sear and sauté food by using the inner pot before cooking under pressure. This "set-and-forget" cooking method allows you to save your time in the kitchen thanks to an air-tight lid that locks into place. Cooking liquids come to a boil under high pressure; they transform to a steam shortly thereafter. Consequently, the Power Pressure Cooker XL, your versatile, digital pressure cooker, is able to cook food more quickly than traditional appliances.

Did you know that pressure cookers became the most widely used household utensils during World War II? As a matter of fact, people needed to save fuel and cook inexpensive food. Simple!

It is obvious that quick cooking times mean less energy use. It is good for personal health and for Mother Earth.

The Power Pressure Cooker XL is a money saving kitchen gadget.
Customers have estimated that you can save hundreds of dollars a year with your Power Pressure Cooker XL. In addition, your Power Pressure Cooker XL will last 20 years or more!

The Power Pressure Cooker XL can cook almost everything, for inexpensive cuts of meat and root vegetables to sophisticated desserts and crowd-pleasing snacks. Even leftovers are made to look fantastic and taste delicious in your Power Pressure Cooker XL. This is the magic of one-pot cooking that will enchant you!

Healthy and flavorful meals.
Many studies have shown that pressure cooking tends to preserve valuable nutrients better than conventional methods such as grilling, frying, steaming, baking or boiling. A pressure cooking actually requires very little fat and water, so that your food retains most of its valuable nutrients. And guess what? The shorter cooking time will help you to cook great meals without nutrient loss.

Flavorful pasta, hearty stew, rich and luxurious dessert, deliciously gooey cake, slurp-worthy chicken soup… You don't necessarily need to give up these gorgeous dishes. You just have to make better food choices. The Power Pressure Cooker XL with its flavor infusion technology will help you find a good balance between indulgence and nutrition!

If you want to cook faster and eat better, but you are confused by all the information out there, this cookbook may help you. It contains 150 recipes with a lot of tasty cooking solutions that won't leave you indifferent! We are going to explore the surprising variety of great dishes you can make in your Power Pressure Cooker XL so you can happily indulge in a cooking experience!

Guide to Using This Recipe Collection

It seems easy to create tasty meals, save time in the kitchen and stay within a grocery budget but we are usually confused by all the information out there! This recipe collection is ready to be your steady kitchen companion. It contains 500 recipes that are divided into 10 categories so it may help you become a great home cook. It is chock-full of the surprising variety of easy dishes, great tips, cooking secrets, serving ideas, crafty tricks, innovations, and so forth.

We'll explore a wide choice of dishes, from elegant vegetable sides to saucy meat and slurp-worthy soups to delectable dessert, and use most wholesome, all-natural ingredients in the process. All the recipes are quite simple to prepare and are written in an easy-to-follow way. Each and every of these 350 recipes will guide you every step of the way in order to prepare the best pressure cooker meals ever. In addition, these recipes contain the nutritional information so you will be able to track your intake and consumption.

The Power pressure cooker XL celebrates the good old rule: Life is too short to eat bad food or drink bad wine!

Power Pressure Cooker XL
Cooking Guide / Specifications

Please note that cooking times are approximate; use them as a guideline only. The Power Pressure Cooker XL requires the addition of liquid in some form. Never fill the inner pot of your Power Pressure Cooker XL above MAX line.

VEGETABLES	Liquid/Cups	Cooking Time in minutes
Asparagus, whole	1	1–2
Beans, fava	1	4
Beans, green	1	2–3
Beans, lima	1	2
Beets	1	10
Broccoli	1	2
Brussel sprouts	1	4
Carrots, sliced	1	4
Corn on-the-cob	1	3
Pearl onions	1	2
Potatoes, chunks	1	6
Potatoes, whole	1	10–11
Squash, acorn	1	7
Squash, summer	1	4
Zucchini	1	4

SEAFOOD/FISH	Liquid/Cups	Cooking Time in minutes
Clams	1	2–3
Lobster, whole	1	2–3
Shrimp	1	1–2
Fish, Soup, Stock	1–4	5–6

MEATS	Liquid/Cups	Cooking Time in minutes
Beef/Veal. roast or brisket	3–4	35–40
Beef meatloaf	1	10–15
Beef, corned	4	50–60
Pork, roast	1	40–45
Pork, ribs	3	20
Leg of lamb	3	35–40
Chicken, whole	3–4	20
Chicken, pieces	3–4	15–20
Cornish hens	1	15
Meat Soup/Stock	4–6	15–20

POULTRY

1. Chicken and Barley Soup

Ready in about 50 minutes
Servings 6

Here's a hearty and rich chicken soup to fill you up! Make the most of grains, meat and vegetables in this main dish soup and delight your family!

Per serving: 585 Calories; 27.3g Fat; 46.1g Carbs; 38.4g Protein; 3.9g Sugars

Ingredients

5 cups homemade broth
1/4 cup tomato puree
4 tablespoons flour
4 tablespoons vegetable oil
1 cup carrots, chopped
2 onions, diced
1 1/3 cups pot barley
1 ½ pounds chicken breasts, boneless, skinless and cubed
1 ¼ cups heavy cream
1 ½ cups celery stalks, chopped
1/2 teaspoon ground black pepper
1/2 teaspoon salt
3/4 teaspoon cayenne pepper
1 teaspoon dry thyme

Directions

- Coat the chicken with flour; season with the salt, ground black pepper, and cayenne pepper. Press the CHICKEN/MEAT key. Set to 40 minutes.
- Now, heat vegetable oil; cook the chicken cubes until they have just browned, 3 minutes per side.
- Add the remaining ingredients, except for the heavy cream. Place the lid on the cooker, lock the lid and switch the pressure release valve to closed.
- Once the timer reaches 0, the cooker will automatically switch to KEEP WARM/CANCEL.
- Switch the pressure release valve to open. When the steam is completely released, remove the cooker's lid.
- Add the heavy cream; give it a good stir. Serve warm in individual bowls.

2. Yummy Chicken and Kale Soup

Ready in about 40 minutes
Servings 8

Turn some basic ingredients into this colorful root vegetable and chicken dish that the whole family will enjoy.

Per serving: 268 Calories; 10.6g Fat; 15.8g Carbs; 27.7g Protein; 5.5g Sugars

Ingredients

1 ½ pounds whole chicken, skin removed
8 cups chicken stock
2 ½ cups frozen kale, thawed
2 cups turnip, chopped
2 cups celery with leaves, chopped
1 teaspoon minced garlic
Salt and freshly ground black pepper, to taste
2 sprigs dry thyme
2 bell peppers, thinly sliced
2 cups carrots, peeled and grated
2 tablespoons olive oil, melted
2 shallots, peeled and diced

Directions

- Press the CHICKEN/MEAT key. Heat the oil; now, sauté the carrots, turnip, celery, shallots, garlic and bell peppers until just tender and fragrant. Press the CANCEL key.
- Now, add stock, salt, black pepper, thyme, and chicken. Press the SOUP/STEW key and cook for 30 minutes.
- Once the timer reaches 0, the cooker will automatically switch to KEEP WARM/CANCEL.
- Switch the pressure release valve to open. Allow the pressure to drop on its own and carefully remove the cooker's lid.
- Stir in thawed kale; allow kale to sit for 4 minutes longer. Serve right away.

3. Juicy Turkey in Ale Sauce

Ready in about 40 minutes
Servings 4

Ale, a drink with fruity and full-bodied taste, gives this sauce a caramel and roasty flavor as well as an impressive texture. Lager works well too, but bear in mind that it is cleaner and mellower than Ale.

Per serving: 321 Calories; 9.9g Fat; 21.3g Carbs; 32.1g Protein; 13.1g Sugars

Ingredients

1 ½ pounds turkey breasts, cut into 8 pieces
10 ounces Ale
1 ¼ cups cup yogurt
1/3 cup arrowroot
2 tablespoons olive oil
1/2 teaspoon dried sage
2 sprigs dried rosemary
2 sprigs dried thyme
1 ½ cups green onions, chopped
Sea salt and freshly ground black pepper, to your liking

Directions

- In a small-sized bowl, combine the arrowroot, salt, and black pepper. Then, dredge the turkey in this mixture.
- Press the CHICKEN/MEAT key. Heat the oil; sauté green onions until softened, about 2 minutes. Now, brown the chicken on all sides, working in batches. Reserve prepared turkey.
- Pour in Ale and bring to a boil; cook for a further 2 minutes. Add browned turkey, along with its juice and dried herbs, to the Power pressure cooker XL.
- Press the SOUP/STEW key and cook for 30 minutes.
- Once the timer reaches 0, the cooker will automatically switch to KEEP WARM/CANCEL.
- Switch the pressure release valve to open. Afterwards, carefully remove the cooker's lid. Stir in yogurt and serve warm.

4. Chicken in Creamy Marinara Sauce

Ready in about 25 minutes
Servings 4

Entertaining your family during the holiday season doesn't have to leave you stuck in the kitchen all day long. The Power pressure cooker XL is here to help! Simply drop all ingredients into the inner pot, press the right button and enjoy!

Per serving: 498 Calories; 37.1g Fat; 17.8g Carbs; 24.6g Protein; 9.8g Sugars

Ingredients

4 chicken drumsticks, trimmed of fat
1 ¾ cups marinara sauce
1 cup sour cream
1 cup grated sharp cheese
1/2 stick butter
1 teaspoon garlic paste
1 teaspoon chipotle powder
1 tablespoon fresh basil leaves, chopped
Sea salt and freshly cracked black pepper, to taste
1/2 teaspoon fresh rosemary, chopped

Directions

- Press the SOUP/STEW key and melt the butter. Press the TIME ADJUSTMENT key to set time to 20 minutes.
- Add the garlic paste, chipotle powder, marinara sauce, rosemary, and basil leaves.
- Sprinkle the chicken drumsticks with the salt and ground black pepper. Nestle the chicken down into the sauce.
- Once the timer reaches 0, the cooker will automatically switch to KEEP WARM/CANCEL.
- Switch the pressure release valve to open. Afterwards, carefully remove the cooker's lid. Stir in the cheese and sour cream and serve right away.

5. Country Poached Chicken with Fennel

Ready in about 25 minutes
Servings 10

Anything pork can do, poultry can do better! Seriously, pressure cooked boneless chicken meat with vegetables will blow your mind!

Per serving: 178 Calories; 6.8g Fat; 1.1g Carbs; 26.5g Protein; 0.3g Sugars

Ingredients

2 pounds chicken meat, boneless
1 cup fennel bulb, chopped
1 cup celery with leaves, chopped
2 ¼ cups vegetable stock

Directions

- Place the chicken, fennel bulb and celery in your Power pressure cooker XL. Add the stock to cover the ingredients.
- Choose the CHICKEN/MEAT function; set time to 15 minutes. Place the lid on the cooker, lock the lid and switch the pressure release valve to closed.
- Once the timer reaches 0, the cooker will automatically switch to KEEP WARM/CANCEL.
- Switch the pressure release valve to open. Afterwards, carefully remove the cooker's lid.
- Taste, adjust the seasonings and serve warm.

6. Saucy Chicken Fillet with Gruyère Cheese

Ready in about 25 minutes
Servings 6

Here's a festive main course your guests will love for sure! The star of this dish is a homemade chipotle salsa that can be prepared in no time.

Per serving: 450 Calories; 24.7g Fat; 5g Carbs; 50.2g Protein; 2.5g Sugars

Ingredients

3 teaspoons olive oil
6 chicken fillets
1/2 teaspoon fennel seeds
2 garlic cloves, minced
Salt and freshly ground black pepper, to your liking
2 tablespoons apple cider vinegar
1 cup Gruyère cheese, shredded

For Homemade Salsa:
12 ounces fire roasted tomatoes
2 fresh ripe tomatoes, chopped
1 medium-sized onion, finely chopped
1 garlic clove, minced
3 chipotle peppers in adobo
1/2 teaspoon kosher salt
1/3 teaspoon freshly ground black pepper
1/3 cup cilantro
2 tablespoons fresh lime juice

Directions

- Press the CHICKEN/MEAT key; set time to 15 minutes. Then, heat olive oil and brown the chicken fillets on all sides.
- Meanwhile, make your salsa by mixing all the salsa ingredients in your food processor; blend until everything is well incorporated.
- Add the fennel seeds, garlic, salt, pepper and vinegar to the Power pressure cooker XL. Add the prepared salsa; place the lid on the cooker, lock the lid and switch the pressure release valve to closed.
- Once the timer reaches 0, the cooker will automatically switch to KEEP WARM/CANCEL. Serve topped with the cheese. Enjoy!

7. Chicken Curry with Apple Chutney

Ready in about 20 minutes
Servings 8

An apple chutney is the perfect condiment that compliments this chicken dish but a mango chutney works well too.

Per serving: 288 Calories; 10.6g Fat; 18.4g Carbs; 29.7g Protein; 12.1g Sugars

Ingredients

2 pounds boneless and skinless chicken, cut into strips
2 tablespoons curry powder
1 ½ cups rice milk, unsweetened
1/4 cup vegetable oil
1/2 teaspoon ground black pepper
1/2 teaspoon sea salt
2 yellow onions, chopped
3/4 cup apple chutney, pureed

Directions

- Press the CHICKEN/MEAT key and heat 1 tablespoon of oil. Then, brown the chicken strips until they're no longer pink. Transfer them to a plate and reserve.
- Heat the remaining oil in your Power pressure cooker XL. Next, sauté the onions for 6 minutes or until tender and translucent. Add the curry powder and stir to combine.
- Add the remaining ingredients. Place the lid on the cooker, lock the lid and switch the pressure release valve to closed.
- Once the timer reaches 0, the cooker will automatically switch to KEEP WARM/CANCEL. Taste, adjust the seasonings and serve warm.

8. Hearty Chicken Stew

Ready in about 35 minutes
Servings 4

With wonderful aromatic spices and ripe tomatoes, this chicken stew is super addicting! You can add another combo of seasonings if desired.

Per serving: 247 Calories; 13.9g Fat; 12.7g Carbs; 21g Protein; 3.1g Sugars

Ingredients

4 chicken legs, skinless
1 cup onions, thinly sliced
2 ripe tomatoes, chopped
1 teaspoon minced garlic
2 tablespoons corn flour
1 ½ cups vegetable stock
1 fennel bulb, chopped
3 teaspoons vegetable oil
1 sprig dried thyme
1/2 teaspoon cayenne pepper
2 sprigs dried rosemary
Sea salt and freshly ground black pepper

Directions

- Press the CHICKEN/MEAT key and heat the oil. Season the chicken legs with salt, black pepper, cayenne pepper, rosemary, and thyme.
- Then, brown the chicken legs for 3 minutes on each side. Stir in the onions and cook for 5 more minutes.
- Add the garlic and cook for 1 minute longer or until fragrant. Sprinkle with the flour and add the stock. Press the CANCEL key.
- Next, stir the tomatoes and fennel into the Power pressure cooker XL. Give it a gentle stir. Place the lid on the cooker, lock the lid and switch the pressure release valve to closed.
- Press the CHICKEN/MEAT key and then, TIME ADJUSTMENT to 20 minutes.
- Once the timer reaches 0, the cooker will automatically switch to KEEP WARM/CANCEL. Serve warm.

9. Lemon Chicken Fillets with Currants

Ready in about 20 minutes
Servings 6

You don't have to heat up your whole stove just for cooking a few chicken fillets. You can get even better chicken in your Power pressure cooker XL.

Per serving: 299 Calories; 15.9g Fat; 4.8g Carbs; 33.6g Protein; 1.1g Sugars

Ingredients

6 lemon slices
1 ½ pounds chicken fillets
1/3 cup currants
2 tablespoons canola oil
1 teaspoon coriander seeds
2 garlic cloves, finely chopped
1/2 teaspoon salt
1 teaspoon ground cumin
1/4 teaspoon freshly cracked black pepper
2 ¼ cups water
1 cup scallions, chopped
1 cup Greek olives, drained and pitted

Directions

- Press the CHICKEN/MEAT key and heat canola oil; sauté the scallions, garlic, cumin, and coriander seeds. Nestle the chicken fillets in this mixture.
- Distribute the currants and olives over the chicken fillets. Sprinkle with salt and black pepper. Top with the lemon slices. Then, pour in the water.
- Place the lid on the cooker, lock the lid and switch the pressure release valve to closed. Cook for 15 minutes.
- Once the timer reaches 0, the cooker will automatically switch to KEEP WARM/CANCEL. Serve warm.

10. Turkey and Green Bean Soup

Ready in about 45 minutes
Servings 6

This is one good-looking bowl of soup. Green bean is considered to be a low-calorie vegetable, but it can add an amazing flavor and a great nutritional value to any soup recipe.

Per serving: 130 Calories; 1.4g Fat; 14.3g Carbs; 14.8g Protein; 7.6g Sugars

Ingredients

1 ½ pounds turkey drumsticks, boneless, skinless and diced
2 cups green beans
2 medium-sized ripe tomatoes, chopped
1 cup carrots, diced
1 cup onions, chopped
1 teaspoon minced garlic
1 turnip, chopped
6 cups turkey stock
2 tablespoons fresh parsley
1/4 teaspoon ground black pepper
1 teaspoon dried oregano
1 teaspoon dried marjoram
1/2 teaspoon kosher salt
1/2 teaspoon dried basil

Directions

- Throw all of the above ingredients, except for green beans, into the Power pressure cooker XL. Press the SOUP/STEW key and then, TIME ADJUSTMENT to 30 minutes.
- Place the lid on the cooker, lock the lid and switch the pressure release valve to closed.
- Remove the cooker's lid and stir in the green beans. Seal the lid again and wait for 10 minutes to blanch the beans. Serve with garlic croutons, if desired.

11. Italian Sausage and Sweet Potato Chowder

Ready in about 35 minutes
Servings 6

Eat well and stay on budget with your Power pressure cooker XL! Simply throw basic ingredients into the inner pot and watch the magic happen!

Per serving: 481 Calories; 25.5g Fat; 38.8g Carbs; 23.5g Protein; 3.9g Sugars

Ingredients

1 pound hot Italian turkey sausage, sliced
6 sweet potatoes, peeled and cubed
3 teaspoons canola oil
6 ½ cups broth
2 yellow onions, chopped
2 cups Swiss chard, stemmed and torn into pieces
3 garlic cloves, minced
1/4 freshly ground black pepper
1/2 teaspoon salt

Directions

- Add all ingredients, except for Swiss chard, to your Power pressure cooker XL. Press the CHICKEN/MEAT button and then, TIME ADJUSTMENT to 20 minutes.
- Once the timer reaches 0, the cooker will automatically switch to KEEP WARM/CANCEL. Then, puree about 1/2 of the cooked mixture.
- Add Swiss chard to the Power pressure cooker XL. Seal the lid again and wait for 10 minutes to blanch Swiss chard. Serve at once and enjoy!

12. Turkey and Carrot Soup with Chickpeas

Ready in about 35 minutes
Servings 6

Turkey meat is the basis for this savory and rich soup, which gets an extra kick from canned chickpeas. Serve with enough crusty bread.

Per serving: 427 Calories; 9.2g Fat; 37g Carbs; 48.2g Protein; 8.2g Sugars

Ingredients

1 ½ pounds turkey thighs, boneless, skinless and diced
1/2 pound carrots, trimmed and diced
8 ounces canned chickpeas
2 ripe tomatoes, chopped
1 cup yams, chopped
1 cup spring onions, chopped
2 cloves garlic, minced
1 teaspoon dried marjoram
2 tablespoons fresh cilantro, roughly chopped
6 cups roasted vegetable stock
1/4 teaspoon ground black pepper
1/3 teaspoon kosher salt
1/2 teaspoon cayenne pepper
1 cup celery with leaves, trimmed and chopped

Directions

- Throw all of the above ingredients, except for canned chickpeas, into the Power pressure cooker XL.
- Choose the CHICKEN/MEAT function. Press the TIME ADJUSTMENT key until you reach 20 minutes.
- Place the lid on the Power pressure cooker XL, lock the lid and switch the pressure release valve to closed.
- Uncover and stir in the chickpeas; cover and allow it to stand for 10 minutes. Serve with a pesto and croutons.

13. Chicken Liver Pâté Spread

Ready in about 15 minutes
Servings 16

Make this pâté a day ahead to allow the flavors to develop. Serve with wheat crackers or warm toast.

Per serving: 80 Calories; 3.9g Fat; 1.2g Carbs; 7.0g Protein; 0.0g Sugars

Ingredients

2 tablespoons butter
2 teaspoons olive oil
1 teaspoon dried basil
1 tablespoon dried sage
2 sprigs dried thyme
1/2 teaspoon ground black pepper, to taste
1 teaspoon salt
1 pound chicken livers
3 anchovies in oil
1 cup leek, roughly chopped
1/3 cup rum

Directions

● Press the "CHICKEN/MEAT" key. Put the olive oil into the Power Pressure Cooker XL; sauté the leeks. Then, add the chicken livers and cook until the livers are seared.
● Pour in the rum. Close and lock the lid of your Power Pressure Cooker XL. Set the cooking time to 10 minutes.
● Switch the pressure release valve to open. When the steam is released completely, remove the lid.
● Add the remaining ingredients and stir to combine. Serve well chilled with your favorite rustic bread.

14. Chicken and Kale Stew

Ready in about 20 minutes
Servings 8

This hearty stew features tender ground chicken simmered with tomatoes, root vegetables and kale. Crisp white wine adds just the right amount of tanginess to this robust stew.

Per serving: 235 Calories; 8.0g Fat; 14.9g Carbs; 23.1g Protein; 2.8g Sugars

Ingredients

1 cup tomatoes, seeded and chopped
1 pound ground chicken
1/4 teaspoon ground black pepper
1/2 teaspoon salt
2 sprigs dried thyme
1 teaspoon red pepper flakes, crushed
1 teaspoon marjoram
3 teaspoons olive oil
1/2 cup celery stalk, chopped
1 cup carrots, diced
1 cup onions, diced
1/3 cup white wine
1 cup kale leaves, chopped
7 cups chicken broth
10 ounces noodles, cooked

Directions

● Press the "SOUP/STEW" key and melt the olive oil. Once hot, add the ground chicken and all seasonings. Cook until the chicken has browned.
● Add the onion, carrot, and celery; cook for about 6 minutes. Pour in the wine to deglaze the pot.
● Add the remaining ingredients, minus the cooked noodles. Stir to combine and place the lid on your Power Pressure Cooker XL and lock. Switch the pressure release valve to closed.
● Set the cooking time to 10 minutes. Once the timer reaches 0, the Power Pressure Cooker XL will automatically switch to "KEEP WARM/CANCEL".
● Switch the pressure release valve to open. When the steam is released completely, remove the lid.
● Serve warm with cooked noodles.

15. Chicken, Artichoke and Rice Casserole

Ready in about 25 minutes
Servings 6

Treat your family to a comforting bowl of something fabulous like this rich and hearty casserole. The casserole is a family-friendly recipe that cooks perfectly in the Power Pressure Cooker XL!

Per serving: 595 Calories; 30.3g Fat; 49.8g Carbs; 30.9g Protein; 4.9g Sugars

Ingredients

1 teaspoon minced garlic
1 cup onions, chopped
1/3 cup rosé wine
1 pound hot Italian sausage, cut into pieces
4 boneless, skinless chicken thighs
3 tablespoons olive oil
1 ½ cups chicken stock
11 ounces artichoke hearts, quartered
1 teaspoon paprika
1/2 teaspoon ground black pepper
1 teaspoon salt
2 Serrano peppers, stemmed, cored, and chopped
26 ounces canned whole tomatoes, roughly chopped
1 ½ cups long-grain white rice

Directions

- Press the "RICE/RISOTTO" key. Heat the olive oil and brown the sausage, turning periodically, for about 5 minutes. Transfer to a large-sized bowl.
- Add the chicken and brown, turning occasionally, for approximately 5 minutes. Transfer to the bowl with the sausage.
- Stir in the onion and Serrano peppers. Cook, while stirring frequently, until the onion is translucent, or about 3 minutes. Add the garlic and cook until aromatic.
- Pour in the wine; bring to a simmer. Continue simmering until the wine has reduced to a thick glaze. Stir in the tomatoes, stock, white rice, artichoke hearts, paprika, salt, and ground black pepper.
- Return the reserved sausage and the chicken to the cooker. Give it a good stir. Lock the lid onto the Power Pressure Cooker XL. Cook for 10 minutes.
- Use a Quick release function and open your Power Pressure Cooker XL. Stir once again before serving.

16. Chicken Curry Soup

Ready in about 25 minutes
Servings 4

If you love curry, the Power Pressure Cooker XL is a great tool to prepare this all-in-one meal while saving you time and money. You can add chopped smoked bacon to enrich the flavor.

Per serving: 320 Calories; 23.4g Fat; 19.4g Carbs; 11.5g Protein; 8.9g Sugars

Ingredients

1 pound chicken breast, chopped
2 ½ cups water
8 ounces frozen okra
1/2 teaspoon ground ginger
1/2 teaspoon curry powder
8 ounces sugar snap peas
1 ½ cups coconut milk
8 ounces frozen carrots

Directions

- Choose the "SOUP/STEW" function. Put all the ingredients into your Power Pressure Cooker XL.
- Place the lid on the Power Pressure Cooker XL and lock. Cook for 20 minutes.
- Once the timer reaches 0, the Power Pressure Cooker XL will automatically switch to "KEEP WARM". Press the "CANCEL" key. Switch the pressure release valve to open.
- When the steam is released completely, remove the lid. Serve hot and enjoy!

17. Country Chicken and Vegetable Soup

Ready in about 40 minutes
Servings 6

We all know that soup is the very important meal, but many of us don't have the time to make healthy and satisfying soup. Don't settle for store-bought instant soup and make this easy, homey soup just like your grandma used to make.

Per serving: 167 Calories; 2.8g Fat; 11.1g Carbs; 23.5g Protein; 3.1g Sugars

Ingredients

1/2 pound potatoes, diced
4 ½ cups chicken stock
1 ½ cups carrots, trimmed and chopped
1 cup onion, peeled and diced
1/2 teaspoon freshly cracked black pepper, to taste
1 teaspoon salt
4 frozen chicken breast halves, boneless and skinless

Directions

- Choose the "CHICKEN/MEAT" function. Simply put all of the above ingredients into your Power Pressure Cooker XL.
- Close and lock the lid. Set the cooking time to 30 minutes. Then switch the pressure release valve to open.
- When the steam is completely released, remove the lid. Serve right away!

18. Delicious Spring Chili

Ready in about 35 minutes
Servings 8

Here's an easy recipe for chicken chili that will nourish your appetite and delight your taste buds! The recipe calls for spring plants but you can make this chili all year long by using winter onions instead of green onions.

Per serving: 317 Calories; 4.1g Fat; 29.1g Carbs; 39.6g Protein; 2.1g Sugars

Ingredients

1 ¾ pounds coarse ground chicken
2 cups water
1 tablespoon green garlic, minced
1 teaspoon cumin powder
1 large-sized green chili, diced
1 teaspoon celery seeds
1 ½ cups green onions, chopped
1 ¾ cups dry pinto beans
16 ounces canned beef broth
1 cup tomato, diced

Directions

- Press the "BEANS/LENTILS" key and the brown ground chicken for 5 minutes; deglaze a pan with beef broth.
- Add the rest of the above ingredients. Place the lid on the Power Pressure Cooker XL and lock the lid; switch the pressure release valve to closed.
- Cook for 25 minutes. Remove the lid according to the manufacturer's instructions.
- Serve right away, topped with fresh chives, if desired.

19. Chicken and Navy Bean Soup

Ready in about 35 minutes
Servings 6

Hearty and filling, a hot bowl of bean soup is sure to warm your body and soul, no matter what the season. Navy beans is a staple food you should always have on hand.

Per serving: 459 Calories; 13.0g Fat; 62.4g Carbs; 26.4g Protein; 6.0g Sugars

Ingredients

3/4 pound cooked chicken breast, chopped
2 cups chicken stock
16 ounces canned stewed tomatoes
1/2 teaspoon cayenne pepper
1/2 teaspoon salt
1/4 teaspoon ground black pepper, chopped
20 ounces canned navy beans, rinsed and drained
3 teaspoons olive oil
1 cup sour cream
1/2 cup fresh cilantro, chopped

Directions

- Choose the "SOUP/STEW" function. Place all the ingredients, except for the cilantro, in the inner pot of the Power Pressure Cooker XL.
- Next, lock the lid; press the time adjustment button until you reach 30 minutes.
- Serve warm garnished with fresh cilantro.

20. Rigatoni with Chicken and Parmesan

Ready in about 20 minutes
Servings 4

It's easy to make the most sophisticated pasta recipes! Just gather the ingredients, throw them all into the Power Pressure Cooker XL, and let them cook while you relax.

Per serving: 643 Calories; 14.2g Fat; 68.8g Carbs; 57.4g Protein; 2.9g Sugars

Ingredients

1 ¾ cups tomato paste
1/2 teaspoon salt
1/2 tablespoon fresh sage
1 teaspoon dried thyme
1/2 tablespoon fresh basil, chopped
1/4 teaspoon ground black pepper, or more to taste
1 ½ pounds chicken, chopped
1 heaping teaspoon minced garlic
1 cup leeks, chopped
1 package dry rigatoni pasta
2 tablespoons peanut oil
1/2 cup Parmesan cheese, grated

Directions

- Press the "CHICKEN/MEAT" key and warm the peanut oil. Cook the chicken, leeks, and garlic till they're thoroughly cooked, approximately 6 minutes. Press the "CANCEL" button.
- Add the rest of the above ingredients, except for the Parmesan cheese. Now, choose the "BEANS/LENTILS" function. Close and lock the lid. Cook for 4 minutes.
- Next, release the pressure by using a Quick pressure release. When the steam is completely released, remove the lid. Serve topped with grated Parmesan cheese.

21. Chicken with Pears and Sweet Onion

Ready in about 25 minutes
Servings 6

Get ready for this unusual sweet and savory chicken to kick things up! If you're not a fan of fruit and meat combo, just substitute the pears for sweet potatoes.

Per serving: 292 Calories; 6.7g Fat; 11.6g Carbs; 44.4g Protein; 7.1g Sugars

Ingredients

1 cup chicken stock
3 teaspoons butter
3 small-sized firm pears, peeled, cored, and sliced
1/2 cup sweet onions, chopped
1/2 teaspoon ground black pepper
1 teaspoon cayenne pepper
1 teaspoon salt
10 boneless, skinless chicken thighs, trimmed
2 tablespoons balsamic vinegar
1 teaspoon dried dill weed

Directions

- Press the "CHICKEN/MEAT" key and melt the butter. Sprinkle the chicken with the salt, cayenne pepper, and black pepper; brown it lightly on both sides, turning once or twice. Set it aside.
- Add the remaining ingredients. Add the browned chicken into the mixture.
- Place the lid on the Power Pressure Cooker XL. Cook about 20 minutes or until the chicken is tender.
- When the steam is completely released, unlock and open the Power Pressure Cooker XL. Stir well and serve.

22. Jalapeño Chicken Thighs

Ready in about 30 minutes
Servings 6

Here is one of the most delicious recipes for spicy chicken thighs! If you're not a fan of spicy wings, adjust the number of jalapeños to your liking. Pair these wings with steamed rice or mashed potatoes.

Per serving: 262 Calories; 7.1g Fat; 2.4g Carbs; 44.5g Protein; 1.1g Sugars

Ingredients

1/2 teaspoon ground black pepper
1 teaspoon ground cumin
1 teaspoon salt
1/2 teaspoon dried thyme
1/3 cup chicken broth
1 cup spring onions, green and white parts, thinly sliced
10 boneless, skinless chicken thighs, trimmed
1 teaspoon minced garlic
1 teaspoon packed dark brown sugar
2 fresh jalapeño chilies, stemmed, seeded, and minced
1 ½ tablespoons balsamic vinegar
1 tablespoon olive oil

Directions

- Press the "CHICKEN/MEAT" key and heat the oil. Mix the chicken, thyme, cumin, salt, and black pepper. Set aside.
- Cook the jalapeño pepper, spring onions, and garlic; stir often until they become soft, approximately 3 minutes.
- Add the chicken mixture, scraping every speck of spice, to the Power Pressure Cooker XL; cook about 5 minutes, stirring occasionally, until lightly browned. Pour in the broth and vinegar; stir in the brown sugar until dissolved.
- Place the lid on the Power Pressure Cooker XL, lock the lid and switch the pressure release valve to closed.
- Cook for a further 17 minutes. Use a Quick release method, unlock, and open the Power Pressure Cooker XL. Stir well and serve immediately. Bon appétit!

23. Classic Chicken Curry

Ready in about 20 minutes
Servings 6

Coconut milk gives a wonderful texture to this classic chicken meal. It contains lauric acid, which has been shown to promote bone health.

Per serving: 491 Calories; 30.4g Fat; 8.7g Carbs; 45.9g Protein; 3.5g Sugars

Ingredients

2 tablespoons canola oil
1 cup carrots, chopped
1 ½ cups coconut milk
2 teaspoons ginger, freshly grated
1/2 teaspoon celery seeds
1/2 teaspoon ground black pepper
1 teaspoon salt
1/2 teaspoon ground cumin
1/2 teaspoon fennel seeds
1 teaspoon ground turmeric
1 teaspoon minced garlic
2 pounds chicken breasts, cut into bite-size chunks
1 cup leeks, chopped
1/2 cup fresh parsley leaves, roughly chopped

Directions

- Press the "CHICKEN/MEAT" key. Now, heat the oil; sauté the leeks, garlic, carrot and ginger in hot oil; cook until they're just tender.
- Add the fennel seeds, celery seeds, cumin, and turmeric, and cook for an additional 3 minutes.
- Stir in the remaining ingredients, except for the parsley.
- Place the lid on the Power Pressure Cooker XL, lock the lid and switch the pressure release valve to closed; cook for 10 minutes.
- Use a Quick release method, unlock, and open the Power Pressure Cooker XL. Serve warm garnished with fresh parsley leaves.

24. Party Hot Chicken Wings

Ready in about 20 minutes
Servings 8

Rich and spicy, this chicken wings call for a combination of hot sauce and butter; feel free to use whatever hot sauce you have on hand.

Per serving: 371 Calories; 9.9g Fat; 0.6g Carbs; 65.9g Protein; 0.0g Sugars

Ingredients

16 chicken wings, frozen
1 sprig thyme
1 cup hot sauce
1/2 teaspoon salt
1/2 teaspoon freshly ground black pepper
2 tablespoons butter, melted

Directions

- Choose the "CHICKEN/MEAT" function. Add the melted butter and hot sauce to the Power Pressure Cooker XL; mix to combine well.
- Add the remaining ingredients. Place the lid on the Power Pressure Cooker XL, lock the lid and switch the pressure release valve to closed.
- Cook for 15 minutes. Press the "CANCEL" key. Switch the pressure release valve to open. When the steam is completely released, remove the lid.
- Serve warm with a dipping sauce of choice.

25. Saucy Turkey Wings

Ready in about 40 minutes
Servings 4

Lots of cranberries and orange juice, plus spices to balance out the sweetness of the fruit, make this recipe a winner for your family lunch!

Per serving: 463 Calories; 29.0g Fat; 13.0g Carbs; 34.6g Protein; 6.4g Sugars

Ingredients

1 pound turkey wings
1 stick butter, at room temperature
2 cups vegetable stock
2 cups cranberries
1/3 cup orange juice
2 onions, sliced into rings
1/2 teaspoon ground black pepper, to your liking
1/2 teaspoon cayenne pepper
1 teaspoon salt

Directions

- Choose the "CHICKEN/MEAT" function and melt the butter. Brown the turkey wings on all sides. Season with the salt, black pepper, and cayenne pepper.
- Now, add the onion rings and cranberries. Pour in the orange juice and the vegetable stock. Place the lid on the Power Pressure Cooker XL, lock the lid and switch the pressure release valve to closed. Cook for 25 minutes.
- Press the "CANCEL" key. Switch the pressure release valve to open. When the steam is completely released, remove the lid.
- Afterwards, preheat a broiler. Cook the wings under the broiler for about 7 minutes.
- While the wings are broiling, press the "CHICKEN/ MEAT" key again and cook the sauce uncovered in order to reduce the liquid content. Spoon the sauce over the wings and serve.

26. Honey Chicken Wings

Ready in about 35 minutes
Servings 5

Honey adds a little bit of sweetness to balance the spices in this recipe. If you like mild-tasting wings you can cut the shallot powder down to 1/2 teaspoon.

Per serving: 346 Calories; 5.5g Fat; 19.0g Carbs; 52.7g Protein; 18.6g Sugars

Ingredients

1/3 cup honey
1/2 teaspoon garlic powder
1 teaspoon coriander
1/2 teaspoon cumin powder
2 tablespoons apple cider vinegar
12 chicken wings
1 tablespoon shallot powder
1/4 teaspoon ground black pepper
1 teaspoon salt

Directions

- Choose the "CHICKEN/MEAT" function. Place the chicken wings in your Power Pressure Cooker XL.
- Place the lid on the Power Pressure Cooker XL, lock the lid and switch the pressure release valve to closed. Cook for 15 minutes. Reserve the liquid.
- Preheat your oven to 390 degrees F.
- Transfer the chicken wings to the oven and roast them until the skin is crispy. Remove the chicken from the oven and set aside in a baking dish, keeping them warm.
- Add the rest of the above ingredients to the Power Pressure Cooker XL with the chicken broth; choose the "CHICKEN/MEAT" function.
- Cook for 12 minutes, stirring continuously. Pour the sauce over the chicken wings, and serve.

27. Fried Rice with Chicken

Ready in about 25 minutes
Servings 6

This is a classic and belly-warming dish that everyone will love. It is also kid-friendly and can be served as a festive dinner and family lunch.

Per serving: 432 Calories; 9.6g Fat; 64.5g Carbs; 19.5g Protein; 1.3g Sugars

Ingredients

1/2 stick butter, softened
3 ½ cups water
2 cups chicken, cut into chunks
2 medium-sized carrots, thinly sliced
2 ½ cups multi-grain rice
2 tablespoons apple cider vinegar
1/2 teaspoon ground black pepper, to taste
1 teaspoon salt
1 teaspoon dried basil
1 teaspoon dried dill weed
1/2 cup green onions, chopped

Directions

- Choose the "RICE/RISOTTO" function. Add all of the above ingredients to your Power Pressure Cooker XL.
- Place the lid on the Power Pressure Cooker XL, lock the lid and switch the pressure release valve to closed. Set the timer for 20 minutes.
- Once the cooking is complete, press the "CANCEL" key.
- When the steam has been released, remove the lid. Serve right now.

28. Chicken and Green Pea Soup

Ready in about 30 minutes
Servings 6

Canned tomatoes, chicken and green peas are natural allies in this healthy and hearty soup. Serve with a generous spoonful of Greek yogurt or mashed cauliflower swirled into each serving.

Per serving: 227 Calories; 3.3g Fat; 21.2g Carbs; 28.4g Protein; 9.8g Sugars

Ingredients

1 cup onions, chopped
1 teaspoon minced garlic
20 ounces canned diced tomatoes
2 chicken breasts, boneless, skinless and diced
1/4 teaspoon ground black pepper
1/2 teaspoon salt
1 teaspoon dried dill weed
1 teaspoon dried marjoram
4 cups vegetable stock
1 cup carrots, diced
1 cup celery rib, chopped
1/2 cup celery stalk, chopped
18 ounces green peas

Directions

- Choose the "SOUP/STEW" function. Add all of the above ingredients, except for the peas, to your Power Pressure Cooker XL. Lock the lid and switch the pressure release valve to closed.
- Cook for 20 minutes; use a Quick release method to drop the pressure.
- Unlock and open the Power Pressure Cooker XL. Stir in the green peas. Then, seal the lid and wait for 7 minutes to warm up and blanch the peas. Serve hot with cornbread.

29. Ground Turkey Bean Chili

Ready in about 20 minutes
Servings 8

Make room for a 5-star meal! No hot sauce here. Just purely rich beans, meat and creamy goodness.

Per serving: 337 Calories; 18.6g Fat; 13.3g Carbs; 35.9g Protein; 2.4g Sugars

Ingredients

2 cups water
2 ½ cups chicken stock
1/2 teaspoon celery seeds
1 cup onions, chopped
1 teaspoon chili powder
30 ounces canned beans, drained and rinsed well
2 tablespoons olive oil
2 pounds ground turkey
30 ounces canned diced tomatoes with green chilies
1/2 teaspoon cumin powder
1/2 cup Monterey Jack cheese, shredded

Directions

- Press the "RICE/RISOTTO" key and melt the oil in your Power Pressure Cooker XL. Then, sauté the onions for 6 minutes. Add the ground turkey and cook until the meat has browned, 6 minutes more.
- Stir in the remaining ingredients, except for the Monterey Jack cheese. Cover and cook for 6 minutes.
- Switch the pressure release valve to open. When the steam is released, remove the cooker's lid.
- Ladle into soup bowls and serve topped with the shredded Monterey Jack cheese. Bon appétit!

30. Chicken with Beans and Tomato

Ready in about 20 minutes
Servings 6

You can use any type of canned beans for this recipe, even though the recipe calls for red kidney beans. Also, if you can use homemade stewed tomatoes, it is absolutely worth the time invested.

Per serving: 349 Calories; 7.6g Fat; 50.1g Carbs; 22.5g Protein; 5.2g Sugars

Ingredients

1 pound chicken breast, chopped
3 teaspoons vegetable oil
16 ounces canned stewed tomatoes
1/4 teaspoon ground black pepper, chopped
1/2 teaspoon salt
1/2 teaspoon paprika
16 ounces canned red kidney beans, rinsed and drained
1/2 cup fresh parsley leaves, coarsely chopped
2 cups vegetable stock
1/3 cup sour cream

Directions

- Choose the "SOUP/STEW" function.
- Place the ingredients, except the parsley leaves, in the inner pot of the Power Pressure Cooker XL.
- Next, place the lid on the Power Pressure Cooker XL; then, press the time adjustment button until you reach 15 minutes.
- Press the "CANCEL" key. Switch the pressure release valve to open. When the steam is released completely, remove the cooker's lid.
- Serve garnished with fresh parsley. Bon appétit!

31. Peppery Chicken Dip

Ready in about 25 minutes
Servings 10

When you are having friends over, the last thing you want to do is spend hours in the kitchen, preparing food. This dipping sauce is ready in less than 30 minutes and you can make it a day or two ahead and keep it in your refrigerator.

Per serving: 136 Calories; 6.3g Fat; 5.7g Carbs; 14.0g Protein; 3.1g Sugars

Ingredients

1 cup tomato puree, chopped
2 tablespoons canola oil
1 ½ teaspoons granulated garlic
3 teaspoons arrowroot
1 cup onion, finely chopped
1 pound ground chicken
1 ½ teaspoons dried basil
1/2 teaspoon ground black pepper to taste
1 teaspoon salt
1/2 teaspoon cayenne pepper
1 teaspoon dried thyme
2 Serrano peppers, seeded and chopped
2 bell peppers, seeded and chopped

Directions

- Choose the "CHICKEN/MEAT" function and warm the canola oil. Cook the chicken in the hot oil for about 6 minutes, or until the meat is no longer pink.
- Add the rest of the above ingredients. Next, place the lid on the Power Pressure Cooker XL; then, press the time adjustment button until you reach 15 minutes.
- Press the "CANCEL" key. Switch the pressure release valve to open. When the steam is released completely, remove the cooker's lid. Serve warm or at room temperature.

32. Saucy Chicken Wings

Ready in about 20 minutes
Servings 8

Here's the recipe for the most delicious and the easiest chicken wings ever! While they're cooking, relax and enjoy a glass of wine as the entire house fills with the wonderful smells.

Per serving: 285 Calories; 8.1g Fat; 0.5g Carbs; 49.5g Protein; 0.0g Sugars

Ingredients

16 chicken wings, frozen
2 tablespoons butter
1 cup hot sauce

Directions

- Choose the "SOUP/STEW" function. Add the butter and the hot sauce to the Power Pressure Cooker XL.
- Throw in the wings. Place the lid on the Power Pressure Cooker XL, lock the lid and switch the pressure release valve to closed.
- Cook for 15 minutes. Press the "CANCEL" key. Switch the pressure release valve to open. When the steam is completely released, remove the lid. Bon appétit!

33. Creamed Chorizo and Kale Soup

Ready in about 15 minutes
Servings 6

This classic chorizo soup cooks quickly and easily in your Power pressure cooker XL. Sprinkle each serving with lemon pepper seasoning and fresh roughly chopped cilantro leaves.

Per serving: 172 Calories; 9.1g Fat; 7.3g Carbs; 12.4g Protein; 1.9g Sugars

Ingredients

3 chicken chorizo, chopped
2 cups kale leaves, torn into pieces
1/2 pound zucchini, sliced
1/2 teaspoon sugar
1 cup brown onion, chopped
1/2 teaspoon dried basil
1 teaspoon red pepper flakes, crushed
1/2 teaspoon dried oregano
3 teaspoons olive oil
1/3 cup heavy cream
2 cloves garlic, peeled and minced
6 ½ cups homemade broth
Salt and ground black pepper, to taste

Directions

- Press the SOUP/STEW key. Set time to 10 minutes. Now, heat the oil until sizzling. Then, sauté the chorizo, garlic and onion, until the sausage is browned, the onion is translucent, and the garlic is fragrant.
- Throw in the rest of the above ingredients, minus the heavy cream.
- Place the lid on the Power pressure cooker XL, lock the lid and switch the pressure release valve to closed.
- Press the CANCEL key. Switch the pressure release valve to open. When the steam is completely released, remove the lid.
- Add the heavy cream just before serving, stir and enjoy!

34. Satisfying Chicken Noodle Soup

Ready in about 45 minutes
Servings 6

Packed full of goodness, this soup uses lots of different vegetables and herbs to enhance the flavor. It is also said to cure the common cold. Enjoy!

Per serving: 305 Calories; 16.5g Fat; 17.2g Carbs; 21.8g Protein; 4.7g Sugars

Ingredients

2 tablespoons olive oil
4 chicken thigh cutlets, chopped, skinned and excess fat trimmed
8 ounces dry egg noodles
2 rosemary sprigs, crushed
2 thyme springs, crushed
2 brown onions, finely chopped
1 zucchini, diced
2 tablespoons sesame oil
1 ripe tomato, chopped
6 ½ cups chicken broth
1/2 cup yogurt
2 tablespoons arrowroot
1 cup celery with leaves, chopped
Salt and ground black pepper, to taste

Directions

- Coat the chicken with the arrowroot, salt and black pepper. Press the SOUP/STEW key, then, the time select key and set to 30 minutes
- Now, heat olive oil and brown the chicken until it's lightly browned, about 6 minutes.
- Stir in the onions and sauté them for 4 more minutes. Add the rest of the above ingredients, minus the yogurt.
- Place the lid on the Power pressure cooker XL, lock the lid and switch the pressure release valve to closed. Press the CANCEL key.
- Let the steam naturally release. When the steam is completely released, remove the cooker's lid.
- Stir in the yogurt and serve immediately.

35. Flavorful Turkey Sausage Stew

Ready in about 2 hours 15 minutes
Servings 8

The most flavorful turkey sausage stew made easily in your Power pressure cooker XL! If you don't have a turkey stock on hand, any type of stock will work.

Per serving: 207 Calories; 13.2g Fat; 3.8g Carbs; 20.6g Protein; 1g Sugars

Ingredients

2 cups turkey breakfast sausage, chopped
1 cup scallions, chopped
1 cup lean ground beef
1 cup Roma tomatoes, chopped
1 cup turkey stock
4 cups water
3 teaspoons corn oil
3 cloves garlic, smashed
1 cup sharp cheese, shaved
1/2 teaspoon cumin powder
1 teaspoon ground bay leaf
1/2 teaspoon fennel seeds

Directions

- Heat the oil in a saucepan over a moderate heat. Then, sauté the scallions and garlic until they're just tender, about 4 minutes.
- Stir in the beef and sausage; cook until the meat is browned, about 6 minutes.
- Transfer this sautéed mixture to the Power pressure cooker XL. Add the remaining ingredients, minus the cheese. Choose the SLOW COOK function.
- Place the lid on the Power pressure cooker XL, lock the lid and switch the pressure release valve to closed. Cook for 2 hours.
- Ladle the stew into individual bowls; serve topped with sharp cheese. Enjoy!

36. Chicken and Sorghum Soup with Green Peas

Ready in about 40 minutes
Servings 6

Sorghum is a gluten-free grain that makes a perfect addition to this great tasting chicken soup with vegetables. Green peas add a touch of spring and refreshment to your meal!

Per serving: 399 Calories; 9.3g Fat; 63.2g Carbs; 18.3g Protein; 4.2g Sugars

Ingredients

6 chicken thighs, boneless
Salt and ground black pepper, to taste
2 cups sorghum grain
1 ½ cups frozen green peas, thawed
2 tablespoons ghee
2 russet potatoes, peeled and sliced
6 ½ cups chicken broth
1 cup carrots, sliced
2 shallots, diced
3 teaspoons corn flour
1/2 teaspoon salt
1 teaspoon cayenne pepper
1/4 teaspoon black pepper

Directions

- Toss the chicken with the corn flour; generously season with salt and ground black pepper.
- Press the SOUP/STEW key; now, use the cook time selector to adjust to 30 minutes.
- Then, warm the ghee until melted. Brown the coated chicken, turning periodically, for 6 minutes or until lightly browned.
- Add the shallots, carrots, and potatoes. Top with sorghum and broth; season with salt, black pepper, and cayenne pepper. Place the lid on the Power pressure cooker XL, lock the lid and switch the pressure release valve to closed.
- Press the CANCEL key. When the steam is completely released, remove the lid.
- Afterwards, stir in green peas; cover and let it stand for 3 minutes. Serve warm.

37. Turkey and Vegetable Risotto

Ready in about 25 minutes
Servings 8

A nutritious and delicious risotto can be prepared quickly with help from your Power pressure cooker XL! Make the most of food and enjoy with your family!

Per serving: 579 Calories; 20.1g Fat; 51.2g Carbs; 44.6g Protein; 2.3g Sugars

Ingredients

2 cups turkey leftovers, chopped
1/2 stick butter, at room temperature
2 cups fresh Swiss chard, torn into pieces
1 cup rutabaga, chopped
1 cup zucchini, chopped
1 cup carrots, chopped
3 cups Arborio rice, rinsed
2 teaspoons soy sauce
5 cups broth

Directions

- Press the RICE/RISOTTO key; use the cook time selector to adjust to 18 minutes.
- Add all ingredients to the Power pressure cooker XL.
- Place the lid on the Power pressure cooker XL, lock the lid and switch the pressure release valve to closed.
- Press the CANCEL key. When the steam is completely released, remove the cooker's lid. Serve warm.

38. Chunky Poultry Chili

Ready in about 20 minutes
Servings 8

This fabulous chili is relatively low in calories but high in protein. It's made with two kinds of peppers, pinto beans and great tasting seasonings.

Per serving: 398 Calories; 12.8g Fat; 41g Carbs; 29.9g Protein; 3.6g Sugars

Ingredients

1 cup tomatoes, chopped
16 ounces canned pinto beans, drained
1 teaspoon minced garlic
1 cup bell peppers, chopped
2 cups water
1 teaspoon dried marjoram
1 cup scallions, finely chopped
1 cup serrano peppers, deveined and chopped
3 teaspoons canola oil
1 cup crème fraiche, to serve
1 pound mix of ground turkey and chicken
2 ½ cups broth

Directions

- Press the MEAT/CHICKEN key. Now, heat the oil until sizzling. Then, sauté the garlic and scallions until they're tender and fragrant.
- Throw in the rest of the above ingredients, minus crème fraiche.
- Place the lid on the Power pressure cooker XL, lock the lid and switch the pressure release valve to closed. Cook for 15 minutes.
- Press the CANCEL key. Switch the pressure release valve to open. When the steam is completely released, remove the cooker's lid.
- Divide your chili among eight serving bowl. Add a dollop of crème fraiche to each serving. Enjoy!

39. Habanero Chicken Soup with Barley

Ready in about 25 minutes
Servings 6

This spicy chicken soup is easy to prepare in the Power pressure cooker. A great choice for your next family meal!

Per serving: 532 Calories; 10.8g Fat; 85.5g Carbs; 27.9g Protein; 14.8g Sugars

Ingredients

1 teaspoon habanero pepper, seeded and finely minced
3/4 pound chicken thighs, boneless, skinless and chopped
3/4 cup cooked barley
1/3 teaspoon ground cumin
Sea salt and ground black pepper, to taste
2 shallots, diced
1 cup celery, sliced
1 quart tomato soup
3 teaspoons olive oil
3 teaspoons corn flour
6 small chapattis

Directions

- Dust the chicken with the corn flour; season with salt and black pepper.
- Press the CHICKEN/MEAT key. Now, heat the oil until sizzling. Then, brown the coated chicken about 6 minutes in your Power pressure cooker XL.
- Then, sauté the shallots, celery, and habanero pepper for 2 minutes. Add the tomato soup, and ground cumin.
- Place the lid on the Power pressure cooker XL, lock the lid and switch the pressure release valve to closed. Cook for 15 minutes.
- Press the CANCEL key. Switch the pressure release valve to open. When the steam is completely released, remove the cooker's lid.
- Stir in barley and serve warm with chapattis.

40. Green Peas and Chicken Soup

Ready in about 25 minutes
Servings 8

Here's an all-time favorite! Now, you've got to find some soft dinner rolls and your meal is ready!

Per serving: 210 Calories; 6.9g Fat; 25.7g Carbs; 12.4g Protein; 8g Sugars

Ingredients

1 teaspoon peanut oil
2 chicken thighs, skin removed
2 chicken drumsticks, boneless and chopped
1 pound carrots, peeled and grated
1/2 pound parsnip, chopped
2 shallots, peeled and chopped
2 dried rosemary sprigs
1 teaspoon minced garlic
4 ½ cups chicken stock
1 teaspoon ground bay leaf
1 cup rutabaga, peeled and finely chopped
1 teaspoon lemon zest
16 ounces frozen green peas, thawed
3 teaspoons corn oil
1 pound jicama, peeled and diced
Salt and freshly ground black pepper, to taste

Directions

- Press the CHICKEN/MEAT key. Now, heat the corn oil and peanut oil.
- Next, sauté the carrots, rutabaga, parsnip, shallots, and chicken meat until just tender. Add the remaining ingredients, minus green peas.
- Place the lid on the Power pressure cooker XL, lock the lid and switch the pressure release valve to closed. Cook for 15 minutes.
- Press the CANCEL key. Switch the pressure release valve to open. When the steam is completely released, remove the cooker's lid.
- Add green peas, cover and let it stand for 6 minutes. Serve warm.

41. Pilaf with Turkey Sausage

Ready in about 25 minutes
Servings 8

You're about to cook the best winter pilaf you've ever eaten! The recipe calls for chili powder but you can also use habanero pepper or ancho chili pepper. When it comes to the mustard, you can use your favorite brand.

Per serving: 347 Calories; 6g Fat; 56.9g Carbs; 14.7g Protein; 2.5g Sugars

Ingredients

2 ½ cups white rice, rinsed
4 turkey sausages, sliced
4 cups spinach, torn into pieces
1 cup bell peppers, seeded and thinly sliced
3 teaspoons olive oil
2 shallots, chopped
1 cup fennel bulb, chopped
1 teaspoon minced garlic
2 tablespoons brown mustard, for garnish
1/2 teaspoon chili powder
1/2 pound carrots, chopped
4 cups vegetable broth
Salt and ground black pepper, to your liking
1/3 cup apple wine

Directions

- Choose the BEANS/LENTILS function; use the cook time selector to adjust to 15 minutes. Heat the oil and sauté the shallots and garlic until just tender and aromatic, about 4 minutes.
- Add the remaining ingredients, minus brown mustard.
- Place the lid on the Power pressure cooker XL, lock the lid and switch the pressure release valve to closed.
- Press the CANCEL key. Switch the pressure release valve to open. When the steam is completely released, remove the cooker's lid.
- Once the pressure has been released, open the lid. Bon appétit!

42. Mushroom and Turkey Soup with Black-Eyed Peas

Ready in about 25 minutes
Servings 8

Turkey thighs pair well with cremini mushrooms. Pressure cooking is one of the best cooking methods to achieve flavors that will blow you away!
Serve with Iceberg salad and croutons for a beautiful presentation.

Per serving: 209 Calories; 8.9g Fat; 15.3g Carbs; 18.7g Protein; 3.6g Sugars

Ingredients

1 ½ cups cremini mushrooms, thinly sliced
3 turkey thighs, skinless and boneless
2 cups black-eyed peas, soaked overnight
1 cup celery with leaves, finely chopped
1 teaspoon minced garlic
2 tablespoons olive oil
2 yellow onions, peeled and diced
1/2 pound carrots, peeled and grated
5 cups chicken stock
2 dried thyme sprigs
2 dried rosemary sprigs
1 cup fennel bulb, peeled and finely chopped
Salt and freshly ground black pepper, to taste

Directions

- Choose the RICE/RISOTTO function; use the cook time selector to adjust to 18 minutes. Heat the oil and sauté the fennel, carrots, celery, onions and garlic until just tender and aromatic, about 6 minutes.
- Add the remaining ingredients. Place the lid on the Power pressure cooker XL, lock the lid and switch the pressure release valve to closed.
- Press the CANCEL key. Switch the pressure release valve to open. When the steam is completely released, remove the cooker's lid.
- Ladle the soup into individual bowls and serve with croutons if desired.

43. Chicken Fillets with Orange Sauce and Cashews

Ready in about 30 minutes
Servings 8

Chicken fillets go well with citrus fruit in every recipe, whatever cooking method you prefer to use. However, making pressure-cooked chicken fillets is easier than you think.

Per serving: 350 Calories; 15.1g Fat; 9.4g Carbs; 42.4g Protein; 5.8g Sugars

Ingredients

2 ½ pounds chicken fillets
2 cups orange juice
1/3 cup cashews, chopped
1/3 cup currants
3 teaspoons olive oil
2 teaspoons corn flour
1/3 teaspoon black pepper, ground
1/2 teaspoon dried dill
1/3 teaspoon salt
1/3 teaspoon ginger powder
1/3 cup cold water

Directions

- Choose the CHICKEN/MEAT function. Warm the oil and fry the chicken fillets for 4 minutes per side.
- Add the remaining ingredients, except for corn flour and cold water. Place the lid on the Power pressure cooker XL, lock the lid and switch the pressure release valve to closed. Cook for 15 minutes.
- Press the CANCEL key. Switch the pressure release valve to open. When the steam is completely released, remove the cooker's lid.
- In a small-sized bowl, while whisking vigorously, combine the corn flour with cold water. Slowly stir the slurry into the Power pressure cooker XL.
- Press the BEANS/LENTILS key and continue cooking for 5 minutes or until the sauce has thickened and thoroughly warmed. Serve.

44. Chicken and Fennel in Tomato Sauce

Ready in about 25 minutes
Servings 8

Here's a sophisticated chicken dish packed with fennel and tomatoes! Make this recipe on a rainy day and invite your friends over. Enjoy memorable moments!

Per serving: 153 Calories; 4.9g Fat; 13.2g Carbs; 15g Protein; 3g Sugars

Ingredients

8 chicken drumsticks
3/4 pound fennel bulb, chopped
2 cups tomato puree
1/2 cup cold water
Kosher salt ground black pepper, to taste
1/4 teaspoon curry powder
3 teaspoons vegetable oil
2 shallots, finely chopped
3 teaspoons ground flaxseed

Directions

- Choose the CHICKEN/MEAT function. Heat the oil and brown the chicken drumsticks for 6 minutes, turning periodically.
- Add the rest of the above ingredients, except for ground flaxseed.
- Place the lid on the Power pressure cooker XL, lock the lid and switch the pressure release valve to closed. Cook for 15 minutes.
- Press the CANCEL key. Switch the pressure release valve to open. When the steam is completely released, remove the cooker's lid.
- Stir in ground flaxseed to thicken the sauce and serve warm.

45. Traditional Chicken Paprikash

Ready in about 45 minutes
Servings 8

This is exactly what you need to warm up during cold and windy days! Add chili powder to enjoy this slurp-worthy paprikash even more!

Per serving: 281 Calories; 15.8g Fat; 7.8g Carbs; 27.5g Protein; 4.1g Sugars

Ingredients

1 ½ pounds chicken wings, boneless
1 cup yellow onions, peeled and diced
1 tablespoon smoked paprika
3 teaspoons canola oil
1/2 cup tomato puree
2 bell peppers, peeled and sliced
2 cups chicken broth
3 cloves garlic, finely minced
1 cup coconut milk
2 teaspoons arrowroot
Salt and freshly ground black pepper, to taste

Directions

- Choose the SOUP/STEW function; use the cook time selector to adjust to 30 minutes. Heat canola oil and sauté the onions, garlic, and bell peppers for 4 minutes.
- Add the chicken wings and continue cooking until they are slightly browned.
- In a mixing bowl, combine together the tomato puree, paprika, and chicken broth. Pour this tomato/broth mixture over the chicken in the Power pressure cooker XL.
- Place the lid on the Power pressure cooker XL, lock the lid and switch the pressure release valve to closed.
- Press the CANCEL key. Switch the pressure release valve to open. When the steam is completely released, remove the cooker's lid.
- Remove the chicken from the cooker by using a slotted spoon. Divide the chicken among serving plates. Combine the arrowroot and coconut milk. Then, stir this mixture into the cooker.
- Press RICE/Risotto key and simmer for 6 minutes, stirring continuously, until the cooking juices have thickened. Salt and pepper to taste; spoon the sauce over the chicken.

46. Porcini and Ground Chicken Risotto

Ready in about 15 minutes
Servings 4

Whip up a fabulous risotto that is not only tasty but nutritious! Plus, you don't have to spend time stirring.

Per serving: 608 Calories; 10.1g Fat; 95.7g Carbs; 32g Protein; 2.3g Sugars

Ingredients

2 cups porcini mushrooms, chopped
2 cups ground chicken
2 ¼ cups basmati rice
2 shallots, chopped
1 cup celery, trimmed and chopped
1/2 teaspoon paprika
3 cups chicken stock
1 teaspoon garlic paste
3 teaspoons olive oil
Sea salt and ground black pepper, to taste

Directions

- Choose the RICE/RISOTTO function. Set time to 6 minutes. Heat the oil and sauté ground chicken, garlic paste, shallots, mushrooms, and celery, until the chicken is lightly browned and the mushrooms are tender and fragrant.
- Stir in the remaining ingredients. Place the lid on the Power pressure cooker XL, lock the lid and switch the pressure release valve to closed.
- Press the CANCEL key. Switch the pressure release valve to open. When the steam is completely released, remove the cooker's lid.
- Let the pressure release gradually and naturally for a few minutes. Serve right away.

47. Rich Winter Meat Dip

Ready in about 20 minutes
Servings 24

Create a delicious party dip in 20 minutes with this easy Power pressure cooker XL recipe! Serve with breadsticks, tortilla chips, veggie sticks.

Per serving: 116 Calories; 7.6g Fat; 5.1g Carbs; 6.9g Protein; 3g Sugars

Ingredients

1 ¼ pounds turkey breasts, boneless and chopped
4 ham slices, cut into strips
1 cup salsa
4 cloves garlic, peeled and finely minced
1/3 cup stock
2 bell peppers, cut into strips
3 teaspoons olive oil
1 ¼ cups cream cheese
1 cup Greek-style yogurt
Salt and freshly ground black pepper, to taste
2 sprigs dry rosemary, crushed
1 cup leeks, coarsely chopped
1/2 cup tomato puree

Directions

- Heat the oil; cook the ham along with the garlic, leeks, and bell peppers for 4 minutes, stirring periodically.
- Next, stir in the salsa, tomato puree, stock, and chopped turkey breast.
- Place the lid on the Power pressure cooker XL, lock the lid and switch the pressure release valve to closed.
- Press the CANCEL key. Switch the pressure release valve to open. When the steam is completely released, remove the cooker's lid.
- Afterwards, fold in the yogurt and cream cheese. Give it a good stir. Season with salt, black pepper, and dried rosemary. Bon appétit!

48. Hot Habanero Chicken Breasts

Ready in about 30 minutes
Servings 6

Here's a speedy, budget friendly dish for your next dinner party! We love habanero sauce here, but feel free to use any other hot sauce of your choice.

Per serving: 311 Calories; 10g Fat; 14.4g Carbs; 39.1g Protein; 11.9g Sugars

Ingredients

6 tablespoons habanero sauce
6 chicken breast halves, skinless
1/3 cup maple syrup
1/2 cup tomato puree
1/2 teaspoon ground black pepper
1/2 teaspoon cumin seeds
1 teaspoon sea salt
1 teaspoon smoked paprika
1/2 teaspoon dried basil
1 ½ cups water

Directions

- Pour the water into the Power pressure cooker XL; place a steamer basket on the bottom.
- Arrange the chicken breast halves in the steamer basket. Press the CHICKEN/MEAT key. Set time to 15 minutes.
- Place the lid on the Power pressure cooker XL, lock the lid and switch the pressure release valve to closed.
- Press the CANCEL key. Switch the pressure release valve to open. When the steam is completely released, remove the cooker's lid.
- In the meantime, prepare the dipping sauce by mixing the rest of the above ingredients.
- Cook chicken breast under the broiler for an additional 6 minutes. Serve hot.

49. Two-Cheese and Pancetta Dip

Ready in about 25 minutes
Servings 24

With its rich flavor and unique texture, lard is prized for its versatility in the kitchen. It will give to this chunky and flavorful dipping sauce a special aroma and an amazing smoothness. You can use a goose fat too. Serve with your favorite dippers and enjoy your party!

Per serving: 102 Calories; 5.9g Fat; 4.3g Carbs; 8g Protein; 1.5g Sugars

Ingredients

1/2 cup Mozzarella cheese, grated
1 cup Ricotta cheese
4 pancetta slices, cut into strips
3/4 pound minced chicken meat
2 shallots, peeled and chopped
1 cup salsa
4 cloves garlic, peeled and minced
4 tablespoons ketchup
1 cup stock
2 bell peppers, cut into strips
3 tablespoons lard, softened
Salt and crushed red pepper flakes, to taste
1 teaspoon dry dill weed

Directions

- Press the CHICKEN/MEAT key. Set time to 15 minutes. Melt the lard and cook pancetta for 2 minutes.
- Then add the garlic, shallots and peppers; cook for a further 4 minutes or until they're fragrant.
- Next, stir in the salsa, ketchup, stock, and minced chicken meat. Add the salt, red pepper flakes, and dill.
- Place the lid on the Power pressure cooker XL, lock the lid and switch the pressure release valve to closed.
- Press the CANCEL key. Switch the pressure release valve to open. When the steam is completely released, remove the cooker's lid.
- Afterwards, fold in both cheeses and stir to combine well. Serve at room temperature.

50. Barbecue Chicken Drumsticks

Ready in about 20 minutes
Servings 6

Don't settle for a boring chicken! Make the most of your Power pressure cooker XL and try these drumsticks that are ready in 20 minutes.

Per serving: 307 Calories; 9g Fat; 22.1g Carbs; 32.3g Protein; 11.3g Sugars

Ingredients

1 cup barbecue sauce
1 ½ pounds chicken drumsticks
3 teaspoons sesame oil
1 cup spring onions, chopped
1/2 teaspoon cayenne pepper
1 teaspoon salt
1/3 teaspoon ground black pepper
1/3 cup all-purpose flour
2 cloves garlic, minced

Directions

- Press the CHICKEN/MEAT key. Season the chicken drumsticks with black pepper, cayenne pepper, and salt.
- Heat sesame oil and sauté the garlic and spring onion. Stir in the seasoned chicken drumsticks and cook until they are browned.
- Then, dust the chicken with flour. Pour in the barbecue sauce.
- Place the lid on the Power pressure cooker XL, lock the lid and switch the pressure release valve to closed.
- Press the CANCEL key. Switch the pressure release valve to open. When the steam is completely released, remove the cooker's lid.
- Lastly, check for doneness and adjust the seasonings. Serve warm.

51. Hot Party Duck Bites

Ready in about 25 minutes
Servings 6

Duck meat is packed with protein, selenium, and vitamins B-5 and B-12. Using a homemade jalapeno sauce is something that your poultry deserves.

Per serving: 388 Calories; 24.1g Fat; 15.3g Carbs; 27.9g Protein; 11.5g Sugars

Ingredients

1 ½ pounds duck, cut up, with bones
1/3 cup tomato puree
1 ½ teaspoons kosher salt
2 teaspoons dry basil
1/2 teaspoon ground black pepper
1/3 cup maple syrup
1 ½ cups water

For Jalapeno Sauce:
2 jalapenos, halved
1/2 cup loosely packed parsley, finely chopped
1/3 cup sour cream
1 clove garlic
2 tablespoons lemon juice
1/4 teaspoon salt
1/4 cup olive oil

Directions

- Pour the water into your Power pressure cooker XL; place a steamer basket in the Power pressure cooker XL.
- Arrange the duck meat in the steamer basket. Press the CHICKEN/MEAT key.
- Place the lid on the Power pressure cooker XL, lock the lid and switch the pressure release valve to closed. Cook for 15 minutes.
- In the meantime, prepare jalapeno sauce by mixing all the sauce ingredients in your food processor.
- Press the CANCEL key. Switch the pressure release valve to open. When the steam is completely released, remove the cooker's lid.
- Add the sauce along with the remaining ingredients to your Power pressure cooker XL. Cook under the broiler for 6 minutes, until they become crisp.

52. Agave-Glazed Chicken Fillets

Ready in about 25 minutes
Servings 6

These sticky chicken fillets will amaze your family and friends! Add a few sprinkles of chili powder to spice up your weeknights!

Per serving: 388 Calories; 21.3g Fat; 6.9g Carbs; 41.3g Protein; 5.2g Sugars

Ingredients

1 cup chicken stock
1/2 teaspoon freshly grated ginger
1/3 cup agave nectar
6 chicken fillets
3 garlic cloves, crushed
1/2 teaspoon cayenne pepper
4 tablespoons olive oil
2 tablespoons sesame seeds
3 teaspoons oyster sauce

Directions

- Prepare your Power pressure cooker XL by adding 1 ½ cups of water and a steamer basket to the bottom. Lay the chicken fillets in the steamer basket.
- Choose the CHICKEN/MEAT function. Place the lid on the Power pressure cooker XL, lock the lid and switch the pressure release valve to closed. Cook for 15 minutes.
- Press the CANCEL key. Switch the pressure release valve to open. When the steam is completely released, remove the cooker's lid.
- Meanwhile, in a mixing bowl, combine the rest of the above ingredients. Coat the chicken with this mixture.
- After that, place the chicken fillets under the broiler for 4 minutes. Serve and enjoy!

53. Old-Fashioned Chicken Stew

Ready in about 40 minutes
Servings 4

Here is a great stew with depths of flavor! In addition, this is a great recipe for using up any leftover chicken that you might have in the kitchen; it will reduce the cooking time. Serve with hot cooked rice.

Per serving: 536 Calories; 15.1g Fat; 47.7g Carbs; 52.3g Protein; 7.7g Sugars

Ingredients

4 chicken thighs, halved
1 ½ cups stock
3 teaspoons olive oil
2 garlic cloves, minced
3/4 pound potatoes, peeled and quartered
1 cup bell peppers, chopped
1 cup scallions, chopped
1 cup celery with leaves, chopped
1 cup turnip, chopped
2 ripe tomatoes, chopped
2 tablespoons apple cider vinegar
1 cup canned black beans, rinsed and drained
1/2 teaspoon ground black pepper
1 teaspoon salt

Directions

- Press the SOUP/STEW key; use the cook time selector to adjust to 30 minutes. Then, heat the oil and cook the scallions, celery, turnip, bell peppers, and garlic.
- Now, cook for 4 minutes or until the vegetables are just tender. Add the rest of the above ingredients.
- Place the lid on the Power pressure cooker XL, lock the lid and switch the pressure release valve to closed.
- Press the CANCEL key. Switch the pressure release valve to open. When the steam is completely released, remove the cooker's lid.
- Remove the chicken thighs and pull the meat off the bones; return the chicken to the Power pressure cooker XL. Serve warm and enjoy!

54. Tangy Chicken Fillets with Peaches

Ready in about 15 minutes
Servings 6

Here are succulent chicken fillets your family will love! This simple and sophisticated dish involves minimal effort for maximum flavor. Try it today!

Per serving: 235 Calories; 8.4g Fat; 5g Carbs; 33g Protein; 4.5g Sugars

Ingredients

1 cup canned peaches in syrup, sliced
1 ½ pounds chicken fillets
2 tablespoons oyster sauce
1/2 tablespoon sugar
1 teaspoon sea salt
1 ½ teaspoons shallot powder
1/3 teaspoon white pepper, or more to taste
1/2 teaspoon cayenne pepper

Directions

- Rub the chicken fillets with all seasonings. Lightly grease the bottom and sides of your Power pressure cooker XL; brown the chicken on all sides.
- Sprinkle the sugar over the chicken; drizzle oyster sauce over everything. Add the peaches along with their syrup.
- Choose the SOUP/STEW function.
- Place the lid on the Power pressure cooker XL, lock the lid and switch the pressure release valve to closed. Cook for 10 minutes.
- Press the CANCEL key. Switch the pressure release valve to open. When the steam is completely released, remove the cooker's lid.
- Transfer everything to a serving platter and serve at once.

55. Aromatic Turkey Breasts

Ready in about 40 minutes
Servings 8

Need more ideas for what to make with turkey breasts?
Try this herbed turkey for an easy mid-week meal.

Per serving: 202 Calories; 5.9g Fat; 0.7g Carbs; 34.2g
Protein; 0.2g Sugars

Ingredients

2 sprigs dry thyme
1 teaspoon dried basil
1 ½ teaspoons garlic powder
2 teaspoons dry sage
Seasoned salt and ground black pepper, to taste
2 pounds turkey breasts, cut into bite-sized chunks
4 garlic cloves, peeled and minced
1 ½ cups broth

Directions

- Choose the SOUP/STEW function; use the cook time
  selector to adjust to 30 minutes. Firstly, brown turkey
  breast on all sides.
- Throw in the remaining ingredients. Place the lid on
  the Power pressure cooker XL, lock the lid and switch
  the pressure release valve to closed.
- Press the CANCEL key. Switch the pressure release
  valve to open. When the steam is completely released,
  remove the cooker's lid.
- Taste the turkey for doneness and serve. Enjoy!

PORK

56. Old-Fashioned Beans

Ready in about 30 minutes
Servings 8

Pinto beans are high in fiber and protein. This amazing food can reduce cholesterol levels, protect your heart and help lower risk of cancer.

Per serving: 516 Calories; 19.4g Fat; 56.1g Carbs; 29.2g Protein; 3.0g Sugars

Ingredients

1 ½ cups water
1 (1 1¼) package onion soup mix
1/4 cup olive oil
1/2 tablespoon brown sugar
1 tablespoon minced garlic
1 ½ pounds pinto beans, soaked overnight
2 teaspoons mustard
1/2 pound bacon slices, chopped
1 cup onions, chopped

Directions

- Choose the "BEANS/LENTILS" function; warm the olive oil and cook the onions, garlic, and bacon for 6 minutes.
- Add the soup mix and 1½ cup of water; cook for 6 more minutes. Now, add the beans and 4 cups of water.
- Stir in the mustard and brown sugar. Place the lid on the Power Pressure Cooker XL, lock the lid and switch the pressure release valve to closed. Cook for an additional 15 minutes.
- Press the "CANCEL" key. Switch the pressure release valve to open. When the steam is completely released, remove the lid. Serve immediately. Bon appétit!

57. Pork Ribs with Pearl Onions

Ready in about 35 minutes
Servings 4

These are deliciously spicy and very addictive pork ribs. Feel free to adjust the amount of spices to your own personal taste.

Per serving: 361 Calories; 20.3g Fat; 11.9g Carbs; 32.0g Protein; 6.8g Sugars

Ingredients

1 ½ cups tomato sauce
1 tablespoon minced garlic
1 ½ cups water
1/2 teaspoon ground black pepper
1 teaspoon salt
1/2 teaspoon dried marjoram
1 ¼ cups pearl onions
1 cup carrots, thinly sliced
1 pound pork ribs

Directions

- Choose the "CHICKEN/MEAT" function.
- Cook the ribs in the Power Pressure Cooker XL until browned. Pour in the water and the tomato sauce. Add the remaining ingredients.
- Place the lid on the Power Pressure Cooker XL, lock the lid and switch the pressure release valve to closed. Press the "TIME ADJUSTMENT" key until you reach 30 minutes.
- When the steam is completely released, remove the lid. Serve warm.

58. Tender Pork Butt with Mushrooms

Ready in about 35 minutes
Servings 4

This is a filling and comforting one-pot meal that is chock-full of nutritious vegetables and protein-packed meat. Making Sunday lunch for the whole family is easier than you think!

Per serving: 254 Calories; 7.8g Fat; 3.9g Carbs; 37.0g Protein; 1.6g Sugars

Ingredients

1/2 cup scallions, chopped
2 cups mushrooms, thinly sliced
1/4 teaspoon ground black pepper, to your liking
1 tablespoon coriander
1/2 teaspoon salt
1/3 cup dry red wine
1/2 cup chicken stock
1 teaspoon crushed garlic
1 pound pork butt, sliced
1/2 cup celery rib, chopped
1 cup celery stalk, chopped

Directions

- Choose the "CHICKEN/MEAT" function.
- Brown the pork in the Power Pressure Cooker XL for 10 minutes on all sides. Now, lay the sliced mushrooms over the ribs.
- Pour in the wine and chicken stock. Throw in the remaining ingredients. Place the lid on the Power Pressure Cooker XL, lock the lid and switch the pressure release valve to closed. Press the "TIME ADJUSTMENT" key until you reach 20 minutes.
- When the steam is completely released, remove the lid. Bon appétit!

59. Melt-in-Your-Mouth Pork Chops with Broccoli

Ready in about 30 minutes
Servings 4

An irresistible and affordable combination of tender pork chops and healthy vegetables that is perfect for cold winter nights when you need something tasty and satisfying.

Per serving: 302 Calories; 20.3g Fat; 5.1g Carbs; 20.8g Protein; 1.5g Sugars

Ingredients

1/2 pound broccoli, chopped
2 medium-sized shallots, chopped
1 tablespoon coriander
1 ½ cups beef stock
1 teaspoon salt
1/2 teaspoon ground black pepper, or more to your liking
1 tablespoon peeled and crushed garlic
1 cup celery stalks, chopped
4 pork chops
1/3 cup sparkling wine

Directions

- Press the "CHICKEN/MEAT" key.
- Brown the pork chops for 10 minutes on all side. Throw in the remaining ingredients.
- Place the lid on the Power Pressure Cooker XL, lock the lid and switch the pressure release valve to closed.
- Press the "TIME ADJUSTMENT" key until you reach 15 minutes.
- When the steam is completely released, remove the cooker's lid. Bon appétit!

60. Pork Tenderloin with Baby Carrots

Ready in about 25 minutes
Servings 4

This finger-licking pork tenderloin will delight your senses! Baby carrots are high in vitamin K, fiber, beta-carotene, potassium and antioxidants.

Per serving: 265 Calories; 4.9g Fat; 17.4g Carbs; 33.2g Protein; 9.2g Sugars

Ingredients

1 cup celery stalks, chopped
1 tablespoon peeled and crushed garlic
1/2 teaspoon red pepper, crushed
1/3 teaspoon fennel seeds
1/2 teaspoon cumin powder
1 pound baby carrots, thinly sliced
1 teaspoon salt
1/2 teaspoon ground black pepper, or more to your liking
1 pound pork tenderloin
1/3 cup dry red wine
2 white onions, chopped
1 ½ cups chicken broth

Directions

- Press the "CHICKEN/MEAT" key. Brown the pork for 8 minutes on all side. Throw in the remaining ingredients.
- Place the lid on the Power Pressure Cooker XL, lock the lid and switch the pressure release valve to closed.
- Press the "TIME ADJUSTMENT" key until you reach 15 minutes.
- When the steam is completely released, remove the cooker's lid.

61. Old-Fashioned Pork Belly

Ready in about 40 minutes
Servings 6

This recipe calls for sweet onions so that you can use Vidalia onions, Peruvian onions, sweet red onions, and so forth. Serve with warm pasta or rice.

Per serving: 550 Calories; 30.6g Fat; 4.0g Carbs; 53.5g Protein; 1.4g Sugars

Ingredients

5 medium-sized cloves garlic, sliced
1/2 teaspoon ground star anise
1 teaspoon grated fresh ginger
1 ½ pounds pork belly, sliced
2 ¼ cups water
1/4 cup cooking wine
1/2 cup sweet onions, peeled and chopped
1/3 cup soy sauce
1 teaspoon sugar

Directions

- Press the "CHICKEN/MEAT" key and sear the pork belly on both sides, about 8 minutes. Add the remaining ingredients.
- Place the lid on the Power Pressure Cooker XL, lock the lid and switch the pressure release valve to closed.
- Press the "TIME ADJUSTMENT" key until you reach 25 minutes; cook until your meat is almost falling apart.
- Once the timer reaches 0, the cooker will automatically switch to "KEEP WARM/CANCEL". Switch the pressure release valve to open.
- When the steam is completely released, remove the cooker's lid. Serve right away!

62. Party Barbecue Pork

Ready in about 55 minutes
Servings 16

You can serve this saucy pork on a plate or make delicious barbecue sandwiches garnished with some pickles, mustard and tomato ketchup. It is good to freeze and pull out as needed.

Per serving: 340 Calories; 7.1g Fat; 13.4g Carbs; 52.0g Protein; 9.5g Sugars

Ingredients

1 ½ teaspoons garlic powder
1/2 teaspoon black pepper, or more to your liking
1 tablespoon onion powder
1 teaspoon sea salt
1/2 teaspoon cumin powder
7 pounds pork butt roast
20 ounces barbecue sauce

Directions

- Press the "CHICKEN/MEAT" key.
- Season the pork with the cumin powder, onion powder, garlic powder, salt and black pepper. Now, fill the cooker with enough water to cover.
- Place the lid on the Power Pressure Cooker XL, lock the lid and switch the pressure release valve to closed.
- Press the "TIME ADJUSTMENT" key until you reach 50 minutes. Switch the pressure release valve to open. When the steam is completely released, remove the cooker's lid.
- Mix 2 cups of cooking juice with the barbecue sauce. Shred your pork and drizzle with the prepared sauce. Serve right now.

63. Pork Cutlets with Vegetables

Ready in about 35 minutes
Servings 4

There are so many ways to cook the pork cutlets, but the secret is to go nicely and slowly. Give this recipe a try and prepare the most appetizing cutlets with little effort.

Per serving: 351 Calories; 4.4g Fat; 45.3g Carbs; 30.6g Protein; 28.6g Sugars

Ingredients

4 pork cutlets
1 cup carrots, thinly sliced
1 cup parsnips, thinly sliced
1 cup onions, slice into rings
1 ½ cups BBQ sauce
1 ½ cups water

Directions

- Press the "CHICKEN/MEAT" key. Place the pork cutlets in your Power Pressure Cooker XL. Pour in 1/2 cup of BBQ sauce and 1 ½ cups of water.
- Add the onions, parsnips, and carrots. Lock the lid and switch the pressure release valve to closed.
- Press the "TIME ADJUSTMENT" key until you reach 30 minutes. Switch the pressure release valve to open. When the steam is completely released, remove the cooker's lid.
- Drizzle with the remaining 1 cup of BBQ sauce and serve right now.

64. Easy Braised Cabbage with Bacon

Ready in about 20 minutes
Servings 8

Here's a tangy, bright and comforting cabbage that you can plan even for busy weeknights. Top-notch chefs make braised cabbage with apples and a splash of balsamic vinegar. Lovely!

Per serving: 103 Calories; 8.5g Fat; 4.4g Carbs; 2.9g Protein; 2.3g Sugars

Ingredients

1 ½ cups beef broth
2 tablespoons lard
1/2 teaspoon ground black pepper
1 teaspoon salt
1 pound cabbage, shredded
4 slices bacon, cut into chunks

Directions

- Press the "BEANS/LENTILS" key and cook the bacon for 6 minutes or until it's browned. Add the lard and stir until melted.
- Add the cabbage to the Power Pressure Cooker XL; pour in the beef broth. Season with the salt and ground black pepper to taste. Stir to combine well.
- Press the "CANCEL" key; then, press the "FISH/VEGETABLE/STEAM" key and increase the cook time to 10 minutes.
- When the steam is completely released, remove the lid and press the "CANCEL" key. Serve warm.

65. Rigatoni with Sausage and Bacon

Ready in about 25 minutes
Servings 4

Everyone loves last minute meals that they can put together with ingredients from their pantry. In addition, if you use the Power Pressure Cooker XL, you will be able to make an amazing one-pot pasta recipe in 25 minutes!

Per serving: 762 Calories; 43.0g Fat; 64.6g Carbs; 38.2g Protein; 3.3g Sugars

Ingredients

1 (16-ounce) package dry rigatoni pasta
2 teaspoons olive oil
1 ¼ pounds sausage meat
2 ¼ cups tomato purée
1/2 teaspoon red pepper flakes crushed
1/2 teaspoon ground black pepper, or more to taste
1 teaspoon salt
4 slices bacon
1 cup leek, chopped
1/2 cup Parmigiano-Reggiano, grated
1 teaspoon fresh basil, chopped
1 teaspoon fresh sage
1 teaspoon minced garlic

Directions

- Press the "BEANS/LENTILS" key and warm the olive oil. Cook the bacon for about 5 minutes. Now, add the sausage meat and cook for an additional 5 minutes, until it is browned and thoroughly cooked.
- Add the leeks and garlic; sauté them for an additional 3 minutes. Now, add the tomato purée, salt, black pepper, and red pepper flakes. Add the rigatoni pasta; pour in the water to cover your pasta.
- Press the "CANCEL" key; then, press the "SOUP/STEW" key and increase the cook time to 8 minutes. Lock the lid and switch the pressure release valve to closed.
- When the steam is completely released, remove the lid. Throw in the sage, basil and the Parmigiano-Reggiano; stir until the cheese is completely melted. Enjoy!

66. Chili Bean Soup

Ready in about 40 minutes
Servings 6

If you're not a fan of spicy food, adjust the number of chili peppers to your liking. For a complete Mexican meal, serve these up with some tortilla chips or Spanish rice.

Per serving: 178 Calories; 4.2g Fat; 21.6g Carbs; 14.6g Protein; 8.4g Sugars

Ingredients

1 ½ cups carrots, diced
16 ounces canned tomatoes, diced
1/2 pound ham bone
2 bay leaves
1 cup celery rib, diced
1 teaspoon kosher salt
1/2 teaspoon ground black pepper, or more to taste
1/2 teaspoon cumin powder
1/2 teaspoon garlic powder
1/2 teaspoon chili powder
1 chili pepper, minced
1 ½ cups dry beans, soaked in water overnight
1 cup red onion chopped

Directions

- Press the "BEANS/LENTILS" key. Drain and rinse your beans.
- Put the beans along with the ham bone and bay leaves into your Power Pressure Cooker XL; now, add just enough water to cover.
- Lock the lid and switch the pressure release valve to closed. Press the "TIME ADJUSTMENT" key until you reach 10 minutes.
- Discard the ham bone and bay leaves; now, add the other ingredients and stir to combine well.
- Press the "SOUP/STEW" key; cook for 25 minutes. When the steam is completely released, remove the lid. Serve and enjoy!

67. Herbed Pasta with Bacon and Cheese

Ready in about 20 minutes
Servings 4

Get ready for rich and unusual pasta dish to kick things up! A perfect mix of flavor and textures in this pasta dish will amaze your family and friends.

Per serving: 652 Calories; 23.3g Fat; 98.5g Carbs; 17.4g Protein; 3.5g Sugars

Ingredients

16 ounces dry pasta
1 cup yellow onions, finely chopped
1 teaspoon minced garlic
1 cup bacon
1/2 tablespoon fresh sage
1 sprig rosemary
1/2 tablespoon fresh basil, chopped
2 ½ cups tomato purée
1/2 teaspoon ground black pepper, or more to taste
1/2 teaspoon salt
1/2 teaspoon paprika
2 teaspoons lard, at room temperature
1/2 cup Cheddar cheese, grated

Directions

- Press the "SOUP/STEW" key and warm the lard; cook the bacon for about 5 minutes. Add the onions and garlic; sauté until tender and fragrant, for 6 more minutes. Press the "CANCEL" key.
- Now, add the tomato purée, paprika, salt, and black pepper.
- Add the dry pasta and enough water to cover your pasta. Add rosemary, sage, and basil.
- Choose the "BEANS/LENTILS" function. Lock the lid and switch the pressure release valve to closed.
- Press the "TIME ADJUSTMENT" key until you reach 8 minutes. Once the timer reaches 0, the Power Pressure Cooker XL will automatically switch to "KEEP WARM/CANCEL".
- Switch the pressure release valve to open. When the steam is completely released, remove the lid. Add the Cheddar cheese and serve.

68. Traditional Pasta with Bolognese Sauce

Ready in about 20 minutes
Servings 6

Traditionally, we use spaghetti for this recipe; however, you can use any type of pasta noodles you like; orzo and farfalle even work well here.

Per serving: 587 Calories; 36.9g Fat; 18.0g Carbs; 43.1g Protein; 5.3g Sugars

Ingredients

2 teaspoons lard, at room temperature
20 ounces pasta noodles
1 ½ pounds tomato pasta sauce
1 teaspoon smashed garlic
1 teaspoon dried oregano
2 sprigs dried rosemary
1/2 teaspoon ground black pepper, to taste
1 teaspoon dried basil
1 teaspoon sea salt
1 pound ground pork
1/3 pound ground beef
1 cup onions, peeled and chopped

Directions

- Press the "SOUP/STEW" key and warm the lard; sauté the onions, garlic, beef, and pork, stirring frequently, until they are tender, about 5 minutes. Press the "CANCEL" key.
- Add the remaining ingredients. Choose the "BEANS/LENTILS". Lock the lid and switch the pressure release valve to closed. Press the "TIME ADJUSTMENT" key until you reach 10 minutes.
- When the steam is completely released, remove the lid. Serve garnished with grated cheese if desired.

69. Christmas Spareribs with Pineapple

Ready in about 35 minutes
Servings 6

You can't go wrong with spareribs at Christmas. You could also try adding some diced chipotle or habanero peppers to give this dish an extra kick.

Per serving: 678 Calories; 27.5g Fat; 44.8g Carbs; 60.6g Protein; 41.1g Sugars

Ingredients

3 pounds spareribs, cut for serving
18 ounces canned pineapple
1/2 teaspoon black pepper, to taste
1/2 teaspoon coriander, ground
1 teaspoon salt
1 cup onions, sliced
1 (1-inch) piece ginger, finely chopped
1/2 teaspoon granulated garlic
1/2 cup tomato paste
3 teaspoons olive oil
1/3 cup tamari (soy) sauce
2 tablespoons apple cider vinegar
Prepared cornstarch slurry

Directions

- Press the "CHICKEN/MEAT" key and heat the olive oil; sauté the onions until tender, about 10 minutes.
- Stir in the other ingredients, except for the cornstarch slurry. Lock the lid and switch the pressure release valve to closed.
- Press the "TIME ADJUSTMENT" key until you reach 20 minutes.
- Once the timer reaches 0, the Power Pressure Cooker XL will automatically switch to "KEEP WARM/CANCEL". Switch the pressure release valve to open.
- When the steam is completely released, remove the lid. Now, add the cornstarch slurry and stir until the sauce has thickened. Serve warm.

70. Rich Ham and Sausage Spaghetti

Ready in about 20 minutes
Servings 6

No matter the style, a great spaghetti recipe is not just about the recipe. It's also about the reliable kitchen tools. The Power Pressure Cooker XL spaghetti is one of the best pasta recipes you've ever tried!

Per serving: 364 Calories; 8.2g Fat; 42.3g Carbs; 31.5g Protein; 9.1g Sugars

Ingredients

24 ounces dried spaghetti
1 ¾ pounds pasta sauce
1/2 teaspoon spicy brown mustard
1 teaspoon crushed garlic
3 slices ham, chopped
2 teaspoons butter, softened
1/4 teaspoon ground black pepper, or more to taste
1 teaspoon dried basil
1/2 teaspoon sea salt
1/2 teaspoon dried oregano
1 cup onions, peeled and chopped
2 teaspoons grapeseed oil
1 pound pork sausage meat

Directions

- Press the "CHICKEN/MEAT" key and melt the grape seed oil and butter.
- Now, sauté the onions, garlic, sausage meat, and ham, stirring frequently, until they are tender, about 6 minutes. Press the "CANCEL" key. Add the remaining ingredients.
- Choose the "BEANS/LENTILS" function. Lock the lid and switch the pressure release valve to closed. Press the "TIME ADJUSTMENT" key until you reach 10 minutes.
- Once the timer reaches 0, the Power Pressure Cooker XL will automatically switch to "KEEP WARM/CANCEL". Switch the pressure release valve to open.
- When the steam is completely released, remove the lid. Serve at once.

71. Slow Cooker Meatloaf

Ready in about 7 hours
Servings 10

There is no such thing as a saucy, slow cooker meatloaf! If you are missing grandma's classic meatloaf, here's the right recipe for you!

Per serving: 315 Calories; 18.7g Fat; 18.9g Carbs; 22.6g Protein; 7.7g Sugars

Ingredients

For the Meatloaf:
Non-stick cooking spray
1 ¼ cups milk
1 cup canned mushrooms, drained and chopped
1/2 teaspoon ground black pepper, or more to taste
1 teaspoon salt
1 cup onions, finely chopped
2 whole egg
2 sprigs dried thyme
1/2 teaspoon onion powder
3/4 teaspoon garlic powder
1 ½ cups rice, cooked
1 ½ pounds ground pork meat

For the Topping:
1 cup ketchup
1 teaspoon brown sugar

Directions

- Press the "SLOW COOK" key. Lightly oil the inner pot of your Power Pressure Cooker XL with a non-stick cooking spray.
- Mix all the ingredients for the meatloaf. Shape the mixture into a round loaf; transfer it to the Power Pressure Cooker XL.
- Then, mix the ingredients for the topping. Place the topping over the meatloaf.
- Lock the lid and switch the pressure release valve to closed. Press the "TIME ADJUSTMENT" key until you reach 7 hours.
- Once the timer reaches 0, the Power Pressure Cooker XL will automatically switch to "KEEP WARM/CANCEL". Switch the pressure release valve to open. When the steam is completely released, remove the lid. Enjoy!

72. Grandma's Juicy Pork Loin

Ready in about 30 minutes
Servings 6

Serve this mouth-watering pork loin as an elegant first course and treat your party guests! You can substitute rice wine vinegar for any white wine vinegar; champagne vinegar works well, too.

Per serving: 613 Calories; 25.6g Fat; 43.2g Carbs; 50.8g Protein; 38.3g Sugars

Ingredients

2 ½ pounds pork loin, cut for serving
16 ounces canned pineapple
1/2 teaspoon black pepper
1/2 teaspoon coriander, ground
1/2 teaspoon ginger, finely chopped
1/3 cup tamari sauce
1/4 cup rice wine vinegar
1/2 teaspoon granulated garlic
1 teaspoon salt
1 cup onions, sliced
1 tablespoon brown sugar
2 tablespoons olive oil
1/2 cup tomato paste
1 tablespoon cornstarch slurry

Directions

- Choose the "SOUP/STEW" function and heat the oil; now, sauté the onions until just tender or about 6 minutes.
- Stir in the rest of the above ingredients, except for the cornstarch slurry.
- Lock the lid and switch the pressure release valve to closed. Cook for 20 minutes.
- Once the timer reaches 0, the Power Pressure Cooker XL will automatically switch to "KEEP WARM/CANCEL". Switch the pressure release valve to open.
- When the steam is completely released, remove the lid. Add the cornstarch slurry and stir until the juice has thickened. Serve warm and enjoy!

73. Maple Beans with Bacon

Ready in about 30 minutes
Servings 6

Loaded with rich and flavorful bacon, this deliciously satisfying beans are just as good as a family lunch, as it is served on weeknights. It's also great when reheated. Use any type of your favorite dry beans.

Per serving: 307 Calories; 9.3g Fat; 36.8g Carbs; 20.2g Protein; 13.3g Sugars

Ingredients

2 slices bacon, chopped
1/2 teaspoon ground black pepper, or more to taste
1 teaspoon sea salt
1 cup onions, diced
3 tablespoons tomato paste
2 ½ cups water
3 cups chicken stock
1 tablespoon maple syrup
3 ½ cups dry beans

Directions

- Soak the beans overnight. Choose the "BEANS/LENTILS" function.
- Then, transfer the soaked beans to your Power Pressure Cooker XL.
- Add the rest of the above ingredients. Place the lid on the Power Pressure Cooker XL, lock the lid and switch the pressure release valve to closed.
- Press the "TIME ADJUSTMENT" key until you reach 25 minutes. Once the timer reaches 0, the Power Pressure Cooker XL will automatically switch to "KEEP WARM/CANCEL".
- Switch the pressure release valve to open. When the steam is completely released, remove the lid. Bon appétit!

74. Holiday Ham with Pineapple

Ready in about 1 hour
Servings 8

It's the holiday season! From now onwards, you can prepare traditional ham in no time and enjoy your holiday to the fullest.

Per serving: 324 Calories; 7.3g Fat; 44.4g Carbs; 21.2g Protein; 33.3g Sugars

Ingredients

1 pound baby potatoes, and cubed
1 cup water
20 ounces canned crushed pineapple
2 tablespoons vegetable oil
2 pounds ham, cubed
5-6 freshly cracked black peppercorns
1 teaspoon salt
2 tablespoons brown sugar

Directions

- Press the "CHICKEN/MEAT" key and heat the oil. Cook the ham cubes until lightly browned or about 6 minutes; add the water.
- Next, stir in the potatoes, crushed pineapple, and brown sugar. Season with salt and black peppercorns.
- Place the lid on the Power Pressure Cooker XL, lock the lid and switch the pressure release valve to closed. Cook for 50 minutes
- When the Beep sounds, perform a Natural pressure release. When the steam is completely released, remove the lid. Bon appétit!

75. Root Vegetable and Pork Soup

Ready in about 40 minutes
Servings 6

A tasty and rich soup that has all the best flavors of the season, made with the healthiest ingredients in the world! Turnip can help you lower blood pressure and fight cancer. Parsnip prevents heart disease, obesity, diverticulitis and stroke.

Per serving: 430 Calories; 21.5g Fat; 21.1g Carbs; 36.3g Protein; 4.6g Sugars

Ingredients

5 cups vegetable broth
1 cup parsnip, chopped
1/2 cup celery stalk, chopped
1 cup turnip, peeled and sliced
1 ½ pounds pork ribs
1/2 teaspoon paprika
1/4 teaspoon black pepper, ground
1/2 tablespoon sea salt
1/2 cup celery rib, finely chopped
2 potatoes, peeled and diced
1 cup carrots, trimmed and sliced
2 cups greens, diced

Directions

- Press the "SOUP/STEW" key. Simply add all the ingredients, minus the greens, to your Power Pressure Cooker XL.
- Place the lid on the Power Pressure Cooker XL, lock the lid and switch the pressure release valve to closed.
- Now, cook approximately 35 minutes. When the steam is released, open your Power Pressure Cooker XL. Add the greens and stir well until they're wilted. Bon appétit!

76. Delicious Pork with Fingerling Potatoes

Ready in about 35 minutes
Servings 6

This combo of pork and veggies is both sophisticated and rustic. You can also use New or Petite potatoes.

Per serving: 297 Calories; 11.4g Fat; 19.5g Carbs; 28.1g Protein; 4.8g Sugars

Ingredients

1 1/3 pounds loin, diced
1 pound fingerling potatoes, peeled
1/2 cup bell pepper, deveined and thinly sliced
1 teaspoon garlic paste
2 white onions, thinly sliced
1 teaspoon chili pepper, deveined and minced
Salt and ground black pepper, to taste
1 cup cream of mushroom soup

Directions

- Press the CHICKEN/MEAT key and brown the pork in small batches for 6 minutes; reserve.
- Next, add the onions, potatoes and peppers to the Power pressure cooked XL; sauté the vegetables in the pan drippings for 5 minutes.
- Pour the cream of mushroom soup into the Power pressure cooker XL. Add the garlic paste, salt, and ground black pepper.
- Place the lid on the Power pressure cooker XL, lock the lid and switch the pressure release valve to closed. Press the TIME ADJUSTMENT key until you reach 20 minutes.
- Press the CANCEL key. Switch the pressure release valve to open. When the steam is completely released, remove the cooker's lid.
- Serve and enjoy!

77. Pork Loin with Apple Sauce

Ready in about 35 minutes
Servings 4

Pressure cooked pork is moist, tender and flavorsome! This versatile meat goes well with cooking apples. In this recipe, the secret lies in the simple approach – brown the pork to enhance the flavor.

Per serving: 380 Calories; 19.5g Fat; 19.2g Carbs; 30.8g Protein; 8g Sugars

Ingredients

1 pound center-cut pork loin
1/2 pound cooking apples, peeled, cored and cut into wedges
2 small-sized leeks, white part only, thinly sliced
2 tablespoons canola oil
1 ¼ cups stock, preferably homemade
1 teaspoon cayenne pepper
1/2 teaspoon salt
1 teaspoon dry rosemary, crushed
1 teaspoon dry thyme, crushed
1/2 teaspoon ground black pepper

Directions

- Press the CHICKEN/MEAT key and warm 1 tablespoon of the oil. Season the pork loin with salt, black pepper and cayenne pepper. Sear the pork loin on all sides about 5 minutes; set it aside.
- Then, warm another tablespoon of oil; sauté the leeks, until they have softened, about 5 minutes. Press the CANCEL key.
- Add the apples, thyme, and rosemary; pour in the stock. Nestle the pork loin among the prepared apples and onions.
- Place the lid on the Power Pressure Cooker XL, lock the lid and switch the pressure release valve to closed. Press the CHICKEN/MEAT key and cook for 20 minutes.
- Once the timer reaches 0, the cooker will automatically switch to KEEP WARM/CANCEL mode. Switch the pressure release valve to open. When the steam is completely released, remove the cooker's lid.
- To serve, arrange your pork on a serving plate; spoon the apple-onion mixture over the pork loin. Bon appétit!

78. Green Beans with Pancetta and Scallions

Ready in about 15 minutes
Servings 6

Steamed vegetables are definitely one of the best options to make you lunch a delicious pleasure. In this recipe, you can substitute ham for pancetta with the same result.

Per serving: 245 Calories; 16.3g Fat; 9g Carbs; 16.3g Protein; 2.3g Sugars

Ingredients

1 pound green beans
1/2 pound pancetta, chopped
1 ½ cups scallions, chopped
3 ½ cups chicken stock
1/2 teaspoon brown sugar
3 cloves garlic, peeled and finely minced
Sea salt and freshly ground black pepper, to your liking

Directions

- Press the SOUP/STEW key and sauté the scallions, garlic, and pancetta for 3 minutes.
- Then, add the green beans and stock; sprinkle with sugar, salt and black pepper. Place the lid on the Power Pressure Cooker XL, lock the lid and switch the pressure release valve to closed.
- Press the FISH/VEGETABLES/STEAM key and cook for 4 minutes.
- Once the timer reaches 0, the cooker will automatically switch to KEEP WARM/CANCEL mode. Switch the pressure release valve to open. When the steam is completely released, remove the cooker's lid.
- Divide among individual bowls and serve right now.

79. Rice with Tomato-Chili Pork

Ready in about 20 minutes
Servings 4

Preparing pork ribs in the Power pressure cooker XL is not only fun, it's also very simple. Pork is quite versatile food so let your imagination run wild!

Per serving: 647 Calories; 21.1g Fat; 80.7g Carbs; 30.4g Protein; 2.6g Sugars

Ingredients

2 cups Arborio rice
1 cup Roma tomatoes, diced
1 chipotle pepper, deveined and finely chopped
1 pound pork ribs
1/2 teaspoon dried oregano
3 cloves garlic, minced
1/2 teaspoon dried basil
3 teaspoons melted lard
3 cups stock
1/2 cup scallions, chopped

Directions

- Press the CHICKEN/MEAT key and heat the lard; then, brown the pork ribs for 4 minutes. Reserve.
- Add the scallions and garlic and continue sautéing, until softened, about 4 minutes. Press the CANCEL key.
- Stir in the chipotle pepper, basil, and oregano; cook until they are aromatic, stirring often. Stir in the canned tomatoes and rice; then, pour in the stock.
- Nestle the pork ribs into the sautéed mixture. Place the lid on the Power Pressure Cooker XL, lock the lid and switch the pressure release valve to closed.
- Press the SOUP/STEW key and cook for 10 minutes.
- Once the timer reaches 0, the cooker will automatically switch to KEEP WARM/CANCEL mode. Switch the pressure release valve to open. When the steam is completely released, remove the cooker's lid.
- Serve warm.

80. Butter Beans and Pork Stew

Ready in about 25 minutes
Servings 4

Butter beans add a great chunky texture to this amazing pork recipe, making your meal less boring and more appealing! One teaspoon of chipotle powder works well with this stew, too.

Per serving: 595 Calories; 35.4g Fat; 26g Carbs; 42.3g Protein; 6.3g Sugars

Ingredients

2 cups canned butter beans, drained and rinsed
1 ¼ pounds pork shoulder, cubed
2 red onions, chopped
3 cloves garlic, minced
3 teaspoons vegetable oil
2 ripe tomatoes, chopped
1/2 cup bell pepper, stemmed, cored, cut into strips
1/2 serrano pepper, stemmed, cored, cut into strips
2 cups chicken broth
2 teaspoons dry thyme
1/3 teaspoon dried oregano
1/2 teaspoon dried basil

Directions

- Press the BEANS/LENTILS key and heat vegetable oil; now, sauté the onions and peppers about 5 minutes, until they have softened.
- Add the garlic, basil, oregano, and thyme and cook until they're just fragrant, for 30 seconds longer.
- Add the beans, tomatoes, broth, and pork. Place the lid on the Power Pressure Cooker XL, lock the lid and switch the pressure release valve to closed. Cook for 15 minutes.
- Once the timer reaches 0, the cooker will automatically switch to KEEP WARM/CANCEL mode.
- Switch the pressure release valve to open. When the steam is completely released, remove the cooker's lid. Give it a good stir. Enjoy!

81. Pork Cutlets with Petite Potatoes

Ready in about 30 minutes
Servings 4

This pork and potato dish is both dinner-worthy and family lunch option. If you don't have petite potatoes on hand, baby potatoes will work, too.

Per serving: 485 Calories; 24g Fat; 51.8g Carbs; 15g Protein; 6.6g Sugars

Ingredients

1 pound pork cutlets
1 pound petite potatoes, cut into wedges
1/3 cup apple cider
1 medium-sized red onion, thinly sliced
1 tablespoon butter
1/2 teaspoon ground black pepper
1/2 teaspoon cayenne pepper
1/2 teaspoon kosher salt
1 teaspoon hot red pepper sauce

Directions

- Press the CHICKEN/MEAT key and melt the butter. Season the pork cutlets with the salt, ground black pepper, and cayenne pepper. Brown pork cutlets for 4 minutes per side.
- Add the onion and potatoes; cook, stirring periodically, until the potatoes have softened and slightly browned, about 5 minutes. Choose the CANCEL function.
- Add the apple cider and red pepper sauce. Nestle the chops into the sautéed mixture.
- Place the lid on the Power Pressure Cooker XL, lock the lid and switch the pressure release valve to closed. Choose the CHICKEN/MEAT function and cook for 15 minutes.
- Once the timer reaches 0, the cooker will automatically switch to KEEP WARM/CANCEL mode.
- Switch the pressure release valve to open. When the steam is completely released, remove the cooker's lid. Serve warm.

82. Hash Browns with Pancetta and Fontina

Ready in about 40 minutes
Servings 4

This casserole is loaded with flavorful pancetta, hash browns and cheese and looks beautiful on your dining table.

Per serving: 516 Calories; 38.3 Fat; 9.8g Carbs; 31.4g Protein; 0.4g Sugars

Ingredients

1 ¼ pounds frozen shredded hash brown potatoes, thawed
12 ounces pancetta, chopped
1 cup fontina cheese, shredded
3 teaspoons vegetable oil
1/4 cup fresh cilantro, chopped
1 teaspoon salt
1/4 teaspoon freshly ground black pepper

Directions

- Choose the MEAT/CHICKEN function and 15-minute cook time. Heat the oil and sauté hash brown potatoes 7 minutes, stirring occasionally, until they are browned.
- Add the cilantro, pancetta, salt, and black pepper. Place the lid on the Power Pressure Cooker XL, lock the lid and switch the pressure release valve to closed.
- Once the timer reaches 0, the cooker will automatically switch to KEEP WARM/CANCEL mode.
- Switch the pressure release valve to open. When the steam is completely released, remove the cooker's lid.
- Transfer the mixture to a baking dish; top with shredded cheese and bake in the preheated oven at 350 degrees F for 15 minutes, until golden brown. Bon appétit!

83. Saucy Pork Shoulder with Celery

Ready in about 50 minutes
Servings 4

This tender pork shoulder can be served on any occasion. Add a pinch of chili powder for some extra oomph!

Per serving: 419 Calories; 31.4g Fat; 5.8g Carbs; 27.2g Protein; 3.8g Sugars

Ingredients

1 pound pork shoulders, trimmed and chopped
1 pound celery, chopped
1/3 cup apple cider
3 teaspoons olive oil
1 tablespoon sesame oil
1/4 teaspoon ground black pepper
1 teaspoon salt
1 teaspoon cayenne pepper
3/4 cup water

Directions

- Press the CHICKEN/ MEAT key and heat the oil.
- Season the pork with the salt, black pepper and cayenne pepper. Then, sear the pork for about 5 minutes. Press the CANCEL key.
- Add the remaining ingredients. Press the SOUP/ STEW key; use the cook time selector to adjust to 40 minutes.
- Place the lid on the Power Pressure Cooker XL, lock the lid and switch the pressure release valve to closed.
- Once the timer reaches 0, the cooker will automatically switch to KEEP WARM/CANCEL mode.
- Switch the pressure release valve to open. When the steam is completely released, remove the cooker's lid. Serve immediately.

84. Rich Ground Pork and Vegetable Dinner

Ready in about 25 minutes
Servings 6

Here's a great Sunday dish! Freshly ground pork and colorful vegetables, well-seasoned and perfectly cooked, in your Power pressure cooker XL!

Per serving: 282 Calories; 3.9g Fat; 31.6g Carbs; 30.1g Protein; 6.6g Sugars

Ingredients

1 1/3 pounds ground pork
4 new potatoes, peeled and sliced
1 cup bell peppers, seeded and thinly sliced
2 ripe tomatoes, chopped
1 cup carrots, thinly sliced
1 cup cabbage, shredded
1/2 cup celery stalks, chopped
2 red onions, finely chopped
1 teaspoon red pepper flakes, crushed
1/3 teaspoon cumin powder
Salt and black pepper, to your liking

Directions

- Press the CHICKEN/MEAT key and cook ground pork about 4 minutes or until no longer pink. Reserve.
- Add the onions, potatoes, carrots, cabbage, celery and bell peppers.
- Add the remaining ingredients, stir and place the lid on the Power Pressure Cooker XL; lock the lid and switch the pressure release valve to closed. Cook for 15 minutes.
- Once the timer reaches 0, the cooker will automatically switch to KEEP WARM/CANCEL mode.
- Switch the pressure release valve to open. When the steam is completely released, remove the cooker's lid. Serve warm.

85. Cherry Tomato and Bacon Omelet

Ready in about 20 minutes
Servings 6

This appetizing omelet showcases cherry tomatoes at their finest. However, you can use any type of fresh tomatoes in this recipe.

Per serving: 216 Calories; 14.9g Fat; 4.4g Carbs; 15.9g Protein; 2.9g Sugars

Ingredients

1 cup cherry tomatoes, halved
6 slices bacon, cooked and chopped
8 whole eggs
3 cloves garlic, peeled and minced
1/2 cup scallions, finely chopped
1/3 cup evaporated milk
1 teaspoon smoked cayenne pepper
2 sprigs dry thyme
Salt and ground black pepper, to taste

Directions

- Start by whisking the eggs with milk. Whisk to combine well.
- Add the remaining items; stir until everything is well mixed. Pour the egg mixture into a heat-resistant dish; cover.
- Add 1 cup of water to the base of your Power pressure cooker XL. Lay the trivet on the bottom of the Power pressure cooker XL. Lower the heat-resistant dish onto the trivet.
- Press the RICE/RISOTTO key and use the cook time selector to adjust to 18 minutes.
- Place the lid on the Power Pressure Cooker XL, lock the lid and switch the pressure release valve to closed.
- Once the timer reaches 0, the cooker will automatically switch to KEEP WARM/CANCEL mode.
- Switch the pressure release valve to open. When the steam is completely released, remove the cooker's lid. Serve warm.

86. Meatballs with Broccoli and Sultanas

Ready in about 20 minutes
Servings 4

One simple word – meatballs! With fresh vegetables, fresh eggs, and lean mixed meat, this recipe is flavorful and extremely comforting.

Per serving: 599 Calories; 18.9g Fat; 63.7g Carbs; 39.5g Protein; 11.9g Sugars

Ingredients

1 pound lean ground pork
1/4 pound lean ground beef
1 pound broccoli, broken into florets
1/4 cup sultanas
1 cup white rice, cooked
2 yellow onions, finely chopped
2 eggs plus 1 egg yolk
2 cups tomato puree
4 garlic cloves, minced
1 tablespoon dry white wine
2 cups water
2 tablespoons fresh parsley, chopped
1 teaspoon salt
1/4 teaspoon cumin seeds
1/2 teaspoon cayenne pepper
1/4 teaspoon ground black pepper

Directions

- Add the broccoli, sultanas, and cumin seeds to the Power pressure cooker XL.
- In a large mixing bowl, combine ground beef, ground pork, cooked rice, onions, egg, egg yolk, fresh parsley, garlic, salt, black pepper, and cayenne pepper. Mix to combine well.
- Form the mixture into 24 meatballs. Nestle the meatballs in the broccoli mixture.
- Whisk the tomato puree, wine and water in a measuring cup or a bowl. Pour the mixture into the Power pressure cooker XL.
- Choose the CHICKEN/MEAT function. Place the lid on the Power Pressure Cooker XL, lock the lid and switch the pressure release valve to closed. Cook for 15 minutes.
- Once the timer reaches 0, the cooker will automatically switch to KEEP WARM/CANCEL mode.
- Switch the pressure release valve to open. When the steam is completely released, remove the cooker's lid. Serve warm.

87. Mom's Gourmet Sauerkraut

Ready in about 25 minutes
Servings 6

Here's an easy and quick way to cook a satisfying meal for you family. Alternatively, you can use some chili powder to add extra warmth to this appetizing dish.

Per serving: 187 Calories; 3.6g Fat; 11.9g Carbs; 26.9g Protein; 5.3g Sugars

Ingredients

4 cups sauerkraut, shredded
1/2 cup chicken stock
4 cloves garlic, finely minced
2 red onions, chopped
1 cup tomato puree
1 ¼ pounds ground pork
1/2 teaspoon ground bay leaf
1/2 teaspoon red pepper, crushed
Salt and freshly ground black pepper, to taste

Directions

- Press the MEAT/CHICKEN key.
- Add the ground pork, onions and garlic to the Power pressure cooker XL; sauté until the meat becomes lightly browned; drain off any rendered fat. Stir in the remaining ingredients.
- Place the lid on the Power Pressure Cooker XL, lock the lid and switch the pressure release valve to closed. Cook for 15 minutes.
- Once the timer reaches 0, the cooker will automatically switch to KEEP WARM/CANCEL mode.
- Switch the pressure release valve to open. When the steam is completely released, remove the cooker's lid. Serve immediately!

88. Delicious Wax Bean and Pork Soup

Ready in about 35 minutes
Servings 8

Yellow wax beans are packed with vitamins, iron, manganese, dietary fiber, and antioxidants. A homemade crusty bread would go well on the side.

Per serving: 261 Calories; 11.8g Fat; 8.1g Carbs; 28.4g Protein; 3.7g Sugars

Ingredients

1 ½ pounds yellow wax beans
1 pound pork tenderloin, trimmed and cut into
1-inch pieces
3 ham hocks
1 cup bell peppers, diced
1/2 cup onions, chopped
1/2 pound celery, diced
1/4 cup dry white wine
1/2 teaspoon dried basil
1/2 teaspoon mustard seed
8 ½ cups water

Directions

- Fill the Power pressure cooker XL with all of the above ingredients, except for the wine. Choose the SOUP/STEW function.
- Place the lid on the Power Pressure Cooker XL, lock the lid and switch the pressure release valve to closed. Cook for 30 minutes.
- Once the timer reaches 0, the cooker will automatically switch to KEEP WARM/CANCEL mode.
- Switch the pressure release valve to open. When the steam is completely released, remove the cooker's lid.
- Add the wine and stir to combine. Serve and enjoy!

89. Pear Cider Pork Chops

Ready in about 25 minutes
Servings 8

These mouthwatering pork chops are seasoned with strong spices and cooked with pears and cider. Serve with warm corn tortillas.

Per serving: 423 Calories; 29.9g Fat; 7.8g Carbs; 25.6g Protein; 5g Sugars

Ingredients

1/2 pound cooking pears, cored and diced
2 ½ cups pear cider
2 pounds pork chops
3 teaspoons coconut oil, melted
1/2 teaspoon allspice
1/2 teaspoon ground bay leaf
Salt and black pepper, to taste

Directions

- Press the CHICKEN/MEAT key and warm the oil; now, season the pork chops with salt and pepper.
- Next, sear the pork chops for 3 minutes per side. Press the CANCEL key.
- Add the pear cider, pears, ground bay leaf and allspice to the Power pressure cooker XL. Place the lid on the Power Pressure Cooker XL, lock the lid and switch the pressure release valve to closed.
- Press the CHICKEN/MEAT key and cook for 15 minutes.
- Once the timer reaches 0, the cooker will automatically switch to KEEP WARM/CANCEL mode.
- Switch the pressure release valve to open. When the steam is completely released, remove the cooker's lid. Serve immediately.

90. Pork and Veggie Risotto

Ready in about 30 minutes
Servings 4

Here's the absolute easiest way to cook pork and vegetables along with rice! This easy pork risotto recipe is perfect for lunch or a potluck party.

Per serving: 565 Calories; 10.5g Fat; 78.7g Carbs; 38.7g Protein; 6.3g Sugars

Ingredients

1 pound trimmed boneless pork butt, cut into bite-size pieces
1 ¾ cups brown rice
4 cups chicken stock
1 cup scallions, chopped
1 cup bell peppers, sliced
1/2 pound red cabbage, shredded
4 garlic cloves, minced
3 teaspoons vegetable oil
1 parsnip, chopped
1 teaspoon sea salt
1/2 teaspoon cayenne pepper
1⁄2 teaspoon black pepper
1/2 teaspoon chipotle powder

Directions

- Press the CHICKEN/MEAT key and heat the oil until sizzling.
- Then, cook the pork along with the garlic, scallions, bell peppers, cabbage, and parsnip for about 5 minutes. Press the CANCEL key.
- Throw in the rest of the above ingredients. Place the lid on the Power Pressure Cooker XL, lock the lid and switch the pressure release valve to closed.
- Press the RICE/RISOTTO key and cook for 18 minutes.
- Once the timer reaches 0, the cooker will automatically switch to KEEP WARM/CANCEL mode.
- Switch the pressure release valve to open. When the steam is completely released, remove the cooker's lid.

91. Savoy Cabbage with Prosciutto

Ready in about 25 minutes
Servings 4

Did you know that Savoy cabbage is high in vitamin C, vitamin B6, vitamin K, potassium, manganese, omega-3 fatty acids and fiber?

Per serving: 250 Calories; 10.3g Fat; 24.6g Carbs; 16.2g Protein; 8.1g Sugars

Ingredients

1 pound savoy cabbage, shredded
1/2 pound prosciutto, diced
4 cloves garlic, minced
2 ½ cups cream of celery soup
2 yellow onions, peeled and chopped
Sea salt and freshly ground black pepper, to taste
1 chipotle pepper, minced

Directions

- Press the CHICKEN/MEAT key and briefly fry the prosciutto until they are nearly crisp, or about 3 minutes.
- Add the remaining ingredients and gently stir with a spoon.
- Place the lid on the Power Pressure Cooker XL, lock the lid and switch the pressure release valve to closed.
- Once the timer reaches 0, the cooker will automatically switch to KEEP WARM/CANCEL mode.
- Switch the pressure release valve to open. When the steam is completely released, remove the cooker's lid. Serve warm and enjoy!

92. Winter Meatball Soup with Farfalle

Ready in about 30 minutes
Servings 6

Did you know that we celebrate National Pasta Day on October 17th? Farfalle, also known as bow-tie pasta, is the perfect addition to this rich and thick meatballs soup. You can use dry egg noodles if desired.

Per serving: 326 Calories; 6.8g Fat; 55.1g Carbs; 12.9g Protein; 7.9g Sugars

Ingredients

12 pork meatballs
1 box farfalle
6 ½ cups stock
2 ½ cups spinach, torn into pieces
1 cup celery with leaves, chopped
3 cloves garlic, minced
2 sweet potatoes, peeled and diced
2 white onions, thinly sliced
3 teaspoons lard, melted
1/2 teaspoon sea salt
1/4 teaspoon ground black pepper, or more to taste
2 tablespoons cider vinegar

Directions

- Press the CHICKEN/MEAT key and warm 1 teaspoon of lard; brown the meatballs for 4 minutes, stirring periodically. Set them aside.
- Then, melt the remaining 2 teaspoons of lard; then, sauté the onions, celery, and potatoes until tender, about 6 minutes.
- Press the CANCEL key. Add the remaining ingredients. Place the lid on the Power Pressure Cooker XL, lock the lid and switch the pressure release valve to closed.
- Choose the SOUP/STEW function; cook for 10 minutes.
- Once the timer reaches 0, the cooker will automatically switch to KEEP WARM/CANCEL mode.
- Switch the pressure release valve to open. When the steam is completely released, remove the cooker's lid. Serve warm and enjoy!

93. Saucy Pork Meatballs with Ziti

Ready in about 25 minutes
Servings 4

Seasoned with Mediterranean herbs and cooked in vegetable sauce, these meatballs have a unique flavor that brings a twist to your everyday meals.

Per serving: 670 Calories; 17.2g Fat; 104.1g Carbs; 29.5g Protein; 15.7g Sugars

Ingredients

3/4 pound lean ground pork
1 box ziti
2 ripe tomatoes, chopped
1 cup vegetable stock
3 teaspoons canola oil
2 small-sized red onions, chopped
2 bell peppers, coarsely chopped
1/3 cup cider
2 cups cauliflower, chopped into small florets
2 sprigs dried rosemary
1/2 tablespoon dried basil
1/2 teaspoon dried marjoram
Sea salt, to your liking
1/3 cup water

Directions

- Thoroughly combine the pork, marjoram, basil and rosemary in a medium-sized mixing bowl. Form the mixture into 16 meatballs.
- Choose the CHICKEN/MEAT function and heat the oil; now, cook the cauliflower, onions and bell peppers, stirring frequently, for 6 minutes. Press the CANCEL key.
- Choose the CHICKEN/MEAT function. Stir in ziti, tomatoes, stock, water, cider, and salt. Throw in the meatballs.
- Place the lid on the Power Pressure Cooker XL, lock the lid and switch the pressure release valve to closed. Cook for 15 minutes.
- Once the timer reaches 0, the cooker will automatically switch to KEEP WARM/CANCEL mode.
- Switch the pressure release valve to open. When the steam is completely released, remove the cooker's lid.
- Stir gently before serving and enjoy!

94. English Muffins with Breakfast Sausage

Ready in about 20 minutes
Servings 8

What could be better than starting your day with warm English muffins and saucy breakfast sausage? You can add Monterey Jack cheese or cheddar cheese if desired.

Per serving: 527 Calories; 28.3g Fat; 33.7g Carbs; 32.8g Protein; 6.4g Sugars

Ingredients

8 toasted English muffins
1 ½ pounds breakfast sausage
1 1/3 cups evaporated milk
1/3 cup wheat flour
1 cup mushrooms, sliced
1 cup bone broth
1 teaspoon salt
1/2 teaspoon mixed peppercorns, freshly cracked
2 sprigs dry thyme
2 sprigs dry rosemary

Directions

- Choose the CHICKEN/MEAT function and cook the mushrooms and breakfast sausage for 6 minutes.
- Sprinkle with rosemary and thyme. Pour in the broth. Place the lid on the Power Pressure Cooker XL, lock the lid and switch the pressure release valve to closed.
- Once the timer reaches 0, the cooker will automatically switch to KEEP WARM/CANCEL mode.
- Switch the pressure release valve to open. When the steam is completely released, remove the cooker's lid.
- In a bowl or a measuring cup, whisk the flour and milk; season with salt and peppercorns. Add this mixture to the Power pressure cooker XL.
- Choose the FISH/VEGETABLES/STEAM function and place the lid on the cooker. Simmer for 2 minutes or until everything is cooked through.
- To serve, spoon the sausage/mushroom gravy over toasted English muffins and enjoy!

95. Pork Butt with Yams

Ready in about 20 minutes
Servings 4

As a starchy vegetable, yam is packed with riboflavin, B-complex vitamins, Vitamin C, niacin, magnesium, iron and calcium. Did you know that there are over 200 varieties of yam?

Per serving: 453 Calories; 17.4g Fat; 35g Carbs; 37.2g Protein; 3.9g Sugars

Ingredients

1 pound pork butt, cut into 4 servings
1 pound yams, peeled and diced
1 ½ cups vegetable stock
1 tablespoon maple syrup
3 teaspoons melted lard
1/2 teaspoon dried sage
1/3 teaspoon ground black pepper
1 teaspoon dried thyme
1/2 teaspoon salt
1/3 teaspoon allspice
1 teaspoon red pepper flakes, crushed

Directions

- Choose the CHICKEN/MEAT function and warm the lard. Season the pork with the salt, black pepper, and red pepper flakes. Then, brown the pork for 5 minutes, turning occasionally. Press the CANCEL key.
- Add the remaining ingredients to the Power pressure cooker XL.
- Press the CHICKEN/MEAT key and set time to 10 minutes. Place the lid on the Power Pressure Cooker XL, lock the lid and switch the pressure release valve to closed.
- Once the timer reaches 0, the cooker will automatically switch to KEEP WARM/CANCEL mode.
- Switch the pressure release valve to open. When the steam is completely released, remove the cooker's lid.
- Transfer prepared pork to a serving platter. Ladle the sauce over the pork.

96. Saucy Morning Bacon

Ready in about 25 minutes
Servings 4

Wake up to the smell of coffee and bacon! Make the most of your breakfast by pairing browned bacon with freshly brewed coffee. It's a unique, cool combination you won't want to miss.

Per serving: 441 Calories; 19.2g Fat; 60.1g Carbs; 7.6g Protein; 7.9g Sugars

Ingredients

8 bacon rashers
1 teaspoon olive oil
4 teaspoons sugar
1 cup brewed coffee

Directions

- Choose the CHICKEN/MEAT function and heat the oil. Cook the bacon for 3 minutes on both sides. Pour in the coffee.
- Place the lid on the Power Pressure Cooker XL, lock the lid and switch the pressure release valve to closed.
- Once the timer reaches 0, the cooker will automatically switch to KEEP WARM/CANCEL mode.
- Switch the pressure release valve to open. When the steam is completely released, remove the cooker's lid.
- Remove prepared bacon to the plates.
- Add the sugar to the Power pressure cooker XL; stir until it dissolves. Pour dissolved sugar over the bacon. Serve with biscuits and fresh fruit juice.

97. Pork Ribs with Walnuts

Ready in about 25 minutes
Servings 4

These flavorful and moist ribs come together in a snap and use only a few basic ingredients. Serve over mashed potatoes.

Per serving: 405 Calories; 28.1g Fat; 2.2g Carbs; 34.2g Protein; 0.4g Sugars

Ingredients

1 pound pork ribs
1/4 cup roasted walnuts, chopped
4 cloves garlic, minced
2 tablespoons apple cider vinegar
3 teaspoons butter, melted
1 ½ cups beef bone broth
1/4 teaspoon ground black pepper
1 teaspoon dried sage
1 teaspoon red pepper flakes, crushed
1/2 teaspoon salt
2 sprigs dried thyme

Directions

- Choose the CHICKEN/MEAT function and warm the butter.,
- Season the pork ribs with the salt, black pepper, red pepper, thyme and sage. Brown the ribs for 5 minutes on all sides, turning once or twice. Press the CANCEL key. Reserve.
- Add the walnuts, garlic, broth, and cider vinegar to the Power pressure cooker XL. Return reserved pork ribs to the Power pressure cooker XL.
- Press the CHICKEN/MEAT key. Set time to 15 minutes. Place the lid on the Power Pressure Cooker XL, lock the lid and switch the pressure release valve to closed.
- Once the timer reaches 0, the cooker will automatically switch to KEEP WARM/CANCEL mode.
- Switch the pressure release valve to open. Allow the pressure to release naturally. Serve warm and enjoy!

98. Yummy Sauerkraut with Kielbasa

Ready in about 25 minutes
Servings 6

Sauerkraut is way more versatile than you think! So fresh, so clean, this recipe will win your heart!

Per serving: 222 Calories; 15.7g Fat; 8.7g Carbs; 12.1g Protein; 4.1g Sugars

Ingredients

5 cups sauerkraut, shredded
1 pound pork kielbasa, thinly sliced
4 cloves garlic, minced
1 ½ cups stock
1 bay leaf
1 cup onions, thinly sliced
1/2 tablespoon sugar
Salt and freshly ground black pepper, to taste

Directions

- Choose the CHICKEN/MEAT function and brown the pork kielbasa for 4 minutes.
- Add the garlic and onions; sauté for 3 minutes more or until they're tender and fragrant. Press the CANCEL key.
- Stir in the rest of the above ingredients. Place the lid on the Power Pressure Cooker XL, lock the lid and switch the pressure release valve to closed.
- Press the SOUP/STEW key and cook for 10 minutes.
- Once the timer reaches 0, the cooker will automatically switch to KEEP WARM/CANCEL mode.
- Switch the pressure release valve to open. Afterwards, allow pressure to release naturally. Serve right now.

99. Home-Style Sunday Meatloaf

Ready in about 1 hour 10 minutes
Servings 10

Pork maple sausage and ground pork pair well in this easy peasy meatloaf! This meatball has a delightful taste thanks to a dose of aromatic spices.

Per serving: 267 Calories; 8.8g Fat; 27.7g Carbs; 18.6g Protein; 10.2g Sugars

Ingredients

For the Meatloaf:
1 pound pork maple sausage
1 pound ground pork
4 garlic cloves, minced
1 cup rice, cooked
2 large-sized eggs
3/4 cup milk
2 small-sized yellow onions, finely chopped
Salt and freshly cracked black pepper, to your liking
1/2 teaspoon turmeric powder
1/2 teaspoon cayenne pepper
1/2 teaspoon dried marjoram
Nonstick cooking spray

For the Topping:
1 cup ketchup
2 tablespoons brown sugar

Directions

- Lightly oil the bottom and sides of your Power pressure cooker XL with a nonstick cooking spray.
- Then, combine all ingredients for the meatloaf. Form your mixture into a round meatloaf; lower it onto the bottom.
- Now, mix the ingredients for the topping. Spread the topping over the meatloaf.
- Choose the SOUP/STEW function; use the cook time selector to adjust to 60 minutes.
- Once the timer reaches 0, the cooker will automatically switch to KEEP WARM/CANCEL mode. Switch the pressure release valve to open. Bon appétit!

100. Fall-Apart-Tender Pork with Cabbage

Ready in about 35 minutes
Servings 4

Here's an old-fashioned recipe that you can find in a grandma's recipe book. It uses pantry staples and cooks fast.

Per serving: 355 Calories; 20.1g Fat; 13g Carbs; 19.7g Protein; 5.8g Sugars

Ingredients

4 pork loin chops, boneless
2 cups red cabbage, shredded
1 cup dry white wine
3 cloves garlic, peeled and crushed
1 cup carrots, coarsely chopped
1/2 cup celery, coarsely chopped
2 yellow onions, sliced
2 cups vegetable stock
2 teaspoons spicy brown mustard
1 teaspoon kosher salt
1/2 teaspoon paprika
1/2 teaspoon ground black pepper, or to your liking

Directions

● Arrange the pork on the bottom of the Power pressure cooker XL. Now, lay the shredded cabbage over the pork.
● Pour in the stock and wine. Add the remaining ingredients.
● Press the SOUP/STEW key and use the cook time selector to adjust to 30 minutes.
● Place the lid on the Power Pressure Cooker XL, lock the lid and switch the pressure release valve to closed.
● Once the timer reaches 0, the cooker will automatically switch to KEEP WARM/CANCEL mode.
● Switch the pressure release valve to open. Bon appétit!

101. Italian-Style Cocktail Meatballs

Ready in about 40 minutes
Servings 10

Here are simple yet creative meatballs that are made from three types of ground meat. Throw in your favorite combination of spices.

Per serving: 230 Calories; 8.1g Fat; 8.4g Carbs; 32.2g Protein; 5.5g Sugars

Ingredients

1 pound ground turkey
1 pound ground pork
1/2 pound ground beef
1/2 cup ketchup
1 ½ cups tomato puree
2 onions, finely chopped
1/3 teaspoon ground black pepper
1/3 teaspoon dried oregano
1 teaspoon seasoned salt
1/2 teaspoon granulated garlic
1/2 teaspoon dried basil
1/2 teaspoon red pepper flakes, crushed

Directions

● In a mixing dish, thoroughly combine the meat, salt, and ground black pepper. Form the mixture into small meatballs (the size of golf balls).
● Choose the CHICKEN/MEAT function and sear the meatballs on all sides, turning occasionally. Press the CANCEL key.
● Next, add all remaining ingredients to the Power pressure cooker XL. Choose the SOUP/STEW function and use the cook time selector to adjust to 30 minutes.
● Place the lid on the Power Pressure Cooker XL, lock the lid and switch the pressure release valve to closed.
● Once the timer reaches 0, the cooker will automatically switch to KEEP WARM/CANCEL mode.
● Switch the pressure release valve to open. Bon appétit!

102. Pancetta and Colby Cheese Frittata

Ready in about 25 minutes
Servings 4

For the very first time, make the recipe as written; later, you can experiment with ingredients according to your taste. Serve with your favorite fixings such as fresh salad or tomato ketchup.

Per serving: 340 Calories; 26.8g Fat; 1.7g Carbs; 22.5g Protein; 0.6g Sugars

Ingredients

6 slices of pancetta, fried and crumbled
1/2 cup Colby cheese, grated
3 tablespoons sour cream
6 eggs, slightly beaten
2 teaspoons butter, melted
1/2 teaspoon ground black pepper, or to your liking
1/2 teaspoon onion powder
1 teaspoon salt

Directions

- Prepare your Power pressure cooker XL by adding the water and rack to the bottom. Treat a baking dish with melted butter.
- In a mixing bowl, beat the eggs together with sour cream. Fold in the crumbled pancetta and grated cheese. Sprinkle with salt, black pepper and onion powder. Beat until everything is well incorporated.
- Pour the mixture into the buttered baking dish. Cover with foil and lower onto the rack.
- Press the CHICKEN/MEAT key and set for 15 minutes.
- Place the lid on the Power Pressure Cooker XL, lock the lid and switch the pressure release valve to closed.
- Once the timer reaches 0, the cooker will automatically switch to KEEP WARM/CANCEL mode.
- Switch the pressure release valve to open. Serve warm.

103. Cheesy Rice with Ham and Peppers

Ready in about 15 minutes
Servings 6

It only takes 15 minutes to throw together this delicious one-pot meal. This recipe cooks the rice until it is just tender, but it is not overcooked sticky mess.

Per serving: 455 Calories; 13.9g Fat; 63.4g Carbs; 15.2g Protein; 4.1g Sugars

Ingredients

2 cups white rice
1/2 pound ham, sliced
2 bell peppers, thinly sliced
2 ½ cups cream of celery soup
2 sprigs dried rosemary, crushed
1/2 teaspoon cayenne pepper
1/2 teaspoon dried basil
1/2 teaspoon salt
1/2 teaspoon freshly cracked black pepper
1/2 teaspoon cumin seeds, ground
1 teaspoon dried oregano
1/2 cup rosé wine
1 cup scallions, chopped
3 teaspoons vegetable oil
1 teaspoon minced garlic
1 ½ cups water
1/2 cup Cheddar cheese, grated

Directions

- Press the CHICKEN/MEAT key and warm the oil. Then, brown the ham for 4 minutes; crumble and reserve.
- Then, sauté the scallions and garlic in the pan drippings until they are tender and fragrant. Add the peppers and continue cooking until they become just tender. Add all seasonings and stir until it's heated through.
- Next, add the wine, soup, water and white rice. Press the RICE/RISOTTO key.
- Place the lid on the Power Pressure Cooker XL, lock the lid and switch the pressure release valve to closed.
- Divide the cooked rice among individual bowls and top each serving with grated cheese. Bon appétit!

104. Pork with Tangy Tomato Sauce

Ready in about 35 minutes
Servings 6

This pork dish is comforting and economical. This is a great option for a family meal if you're in a hurry. If you are not, use the SLOW COOK function and cook the pork for 6 hours.

Per serving: 497 Calories; 37.9g Fat; 9.6g Carbs; 29.3g Protein; 3.7g Sugars

Ingredients

1 ½ pounds pork shoulder, cubed
1 cup tomato puree
1 ½ cups sour cream
2 yellow onions, diced
2 teaspoons lard, melted
1/3 teaspoon cayenne pepper
3 cloves garlic, minced
1/2 teaspoon chili powder
1/2 tablespoon coriander
Salt and black pepper, to taste

Directions

- Press the SOUP/STEW key and warm the lard. Use the cook time selector to adjust to 30 minutes.
- Sauté the onions and minced garlic until they have softened.
- Add the remaining ingredients, except for the sour cream, to the Power pressure cooker XL.
- Place the lid on the Power Pressure Cooker XL, lock the lid and switch the pressure release valve to closed.
- Once the timer reaches 0, the cooker will automatically switch to KEEP WARM/CANCEL mode.
- Switch the pressure release valve to open. Afterwards, add the sour cream and stir until everything is well incorporated. Serve warm.

105. Cocktail Meatballs in Herbed Sauce

Ready in about 30 minutes
Servings 12

Tangy apple juice is a great addition to these unique and cool meatballs! Add cocktail sticks and delight your family!

Per serving: 204 Calories; 4.4g Fat; 8.9g Carbs; 30.4g Protein; 2.3g Sugars

Ingredients

2 ½ pounds ground pork
1/2 tablespoon dried thyme
1/4 cup tamari sauce
3 cloves garlic, minced
1/4 cup apple juice
1/2 cup onions, diced
1 cup bread crumbs
2 teaspoons honey
2 tablespoons fresh chopped chives
1 ½ cups water

Directions

- Place the apple juice, honey, thyme, water, and tamari sauce in your Power pressure cooker XL; stir to combine. Press the SOUP/STEW key and cook for 10 minutes or until the sauce has thickened. Press the CANCEL key.
- In a bowl, combine ground pork, garlic, onions, and bread crumbs; mix until everything is incorporated.
- Now shape the mixture into 24 equal meatballs; carefully transfer the meatballs to the Power pressure cooker XL.
- Choose the CHICKEN/MEAT function and 15-minute cook time.
- Place the lid on the Power Pressure Cooker XL, lock the lid and switch the pressure release valve to closed.
- Once the timer reaches 0, the cooker will automatically switch to KEEP WARM/CANCEL mode.
- Switch the pressure release valve to open. Transfer to a large serving platter. Sprinkle with fresh chopped chives and serve warm.

106. Biscuits with Pork and Cider Gravy

Ready in about 30 minutes
Servings 8

Make this all-star gravy by using only one revolutionary kitchen gadget – the Power pressure cooker XL! This crowd-pleasing gravy is quick and easy enough to cook on a weeknight.

Per serving: 387 Calories; 14g Fat; 36.6g Carbs; 27.8g Protein; 6.5g Sugars

Ingredients

8 biscuits
1 ½ pounds ground pork
3/4 cup cider
3 teaspoons lard
1/2 cup white flour
1 1/3 cups milk
1/2 cup chopped onions
4 garlic cloves, minced
2 sprigs dry thyme
2 sprigs dry rosemary
Sea salt and black pepper, to taste

Directions

- Choose the CHICKEN/MEAT function and melt the lard. Then, cook the pork, breaking it up with a spoon, until no longer pink, about 5 minutes.
- Stir in the garlic and chopped onions and cook for 2 minutes more or until fragrant. Press the CANCEL key.
- Add the rosemary, thyme, and cider. Press the CHICKEN/MEAT key. Set the time to 15 minutes.
- Place the lid on the Power Pressure Cooker XL, lock the lid and switch the pressure release valve to closed.
- Once the timer reaches 0, the cooker will automatically switch to KEEP WARM/CANCEL mode.
- Switch the pressure release valve to open. Once the pressure is completely released, remove the cooker's lid.
- In a mixing bowl, combine the milk and flour; whisk until everything is well combined. Add the milk mixture to your Power pressure cooker XL.
- Press the BEANS/LENTILS key and let it simmer for 5 minutes, or until the sauce has thickened. Season with salt and black pepper. To serve, spoon prepared gravy over the biscuits.

107. Fontina and Bacon Delight

Ready in about 20 minutes
Servings 4

Embrace your inner grandma and check out this amazing family recipe! Prepare lots of warm crusty bread for dunking.

Per serving: 472 Calories; 41.9g Fat; 1.2g Carbs; 21.6g Protein; 0.9g Sugars

Ingredients

3 teaspoons bacon grease
1/2 cup Fontina cheese, shredded
4 thick slices bacon
8 eggs
2 tablespoons fresh cilantro, chopped
1 cup water

Directions

- Prepare your Power pressure cooker XL by adding the water and the trivet.
- Brush the bottom and sides of four ramekins with the bacon grease. Then, lay the bacon slices at the bottom. Now break 2 eggs into each ramekin.
- Top with shredded cheese. Lay ramekins on the trivet. Press the CHICKEN/MEAT key. Set the time to 15 minutes.
- Place the lid on the Power Pressure Cooker XL, lock the lid and switch the pressure release valve to closed.
- Once the timer reaches 0, the cooker will automatically switch to KEEP WARM/CANCEL mode.
- Switch the pressure release valve to open. Once the pressure is completely released, remove the cooker's lid. Sprinkle with fresh cilantro. Serve immediately and enjoy!

108. Penne with Pancetta and Cheese

Ready in about 30 minutes
Servings 6

The Power pressure cooker XL transforms penne and regular pancetta into a magical satisfying pasta dish in record time. If you can't find penne, use whatever pasta you've got on hand!

Per serving: 529 Calories; 28.6g Fat; 1.2g Carbs; 21.6g Protein; 0.9g Sugars

Ingredients

1 ½ box penne pasta
6 slices pancetta, fried and crushed
1/2 cup Cheddar cheese, grated
1 cup Ricotta cheese
3 teaspoons olive oil
2 tablespoons butter
1 cup red onions, finely chopped
3 garlic cloves, finely minced
3 ½ cups stock
1 ½ cups water
2 sprigs dry rosemary
1/2 teaspoon mustard seeds
Salt and freshly ground black pepper, to taste

Directions

- Press the CHICKEN/MEAT key. Set the time to 15 minutes; then, heat olive oil.
- Next, stir in penne, stock, water, salt, black pepper, rosemary, and mustard seeds.
- Place the lid on the Power Pressure Cooker XL, lock the lid and switch the pressure release valve to closed.
- Once the timer reaches 0, the cooker will automatically switch to KEEP WARM/CANCEL mode.
- Switch the pressure release valve to open. Once the pressure is completely released, remove the cooker's lid. Reserve.
- Press the CHICKEN/MEAT key and warm the butter; sauté the onions and garlic until just fragrant, about 4 minutes.
- Add the pancetta and both kinds of cheese; add the penne mixture back to the Power pressure cooker XL and gently toss until everything is well incorporated. Serve and enjoy.

109. Pork and Cheese Frittata

Ready in about 20 minutes
Servings 4

Here's a great idea for a winter breakfast! If you want to cut calories but still have the pork in your frittata, leave out the cheese and add an extra cup of tomato puree instead.

Per serving: 342 Calories; 23.3g Fat; 1.1g Carbs; 60.1g Protein; 0.6g Sugars

Ingredients

6 eggs, lightly beaten
2 teaspoons bacon grease
1/2 pound ground pork, cooked and crumbled
1/4 cup Cottage cheese, crumbled
1/2 cup Provolone cheese, grated
2 tablespoons fresh chives, coarsely chopped
1 teaspoon red pepper flakes, crushed
Salt and ground black pepper, to your liking
1 teaspoon smoked cayenne powder
1 cup water

Directions

- Add the water to the Power pressure cooker XL; place a steamer rack on the bottom. Then, brush a soufflé dish with the bacon grease.
- In a mixing dish, whisk the eggs and Cottage cheese. Fold in the ground pork and Provolone cheese. Season with salt, black pepper, red pepper, and smoked cayenne powder.
- Scrape the mixture into the greased soufflé dish. Cover the dish with foil and lower it onto the steamer rack.
- Press the RICE/RISOTTO key and then, use the cook time selector to adjust to 18 minutes.
- Place the lid on the Power Pressure Cooker XL, lock the lid and switch the pressure release valve to closed.
- Once the timer reaches 0, the cooker will automatically switch to KEEP WARM/CANCEL mode.
- Switch the pressure release valve to open. Once the pressure is completely released, remove the cooker's lid.
- Serve in individual serving dishes topped with fresh chopped chives. Enjoy!

110. Spring Pork Liver Spread

Ready in about 25 minutes
Servings 10

Forget store-bought pate and try an easy-to-make, old-fashion liver recipe! Sit back and dip into this amazing and fun spread, which is perfect for any gathering!

Per serving: 118 Calories; 4.8g Fat; 5.9g Carbs; 12.6g Protein; 1.2g Sugars

Ingredients

4 spring onions, chopped
1 pound pork liver, chopped
4 cloves garlic, sliced
2 large-sized tomatoes, chopped
3 tablespoons flour
2 tablespoons grapeseed oil
1/2 teaspoon ground black pepper, or more to taste
1 teaspoon sea salt
1 ½ teaspoons dried basil

Directions

- Press the RICE/RISOTTO key. Set the time to 18 minutes. Heat the oil and brown the pork liver for 3 minutes, stirring periodically. Add the remaining ingredients.
- Place the lid on the Power Pressure Cooker XL, lock the lid and switch the pressure release valve to closed.
- Once the timer reaches 0, the cooker will automatically switch to KEEP WARM/CANCEL mode.
- Switch the pressure release valve to open. Once the pressure is completely released, remove the cooker's lid.
- Serve with tortilla chips. Enjoy!

BEEF

111. Tomato Cabbage Rolls

Ready in about 55 minutes
Servings 6

White rice gives a wonderful texture to these cabbage rolls that will welcome you home when the days are cold and windy. However, you can make this recipe all year long.

Per serving: 495 Calories; 7.9g Fat; 62.6g Carbs; 41.5g Protein; 8.2g Sugars

Ingredients

10 cabbage leaves, blanched
1/2 teaspoon cayenne pepper
1 ½ pounds ground beef
15 ounces canned tomato sauce
1 tablespoon minced garlic
2 cups rice
5-6 whole black peppercorns, to taste
22 ounces canned tomatoes, diced
1/2 teaspoon sea salt, or more to taste
2 onions, chopped

Directions

- Press the "CHICKEN/MEAT" key.
- Combine the garlic, onions, beef, rice, tomato sauce, cayenne pepper, and salt in a mixing bowl; mix until everything is well combined.
- Divide the meat mixture among the softened cabbage leaves. Roll the cabbage leaves up to form logs.
- Place the rolls in your Power Pressure Cooker XL. Add the peppercorns and diced tomatoes.
- Place the lid on the Power Pressure Cooker XL, lock the lid and switch the pressure release valve to closed. Now, cook for 50 minutes. Use a Quick release pressure.
- When the steam is released, open your Power Pressure Cooker XL. Serve warm.

112. Herbed Pot Roast

Ready in about 50 minutes
Servings 8

This old-fashioned meal is easy to throw together into a revolutionary programmable Power Pressure Cooker XL. Feel free to pick another combo of spices. Mustard powder, marjoram and coriander work well, too.

Per serving: 397 Calories; 13.8g Fat; 15.1g Carbs; 49.1g Protein; 3g Sugars

Ingredients

1 pound red potatoes
1/3 cup red wine
1 tablespoon minced garlic
1/2 cup celery stalk, thinly sliced
1/2 cup parsnip, peeled and thinly sliced
1 teaspoon salt
1/4 teaspoon ground black pepper, to taste
2 ½ pounds chuck roast
2 tablespoons tomato paste
1 ½ cups beef stock
2 sprigs thyme
1 teaspoon rosemary
3 teaspoons canola oil
1 cup onions, thinly sliced
2 carrots, peeled and thinly sliced

Directions

- Press the "CHICKEN/MEAT" key. Season the chuck roast with salt and ground black pepper.
- Warm the canola oil in and sear the beef on all sides. Reserve the beef.
- Add the vegetables to the Power Pressure Cooker XL and cook for about 5 minutes. Add the beef back to the Power Pressure Cooker XL, along with the rest of the above ingredients.
- Place the lid on the Power Pressure Cooker XL, lock the lid and switch the pressure release valve to closed. Cook for 40 minutes.
- Switch the pressure release valve to open. When the steam is released, open your Power Pressure Cooker XL. Bon appétit!

113. Delicious Beef Ribs with Vegetables

Ready in about 55 minutes
Servings 8

Root vegetables, tomato paste and beef ribs are natural allies in this rich family lunch that demands to be served with horseradish sauce and lots of cornbread.

Per serving: 388 Calories; 11g Fat; 23.8g Carbs; 46.5g Protein; 5.5g Sugars

Ingredients

1 ½ cups vegetable broth
1 ½ pounds potatoes, small
3 teaspoons vegetable oil
2 medium-sized red onions, chopped
2 bay leaves
1/4 cup tomato paste
2 sprigs rosemary
2 ½ pounds beef ribs, excess fat trimmed
1/2 pound carrots, peeled and thinly sliced
1/2 cup water
1/2 teaspoon freshly ground black pepper
1 teaspoon sea salt
1 cup parsnip, chopped
2 cloves garlic, peeled and finely minced

Directions

- Choose the "CHICKEN/MEAT" function. Generously season the short ribs with sea salt and black pepper.
- Warm the vegetable oil and brown the ribs on all sides. Reserve the ribs.
- Add the parsnip, carrots, garlic, and onion; sauté for 5 more minutes.
- Add the reserved browned ribs back to the Power Pressure Cooker XL; stir in the other ingredients.
- Place the lid on the Power Pressure Cooker XL, lock the lid and switch the pressure release valve to closed. Cook for 45 minutes.
- Once the timer reaches 0, the cooker will automatically switch to "KEEP WARM/CANCEL". Switch the pressure release valve to open. When the steam is completely released, remove the lid. Bon appétit!

114. Family Beef Stew

Ready in about 35 minutes
Servings 6

This classic dish may become your family favorite. You can make this wonderful stew a few days ahead because it freezes great as well.

Per serving: 269 Calories; 9.6g Fat; 22.6g Carbs; 22.8g Protein; 6.4g Sugars

Ingredients

10 ounces canned tomato sauce
1/2 cup water
1 teaspoon minced garlic
1 pound potatoes, diced
1/2 cup green bell pepper, sliced
1/2 cup red bell pepper, sliced
3 teaspoons vegetable oil
1 cup onions, slice into rings
2 teaspoons Worcestershire sauce
3 teaspoons cornstarch
1/2 pound carrots, chopped
2 ½ pounds beef chuck roast, cubed
2 ½ cups vegetable stock
1 teaspoon dried dill weed
1/2 teaspoon sea salt
1/4 teaspoon ground black pepper, to taste
1/2 teaspoon dried thyme

Directions

- Press the "SOUP/STEW" key. Heat the oil and sear the meat.
- Deglaze the Power Pressure Cooker XL with a splash of broth. Add the garlic and onion, and continue sautéing for an additional 1 ½ minutes. Press the "CANCEL" key.
- Add the remaining ingredients. Place the lid on the Power Pressure Cooker XL, lock the lid and switch the pressure release valve to closed. Cook for 30 minutes.
- Switch the pressure release valve to open. When the steam is completely released, remove the lid. Serve warm, dolloped with sour cream if desired.

115. Classic Pasta with Ground Beef Sauce

Ready in about 15 minutes
Servings 6

There is a creamier version of this classic pasta dish. Top each portion with a few tablespoons of grated yellow cheese if you want to bulk it up even more.

Per serving: 319 Calories; 7.1g Fat; 34g Carbs; 29.1g Protein; 5g Sugars

Ingredients

22 ounces dried egg noodles
1 teaspoon dried basil
1/4 teaspoon ground black pepper, or more to taste
1/2 teaspoon sea salt
1 teaspoon dried dill weed
1 ½ pounds tomato pasta sauce
2 onions, peeled and chopped
1 teaspoon smashed
1 pound ground beef

Directions

- Choose the "CHICKEN/MEAT" function and brown the beef, stirring frequently. Press the "CANCEL" key.
- Add the remaining ingredients. Choose the "BEANS/ LENTILS" function. Place the lid on the Power Pressure Cooker XL, lock the lid and switch the pressure release valve to closed. Cook for 10 minutes.
- Switch the pressure release valve to open. When the steam is completely released, remove the lid.
- Divide among individual serving dishes and serve warm.

116. Festive Rump Roast

Ready in about 1 hour 5 minutes
Servings 8

This super-easy pot roast cooks perfectly in your Power Pressure Cooker XL. Serve with a cold glass of quality beer.

Per serving: 330 Calories; 11.7g Fat; 1.6g Carbs; 54.1g Protein; 0.8g Sugars

Ingredients

2 cups beef broth
1 cup onions, chopped
3 pounds rump roast
1 bay leaf
2 teaspoons olive oil
1/2 teaspoon ground black pepper, or more to taste
1 teaspoon salt

Directions

- Choose the "CHICKEN/MEAT" function. Pat the rump roast dry and season with salt and black pepper.
- Heat the oil and brown the meat on all sides. Remove your roast from the Power Pressure Cooker XL.
- Now, add the onions, beef broth, and bay leaf; add the water to cover the ingredients. Add the roast back to the Power Pressure Cooker XL.
- Place the lid on the Power Pressure Cooker XL, lock the lid and switch the pressure release valve to closed. Cook for 1 hour.
- Switch the pressure release valve to open. When the steam is completely released, remove the lid.
- Move the prepared roast to a serving platter. You can thicken the juices with a slurry of water and cornstarch.

117. Easiest Beef Stroganoff

Ready in about 35 minutes
Servings 6

You can substitute the sour cream with crème fraîche. What are the differences? Sour cream has a fat content of about 20% and it contains some thickeners. Crème fraîche has a fat content of about 30% and richer flavor.

Per serving: 471 Calories; 21g Fat; 6.4g Carbs; 62.9g Protein; 2.8g Sugars

Ingredients

2 ½ cups beef stock
1 ½ pounds mushrooms, sliced
2 ½ pounds beef sirloin, sliced
1 sprig dried rosemary
1 sprig dried thyme
2 tablespoons olive oil
1 cup red onion, peeled and finely chopped
1/2 cup sour cream
2 bay leaves

Directions

- Choose the "CHICKEN/MEAT" function and heat the olive oil; sear the meat for 5 minutes.
- Add the other ingredients, except for the sour cream.
- Place the lid on the Power Pressure Cooker XL, lock the lid and switch the pressure release valve to closed. Cook for 25 minutes.
- Switch the pressure release valve to open. When the steam is completely released, remove the lid.
- Serve dolloped with sour cream. Enjoy!

118. Beef Ribs with Mushrooms

Ready in about 45 minutes
Servings 8

Here's one of the best winter-worthy dishes that is chock full of protein packed mushrooms, vegetables and aromatic seasonings. Sure, you don't have to wait for winter to try this recipe!

Per serving: 296 Calories; 13.7g Fat; 6.8g Carbs; 35.7g Protein; 4.1g Sugars

Ingredients

2 cups mushrooms, quartered
1 teaspoon minced garlic
1 cup carrots, peeled and thinly sliced
1/4 cup olive oil
2 ½ cups vegetable stock
1/4 cup tomato ketchup
2 sprigs rosemary
2 yellow onions, peeled and chopped
2 pounds beef ribs, excess fat trimmed
1/4 teaspoon ground black pepper
1/2 teaspoon salt

Directions

- Choose the "CHICKEN/MEAT" function and heat the olive oil.
- Now, season the short ribs with salt and ground black pepper. Brown your short ribs on all sides. Set the ribs aside.
- Add the mushrooms, onion, carrots, and garlic to the Power Pressure Cooker XL; then, sauté for 5 minutes.
- Next, add the ribs back to the Power Pressure Cooker XL along with the rest of the above ingredients. Cook for 35 minutes.
- Switch the pressure release valve to open. When the steam is completely released, remove the lid. Transfer to a serving platter and enjoy!

119. Penne Pasta with Feta and Sausage

Ready in about 25 minutes
Servings 6

Penne pasta and beef combine very well and this meal is attractive in appearance as well. Did you know that Feta cheese is much easier to digest than cow's milk cheeses?

Per serving: 783 Calories; 40.4g Fat; 77.1g Carbs; 30.6g Protein; 14g Sugars

Ingredients

1 ¼ pounds beef sausage
1/3 cup olives, pitted and sliced
3 cloves garlic, minced
20 ounces penne pasta
1/2 teaspoon dried basil
1/2 cup Feta cheese, crumbled
1/2 teaspoon ground black pepper, to your liking
1 teaspoon salt
2 ½ cups tomato paste
1/2 cup scallions, finely chopped

Directions

- Choose the "CHICKEN/MEAT" function and brown the sausage for 5 minutes or until thoroughly cooked.
- Add the scallions and garlic; sauté them for 5 more minutes or until fragrant and tender. Press the "CANCEL" key. Add the rest of the above ingredients, except for the Feta cheese.
- Next, choose the "BEANS/LENTILS" function. Place the lid on the Power Pressure Cooker XL, lock the lid and switch the pressure release valve to closed; cook for 10 minutes.
- Use a Quick release method, unlock, and open the Power Pressure Cooker XL. Garnish with the Feta cheese. Bon appétit!

120. Risotto with Beef Bacon and Cheese

Ready in about 30 minutes
Servings 4

This one-pot meal is best enjoyed warm and it also has the advantage of being simple to prepare. Feta cheese makes an excellent addition to this rich beef risotto.

Per serving: 526 Calories; 17.5g Fat; 70.9g Carbs; 19g Protein; 2.5g Sugars

Ingredients

4 cups chicken stock
1/2 cup Feta cheese, crumbled
1/4 teaspoon freshly ground black pepper, to your liking
1 teaspoon salt
1 teaspoon dried dill weed
1 cup leeks, chopped
3 garlic cloves, chopped
1 ¾ cups rice
1/2 tablespoon olive oil
2 tablespoons apple cider vinegar
2 sprigs dried thyme
1 teaspoon dried basil
1/2 teaspoon mustard powder
1 cup beef bacon, diced

Directions

- Press the "RICE/RISOTTO" key and heat the oil; sauté the leeks and garlic until they are tender, about 5 minutes.
- Stir in the bacon, rice, and chicken stock. Add the apple cider vinegar, thyme, basil, dill weed, and mustard powder. Season with salt and black pepper; stir to combine well.
- Place the lid on the Power Pressure Cooker XL, lock the lid and switch the pressure release valve to closed; cook for 20 minutes.
- Once the timer reaches 0, the Power Pressure Cooker XL will automatically switch to "KEEP WARM/CANCEL". Switch the pressure release valve to open.
- When the steam is completely released, remove the lid. Serve topped with crumbled Feta cheese. Bon appétit!

121. Delicious Country Stew

Ready in about 50 minutes
Servings 8

Here's a hearty and savory stew with the best aromatics that cooks to perfection every time in the Power Pressure Cooker XL. Yummy!

Per serving: 297 Calories; 8.5g Fat; 15.5g Carbs; 37.8g Protein; 3.9g Sugars

Ingredients

1/4 cup tomato paste
1 cup carrots, chopped
1/2 teaspoon celery seeds
1 cup celery stalks, chopped
1/2 teaspoon cumin powder
1/2 tablespoon lard
1/2 teaspoon red pepper flakes, crushed
1 teaspoon sea salt
1/4 teaspoon black pepper, ground
2 bay leaves
1 pound potatoes, chopped
1 teaspoon minced garlic
2 onions, finely chopped
2 pounds beef stew meat
3 teaspoons arrowroot flour
2 ½ cups beef bone broth

Directions

- Choose the "CHICKEN/MEAT" function and sauté the beef, onion and garlic until the meat is no longer pink, approximately 5 minutes.
- Add the remaining ingredients, except for the arrowroot flour.
- Place the lid on the Power Pressure Cooker XL, lock the lid and switch the pressure release valve to closed; cook for 40 minutes.
- Once the timer reaches 0, the Power Pressure Cooker XL will automatically switch to "KEEP WARM/CANCEL". Switch the pressure release valve to open.
- When the steam is completely released, remove the lid.
- To make the slurry, combine 1/4 of the cooking liquid with the arrowroot flour. Add the slurry back to the Power Pressure Cooker XL. Serve warm.

122. Pasta with Beef and Mushrooms

Ready in about 25 minutes
Servings 4

Here's a gorgeous autumn meal! For a little more kick, use jalapeno or another green chili pepper.

Per serving: 428 Calories; 10.6g Fat; 49.9g Carbs; 35.6g Protein; 11.4g Sugars

Ingredients

1 pound dried egg noodles
3/4 pound lean ground beef
2 cups mushrooms, chopped
3 cups tomato puree
1/2 teaspoon black pepper, ground
1 teaspoon salt
1/2 teaspoon dried basil leaves
1 teaspoon dried oregano
2 teaspoons olive oil
1 teaspoon minced garlic
1 cup onions, chopped

Directions

- Choose the "RICE/RISOTTO" function and heat the oil; now, brown the ground beef for about 4 minutes.
- Then, sauté the onions and garlic until they're tender, an additional 4 minutes. Press the "CANCEL" key.
- Throw in the rest of the above ingredients. Choose the "BEANS/LENTILS" function.
- Place the lid on the Power Pressure Cooker XL, lock the lid and switch the pressure release valve to closed; cook for 10 minutes.
- Press the "CANCEL" key. Switch the pressure release valve to open. When the steam is released completely, remove the cooker's lid. Bon appétit!

123. Meat Dipping Sauce

Ready in about 25 minutes
Servings 12

This dipping sauce is perfect on a cold windy night when you and your guests need a rich and hearty snack. You can substitute chipotle peppers for minced habanero peppers.

Per serving: 104 Calories; 4.7g Fat; 3.2g Carbs; 12g Protein; 0.4g Sugars

Ingredients

1 pound ground meat
4 cloves garlic, sliced
1 can tomatoes, crushed
1/4 teaspoon ground black pepper, or more to taste
1/2 teaspoon salt
2 medium-sized shallots, chopped
1/2 teaspoon paprika
2 tablespoons vegetable oil
1 teaspoon minced chipotle peppers

Directions

- Choose the "CHICKEN/MEAT" function and heat the vegetable oil. Now, sauté the shallots and garlic for 5 minutes. Stir in the chipotle pepper and the ground meat; cook until they are browned, an additional 5 minutes.
- Add the tomatoes, paprika, salt, and ground black pepper.
- Place the lid on the Power Pressure Cooker XL, lock the lid and switch the pressure release valve to closed; cook for 13 minutes.
- Allow the pressure to release gradually and naturally. When the steam is released completely, remove the cooker's lid. Serve warm.

124. Rice with Mushrooms and Beef Roast

Ready in about 25 minutes
Servings 6

The next time you fancy a festive family lunch, try this mouth-watering rice recipe. You can substitute brown rice for white rice, if it is like that, reduce the cooking time to 6 minutes.

Per serving: 498 Calories; 10.4g Fat; 81.6g Carbs; 18.9g Protein; 1.4g Sugars

Ingredients

3 teaspoons vegetable oil
1 cup yellow onion, chopped
1 cup beef roast, cut into chunks
2 cups mushrooms, sliced
3 ¼ cups brown rice
1/2 teaspoon mustard seeds
1/2 teaspoon salt
1 teaspoon cayenne pepper
1/4 teaspoon ground black pepper, or more to taste
3 ½ cups water
1/2 teaspoon fennel seeds
1/2 cup celery stalk, thinly sliced

Directions

- Choose the "RICE/RISOTTO" function. Press the "TIME ADJUSTMENT" key until you reach 18 minutes.
- Simply throw all of the above ingredients into the Power Pressure Cooker XL. Lock the lid and switch the pressure release valve to closed.
- Press the "CANCEL" key. Switch the pressure release valve to open. When the steam is released completely, remove the cooker's lid. Bon appétit!

125. Pasta with Beef and Tomato Sauce

Ready in about 25 minutes
Servings 6

Lean ground beef releases its juices during pressure cooking in this amazing pasta, flavored with dry aromatics. Try serving with some extra tomato ketchup and freshly grated Parmigiano Reggiano cheese.

Per serving: 375 Calories; 9.4g Fat; 30.9g Carbs; 40.7g Protein; 4.6g Sugars

Ingredients

2 cups fresh mushrooms, chopped
1 ½ pounds lean ground beef
20 ounces pound dry egg noodles
1 cup onions, chopped
1 teaspoon minced garlic
1 teaspoon dry basil
1 teaspoon dry dill weed
1/2 teaspoon ground black pepper, or more to taste
1 teaspoon sea salt
1 ½ pounds tomato paste

Directions

- Choose the "RICE/RISOTTO" function and brown the beef for about 4 minutes, stirring continuously. Press the "CANCEL" key.
- Add the other ingredients. Now, choose the "BEANS/LENTILS" function. Place the lid on the Power Pressure Cooker XL, lock the lid and switch the pressure release valve to closed.
- Press the "TIME ADJUSTMENT" key until you reach 15 minutes. Switch the pressure release valve to open.
- When the steam is completely released, remove the cooker's lid. Bon appétit!

126. Beef Soup with Peas and Kumara

Ready in about 45 minutes
Servings 6

As a matter of fact, sweet potato is called kūmara in New Zealand. It is high in vitamins, minerals and fiber, but low in calories and fat.

Per serving: 314 Calories; 7.2g Fat; 25.5g Carbs; 35.9g Protein; 9.9g Sugars

Ingredients

1 ¼ pounds lean beef chuck, coarsely chopped
10 ounces green peas
2 kumara, peeled and cut into bite-sized pieces
2 ripe tomatoes, chopped
1 cup carrots, diced
6 cups bone broth
2 onions, chopped
1/2 cup corn kernels
1/4 teaspoon ground black pepper
1/2 teaspoon smoked paprika
1/2 teaspoon sea salt

Directions

- Press the CHICKEN/MEAT key; brown the beef for 4 minutes. Press the CANCEL key.
- Add the remaining ingredients, minus green peas and corn kernels. Choose the SOUP/STEW function and use the cook time selector to adjust to 30 minutes.
- Place the lid on the Power Pressure Cooker XL, lock the lid and switch the pressure release valve to closed.
- Once the timer reaches 0, the cooker will automatically switch to KEEP WARM/CANCEL mode.
- Switch the pressure release valve to open. Once the pressure is completely released, remove the cooker's lid.
- Stir in the green peas and corn. Cover and let it stand for 10 minutes. Enjoy!

127. Hearty Beef and Wild Rice Soup

Ready in about 35 minutes
Servings 6

Beef soup is an all-time favorite, isn't it? Very economical and practical, this recipe serves a crowd. It also freezes and reheats well.

Per serving: 388 Calories; 8.1g Fat; 43g Carbs; 35.7g Protein; 8.7g Sugars

Ingredients

1 pound beef stew meat
1 ½ cups wild rice
2 carrots, chopped
1 rutabaga, chopped
6 ½ cups vegetable broth
2 teaspoons butter, at room temperature
2 cups shredded cabbage
2 onions, chopped
1/2 teaspoon crushed red pepper flakes
2 teaspoons garlic paste
1/2 teaspoon seasoned salt
1/3 teaspoon ground allspice

Directions

- Press the CHICKEN/MEAT key and warm the butter. Then, brown the beef stew meat on all sides, turning occasionally. Transfer to a large-sized bowl and reserve.
- Stir in the onions, carrot, and rutabaga; cook, stirring frequently, until the onion is translucent.
- Add the remaining ingredients. Now add reserved beef back to the Power pressure cooker XL.
- Now, choose the SOUP/STEW function and use the cook time selector to adjust to 30 minutes.
- Place the lid on the Power Pressure Cooker XL, lock the lid and switch the pressure release valve to closed.
- Once the timer reaches 0, the cooker will automatically switch to KEEP WARM/CANCEL mode.
- Switch the pressure release valve to open. Once the pressure is completely released, remove the cooker's lid. Serve.

128. Country Yam and Beef Soup

Ready in about 35 minutes
Servings 6

There are so many ways to cook the beef shank rounds, but the secret is to go nicely and slowly. If you like simplifying things, this recipe will be your next favorite.

Per serving: 255 Calories; 6.7g Fat; 15.7g Carbs; 31.4g Protein; 3.6g Sugars

Ingredients

1 pound beef shank rounds
1 ½ cups yams, diced
2 ripe tomatoes, chopped
1 cup celery with leaves, chopped
1 cup carrots, thinly sliced
1 cup scallions, chopped
5 cups broth
Sea salt and ground black pepper
1/3 cup loosely packed fresh cilantro, chopped

Directions

- Firstly, mix the broth and chopped tomatoes in your Power pressure cooker XL. Stir in the remaining ingredients.
- Now, choose the SOUP/STEW function and use the cook time selector to adjust to 30 minutes.
- Place the lid on the Power Pressure Cooker XL, lock the lid and switch the pressure release valve to closed.
- Once the timer reaches 0, the cooker will automatically switch to KEEP WARM/CANCEL mode.
- Switch the pressure release valve to open. Once the pressure is completely released, remove the cooker's lid.
- Slice the meat off the bones. Chop the meat and stir it into the soup. Bon appétit!

129. Tangy Beef and Potato Soup

Ready in about 40 minutes
Servings 8

Looking for a perfect winter warmer? As a serious comfort food, this meaty and nutritious soup will fit the bill!

Per serving: 356 Calories; 10.4g Fat; 11.6g Carbs; 49.2g Protein; 2.9g Sugars

Ingredients

1¼ pounds ground beef
2 cups yellow potatoes, peeled and chopped
2 ½ tablespoons oyster sauce
1/4 cup dry sherry
1/3 cup cider vinegar
2 carrots, chopped
2 tomatoes, chopped
8 cups stock
1/4 teaspoon ground black pepper
1/2 teaspoon sea salt
1 bay leaf
1/4 teaspoon cayenne pepper
1/2 teaspoon dry mustard

Directions

- Press the CHICKEN/MEAT key and brown the meat for 4 minutes, stirring periodically.
- Combine everything in your Power pressure cooker XL. Now, choose the SOUP/STEW function and use the cook time selector to adjust to 30 minutes.
- Place the lid on the Power Pressure Cooker XL, lock the lid and switch the pressure release valve to closed.
- Once the timer reaches 0, the cooker will automatically switch to KEEP WARM/CANCEL mode.
- Switch the pressure release valve to open. Once the pressure is completely released, remove the cooker's lid.
- Give it a good stir. Serve.

130. Beef and Cabbage Medley with Gorgonzola

Ready in about 50 minutes
Servings 6

This meat and vegetable medley is made with carefully selected, tasty and nutritious ingredients. This dish is packed with fiber so it will keep you feeling full for a longer time.

Per serving: 416 Calories; 13.1g Fat; 23.6g Carbs; 52.3g Protein; 8.4g Sugars

Ingredients

1 pound sirloin steak, about 1-inch thick
1/2 head green cabbage, diced
6 ounces gorgonzola cheese
2 small-sized yellow onions, diced
1 cup parsnip, chopped
2 cups canned tomatoes with their juices
1 ½ cups carrots, thinly sliced
2 bell peppers, finely chopped
1 quart bone broth
1 teaspoon smashed garlic
Sea salt and ground black pepper, to your liking

Directions

- Preheat the oven to broil. Broil the steak for 5 minutes per side. Cut into thin slices and transfer to the Power pressure cooker XL.
- Throw in the remaining ingredients, minus gorgonzola cheese. Choose the CHICKEN/MEAT function; use the cook time selector to adjust to 40 minutes.
- Place the lid on the Power Pressure Cooker XL, lock the lid and switch the pressure release valve to closed.
- Once the timer reaches 0, the cooker will automatically switch to KEEP WARM/CANCEL mode.
- Switch the pressure release valve to open. Once the pressure is completely released, remove the cooker's lid.
- Serve warm, topped with gorgonzola and enjoy!

131. Old-Fashioned Beef Stew with Sweet Potatoes

Ready in about 50 minutes
Servings 6

Beef stew doesn't have to be laborious because you can cook with the Power pressure cooker XL. This one uses leeks, but you can use any type of seasonal onions. Feel free to add a chile powder if desired.

Per serving: 399 Calories; 5.7g Fat; 52.5g Carbs; 30.7g Protein; 6.1g Sugars

Ingredients

1 pound beef brisket, cut into pieces
4 sweet potatoes, diced
2 cups Ale
4 cups beef bone broth
1 tablespoon cider vinegar
1 cup leeks, chopped
1/4 cup soy sauce
4 carrots, thinly sliced
3 cloves garlic, minced
2 parsnips, chopped
1 tablespoon cornstarch slurry
Sea salt and black pepper, to taste

Directions

- Choose the CHICKEN/MEAT function and brown the beef for 6 minutes.
- Add the remaining ingredients, except for the cornstarch slurry. Next, choose the SOUP/STEW function and use the cook time selector to adjust to 30 minutes.
- Place the lid on the Power Pressure Cooker XL, lock the lid and switch the pressure release valve to closed.
- Once the timer reaches 0, the cooker will automatically switch to KEEP WARM/CANCEL mode.
- Switch the pressure release valve to open. Once the pressure is completely released, remove the cooker's lid.
- Add the cornstarch slurry and place the lid on the Power pressure cooker XL; allow it to sit for 10 minutes before serving. Enjoy!

132. Easy Sloppy Joes

Ready in about 50 minutes
Servings 8

Sloppy Joes are a fully satisfying comfort food. It can be served alongside a pickled or fresh salad.

Per serving: 296 Calories; 7.5g Fat; 44.8g Carbs; 12.1g Protein; 7.6g Sugars

Ingredients

3 teaspoons canola oil
1 ½ pounds ground chuck, crumbled
2 tomatoes, crushed
1 teaspoon chili powder
1/4 cup Worcestershire sauce
1/4 cup tomato ketchup
3 cloves garlic, minced
2 tablespoons brown sugar
1/3 cup pot barley
1 cup scallions, chopped
8 Kaiser rolls
1/2 tablespoon cayenne pepper

Directions

- Add the pot barley and 3 cups of water to the Power pressure cooker XL. Choose the RICE/RISOTTO function and use the cook time selector to adjust to 25 minutes.
- Place the lid on the Power Pressure Cooker XL, lock the lid and switch the pressure release valve to closed.
- Once the timer reaches 0, the cooker will automatically switch to KEEP WARM/CANCEL mode. Drain the barley and reserve.
- Choose the CHICKEN/MEAT function and 15-minute cook time. Warm canola oil and sauté the scallions and garlic.
- Place the lid on the Power Pressure Cooker XL, lock the lid and switch the pressure release valve to closed.
- Once the timer reaches 0, the cooker will automatically switch to KEEP WARM/CANCEL mode.
- Switch the pressure release valve to open. Once the pressure is completely released, remove the cooker's lid.
- Stir in the barley; stir to combine. Serve over Kaiser rolls.

133. Winter Beef Chili

Ready in about 25 minutes
Servings 6

Here's an all-time favorite and one of the best comforting winter recipes. Serve with some warm flatbreads and grated cheese, if you like.

Per serving: 284 Calories; 9g Fat; 13.4g Carbs; 37.7g Protein; 3.9g Sugars

Ingredients

1 ½ pounds ground beef
1 tablespoon chili powder
2 bell peppers, stemmed, seeded, and chopped
1 teaspoon minced garlic
2 tomatoes, chopped
2 cups canned beans, drained and rinsed
1 cup shallots, chopped
1 cup beef bone broth
2 teaspoons butter, at room temperature
1/2 teaspoon dried oregano
1/2 teaspoon dried basil
2 sprigs dried thyme

Directions

- Press the CHICKEN/MEAT key and melt the butter. Then, sauté the shallots and bell peppers, stirring frequently, until the shallots are translucent, about 5 minutes.
- Stir in the garlic and cook until just fragrant, 30 seconds more. Press the CANCEL key. Add the remaining ingredients.
- Press the BEANS/LENTILS key and use the cook time selector to adjust to 15 minutes.
- Place the lid on the Power Pressure Cooker XL, lock the lid and switch the pressure release valve to closed.
- Once the timer reaches 0, the cooker will automatically switch to KEEP WARM/CANCEL mode.
- Switch the pressure release valve to open. Once the pressure is completely released, remove the cooker's lid. Serve warm.

134. Mediterranean-Style Pot Roast

Ready in about 1 hour
Servings 6

See how to make this flavorful pot roast with no fuss! Easy to cook and easy to serve! In this recipe, rump roast will work well too.

Per serving: 463 Calories; 12.7g Fat; 33.5g Carbs; 51.4g Protein; 11.7g Sugars

Ingredients

2 pounds pot roast, cubed
1/2 pound baby carrots, chopped
2 yams, chopped
1 ½ cups beef bone broth
4 cloves garlic, minced
3 teaspoons canola oil
1/2 pound celery, chopped
2 bell peppers, sliced
1 cup tomato paste
2 medium-sized red onions, chopped
1/4 cup dry white wine
1 ½ cups water
3 teaspoons flour
1/2 teaspoon dried basil
2 sprigs dried thyme
Kosher salt and ground black pepper, to taste

Directions

- Press the CHICKEN/MEAT key and heat canola oil; then, sear the beef for 4 minutes.
- Deglaze the pot with a splash of beef bone broth. Add the onions and garlic; continue sautéing an additional 3 minutes. Press the CANCEL key.
- Add the remaining ingredients, except for the flour. Press the CHICKEN/MEAT key; use the cook time selector to adjust to 40 minutes.
- Place the lid on the Power Pressure Cooker XL, lock the lid and switch the pressure release valve to closed.
- Once the timer reaches 0, the cooker will automatically switch to KEEP WARM/CANCEL mode.
- Switch the pressure release valve to open. Once the pressure is completely released, remove the cooker's lid.
- Now, make the slurry by whisking the flour with 1 tablespoon of water. Add to the Power pressure cooker XL and place the lid on the cooker; allow it to sit for 10 minutes. Serve warm.

135. Basic Beef Broth

Ready in about 1 hour 10 minutes
Servings 12

What could be better than a homey, nourishing broth? You can use meat and marrow bones like short ribs or knuckle bones as well.
Keep your broth 1 or 2 days in the refrigerator or 3 months in the freezer.

Per serving: 197 Calories; 9.5g Fat; 3g Carbs; 24.3g Protein; 1.2g Sugars

Ingredients

1 pound bone-in beef
1 ½ pounds oxtail, cut in half
2 celery stalks, cut and chopped
2 teaspoons olive oil
2 carrots, peeled and chopped
1 cup yellow onions, slice into rings
1/2 cup parsnip, peeled and chopped
1 tablespoon cider vinegar
6 cups water

Directions

- Press the CHICKEN/MEAT key and heat the oil; then, brown the beef on all sides for 5 minutes, turning a few times.
- Add the remaining ingredients. Choose the SOUP/STEW function; set the time to 60 minutes.
- Place the lid on the Power Pressure Cooker XL, lock the lid and switch the pressure release valve to closed.
- Once the timer reaches 0, the cooker will automatically switch to KEEP WARM/CANCEL mode.
- Switch the pressure release valve to open. Once the pressure is completely released, remove the cooker's lid.
- Next, remove the meat and beef bones with a slotted spoon. Discard the bones.

136. Grandma's Beef Stew

Ready in about 40 minutes
Servings 8

You can give this amazing stew your own twist by adding ground cumin, red pepper flakes or smoked paprika. Keep this old-fashioned recipe in your back pocket.

Per serving: 275 Calories; 7g Fat; 20.9g Carbs; 27.8g Protein; 6.8g Sugars

Ingredients

1 ½ pounds beef stew meat, cubed
1/2 pound potatoes, diced
3/4 cup dry red wine
1 tablespoon butter, melted
2 onions, diced
1 pound carrots, diced
1 cup bell pepper, peeled and thinly sliced
2 parsnips, diced
2 teaspoons cocoa powder
3 cloves garlic, minced
1 sprig fresh rosemary, minced
1/4 teaspoon black pepper
1/2 teaspoon sea salt
1 teaspoon cayenne pepper

Directions

- Press the CHICKEN/MEAT key and warm the butter. Now, sauté the onion, carrots, potatoes, parsnip, garlic, and bell peppers for 3 minutes.
- Add the rosemary and meat; continue cooking for 4 minutes more. Add the salt, black pepper, cayenne pepper, cocoa powder and wine.
- Stir in the remaining ingredients. Choose the SOUP/STEW function; set the time to 30 minutes.
- Place the lid on the Power Pressure Cooker XL, lock the lid and switch the pressure release valve to closed.
- Once the timer reaches 0, the cooker will automatically switch to KEEP WARM/CANCEL mode.
- Switch the pressure release valve to open. Once the pressure is completely released, remove the cooker's lid.

137. Hearty Ground Chuck Soup

Ready in about 40 minutes
Servings 6

There are so many ways to cook a chunky beef soup. For instance, you can swap out the ground chuck for equal amounts of mixed ground meat or beef sausage.

Per serving: 373 Calories; 19.1g Fat; 18.7g Carbs; 29.9g Protein; 6.7g Sugars

Ingredients

1 ¼ pounds ground chuck
3 teaspoons vegetable oil
1/2 pound carrots, sliced
2 small-sized onions, peeled and diced
2 cups kale
2 parsnips, chopped
1/3 cup yogurt
3 cloves garlic, peeled and minced
6 ½ cups broth
1/2 teaspoon dried oregano
2 sprigs dried thyme
Salt and ground black pepper, to taste

Directions

- Press the CHICKEN/MEAT key and heat the oil until sizzling; now, brown ground meat for 4 minutes.
- Next, stir in the garlic and onions, and cook until they're just tender, about 4 minutes. Press the CANCEL key.
- Add the remaining ingredients, except for the yogurt. Choose the SOUP/STEW function; set the time to 30 minutes.
- Place the lid on the Power Pressure Cooker XL, lock the lid and switch the pressure release valve to closed.
- Once the timer reaches 0, the cooker will automatically switch to KEEP WARM/CANCEL mode.
- Switch the pressure release valve to open. Once the pressure is completely released, remove the cooker's lid.
- To serve, pour in the yogurt and stir to combine well.

138. Winter Black Bean Chili

Ready in about 40 minutes
Servings 6

Here's the best way to incorporate beans into your diet. This traditional chili is made with simple and rich ingredients.

Per serving: 482 Calories; 11g Fat; 58.4g Carbs; 39.4g Protein; 14g Sugars

Ingredients

2 cups black beans, soaked overnight
2 teaspoons chili powder
1 pound ground beef
1 quart stock
3 cloves garlic, minced
2 bell peppers chopped
2 tablespoons vegetable oil
1 tablespoon red wine vinegar
1 cup scallions, chopped
1 cup tomato puree
1 can tomatoes with juices
1/4 cup brown sugar
Kosher salt and black pepper, to taste

Directions

- Drain and rinse your beans. Then, press the CHICKEN/MEAT function and heat the oil until sizzling. Then, cook the beef, garlic, and scallions for 6 minutes. Press the CANCEL key.
- Add the remaining ingredients; press the BEANS/LENTILS key. Set the time to 30 minutes.
- Place the lid on the Power Pressure Cooker XL, lock the lid and switch the pressure release valve to closed.
- Once the timer reaches 0, the cooker will automatically switch to KEEP WARM/CANCEL mode.
- Switch the pressure release valve to open. Once the pressure is completely released, remove the cooker's lid. Serve warm.

139. Traditional Italian Spaghetti

Ready in about 20 minutes
Servings 6

Here is a delicious, meaty spaghetti recipe for all pasta lovers. Top with grated pecorino cheese and enjoy!

Per serving: 427 Calories; 9.5g Fat; 43.2g Carbs; 41.3g Protein; 12.1g Sugars

Ingredients

1 ½ box spaghetti
1 ½ pounds ground beef
2 teaspoons brown sugar
2 tomatoes, chopped
1 cup scallions, finely minced
3 garlic cloves, minced
1 cup ketchup
2 teaspoons butter, melted
1 teaspoon sea salt
1/2 teaspoon freshly ground black pepper, or to taste
1 teaspoon cayenne pepper
1 teaspoon dried basil
1 teaspoon dried oregano
2 sprigs dried thyme

Directions

- Choose the RICE/RISOTTO function and melt the butter. Set time to 8 minutes. Next, cook the scallions, garlic, beef and sugar for 5 minutes.
- Add the remaining ingredients and stir to combine well.
- Place the lid on the Power pressure cooker XL, lock the lid and switch the pressure release valve to closed.
- Once the timer reaches 0, the cooker will automatically switch to KEEP WARM/CANCEL. When the steam is completely released, carefully remove the cooker's lid.
- Serve at once and enjoy!

140. Mom's Beef Sausage Casserole

Ready in about 40 minutes
Servings 4

Here's a family favorite! Now, you've got to find some good-quality mustard and your dinner is ready!

Per serving: 588 Calories; 7.7g Fat; 97.6g Carbs; 24.2g Protein; 10.4g Sugars

Ingredients

3/4 pound beef sausage, chopped
1 package egg noodles
1 bottle amber lager
2 clove garlic, minced
1 ½ cups green peas, frozen
1/2 habanero pepper, seeded and chopped
1 cup pinto beans, soaked overnight
2 bell peppers, seeded and chopped
2 teaspoons canola oil
1 cup scallions, chopped
2 cups canned tomatoes, crushed
1/2 tablespoon cayenne pepper
1/2 teaspoon dried basil
1/2 teaspoon dried oregano
1/2 teaspoon ground cumin
1/2 teaspoon chipotle pepper, minced
1 teaspoon salt
1/3 teaspoon ground black pepper
Fresh parsley, for garnish

Directions

- Choose the RICE/RISOTTO function and set time to 25 minutes. Now, heat the oil; sauté the scallions, peppers, and garlic for 4 minutes, until just tender.
- Stir in the beef sausage. Cook, until it has lightly browned, an additional 4 minutes.
- Add the tomatoes, green peas, pinto beans, lager, cayenne pepper, basil, oregano, cumin, chipotle pepper, salt, and black pepper. Stir in the egg noodles.
- Place the lid on the Power pressure cooker XL, lock the lid and switch the pressure release valve to closed.
- Once the timer reaches 0, the cooker will automatically switch to KEEP WARM/CANCEL. When the steam is completely released, carefully remove the cooker's lid.
- Give it a good stir, sprinkle with fresh parsley and serve.

141. Family Beef Stew

Ready in about 40 minutes
Servings 8

You're about to cook the best beef stew you've ever eaten! The recipe calls for yams but you can use any type of potatoes as well.

Per serving: 282 Calories; 9.2g Fat; 19.5g Carbs; 29.8g Protein; 5.1g Sugars

Ingredients

1 ½ pounds chuck roast, cut into bite-sized chunks
2 cups stock, preferably homemade
1/2 pound baby carrots, diced
2 parsnips, diced
2 bell peppers, seeded and diced
1 cup scallions, chopped
1/2 pound yams, peeled and diced
1 tablespoon olive oil
1 teaspoon red pepper flakes, crushed
1 sprig dry thyme, minced
Sea salt and ground black pepper, to taste

Directions

- Choose the SOUP/STEW function and use the cook time selector to adjust to 30 minutes. Then, heat the oil; now, sauté the scallions, carrots, parsnips, pepper, and yams for 6 minutes.
- Place the lid on the Power pressure cooker XL, lock the lid and switch the pressure release valve to closed.
- Once the timer reaches 0, the cooker will automatically switch to KEEP WARM/CANCEL. When the steam is completely released, carefully remove the cooker's lid.
- Ladle into serving dishes and enjoy!

142. Risotto with Beef and Peppers

Ready in about 25 minutes
Servings 4

Pressure cooking is one of the best cooking methods to achieve flavors that will amaze your family! Serve with chicory salad or pickled peppers.

Per serving: 375 Calories; 8g Fat; 45.1g Carbs; 23.8g Protein; 4.6g Sugars

Ingredients

1 cup white rice
3/4 pound pot roast, cut into chunks
1 cup bell peppers, stemmed, cored, and chopped
1 cup sweet onions, chopped
3 teaspoons canola oil
2 medium-sized ripe tomatoes, peeled and chopped
1/2 cup cooking wine
1/2 teaspoon dried oregano
1/2 teaspoon dried marjoram
2 sprigs thyme, minced
1 teaspoon cayenne pepper
1 teaspoon fennel seeds
Sea salt and black pepper, to your liking

Directions

- Press the RICE/RISOTTO key. Heat the oil and cook the beef, stirring often, until it softens, about 10 minutes. Reserve.
- Add sweet onions and bell peppers to the Power pressure cooker XL; cook, stirring frequently, until they soften. Press the CANCEL key.
- Stir in the oregano, marjoram, thyme, cayenne pepper, fennel seeds, salt, and black pepper.
- Stir in wine, tomatoes, and rice. Place the lid on the Power pressure cooker XL, lock the lid and switch the pressure release valve to closed. Cook for 6 minutes.
- Once the timer reaches 0, the cooker will automatically switch to KEEP WARM/CANCEL. When the steam is completely released, carefully remove the cooker's lid. Serve immediately.

143. Easiest Steak with Veggies Ever

Ready in about 50 minutes
Servings 8

Steak is the most popular, number-one dish of a festive holiday menu. Use another combo of veggies if desired; just make sure to consult the cooking chart.

Per serving: 394 Calories; 7.8g Fat; 41.8g Carbs; 39.5g Protein; 14.1g Sugars

Ingredients

2 pounds beef steak, cut into serving-sized portions
2 sweet onions, peeled and sliced
1 pound sweet potatoes, peeled and diced
1/2 tablespoon habanero pepper, deveined and thinly sliced
2 large-sized bell peppers, deveined and thinly sliced
1 cup celery with leaves, chopped
1/2 cup Ale
3 cloves garlic, peeled and minced
2 bouillon chicken cubes, dissolved in 2 cups of water
2 medium-sized carrots, diced
1 ½ cups tomato puree
Salt and ground black pepper, to taste

Directions

- Choose the MEAT/CHICKEN function and sear the steak on all sides for 10 minutes.
- Arrange the vegetables in the bottom of your Power pressure cooker XL. Lay the beef steak on the vegetable layer.
- In a mixing bowl, combine the rest of the above ingredients; mix well to combine; pour the mixture into the Power pressure cooker XL.
- Press the SOUP/STEW key and use the cook time selector to adjust to 30 minutes.
- Place the lid on the Power pressure cooker XL, lock the lid and switch the pressure release valve to closed.
- Once the timer reaches 0, the cooker will automatically switch to KEEP WARM/CANCEL. When the steam is completely released, carefully remove the cooker's lid. Serve right away.

144. Pot Roast with Savoy Cabbage

Ready in about 50 minutes
Servings 6

Savoy cabbage is high in antioxidants, vitamin C, vitamin E, minerals and fiber. This recipe is super healthy and easy to make. Win-win!

Per serving: 275 Calories; 15.9g Fat; 12.5g Carbs; 17.8g Protein; 6.6g Sugars

Ingredients

1 pound pot roast
1 head of Savoy cabbage, shredded
1/2 cup dry white wine
2 ripe tomatoes, chopped
1 tablespoon tallow
2 sweet onions, chopped
1/2 teaspoon cayenne pepper
Salt and freshly ground black pepper, to taste

Directions

- Press the CHICKEN/MEAT key and melt the tallow; now, sear the beef for 3 minutes; flip to sear another side. Press the CANCEL key.
- Stir in the rest of the above ingredients. Press the CHICKEN/MEAT key and then, use the cook time selector to adjust to 40 minutes.
- Place the lid on the Power pressure cooker XL, lock the lid and switch the pressure release valve to closed.
- Once the timer reaches 0, the cooker will automatically switch to KEEP WARM/CANCEL. When the steam is completely released, carefully remove the cooker's lid. Serve right away.

145. Barbecue Beef Brisket

Ready in about 1 hour
Servings 6

Cooking the barbecue-style beef is easy thanks to this set-it-and-forget-it pressure-cooker method. You can use another combo of aromatics such as thyme, marjoram, or ground bay leaf.

Per serving: 229 Calories; 7.3g Fat; 3.6g Carbs; 34.8g Protein; 2.9g Sugars

Ingredients

1 ½ pounds beef brisket, cut to fit an inner pot and trimmed of fat
2 spring onions, sliced
1 tablespoon Worcestershire sauce
1 tablespoon ketchup
2 garlic cloves, finely minced
1 tablespoon packed brown sugar
2 tablespoons apple cider vinegar
2 cups stock
1/3 teaspoon ground black pepper
1/2 teaspoon salt
1/2 tablespoon cayenne pepper

Directions

- In a small-sized mixing bowl, combine the minced garlic, salt, black pepper, and cayenne pepper. Rub the mixture over the surface of your beef brisket.
- Arrange rubbed beef brisket in the bottom of your cooker; top with the spring onions; add the stock and ketchup to the Power pressure cooker XL.
- Press the CHICKEN/MEAT key and then, use the cook time selector to adjust to 40 minutes.
- Place the lid on the Power pressure cooker XL, lock the lid and switch the pressure release valve to closed.
- Once the timer reaches 0, the cooker will automatically switch to KEEP WARM/CANCEL. When the steam is completely released, carefully remove the cooker's lid.
- Meanwhile, prepare the sauce by mixing Worcestershire sauce, brown sugar and vinegar.
- Lastly, grill cooked beef for about 12 minutes, turning once or twice, basting with the prepared sauce.

146. Bacon and Sausage Soup

Ready in about 40 minutes
Servings 6

This is one of the favorite family soups that reheats well. Add a steak sauce and Dijon mustard to enhance the flavor if you like.

Per serving: 344 Calories; 25.5g Fat; 16.4g Carbs; 11.9g Protein; 8.7g Sugars

Ingredients

3 slices bacon, cut into bite-sized chunks
1 ½ pounds beef sausages
1 cup tomato paste
3 teaspoons flour
6 cups stock
1 cup bell peppers, chopped
2 onions, chopped
1/2 stick butter
1/3 cup dry white wine
1/2 pimiento pepper, chopped
1/2 teaspoon ground black pepper
1/2 teaspoon cayenne pepper
1 teaspoon salt
2 sprigs dried thyme

Directions

- Press the CHICKEN/MEAT key and melt the butter; now, sauté the onions and peppers until they are softened, about 6 minutes. Crumble in the bacon and sausage and cook for 3 minutes more.
- Whisk in the flour and cook for 1 minute 30 seconds, whisking until the vegetables are thoroughly coated.
- Pour in the stock in a slow, steady stream, whisking continuously. Add the wine and continue whisking for 1 minute more.
- Stir in the thyme, cayenne pepper, salt, and ground black pepper. Afterwards, add the tomato paste.
- Place the lid on the Power pressure cooker XL, lock the lid and switch the pressure release valve to closed.
- Press the TIME ADJUSTMENT key until you reach 20 minutes. Once the timer reaches 0, the cooker will automatically switch to KEEP WARM/CANCEL.
- When the steam is completely released, carefully remove the cooker's lid. Serve with the garlic croutons.

147. Easy One-Pot Beef Dinner

Ready in about 50 minutes
Servings 8

Here's an easy, melt in your mouth chuck roast! Serve with fresh and crisp lettuce leaves, yogurt sauce and lots of cornbread.

Per serving: 322 Calories; 11.3g Fat; 12.8g Carbs; 40g Protein; 4.3g Sugars

Ingredients

2 pounds chuck roast, sliced into thin strips
2 (1-ounce) packages dry Italian salad dressing mix
1 cup leeks, chopped
1/4 cup tomato ketchup
1 teaspoon minced garlic
1 turnip, chopped
1/2 pound carrots, chopped
2 ½ cups vegetable broth
2 teaspoons lard
3 teaspoons corn flour
1 teaspoon grated ginger
1/2 teaspoon celery seeds
1/4 teaspoon black pepper, ground
1/2 teaspoon smoked cayenne pepper

Directions

- Press the CHICKEN/MEAT key use the cook time selector to adjust to 40 minutes; melt the lard. Then, brown the meat for 3 minutes, stirring periodically.
- Add the remaining ingredients and stir to combine. Place the lid on the Power pressure cooker XL, lock the lid and switch the pressure release valve to closed.
- Once the timer reaches 0, the cooker will automatically switch to KEEP WARM/CANCEL.
- When the steam is completely released, carefully remove the cooker's lid.
- To make the slurry, in a small-sized mixing bowl, whisk together the corn flour with 1/4 cup of the cooking liquid.
- Add the slurry back to the cooker. Stir until everything is well combined and serve warm.

148. Hungarian Beef Stew

Ready in about 50 minutes
Servings 6

Make sure to cut the beef and veggies into roughly equal-sized pieces so they'll cook evenly in your Power pressure cooker XL. This stew freezes and reheats well.

Per serving: 369 Calories; 11.2g Fat; 29.1g Carbs; 36.1g Protein; 5.7g Sugars

Ingredients

1 1/3 pounds stewing beef, cut into ½ inch pieces
2 slices thick-cut bacon, diced
2 teaspoons Hungarian paprika
3 garlic cloves, smashed
2 bell peppers, finely minced
4 potatoes, peeled and diced
1 tablespoon lard, at room temperature
2 yellow onions, peeled and chopped
2 tablespoons apple cider vinegar
1 tablespoon fish sauce
4 cups roasted-vegetable stock, preferably homemade
2 ripe tomatoes, finely chopped
1 teaspoon chili pepper, finely minced
2 teaspoons sweet paprika
1/2 teaspoon caraway seeds

Directions

- Press the CHICKEN/MEAT key and use the cook time selector to adjust to 40 minutes; melt the lard. Then, sear the beef and bacon for 4 minutes, stirring periodically.
- Stir in the rest of the above ingredients. Place the lid on the Power pressure cooker XL, lock the lid and switch the pressure release valve to closed.
- Once the timer reaches 0, the cooker will automatically switch to KEEP WARM/CANCEL.
- When the steam is completely released, carefully remove the cooker's lid. Serve hot.

149. Creamed Burger and Lentil Soup

Ready in about 40 minutes
Servings 8

You can't go wrong with pressure cooked and well-seasoned beef soup. This soup is cooked in less than 40 minutes and it has a rich flavor and perfect texture.

Per serving: 305 Calories; 7.8g Fat; 22.3g Carbs; 34.5g Protein; 5.5g Sugars

Ingredients

1 ½ pounds lean ground beef
1 cup red lentils, soaked overnight
1 cup yogurt
3 teaspoons olive oil
3 cloves garlic, minced
1/2 pound baby carrots, diced
2 yellow onions, finely chopped
1 quart vegetable stock
2 teaspoons cayenne pepper
Salt and fresh ground black pepper to taste
3 cups water

Directions

- Choose the SOUP/STEW function and use the cook time selector to adjust to 30 minutes. Heat the oil and cook the ground beef until browned.
- Add the onions, garlic and baby carrots and sauté for 4 minutes, until they're just tender.
- Stir in the remaining ingredients, except for the yogurt. Place the lid on the Power pressure cooker XL, lock the lid and switch the pressure release valve to closed.
- Once the timer reaches 0, the cooker will automatically switch to KEEP WARM/CANCEL.
- When the steam is completely released, carefully remove the cooker's lid. Pour in the yogurt. Stir until it is well mixed.
- Puree the mixture with an immersion blender until smooth. Enjoy!

150. Chuck Roast and Kidney Bean Casserole

Ready in about 40 minutes
Servings 4

Here's a great dish with several layers of flavor for your next festive menu! People will ask you for the recipe.

Per serving: 565 Calories; 10g Fat; 75.2g Carbs; 36.8g Protein; 8.8g Sugars

Ingredients

3 teaspoons butter
3/4 pound chuck roast, cut into 1-inch cubes
1 cup canned kidney beans, drained and rinsed
1 bottle amber lager
2 ripe tomatoes, diced
2 onions, thinly sliced
2 sweet potatoes, peeled and diced
2 bell peppers, stemmed, seeded, and chopped
2 cloves garlic, minced
1/2 box dry noodles
1/2 habanero pepper, stemmed, seeded and chopped
1/2 tablespoon cayenne pepper
1/2 teaspoon dried basil
1/3 teaspoon sea salt
1/2 teaspoon ground cumin

Directions

- Choose the SOUP/STEW function and use the cook time selector to adjust to 30 minutes. Warm the butter and cook the meat until browned, about 5 minutes.
- Stir in the remaining ingredients. Place the lid on the Power pressure cooker XL, lock the lid and switch the pressure release valve to closed.
- Once the timer reaches 0, the cooker will automatically switch to KEEP WARM/CANCEL.
- When the steam is completely released, carefully remove the cooker's lid. Serve warm.

151. Beef and Chile Stew

Ready in about 50 minutes
Servings 8

Here's a robust stew packed with tomatoes and baby carrots! This unique beef stew recipe will give your taste buds a tasty kick that you won't forget!

Per serving: 301 Calories; 4.6g Fat; 56.5g Carbs; 27.5g Protein; 20.8g Sugars

Ingredients

2 pounds lean beef stew meat, cut into cubes
1 (7-ounce) can diced green chiles, drained
2 teaspoons fish sauce
2 tablespoons ground flaxseed
2 (14.5-ounce) cans ready-cut tomatoes with juice
2 (8-ounce) bags baby-cut carrots, diced
1/2 teaspoon red pepper flakes, crushed
Salt and freshly ground black pepper, to your liking
2 ½ cups water

Directions

- Choose the SOUP/STEW function and use the cook time selector to adjust to 40 minutes. Sear the beef for 6 minutes, stirring occasionally.
- Add the remaining ingredients, minus ground flaxseed. Place the lid on the Power pressure cooker XL, lock the lid and switch the pressure release valve to closed.
- Once the timer reaches 0, the cooker will automatically switch to KEEP WARM/CANCEL.
- When the steam is completely released, carefully remove the cooker's lid. Stir in ground flaxseed, cover, and let it sit about 10 minutes before serving.
- Adjust the seasonings and serve warm.

152. Nana's Beef Stew with Dumplings

Ready in about 1 hour
Servings 4

Thanks to your Power pressure cooker XL, you can have the most tender beef for an old-fashioned recipe by using an inexpensive cut of meat. That's a bargain!

Per serving: 444 Calories; 15.4g Fat; 32.5g Carbs; 42.1g Protein; 42.1g Sugars

Ingredients

1 pound beef sirloin, cubed
1 pound mixed vegetables, peeled and diced
1 tablespoon tallow, at room temperature
4 cloves garlic, peeled and crushed
1 ½ cups tomatoes, chopped
2 onions, thinly sliced
1/4 cup cider vinegar
2 cups stock
2 sprigs dried rosemary
1/2 teaspoon dried oregano
1/2 teaspoon dried sage
1/2 teaspoon dried basil
Salt and black pepper, to taste
1/2 teaspoon smoked cayenne pepper

For the Nanas' Dumplings:
1/2 tablespoon shortening
3/4 cup biscuit mix
1 small-sized egg, beaten
1/2 cup milk

Directions

- Choose the SOUP/STEW function and use the cook time selector to adjust to 40 minutes. Warm the tallow and sauté the onions and garlic until they're tender, approximately 4 minutes.
- Then, add the meat and continue cooking until just browned, about 5 minutes.
- Stir in the remaining ingredients for the stew; give it a good stir with a large spoon. Place the lid on the Power pressure cooker XL, lock the lid and switch the pressure release valve to closed.
- Once the timer reaches 0, the cooker will automatically switch to KEEP WARM/CANCEL.
- When the steam is completely released, carefully remove the cooker's lid.
- To make the Nana's famous dumplings, combine the shortening and biscuit mix until crumbly. Then, whisk the egg and milk and add to dry mixture. Stir until everything's well incorporated.
- Drop by tablespoons in bubbling stew. Press the BEANS/LENTILS key and place the lid on the cooker. Cook for 5 minutes. Allow the pressure to release on its own and serve hot!

153. Ground Beef and Wild Rice Delight

Ready in about 30 minutes
Servings 6

Stew is a comfort food that always reminds us of a family lunch. This hearty beef stew is loaded with tomatoes, ground beef, and sour cream.

Per serving: 541 Calories; 14.2g Fat; 57.9g Carbs; 46.2g Protein; 3.4g Sugars

Ingredients

1 ½ pounds ground beef
2 ½ cups cooked wild rice
2 teaspoons melted lard
3/4 cup sour cream
2 tomatoes, chopped
1 tablespoon ketchup
1 cup shallots, thinly sliced
3 cloves garlic, minced
1/2 teaspoon sea salt
1/3 teaspoon freshly ground black pepper
1/2 teaspoon ground coriander
1/2 teaspoon red pepper flakes, crushed

Directions

- Press the CHICKEN/MEAT key and warm the lard. Sauté the shallot and garlic for 4 minutes. Now, cook ground beef for 4 minutes, crumbling it with a wooden spatula.
- Add the rest of the above ingredients, minus sour cream and rice. Place the lid on the Power pressure cooker XL, lock the lid and switch the pressure release valve to closed. Cook for 15 minutes.
- Once the timer reaches 0, the cooker will automatically switch to KEEP WARM/CANCEL.
- When the steam is completely released, carefully remove the cooker's lid. Stir in sour cream; stir until everything is well combined.
- Serve over prepared wild rice.

154. Holiday Beef Sirloin Steak

Ready in about 50 minutes
Servings 8

Don't let the simplicity fool you – this beef dish is packed with flavor and nutrients. Making a holiday dinner has never been easier!

Per serving: 297 Calories; 7.8g Fat; 18.4g Carbs; 37.2g Protein; 10.1g Sugars

Ingredients

2 pounds beef sirloin steak, cut into serving-sized portions
1 cup mushrooms, chopped
1 rutabaga, diced
1 cup celery with leaves, diced
1 bell pepper, seeded and thinly sliced
1/2 cup onions, peeled and sliced
4 carrots, chopped
3 cloves garlic, peeled and minced
1 (10.5-ounces) can French onion soup
1 (10.75-ounces) can tomato soup
1 ½ cups water
1/2 teaspoon cayenne pepper
1/2 teaspoon dried rosemary
Salt and ground black pepper, to taste

Directions

- Arrange the vegetables on the bottom of your Power pressure cooker XL. Place the sirloin steak on the vegetable layer.
- In a mixing bowl, combine the remaining ingredients; mix well to combine. Now, pour the mixture into the Power pressure cooker XL.
- Choose the CHICKEN/MEAT function. Place the lid on the Power pressure cooker XL, lock the lid and switch the pressure release valve to closed. Cook for 40 minutes.
- Once the timer reaches 0, the cooker will automatically switch to KEEP WARM/CANCEL.
- When the steam is completely released, carefully remove the cooker's lid. Transfer the meat and vegetables to a serving platter. Serve and enjoy!

155. Saucy Beef with Sour Cream

Ready in about 35 minutes
Servings 6

This isn't an average recipe for beef. This beef is wonderfully tender, moist and juicy so that it might become your weeknight favorite. Make it tonight and enjoy!

Per serving: 467 Calories; 37.3g Fat; 8g Carbs; 24.9g Protein; 1.6g Sugars

Ingredients

1 ½ pounds chuck pot roast, cubed
1 ½ cups sour cream
1 can cream of mushroom soup
1 cup yellow onions, diced
1 tablespoon garlic, minced
2 teaspoons ghee, at room temperature
1/3 teaspoon cardamom
1/2 tablespoon cumin
1/2 teaspoon chili powder
1/2 tablespoon coriander
Salt and black pepper, to taste

Directions

- Choose the CHICKEN/MEAT function. Then, melt the ghee and sauté the onion and garlic until they are softened.
- Then, brown the meat for 5 to 6 minutes or until it is no longer pink. Add the remaining ingredients, except for the sour cream, to your Power pressure cooker XL.
- Place the lid on the Power pressure cooker XL, lock the lid and switch the pressure release valve to closed. Cook for 15 minutes.
- Once the timer reaches 0, the cooker will automatically switch to KEEP WARM/CANCEL.
- When the steam is completely released, carefully remove the cooker's lid. Add the sour cream and choose the FISH/VEGETABLES/STEAM function. Now, simmer until the cooking liquid has thickened, for 4 minutes. Serve warm.

156. Ground Beef and Sauerkraut

Ready in about 50 minutes
Servings 6

This traditional dish is simple, it uses basic ingredients and tastes just incredible. Sauerkraut is loaded with probiotics that boost the immune, digestive and cognitive functions of your body.

Per serving: 269 Calories; 7.5g Fat; 13.1g Carbs; 36.3g Protein; 6g Sugars

Ingredients

1 ½ pound lean ground beef
3 cups sauerkraut
1 cup leeks, chopped
1 (10.75-ounces) can tomato soup
1 tablespoon smashed garlic
1 tablespoon lard, melted
1 teaspoon mustard powder
1 bay leaf
Sea salt and ground black pepper, to taste

Directions

- Treat the inside of the Power pressure cooker XL with the melted lard. Arrange the leeks on the bottom of your cooker.
- Add the beef, tomato soup, garlic, mustard and sauerkraut. Now, add the bay leaf, salt and black pepper.
- Press the SOUP/STEW key and use the cook time selector to adjust to 30 minutes.
- Place the lid on the Power pressure cooker XL, lock the lid and switch the pressure release valve to closed. Cook for 15 minutes.
- Once the timer reaches 0, the cooker will automatically switch to KEEP WARM/CANCEL.
- When the steam is completely released, carefully remove the cooker's lid.

157. Saucy Corned Beef Brisket

Ready in about 50 minutes
Servings 6

Beef brisket dishes are amazing because they're filling and healthy. Additionally, they reheat well the next day.

Per serving: 275 Calories; 18.6g Fat; 9.9g Carbs; 16.9g Protein; 3.5g Sugars

Ingredients

1 ½ pounds corned beef brisket
1 tablespoon browning sauce
1 ½ cups cream of celery soup
3 cloves garlic, minced
2 ripe tomatoes, chopped
2 teaspoons vegetable oil
2 medium-sized onions, peeled and thinly sliced
1 teaspoon salt
1/4 teaspoon cloves, ground
1/4 teaspoon freshly ground black pepper
1/3 teaspoon ground coriander

Directions

- Choose the CHICKEN/MEAT function and heat the oil. Brush your brisket with the browning sauce on both sides.
- Brown the brisket on both sides, about 6 minutes. Add the rest of the above ingredients to your Power pressure cooker XL.
- Place the lid on the Power pressure cooker XL, lock the lid and switch the pressure release valve to closed. Cook for 40 minutes.
- Once the timer reaches 0, the cooker will automatically switch to KEEP WARM/CANCEL.
- Serve over hot cooked noodles.

158. Country Chuck Roast and Carrot Stew

Ready in about 1 hour
Servings 4

This is another one of those stew recipes that are hearty and so easy to make. Best of all, this delicious stew can be made in your Power pressure cooker XL, so there's minimal cooking effort required.

Per serving: 437 Calories; 14.9g Fat; 23.3g Carbs; 49.7g Protein; 12.3g Sugars

Ingredients

1 ¼ pounds chuck roast, cut into 1-inch cubes
1 pound carrots, diced
1 ¼ cups chicken stock
2 cloves garlic, peeled and minced
3 teaspoons butter
2 onions, thinly sliced
1 (16-ounce) can whole peeled tomatoes, undrained
1/2 cup white vinegar
1/2 teaspoon dried oregano
1 teaspoon dried basil
Sea salt and black pepper, to taste

Directions

- Choose the CHICKEN/MEAT function and warm the butter; now, sauté the beef, onions and garlic until the meat has browned and the onion becomes translucent.
- Add the remaining ingredients; use the cook time selector to adjust to 40 minutes. Place the lid on the Power pressure cooker XL, lock the lid and switch the pressure release valve to closed. Cook for 15 minutes.
- Once the timer reaches 0, the cooker will automatically switch to KEEP WARM/CANCEL.
- When the steam is completely released, carefully remove the cooker's lid. Serve right away.

159. Savoy Cabbage and Beef Sausage Casserole

Ready in about 25 minutes
Servings 4

This hearty beef and vegetable stew combines flavors for a wonderfully warm winter meal. The potatoes in this stew make this a filling dish and because it's made in a pressure cooker, it's a super-easy recipe.

Per serving: 406 Calories; 15.4g Fat; 55.9g Carbs; 12.5g Protein; 8.8g Sugars

Ingredients

1 pound Savoy cabbage, shredded
1 pound beef sausage, crumbled
4 cloves garlic, minced
1 ½ cups tomato puree
1 cup cooked rice
1 cup scallions, minced
1 tablespoon cider vinegar
1 teaspoon salt
1/2 teaspoon fennel seeds
1/4 teaspoon ground black pepper
1/3 cup fresh cilantro, chopped
1 cup water

Directions

- Stir the Savoy cabbage and fennel seeds in a mixing bowl. Use 1/2 of this mixture to make a bed in the bottom of the Power pressure cooker XL.
- In another bowl, combine the sausage, cooked rice, scallions, fresh cilantro, garlic, salt, and ground black pepper. Mix to combine well.
- Lay half of this mixture over the cabbage mixture; then, top with a layer of the remaining cabbage mixture. Top with the remaining meat mixture.
- Whisk the tomato puree, cider vinegar and water in a large-sized mixing bowl; add to the cooker.
- Press the MEAT/CHICKEN key. Place the lid on the Power pressure cooker XL, lock the lid and switch the pressure release valve to closed. Cook for 15 minutes.
- Once the timer reaches 0, the cooker will automatically switch to KEEP WARM/CANCEL.
- When the steam is completely released, carefully remove the cooker's lid. Serve in individual serving bowls. Enjoy!

160. Beef with Barley and Provolone Cheese

Ready in about 45 minutes
Servings 6

When you just feel like being lazy on Sunday, throw this dinner together and allow your Power pressure cooker to cook it for you. It couldn't be easier.

Per serving: 421 Calories; 15.3g Fat; 33.5g Carbs; 38.3g Protein; 3.6g Sugars

Ingredients

1 pound chuck roast, trimmed of fat and cut into 1-inch cubes
1 cup pot barley
1 cup Provolone cheese, shredded
1 serrano pepper, deveined and minced
2 small-sized onions, chopped
3 cups beef bone broth
1 tablespoon lard, at room temperature
1/2 cup loosely packed fresh spinach, torn into small pieces
3 cloves garlic, minced
1/3 teaspoon ground cumin
1 tablespoon chipotle powder

Directions

- Press the SOUP/STEW key and use the cook time selector to adjust to 30 minutes. Then, warm the lard; now, sauté the onions, pepper, and garlic until fragrant, about 4 minutes.
- Throw in the beef and continue cooking until it's no longer pink, about 5 minutes.
- Add the remaining ingredients, minus Provolone cheese. Place the lid on the Power pressure cooker XL, lock the lid and switch the pressure release valve to closed.
- Once the timer reaches 0, the cooker will automatically switch to KEEP WARM/CANCEL.
- When the steam is completely released, carefully remove the cooker's lid. Top with Provolone cheese and serve immediately.

VEGETABLES & SIDE DISHES

161. Saucy Swiss Chard with Sunflower Seeds

Ready in about 30 minutes
Servings 4

Swiss chard is a super-food widely used in a Mediterranean diet; it is a powerhouse of vitamins, minerals and dietary fiber.
Serve with avocado slices, crushed tortilla chips or brown rice.

Per serving: 60 Calories; 4.4g Fat; 4.3g Carbs; 1.8g Protein; 1.3g Sugars

Ingredients

1/4 cup red onions, chopped
1/4 teaspoon ground black pepper, or more to taste
1/3 teaspoon dry basil
1/3 teaspoon kosher salt
2 cloves garlic, minced
1/2 teaspoon dried red pepper flakes
1 cup homemade stock
7 cups Swiss chard leaves, torn into pieces
1 cup water
3 teaspoons canola oil
3 teaspoons sunflower seeds

Directions

- Press the BEANS/LENTILS key and warm canola oil. Use the cook time selector to adjust to 15 minutes.
- Sweat the onions and garlic for 2 minutes; now, stir in dry basil, seeds and red pepper flakes.
- Pour in the stock and water. Place the lid on the cooker and switch the pressure valve to closed.
- Once the timer reaches 0, the Power pressure cooker XL will automatically switch to KEEP WARM. Press the CANCEL key and remove the lid.
- Afterwards, add the salt, black pepper and Swiss chard. Give it a gentle stir and put the lid back on for 10 minutes or until the chard leaves have wilted. Serve warm.

162. Cheesy Millet with Cremini Mushrooms

Ready in about 20 minutes
Servings 6

Thanks to their firm texture and rich taste, cremini mushrooms go perfectly with millet in this easy cheesy recipe. For the best results, soak your millet overnight.

Per serving: 393 Calories; 12.5g Fat; 57g Carbs; 13.3g Protein; 3.9g Sugars

Ingredients

1 cup Colby cheese, grated
2 cups millet, rinsed in a colander
2 cups cremini mushrooms, chopped
2 small-sized carrots, thinly sliced
1/2 teaspoon cayenne pepper
Sea salt and freshly cracked black pepper, to taste
1/4 cup fresh cilantro, chopped
2 medium-sized yellow onions, chopped
1 ½ tablespoons coconut oil
1 ½ cups stock
2 ½ cups water

Directions

- Press the RICE/RISOTTO button. Melt the coconut oil and sauté the onions until they are softened, approximately 2 minutes.
- Stir in the mushrooms and carrots; cook for 4 minutes longer. Stir in the millet; continue cooking until lightly toasted, for 1 minute 30 seconds.
- Stir in the water, stock, cayenne pepper, sea salt, and black pepper. Next, close and lock the lid and cook for 6 minutes.
- Once the timer reaches 0, the Power pressure cooker XL will automatically switch to KEEP WARM. Once the steam is completely released, remove the cooker's lid.
- Divide the mixture among individual bowls. Sprinkle with grated cheese and fresh cilantro. Serve warm or at room temperature. Bon appétit!

163. Garden Breakfast Salad

Ready in about 30 minutes
Servings 6

Have you ever prepared barley in the Power pressure cooker XL? Here is a great opportunity to use this versatile grain for a colorful and refreshing salad!

Per serving: 411 Calories; 11.9g Fat; 70.4g Carbs; 9.4g Protein; 3.8g Sugars

Ingredients

1 cup carrots, chopped
1 bell pepper, deveined and chopped
1 serrano pepper, deveined and chopped
1 teaspoon seasoned salt
3 teaspoons canola oil
2 zucchini, diced
6 cups water
2 ½ cups pot barley, rinsed and drained

For the Dressing:
Sea salt and freshly ground black pepper, to your liking
1 tablespoon fresh lime juice
1/4 cup extra-virgin olive oil
1 teaspoon lime zest

Directions

- Combine pot barley, seasoned salt, canola oil, and water in your Power pressure cooker XL.
- Press the RICE/RISOTTO key and lock the lid; cook for 25 minutes.
- Drain and fluff your barley. Allow it to cool completely. Now, add zucchini, peppers and carrots. Stir to combine.
- In a mixing bowl, combine all the dressing ingredients; whisk until everything is well mixed. Drizzle the dressing over your salad. Serve well-chilled and enjoy!

164. French-Style Kamut Salad

Ready in about 15 minutes + chilling time
Servings 6

Looking for a surprisingly sensational and refreshing salad to amaze your guests? This spring-like salad is sure to please. Bon appétit!

Per serving: 320 Calories; 11.9g Fat; 49.5g Carbs; 8.9g Protein; 2.3g Sugars

Ingredients

1/4 cup extra-virgin olive oil
1/4 cup fresh basil, minced
1/3 teaspoon sea salt
1 teaspoon cayenne pepper
5 cups water
3 teaspoons vegetable oil
1/4 cup fresh lemon juice
2 cups kamut, rinsed and drained
1/2 cup red bell pepper, seeded and chopped
1 cup red onions, minced
1 ½ cups zucchini, diced
Sea salt and freshly cracked black pepper

Directions

- Place your kamut, sea salt, and cayenne in the Power pressure cooker XL. Add the water and vegetable oil. Press the RICE/RISOTTO key.
- Place the lid on the cooker and cook for 8 minutes. Once the timer reaches 0, the Power pressure cooker XL will automatically switch to KEEP WARM/CANCEL.
- Let the steam naturally release and remove the cooker's lid. Add the remaining ingredients, give it a good stir and serve well-chilled.

165. Brown Rice Risotto with Porcini and Tomato

Ready in about 25 minutes
Servings 6

For a light summer risotto, try this flavorful and low-calorie version with your favorite salad on the side.

Per serving: 366 Calories; 9.9g Fat; 59.3g Carbs; 8.7g Protein; 3.5g Sugars

Ingredients

1 cup Porcini mushrooms, chopped
2 cups canned tomatoes, chopped
2 cups brown rice
1 teaspoon fresh or dry basil
1/4 cup butter, cut into small pieces
1/3 teaspoon salt
2 small-sized yellow onions, peeled and finely chopped
2 tablespoons fresh chives
4 cups stock, preferably homemade
1/3 teaspoon turmeric powder

Directions

- Press the RICE/RISOTTO key. Choose the TIME ADJUSTMENT function until you reach 18 minutes.
- Then, sauté the onions and mushrooms until the onions are translucent and the mushrooms are just tender, about 4 minutes.
- Add the remaining ingredients to the Power pressure cooker XL.
- Lock the lid onto the cooker. Press the CANCEL key and let the steam release on its own. Afterwards, remove the cooker's lid.
- Taste and adjust the seasonings. Serve right now.

166. Spiced Collards with Prosciutto

Ready in about 20 minutes
Servings 6

Try these healthy and delicious greens – they are cooked in your Power pressure cooker XL so that you don't have to spend time stirring.

Per serving: 125 Calories; 4.4g Fat; 4.3g Carbs; 16.7g Protein; 0.9g Sugars

Ingredients

1 ½ cups collards, stems trimmed off and chopped
2 cloves garlic, minced
1 ½ cups scallions, diced
1/4 teaspoon allspice
1 pound prosciutto, diced
Sea salt and freshly ground black pepper, to your liking
2 ½ cups vegetable stock
1/3 teaspoon red pepper flakes, crushed

Directions

- Press the FISH/VEGETABLES/STEAM key. Now, brown the prosciutto and scallions for 4 minutes.
- Then, add the collards and vegetable stock; cook until your greens have wilted or 3 minutes longer. Add the garlic, red pepper, allspice, salt, and ground black pepper.
- Close and lock the lid and cook for 10 minutes.
- Press the CANCEL key and let the steam release on its own. Afterwards, remove the cooker's lid.
- Serve immediately.

167. Super Creamy Potato Salad

Ready in about 25 minutes +
chilling time
Servings 6

With rich and creamy winter salad like this, everything is looking and tasting good. Use waxy potatoes like New, Red Bliss or Yukon Gold and avoid starchy potatoes, which have a tendency to fall apart during pressure cooking.

Per serving: 225 Calories; 7.7g Fat; 39.6g Carbs; 7g Protein; 6.6g Sugars

Ingredients

2 carrots, chopped
2 cups water
2 teaspoons wine vinegar
1/3 teaspoon black pepper, freshly cracked
1/2 teaspoon cayenne pepper
1/3 teaspoon sea salt
2 sprigs rosemary, crushed
1/3 cup mayonnaise
1 cup celery, chopped
1 ½ pounds Red Bliss potatoes, scrubbed
2 small-sized leeks, chopped
4 eggs

Directions

- Place the potatoes along with water in your Power pressure cooker XL. Press the SOUP/STEW key and lock the lid; switch the pressure valve to closed.
- Cook for 10 minutes. Now, allow the steam to release completely; remove the cooker's lid.
- Allow the potatoes to cool enough to handle. Peel and slice them. Place a single layer of potatoes in a bowl.
- Alternate potato layers with leeks, carrot, and celery layers. Sprinkle each layer with cayenne pepper, rosemary, salt, and freshly cracked black pepper.
- In a mixing bowl, mix together the mayonnaise and vinegar. Add the mixture to the salad and stir gently with a wooden spoon.
- Press the RICE/RISOTTO key; add a wire rack and 1 ½ cups water to the Power pressure cooker XL. Place the eggs on the prepared wire rack and cook for 6 minutes.
- Once the timer reaches 0, the Power pressure cooker XL will automatically switch to KEEP WARM/CANCEL.
- Top your salad with the chopped eggs. Allow the salad to chill in a refrigerator before serving. Bon appétit!

168. Spicy Hash Browns

Ready in about 20 minutes
Servings 4

This is the perfect hash browns for those short on time. Omit the butter and increase the oil accordingly if you are going vegan.

Per serving: 162 Calories; 9.5g Fat; 18g Carbs; 2g Protein; 1.3g Sugars

Ingredients

1 teaspoon hot paprika
1 pound potatoes, peeled and grated
1 teaspoon sea salt
1/2 teaspoon freshly ground black pepper
1 ½ tablespoons clarified butter
1 ½ tablespoons corn oil

Directions

- Press the SOUP/STEW key and set for 10 minutes. Now, warm the oil and butter.
- Add the potatoes to the Power pressure cooker XL.
- Cook for 6 minutes, stirring periodically, until the potatoes are just browned. Season with hot paprika, salt, and black pepper.
- Next, press the potatoes down firmly with a wide metal spatula; lock the cooker's lid and switch the pressure valve to closed.
- Switch the pressure valve to rapid release. When the steam is completely released, remove the cooker's lid. Adjust the seasonings and serve right now.

169. Party Tomato Chutney

Ready in about 20 minutes
Servings 12

Pimentón gives a wonderful, smoky flavor to this tomato chutney. This is a great idea for your next dinner party; you can serve this chutney with beef sausages or combine it with cream cheese and make a crowd-pleasing party spread.

Per serving: 131 Calories; 0.7g Fat; 29.9g Carbs; 1.2g Protein; 27.4g Sugars

Ingredients

3/4 cup high-quality cider vinegar
1/3 teaspoon ground cloves
1/2 tablespoon curry paste
1/2 teaspoon ground ginger
2 cloves garlic, peeled and minced
3 ounces cups light muscovado sugar
1 cup onions, peeled and diced
3 ½ pounds mixed-color tomatoes, blanched and chopped
1 teaspoon ground coriander
1 tablespoon hot pimentón
2 tablespoons sultanas

Directions

- Purée the tomatoes in a food processor or blender.
- Add the puréed tomatoes to the Power pressure cooker XL. Stir in the remaining ingredients. Stir to combine, press the CHICKEN/MEAT key and lock the lid.
- Now, cook for 15 minutes. Allow the pressure to release naturally. When the steam has been released, carefully remove the cooker's lid.
- Serve chilled over flat bread and enjoy.

170. Wheat Berry and Vegetable Breakfast

Ready in about 30 minutes
Servings 6

For this healthy breakfast, wheat berries are cooked gently and tossed with vegetables and Feat cheese – a winning combination!

Per serving: 188 Calories; 10.3g Fat; 19.6g Carbs; 6.0g Protein; 2.7g Sugars

Ingredients

4 ounces Feta cheese
1 cup cucumber, thinly sliced
1 ½ cups cherry tomatoes, halved
4 ½ cups water
2 teaspoons lemon rind, grated
1/2 cup red onions, chopped
2 ½ tablespoons grapeseed oil
1/2 teaspoon salt
2 cups dry wheat berries
1/2 teaspoon dried oregano
2 tablespoons balsamic vinegar

Directions

- Press the "RICE/RISOTTO" key. Add the oil, wheat berries, water and salt to your Power Pressure Cooker XL; cook under HIGH pressure for 25 minutes.
- Once the timer reaches 0, the cooker will automatically switch to "KEEP WARM". Press the "CANCEL" key. Switch the pressure release valve to open. When the steam is completely released, remove the lid.
- Drain the wheat berries and rinse them through a colander. Place the wheat berries in a serving dish. Toss with the remaining ingredients. Serve chilled and enjoy.

171. Two-Mushroom Pâté

Ready in about 30 minutes +
chilling time
Servings 16

This mushroom spread is quick to prepare. You can use it to make a grab-and-go quick snack or an elegant party dinner.

Per serving: 39 Calories; 2.3g Fat; 3.0g Carbs; 1.6g Protein; 1.4g Sugars

Ingredients

1/3 cup dry white wine
2 onions, peeled and sliced
1 ½ pounds fresh mushrooms, thinly sliced
1 ½ cups boiling water
1/2 teaspoon kosher salt
1/4 teaspoon black pepper, freshly cracked
1 cup dry mushrooms, rinsed
3 tablespoons butter

Directions

- Press the "FISH/VEGETABLES/STEAM" key. In a heat-proof measuring cup, combine the dry mushrooms and boiling water. Cover and set aside. The mushrooms will soak up the water.
- When your Power Pressure Cooker XL is hot, warm the butter. Now, sauté the onions until they're softened, about 5 minutes. Then, stir in the fresh mushrooms; sauté them until fragrant and golden brown, for 5 minutes longer.
- Pour in the white wine; allow the wine to evaporate completely. Add the soaked mushrooms and stir to combine. Season with salt and pepper.
- Close and lock the cooker's lid. Set the cooking time to 10 minutes. When the steam is completely released, remove the lid.
- To make the pâté: mix the ingredients with an immersion blender for 5 minutes. Transfer to a refrigerator in order to chill completely before serving.

172. Sweet Potato Casserole with Marshmallows

Ready in about 30 minutes
Servings 6

Need more ideas for what to make with sweet potatoes? You'll be eating this casserole all day long – for breakfast, lunch, and dinner.

Per serving: 39 Calories; 2.3g Fat; 3.0g Carbs; 1.6g Protein; 1.4g Sugars

Ingredients

2 cups water
1/4 teaspoon freshly ground black pepper
1/2 teaspoon sea salt
1 teaspoon cayenne pepper
3 ½ pounds sweet potatoes, peeled and cut into quarters

For marshmallow-pecan topping:
1 cup brown sugar
1/3 cup walnuts, chopped
1/4 teaspoon freshly grated nutmeg
2 ½ tablespoons butter, melted
1/2 cup all-purpose flour
1 ¾ cups mini marshmallows

Directions

- Press the "SOUP/STEW" key. Add the sweet potatoes, water, sea salt, cayenne pepper, and black pepper to the inner pot of your Power Pressure Cooker XL.
- Lock the lid. Adjust the timer to 15 minutes.
- When the steam is released, open your Power Pressure Cooker XL. Mash the cooked sweet potatoes; taste and adjust the seasonings if needed. Transfer this sweet potato puree to an oven-safe casserole dish.
- Next, mix the flour, brown sugar, nutmeg, and butter to make the topping. Fold in the walnuts. Spread this topping mixture over the sweet potato puree. Top with mini marshmallows.
- Bake at 400 degrees F in the preheated oven for 12 minutes. Enjoy!

173. Cheesy Broccoli Soup

Ready in about 40 minutes
Servings 6

Looking for creative ways to cook with broccoli? This silky soup is both healthy and gourmet. Enjoy!

Per serving: 101 Calories; 4.1g Fat; 10.7g Carbs; 6.4g Protein; 4.1g Sugars

Ingredients

2 ¾ cups vegetable broth
1/2 cup onions, chopped
1/2 cup parsnip, finely chopped
1 cup carrots, sliced
1 teaspoon paprika
1/4 cup ground black pepper, to taste
1 teaspoon salt
1 cup bell pepper, seeded and chopped
1 cup celery stalks, finely chopped
1/2 cup celery rib, finely chopped
2 cups broccoli, broken into small florets
1/2 cup Cheddar cheese, grated

Directions

- Press the "SOUP/STEW" key. Place all of the above ingredients, except for the Cheddar cheese, in your Power Pressure Cooker XL.
- Now, set the timer for 35 minutes. Place the lid on the Power Pressure Cooker XL.
- Once the timer reaches 0, press the "CANCEL" key. Switch the pressure release valve to open. When the steam is completely released, carefully open your Power Pressure Cooker XL.
- Puree the soup with an immersion blender. Serve the soup in individual bowls topped with the grated Cheddar cheese. Enjoy!

174. Winter Jalapeño Soup

Ready in about 45 minutes
Servings 6

Jalapeño pepper is a powerhouse of vitamins C and A. Keep in mind that cooking decreases the heat of jalapeño peppers. In this recipe, use crunchy and tangy pickled jalapeño to enhance the flavor of your soup.

Per serving: 150 Calories; 9.0g Fat; 12.8g Carbs; 4.7g Protein; 3.8g Sugars

Ingredients

2 pickled jalapeño peppers, chopped
1/2 teaspoon ground cumin
1/2 teaspoon dried thyme
1 cup turnip, chopped
2 small-sized onions, finely chopped
1/2 stick butter, softened
1 cup parsnips, chopped
1 ½ cups carrots, chopped
1/2 cup celery stalk, chopped
1 quart chicken broth
4 ½ cups water
1 cup croutons, for garnish

Directions

- Press the "SOUP/STEW" key and melt the butter for a minute or so. Then, add the celery, parsnips, turnip, carrots, onion and jalapeño; sauté the vegetables for about 6 minutes.
- Add the rest of the above ingredients, except for the croutons. Seal the lid and set the timer for 35 minutes.
- Once the timer reaches 0, press the "CANCEL" key. Switch the pressure release valve to open. Carefully remove the lid.
- Ladle your soup into six individual bowls. Serve hot with croutons.

175. Smoky Red Lentil Soup

Ready in about 30 minutes
Servings 6

Red lentils are inexpensive and rich in protein, vitamin B, fiber, and iron. This stress-free lentil recipe may become a family favorite!

Per serving: 317 Calories; 0.9g Fat; 58.1g Carbs; 20.3g Protein; 4.1g Sugars

Ingredients

2 ¼ cups red lentils, rinsed
1/2 cup red bell pepper, seeded and coarsely chopped
2 pounds Yukon Gold potatoes, diced
1 bay leaf
1/2 teaspoon freshly ground black pepper, to taste
1 teaspoon salt
1/2 teaspoon smoked paprika
1 cup carrots, thinly sliced
1 cup onions, chopped
6 cups water
1 teaspoon minced garlic

Directions

- Choose the "BEANS/LENTILS" function on the Power Pressure Cooker XL. Sauté the garlic, onions, paprika, bell pepper, carrots, potatoes, salt, black pepper for about 6 minutes; make sure to stir constantly.
- Stir in the red lentils, bay leaves, and water.
- Cover the pot and bring to HIGH pressure; cook for 20 minutes. Afterwards, use the quick-release method to release the pressure and remove the lid.
- Taste and adjust the seasonings. Serve warm and enjoy!

176. Cauliflower Chowder with Velveeta Cheese

Ready in about 20 minutes
Servings 8

A rich and satisfying, this cheesy chowder is guaranteed to make your meals so much better. Serve this as a light lunch on a brisk and rainy autumn days.

Per serving: 119 Calories; 6.4g Fat; 9.5g Carbs; 7.8g Protein; 4.5g Sugars

Ingredients

2 ½ pounds cauliflower florets
1 teaspoon dried dill weed
1 shallot, chopped
1/2 teaspoon cumin powder
1/2 teaspoon ground black pepper, or more to your liking
1 teaspoon sea salt
1 ¼ cups Velveeta cheese
5 cups vegetable stock

Directions

- Choose the "FISH/VEGETABLES/STEAM" function. Simply drop all the ingredients, except the cheese, in the Power Pressure Cooker XL.
- Now, place the lid on, and set the cooking time to 10 minutes. Afterwards, remove the lid according to the manufacturer's directions.
- Add the Velveeta cheese; stir until the Velveeta cheese is completely melted. Use your immersion blender to blend the soup for 3 minutes.

177. Creamed Summer Squash Soup

Ready in about 40 minutes
Servings 8

This soup recipe is sure to please vegans and vegetable lovers alike. In this recipe, you can substitute regular onions with the shallots and even Vidalia onions.

Per serving: 120 Calories; 2.2g Fat; 19.6g Carbs; 7.9g Protein; 6.5g Sugars

Ingredients

2 cups boiling water
1 cup bell peppers, diced
2 potatoes, diced
4 zucchinis, shredded
1/2 teaspoon paprika
1/2 teaspoon cumin powder
16 ounces silken tofu, pressed
2 cups vegetable stock
1 cup onions, peeled and chopped
2 pounds yellow summer squashes, shredded

Directions

● Choose the "SOUP/STEW" function. Add the onions to your Power Pressure Cooker XL; then, sauté the onions until tender and translucent, about 5 minutes.
● Add the remaining ingredients; place the lid on the Power Pressure Cooker XL and lock; cook for 30 minutes.
● Remove the lid according to the manufacturer's directions. Allow it to cool before puréeing with an immersion blender.
● Serve topped with freshly chopped parsley if desired. Enjoy!

178. Purple Cabbage and Apple Dinner

Ready in about 30 minutes
Servings 4

Amaze your family with this sweet and tart dinner. You can add a few drizzles of vinegar to lock in the fantastic purple color of your cabbage.

Per serving: 157 Calories; 3.7g Fat; 24.0g Carbs; 2.6g Protein; 11.6g Sugars

Ingredients

1 pound purple cabbage, shredded and stems removed
1/2 teaspoon brown sugar
1 ½ cups chicken stock
1/2 cup dry red wine
1 cup onions, diced
1/4 teaspoon allspice
1/2 teaspoon ground black pepper
1 teaspoon salt
1 teaspoon dried thyme
1 tablespoon lard, room temperature
1 cup tart apples, peeled, cored and diced
1 ½ tablespoons all-purpose flour
1 ½ tablespoons cornstarch dissolved in 6 teaspoons dry red wine

Directions

● Choose the "FISH/VEGETABLES/STEAM" function on your Power Pressure Cooker XL. Warm the lard until it's completely melted.
● Then, sauté the onions and apples until soft, about 7 minutes. Add the remaining ingredients, except the cornstarch slurry.
● Dust with flour and give it a gentle stir. Set the cooking time to 15 minutes. Perform a quick-release and open the Power Pressure Cooker XL.
● Next, press the "CHICKEN/MEAT" key and bring to a boil; add the prepared cornstarch slurry.
● Then, boil for 4 minutes, uncovered, or until the cooking liquids have thickened. Serve warm.

179. Summer Wheat Berry Salad

Ready in about 30 minutes + chilling time
Servings 6

Here's a million-dollar salad you will crave during summer days! Toss together these healthy and fresh ingredients and serve the best wheat berry salad ever!

Per serving: 218 Calories; 12.0g Fat; 21.4g Carbs; 9.1g Protein; 3.4g Sugars

Ingredients

2 cups dry wheat berries
1 ½ cups cherry tomatoes, halved
1/2 cup red onions, chopped
3 tablespoons olive oil
1/2 teaspoon salt
1 teaspoon olive oil
2 tablespoons balsamic vinegar
2 ½ cups water
1/2 teaspoon dried oregano
2 sprigs dried rosemary
1/2 teaspoon orange rind, grated
1 cup red bell pepper, cut into strips
1/2 cup green bell pepper, cut into strips
4 ounces Mozzarella cheese
2 ½ cups vegetable stock

Directions

- Press the "RICE/RISOTTO" key. Add 2 tablespoons of olive oil, wheat berries, water, vegetable stock and salt to your Power Pressure Cooker XL; cook for 25 minutes.
- Once the timer reaches 0, the cooker will automatically switch to "KEEP WARM". Press the "CANCEL" key. Switch the pressure release valve to open. When the steam is completely released, remove the lid.
- Drain the wheat berries and rinse them through a colander. Place the wheat berries in a serving bowl. Toss with the remaining ingredients. Serve chilled and enjoy.

180. Spiced Vegetable Soup

Ready in about 45 minutes
Servings 6

This immunity-boosting soup is full of amazing, valuable nutrients. You can substitute chicken broth for a vegetable stock.

Per serving: 134 Calories; 7.0g Fat; 14.2g Carbs; 4.7g Protein; 6.2g Sugars

Ingredients

2 ½ tablespoons grapeseed oil, softened
1 quart chicken broth
1 cup celery stalk, chopped
4 ½ cups water
1/2 pound carrots, chopped
1 cup yellow bell pepper, seeded and chopped
1 cup red bell pepper, seeded and chopped
1/2 teaspoon fennel seeds
1 teaspoon celery seeds
1/4 teaspoon ground cumin
1 cup parsnips, chopped
1 cup leeks, finely chopped

Directions

- Choose the "SOUP/STEW" function and warm the grape seed oil for a minute or so. Then, stir in the parsnips, bell peppers, carrots, celery and leek; sauté the vegetables for approximately 7 minutes.
- Stir in the remaining ingredients. Place the lid on the Power Pressure Cooker XL and lock. Now, set the timer for 35 minutes.
- When the steam is released completely, remove the lid. Serve hot and enjoy.

181. Lasagna with Mushrooms and Cottage Cheese

Ready in about 35 minutes
Servings 6

If you have never had a vegetarian lasagna in the Power Pressure Cooker XL, here is a great idea! Mushrooms can be a great source of protein so you don't need any meat for this delicious lasagna.

Per serving: 578 Calories; 6.4g Fat; 99.0g Carbs; 30.4g Protein; 8.1g Sugars

Ingredients

3 cloves garlic, minced
2 cups pasta sauce
2 cups Cottage cheese
2 sprigs dried rosemary
1 teaspoon red pepper flakes, crushed
1/2 teaspoon sea salt
1/2 teaspoon dried basil
1/2 teaspoon dried oregano
1/2 teaspoon ground black pepper
2 cups mushrooms, thinly sliced
2 pounds dry lasagna noodles

Directions

- Choose the "FISH/VEGETABLES/STEAM" function. Treat a spring-form pan with a nonstick cooking spray.
- Add the lasagna noodles to the bottom of the pan. Spread the pasta sauce. Lay the Cottage cheese.
- Top with the sliced mushrooms. Sprinkle with some minced garlic, spices, and herbs. Repeat the layers until you run out of ingredients. Cover with an aluminum foil.
- Next, place the wire rack on the bottom of your Power Pressure Cooker XL. Pour in 1 cup of water.
- Lower the spring-form pan onto the wire rack; lock the cooker's lid and switch the pressure release valve to closed. Set the cooking time to 25 minutes.
- Once the cooking is done, switch the pressure release valve to open. When the steam is completely released, remove the cooker's lid. Serve warm.

182. Colorful Brown Rice Salad

Ready in about 25 minutes +
chilling time
Servings 4

Looking for a last-minute recipe for a family dinner? This stunning rice salad will fit the bill! Wild rice works well in this recipe, too; just increase the cooking time to 25 minutes.

Per serving: 398 Calories; 8.3g Fat; 70.9g Carbs; 11.8g Protein; 9.2g Sugars

Ingredients

2 medium-sized tomatoes, diced
2 cups water
1/2 teaspoon white pepper, or more to your liking
1 teaspoon salt
1 cup red bell pepper, thinly sliced
2 Serrano peppers, thinly sliced
2 cucumbers, cored and diced
2 red onions, chopped
1 ½ cups brown rice
3/4 cup crumbled Feta cheese

Directions

- Choose the "RICE/RISOTTO" function. Add the rice and water to the Power Pressure Cooker XL. Close and lock the lid. Set the cooking time to 18 minutes.
- Open the cooker using a Natural pressure release. Allow the rice to cool completely.
- Add the remaining ingredients. Give it a gentle stir; serve well-chilled. Bon appétit!

183. Pumpkin Quinoa Delight

Ready in about 15 minutes
Servings 4

You can chill the cooked quinoa and use this as a base for an easy and healthy salad. Please bear in mind that quinoa easily picks up flavors of the ingredients it's cooked with.

Per serving: 185 Calories; 2.9g Fat; 33.9g Carbs; 6.9g Protein; 2.6g Sugars

Ingredients

1 ¼ cups canned pumpkin puree
1/2 teaspoon ground cloves
1/2 teaspoon freshly grated nutmeg
1/4 teaspoon salt
1/3 teaspoon ground cinnamon
1 ½ cups water
1 cup uncooked quinoa, well rinsed

Directions

- Choose the "FISH/VEGETABLES/STEAM" function. Add all the components to the Power Pressure Cooker XL. Next, lock the lid and switch the pressure release valve to closed.
- Set the cooking time to 2 minutes. Let the quinoa stand for 10 minutes.
- Now, use a Quick pressure release and remove the lid according to the manufacturer's directions.
- Taste and adjust the seasonings. Serve at once and enjoy!

184. Mediterranean Tomato-Basil Soup

Ready in about 30 minutes
Servings 6

Ripe tomatoes, potatoes, and aromatic herbs are all cooked together in this hearty soup for an appetizing lunch. You can substitute basil leaves for fresh chopped chives. Enjoy!

Per serving: 130 Calories; 3.0g Fat; 24.2g Carbs; 4.0g Protein; 8.5g Sugars

Ingredients

3 garlic cloves, peeled and finely minced
2 potatoes, peeled and chopped
1 cup onions, chopped
1 teaspoon dried oregano
1/2 teaspoon salt
1/2 teaspoon ground cumin
1 teaspoon celery seeds
1/2 teaspoon grated nutmeg
1 teaspoon fennel seeds
3 pounds tomatoes, chopped
1/2 cup packed fresh basil leaves
1 cup cream

Directions

- Choose the "SOUP/STEW" function. Place the tomatoes, onions, potatoes, garlic, dried oregano, and salt into the Power Pressure Cooker XL; now, add the cumin, celery seeds, nutmeg, and fennel seeds.
- After that, pour in 2 cups of water. Lock the lid onto the pot.
- Set the cooking time to 22 minutes. Reduce the pressure naturally.
- Carefully open the Power Pressure Cooker XL. Afterwards, stir in the cream and basil leaves. Serve at once and enjoy!

185. Autumn Harvest Soup

Ready in about 45 minutes
Servings 6

Never underestimate the importance of a good healthy soup at lunchtime. Be inspired by root vegetables and amaze your family!

Per serving: 145 Calories; 8.7g Fat; 12.8g Carbs; 4.7g Protein; 3.3g Sugars

Ingredients

4 cups chicken broth
3 ½ cups water
1 cup celery stalks, chopped
1 cup parsnips, chopped
1 cup shallots, finely chopped
2 Serrano peppers, seeded and chopped
1 ½ cups carrots, chopped
1/2 teaspoon ground cumin
1/2 teaspoon fennel seeds
1 teaspoon granulated garlic
1/2 stick butter, softened

Directions

- Choose the "SOUP/STEW" function and melt the butter for a minute or so. Then, stir in the Serrano peppers, shallots, parsnip, carrots, and celery; sauté the ingredients for 6 minutes.
- Stir in the rest of the above ingredients. Now, lock the lid and switch the pressure release valve to closed; set the timer for 35 minutes.
- Once the cooking is complete, the Power Pressure Cooker XL will automatically switch to "KEEP WARM/CANCEL". When the steam is completely released, remove the cooker's lid.
- Serve hot and enjoy.

186. Classic Italian Caponata

Ready in about 40 minutes
Servings 4

Caponata is a traditional Sicilian eggplant (aubergine) dish that is cooked perfectly in the Power Pressure Cooker XL. Serve with olives at room temperature.

Per serving: 171 Calories; 16.9g Fat; 6.0g Carbs; 0.9g Protein; 2.5g Sugars

Ingredients

1 cup red onion, sliced
2 tablespoons red wine vinegar
1/3 cup olive oil
2 cups eggplant, unpeeled and cubed
1 tablespoon salt
3 garlic cloves, chopped
1/2 cup fresh basil, chopped

Directions

- Firstly, generously sprinkle the eggplant cubes with salt; let them stand in a colander at least 30 minutes. Rinse the eggplant in water; squeeze them and reserve.
- Choose the "FISH/VEGETABLES/STEAM" function; heat the oil and sauté the eggplant, garlic, and red onion until they are tender.
- Stir in the red wine. Cover with the lid and set the cooking time to 7 minutes. Switch the pressure release valve to open. When the steam is completely released, remove the cooker's lid.
- Serve sprinkled with fresh basil leaves and olives if desired. Bon appétit!

187. Creamy Potato Soup

Ready in about 45 minutes
Servings 6

A thick and creamy vegetarian soup to get you through busy days. The recipe is very easy to make and yields even 6 servings. Serve with homemade cornbread if desired.

Per serving: 195 Calories; 4.3g Fat; 30.5g Carbs; 9.0g Protein; 4.9g Sugars

Ingredients

4 cups vegetable broth
1 ½ cups carrots, sliced
1 cup celery, chopped
1 cup celery stalk, thinly sliced
1 cup yellow onion, chopped
1 teaspoon red pepper flakes, crushed
1 ½ tablespoons ground chia seeds
1/2 teaspoon ground black pepper, to taste
1 teaspoon salt
2 tablespoons fresh basil leaves, finely chopped
2 pounds potatoes, peeled and diced
1 cup spinach leaves, chopped
1/2 cup sharp Cheddar cheese, grated

Directions

- Press the "SOUP/STEW" key. Simply throw all the ingredients, except for the cheese, into the Power Pressure Cooker XL.
- Place the lid on the Power Pressure Cooker XL, lock the lid and switch the pressure release valve to closed. Now, adjust the timer to 40 minutes.
- When the steam is completely released, remove the cooker's lid.
- Lastly, puree the soup with an immersion blender. Ladle the soup into six bowls; top with the grated Cheddar cheese.

188. Garden Vegetable Soup

Ready in about 20 minutes
Servings 8

Feed a crowd with this hearty and healthy soup that is made of vitamin-packed veggies. Serve with hot, crusty rolls.

Per serving: 120 Calories; 6.0g Fat; 13.0g Carbs; 5.5g Protein; 3.8g Sugars

Ingredients

2 cups canned diced tomatoes
1 cup fennel bulb, trimmed and chopped
3/4 pound green beans, trimmed and cut into 1-inch pieces
5 cups vegetable broth
2 tablespoons butter
1 tablespoon olive oil
1/2 teaspoon ground black pepper
1/2 teaspoon salt
1/2 teaspoon dill weed
1 cup onions, cut into rings
1 ½ cups fresh corn kernels

Directions

- Press the "SOUP/STEW" key and melt the oil and butter. Sauté the onion, stirring often, until softened, about 4 minutes. Stir in the vegetable broth, tomatoes, fennel bulb, dill, salt, and the black pepper.
- Place the lid on the Power Pressure Cooker XL, lock the lid and switch the pressure release valve to closed. Cook for 10 minutes.
- Use a quick release and open the cooker. Stir in the corn kernels and green beans.
- Lock the lid back onto your Power Pressure Cooker XL. Continue cooking for 5 minutes longer. Use a quick release and carefully remove the lid. Serve in individual bowls.

189. Wheat Berry with Veggies and Greek Yogurt

Ready in about 30 minutes
Servings 4

Greek yogurt is much creamier than regular yogurt; it has less sugar and more carbs. Greek yogurt is packed with proteins, calcium, probiotics, vitamin B12, and potassium.

Per serving: 150 Calories; 11.9g Fat; 8.3g Carbs; 2.6g Protein; 5.1g Sugars

Ingredients

1 cup sweet onions, peeled and sliced
1 cup celery stalks, chopped
1/2 stick butter
1/4 teaspoon black pepper, or more to taste
1 teaspoon salt
1 cup carrots, thinly sliced
1 ½ cups white wheat berries, soaked overnight in lots of water
1/2 cup Greek yogurt, for garnish

Directions

- Choose the "RICE/RISOTTO" function. In your Power Pressure Cooker XL, combine the white wheat berries with 6 cups water.
- In a pan, melt the butter over medium heat. Then, sauté the sweet onions until tender and translucent. Add the salt and ground black pepper.
- Place the lid on the Power Pressure Cooker XL. Cook the wheat berries together with the carrots and celery until they are tender, about 25 minutes. Switch the pressure release valve to open.
- When the steam is released completely, remove the lid. Now, add the sautéed sweet onions and stir well.
- Serve topped with Greek yogurt.

190. Veggie and Spelt Berry Salad

Ready in about 30 minutes
Servings 8

Enjoy this "good-for-you" salad that is chock-full of colorful vegetables, great aromatics, and amazing grains. Serve well-chilled with bite-sized cubes of your favorite goat cheese.

Per serving: 218 Calories; 13g Fat; 26.6g Carbs; 4.5g Protein; 6.5g Sugars

Ingredients

6 cups water
2 cups spelt berries
1 cup celery, finely diced
1 cup scallions, chopped
1 cup sun-dried tomatoes, diced
3 teaspoons olive oil
1/3 cup wine vinegar
1/3 cup extra-virgin olive oil
1 tablespoon serrano pepper, chopped
1 cup zucchini, chopped
1/2 cup bell pepper, seeded and diced
1/4 teaspoon freshly ground black pepper
2 tablespoons fresh cilantro, chopped
2 teaspoons muscovado sugar
1/2 teaspoon sea salt
1 ¼ cups frozen green peas, thawed

Directions

- Add the olive oil, water, and spelt berries to your Power pressure cooker XL. Place the lid on the cooker, lock the lid and switch the pressure release valve to closed.
- Press the RICE/RISOTTO key. Cook for 25 minutes.
- In the meantime, make the dressing by processing the sugar, black pepper, salt, vinegar, extra-virgin olive oil and scallions in your blender.
- Toss prepared berries with the remaining ingredients. Dress the salad and refrigerate for up to 3 days.

191. Family Green Soup with Beans

Ready in about 40 minutes
Servings 4

Pinto beans work greatest for this recipe but you can freely use any kind of kidney beans. Keep in mind that Power pressure cooker XL reaches the temperature and pressure depending on the temperature of your vegetables, i.e. whether or not they are frozen.

Per serving: 456 Calories; 5.6g Fat; 83.9g Carbs; 19.8g Protein; 6.9g Sugars

Ingredients

1 ½ cups kale, sliced into thin strips
12 ounces pinto beans, soaked overnight
3 cloves garlic, minced or pressed
1/2 teaspoon cayenne pepper
1/3 teaspoon dried thyme
4 sweet potatoes, peeled and cut into chunks
1 cup parsnips, cut into chunks
1/3 teaspoon ground black pepper, to taste
1/3 teaspoon kosher salt
1 bell pepper, diced
1 cup leeks, chopped
3 teaspoons canola oil
5 cups stock

Directions

- Press the BEANS/LENTILS key; use the cook time selector to adjust to 30 minutes. Now, warm canola oil and sauté the leeks and garlic, until softened, about 4 minutes.
- Add sweet potatoes, parsnips, and stock. Add the seasonings.
- Stir in the beans and red bell peppers. Close and lock the cooker's lid. Once the timer reaches 0, the Power pressure cooker XL will automatically switch to KEEP WARM/CANCEL.
- Add kale, lock the lid and allow it to sit until wilted, about 5 minutes. Serve warm and enjoy!

192. Cheesy Vegetable Broth

Ready in about 20 minutes
Servings 16

Homemade broth is better and cheaper than the store-bought versions. This rich and unusual vegetarian broth cooks quickly in your Power pressure cooker XL. Win-win!

Per serving: 60 Calories; 4.7g Fat; 2.4g Carbs; 2.5g Protein; 1g Sugars

Ingredients

1 ¼ cups Colby cheese, cut into pieces
1/3 cup fresh cilantro, chopped
1 cup celery with leaves, chopped
1 cup leeks, chopped
1 cup turnip, sliced
2 tomatoes, chopped
3 cloves garlic, peeled and crushed
1/2 teaspoon black peppercorns
1 bay leaf
9 cups water, to cover
1 teaspoon dried Italian herb blend
2 tablespoons canola oil

Directions

- Press the SOUP/STEW key and heat the oil.
- Then, sweat the leeks, garlic, turnip, and celery; cook, stirring periodically, until your veggies begin to soften.
- Place the tomato and cilantro on top of the vegetables; top with cheese pieces. Add bay leaf, Italian herb blend and black peppercorns.
- Pour the water into your Power pressure cooker XL. Place the lid on the Power pressure cooker XL, lock the lid and switch the pressure release valve to closed. Cook for 10 minutes.
- When the steam is completely released, remove the cooker's lid.
- Set a colander lined with a double layer of cheesecloth over a large-sized bowl; then, pour the broth through to strain; press the vegetables to extract all the liquid. Your broth is ready to use.

193. Creamy Broccoli Soup with Cheese

Ready in about 20 minutes
Servings 6

Broccoli is loaded with antioxidants, vitamin C, calcium, and selenium. Broccoli improves bone health and natural detoxification. This fantastic vegetable protects your body from coronary heart disease, hypertension, obesity, and certain gastrointestinal diseases.

Per serving: 304 Calories; 19.5g Fat; 17.5g Carbs; 18.9g Protein; 3g Sugars

Ingredients

1 pound broccoli, chopped into small florets
1 ¼ cups Parmesan cheese, freshly grated
5 cups vegetable stock
2 shallots, sliced
3/4 cup heavy cream
1 parsnip, trimmed and chopped
1 ½ tablespoons canola oil
1/3 teaspoon allspice
Salt and freshly cracked black pepper, to taste
1/3 teaspoon cumin powder
1 teaspoon red pepper flakes, crushed
1/2 teaspoon garlic powder

Directions

- Press the SOUP/STEW key and warm the oil until sizzling. Then, sauté the shallots until translucent.
- Then, stir in the broccoli florets, parsnip, stock, red pepper, garlic powder, cumin and allspice.
- Place the lid on the Power pressure cooker XL, lock the lid and switch the pressure release valve to closed. Cook for 10 minutes.
- Lastly, release the cooker's pressure according to manufacturer's directions.
- Stir in heavy cream and cheese; season with salt and black pepper to taste. Serve warm.

194. Vegetable Soup with Tortillas and Cheese

Ready in about 30 minutes
Servings 4

A rich tortilla soup is the easiest way to warm up. Each ingredient in this soup plays a part in its rich and incredible flavor. If you want to skip baking these tortillas, use tortilla chips.

Per serving: 426 Calories; 21.1g Fat; 48.5g Carbs; 15.8g Protein; 12.7g Sugars

Ingredients

2 cups water
1/2 stick melted butter
2 ½ cups vegetable stock
1 cup shallots, chopped
1/4 cup fresh lime juice
6 ounces frozen green peas
1 ½ cups canned pumpkin puree
1/2 habanero pepper, seeded and diced
2 green bell peppers, seeded and diced
1 cup summer squash, cut into bite-size pieces
3 cloves garlic, minced
Non-stick cooking spray
6 corn tortillas, cut into wide strips
2 ripe tomatoes, chopped
1/4 teaspoon ground black pepper
1/2 teaspoon ground cumin
1/3 teaspoon dried basil
1 teaspoon sea salt
1/2 teaspoon chili powder
1/2 teaspoon dried oregano
Shredded Swiss cheese, for serving

Directions

- Preheat the oven to 400 degrees F. Then, line a baking sheet with parchment paper. Lightly spray both sides of each tortilla with a nonstick cooking spray. Then, cut the tortillas into strips using a knife.
- Spread the tortilla strips onto the baking sheet. Bake until they are crisp, turning once halfway through baking. It will take about 9 minutes.
- Press the SOUP/STEW key and warm the butter; sauté the shallots for about 3 minutes.
- Add the squash, peppers, garlic, and lime juice; bring to a boil and let the liquid reduce by half. Add the tomatoes, pumpkin puree, herbs, spices, water, and vegetable stock.
- Place the lid on the Power pressure cooker XL, lock the lid and switch the pressure release valve to closed. Cook for 10 minutes.
- Stir in the peas; let it simmer, uncovered, approximately 3 minutes.
- To serve, place tortilla chips on the bottom of each serving bowl; ladle the soup over them. Sprinkle with shredded Swiss cheese. Serve immediately.

195. Chunky Potato and Corn Soup

Ready in about 20 minutes
Servings 6

If you are craving a spoon-clinging, rich and creamy soup, give this recipe a try! You can puree just a cup or two of the soup with an immersion blender to make your soup creamier.

Per serving: 136 Calories; 3.3g Fat; 24.7g Carbs; 4.5g Protein; 3.6g Sugars

Ingredients

1 ½ pounds Yukon Gold potatoes, peeled and diced
2 cups frozen sweet corn
2 shallots, chopped
5 ½ cups vegetable stock
3 teaspoons canola oil
1/3 cup yogurt
Salt and freshly ground black pepper, to taste
1/2 teaspoon ground bay leaves

Directions

● Press the CHICKEN/MEAT key and heat the oil. Then, sauté the shallots for 3 minutes. Choose the CANCEL function.
● Pour in the stock. Add the potatoes and spices. Press the SOUP/STEW key.
● Place the lid on the Power pressure cooker XL, lock the lid and switch the pressure release valve to closed. Cook for 10 minutes.
● Stir in frozen sweet corn and yogurt; stir until everything is well combined and serve.

196. Hearty Cauliflower with Green Peas

Ready in about 25 minutes
Servings 8

What could be better than a bowl of hearty vegetables for winter weeknights? Pamper your senses and add your favorite aromatics.

Per serving: 148 Calories; 4.1g Fat; 24.3g Carbs; 5.8g Protein; 6.9g Sugars

Ingredients

2 pounds cauliflower, cut into small florets
2 ¼ cups fresh green peas
2 ripe tomatoes, diced
2 tablespoons green garlic, finely minced
1/2 teaspoon salt
1/3 teaspoon red pepper flakes, crushed
1/3 teaspoon ground black pepper
1 cup spring onions, white parts only and thinly sliced
2 teaspoons ghee
2 yams, peeled and cubed
1 ½ tablespoons vegetable oil
7 cups vegetable stock

Directions

● Press the RICE/RISOTTO key. Melt the ghee and oil. Add spring onions and sauté them, stirring often, until softened.
● Stir in the stock, tomatoes, cauliflower, green garlic, salt, black pepper, and red pepper.
● Place the lid on the Power pressure cooker XL, lock the lid and switch the pressure release valve to closed. Cook for 6 minutes. Choose the CANCEL function.
● Press the FISH/VEGETABLE/STEAM key. Stir in the peas and yams. Lock the lid back onto the Power pressure cooker XL and cook for 10 minutes more.
● When the steam is completely released, remove the cooker's lid. Serve hot.

197. Baby Spinach and Mushroom Soup

Ready in about 30 minutes
Servings 6

This is one of the favorite mushroom soups that reheats well. In this recipe, you can also use the crushed smoked paprika and dry Mediterranean herbs. Enjoy!

Per serving: 183 Calories; 2.7g Fat; 36g Carbs; 5.2g Protein; 3.7g Sugars

Ingredients

2 ½ cups baby spinach, torn into pieces
10 ounces button mushrooms, sliced
2 cloves garlic, minced
1 cup parsnip, finely chopped
6 ½ cups roasted vegetable stock
2 tablespoons soy sauce
1 cup carrots, diced
Salt and ground black pepper, to your liking
1 pound sweet potatoes, peeled and diced
1 cup scallions, chopped
3 teaspoons vegetable oil
2 tablespoons loosely packed fresh rosemary leaves, minced

Directions

- Press the RICE/RISOTTO key and heat the oil. Use the cook time selector to adjust to 18 minutes. Then, sauté the mushrooms, scallions and garlic for 6 minutes.
- Stir in the parsnip, carrots, rosemary leaves, salt, and black pepper; cook for an additional 2 minutes. Pour in the stock.
- Add diced sweet potatoes and soy sauce. Stir well to combine. Place the lid on the Power pressure cooker XL, lock the lid and switch the pressure release valve to closed.
- Press the CANCEL key. When the steam is completely released, remove the cooker's lid.
- Stir in baby spinach. Lock the lid back onto the Power pressure cooker XL and; let it stand for 6 minutes or until baby spinach leaves are wilted. Enjoy!

198. Brussels Sprout and Endive Soup

Ready in about 20 minutes
Servings 8

Discover this endive soup, an exciting, hearty dish with Brussels sprouts, tomatoes, butter, and aromatics. Serve it as a starter or as the main course with homemade corn bread for an easy dinner.

Per serving: 147 Calories; 6.1g Fat; 19.8g Carbs; 4.8g Protein; 1.6g Sugars

Ingredients

1/2 pound Brussels sprouts, quartered
1 ½ pounds frozen endive, chopped
2 ripe tomatoes, chopped
2 shallots, chopped
7 cups vegetable stock
1/2 teaspoon salt
1 sprig dry thyme, leaves crushed
1 teaspoon cayenne pepper
1/3 teaspoon freshly cracked black pepper
3 garlic cloves, minced
1/2 stick butter

Directions

- Press the BEANS/LENTIL key and melt the butter; sauté the shallots and garlic, stirring often, until they're just softened, about 3 minutes. Choose the CANCEL function.
- Add the stock, Brussels sprouts, tomatoes, salt, thyme, black pepper, cayenne pepper, and endive.
- Choose the RICE/RISOTTO function. Place the lid on the Power pressure cooker XL, lock the lid and switch the pressure release valve to closed. Cook for 6 minutes.
- Once the timer reaches 0, the Power pressure cooker XL will automatically switch to KEEP WARM/CANCEL. Carefully remove the cooker's lid.
- Stir just before serving. Enjoy!

199. Herbed Bow Tie Pasta with Acorn Squash

Ready in about 20 minutes
Servings 4

This pasta dish could not be easier to make. Just sauté your vegetables and add the remaining ingredients. Serve with chopped fresh chives and a freshly grated Parmigiano-Reggiano.

Per serving: 540 Calories; 13.5g Fat; 98.4g Carbs; 17.2g Protein; 6.9g Sugars

Ingredients

1 package bow tie pasta
2 medium-sized Acorn squash, stemmed and diced
2 tablespoons wine vinegar
1 cup chopped leeks, white parts only
1 cup bell peppers, stemmed, cored, and chopped
1 1/3 cups vegetable stock
1 sprig dry rosemary, crushed
1/4 teaspoon ground black pepper
1/4 teaspoon salt, or more to your liking
1/2 tablespoon capers, minced
1/2 teaspoon garlic powder
3 teaspoons grape seed oil
20 ounces canned diced tomatoes

Directions

- Press the RICE/RISOTTO key and heat grape seed oil in your Power pressure cooker XL. Add the leeks and capers; cook, stirring often, for about 3 minutes.
- Add the squash and bell peppers; continue cooking for an additional 2 minutes. Stir in the tomatoes, stock, rosemary, garlic powder, salt, black pepper, and wine vinegar. Press the CANCEL key.
- Stir in the pasta; stir with a wooden spoon until it is well coated. Place the lid on the Power pressure cooker XL, lock the lid and switch the pressure release valve to closed. Cook for 8 minutes.
- Once the timer reaches 0, the cooker will automatically switch to KEEP WARM. Switch the pressure release valve to open. When the steam is completely released, remove the lid.
- Stir well and serve.

200. Summer Zucchini and Sweet Potato Stew

Ready in about 20 minutes
Servings 4

The Power pressure cooker XL ensures you get a quick and tasty summer stew without losing any nutrition and flavor from your vegetables. It might become a staple in your summer kitchen. If you want to thicken the stew, blend just a cup or two of the stew until it all is a smooth puree.

Per serving: 226 Calories; 5.5g Fat; 42.3g Carbs; 4.2g Protein; 6.2g Sugars

Ingredients

2 cups zucchini, diced
1 pound sweet potatoes, diced
1 cup vegetable stock
1/2 teaspoon cayenne pepper
1 cup yellow onions, chopped
4 teaspoons canola oil
2 cloves garlic, minced
1/2 tablespoon celery seeds
1/2 teaspoon ground black pepper
1/3 teaspoon seasoned salt
4 tomatoes, finely chopped

Directions

- Press the CHICKEN/MEAT key. Heat the oil and sweat the onions for 4 minutes.
- Stir in the garlic and cayenne pepper until aromatic, about 1 minute. Press the CANCEL key.
- Stir in the tomatoes; pour in the stock. Add the remaining ingredients; stir well to combine.
- Place the lid on the Power pressure cooker XL, lock the lid and switch the pressure release valve to closed. Press the SOUP/STEW key and cook for 10 minutes.
- Once the timer reaches 0, the cooker will automatically switch to KEEP WARM/CANCEL. When the steam is completely released, remove the cooker's lid. Serve warm.

201. Garam Masala Potatoes with Brussels Sprouts

Ready in about 20 minutes
Servings 6

Yukon Gold are potatoes with yellow-tinged flesh that are perfect for this Indian-inspired dish. They make a great substitute for other types of starchy foods, adding nutritional value to your meals.

Per serving: 114 Calories; 7g Fat; 12.2g Carbs; 2.4g Protein; 1.3g Sugars

Ingredients

1/2 pound Brussels sprouts, cut into halves
1 ½ pounds Yukon Gold potatoes, peeled and cubed
3/4 teaspoon Garam masala
1/4 teaspoon ground black pepper
3/4 teaspoon ginger, minced
1/2 teaspoon salt
3 cloves garlic, minced
1/4 cup yellow onions, chopped
3 tablespoons corn oil

Directions

- Press the SOUP/STEW key. Heat the oil and sauté the onions and garlic until aromatic, about 3 minutes. Now, add fresh ginger and Garam masala and cook for 1 minute more. Choose the CANCEL function.
- Add the salt, black pepper, potatoes and Brussels sprouts to the Power pressure cooker XL. Cover them with water.
- Place the lid on the Power pressure cooker XL, lock the lid and switch the pressure release valve to closed.
- Choose the RICE/RISOTTO function. Set to 8 minutes.
- Once the timer reaches 0, the cooker will automatically switch to KEEP WARM/CANCEL. When the steam is completely released, remove the cooker's lid. Bon appétit!

202. Scallion and Rutabaga Salad

Ready in about 15 minutes
Servings 4

Rutabaga has a lot of health and beauty benefits such as antiaging and antioxidant properties. It can improve your digestions, boost the immune system and regulate blood pressure. Awesome!

Per serving: 185 Calories; 13g Fat; 17.5g Carbs; 2.8g Protein; 11.4g Sugars

Ingredients

1 cup scallions, minced
2 rutabaga, peeled and cubed
1/4 cup olive oil
Salt and freshly ground white pepper, to taste
1/2 teaspoon smoked cayenne pepper
3 teaspoons orange juice
1 cup water

Directions

- Add rutabaga and water to the Power pressure cooker XL.
- Press the BEANS/LENTILS key and lock the lid. Cook for 5 minutes. When the steam is completely released, carefully remove the cooker's lid.
- Transfer rutabaga chunks to a platter and reserve.
- To make the dressing: In a measuring cup, whisk together the rest of the above ingredients. Dress your rutabaga and serve.

203. Easy Traditional Borscht

Ready in about 40 minutes
Servings 6

There are dozens of versions of a traditional beetroot soup – Borscht. This recipe uses lots of winter vegetables and a beef meat for an even richer flavor. Serve with hard-boiled eggs.

Per serving: 261 Calories; 8.8g Fat; 21.1g Carbs; 25.5g Protein; 12.9g Sugars

Ingredients

1 pound brisket, cut into bite-sized pieces
1 ¼ pounds red beets, peeled, diced and rinsed
1 cup leeks, peeled and diced
2 tablespoons minced parsley root
2 cups white cabbage, chopped
3 tablespoons apple cider vinegar
2 cups tomato puree
2 tablespoons butter
3 cloves garlic, peeled and minced
6 ½ cups beef bone broth, preferably homemade
Sea salt and freshly ground black pepper, to taste

Directions

- Press the CHICKEN/MEAT key and melt the butter; then, brown the brisket for 3 minutes, stirring constantly.
- Now, add the leeks and garlic and continue sautéing until fragrant, about 3 minutes. Press the CANCEL key.
- Then, add the parsley root, red beets, white cabbage, tomato puree, broth and vinegar to the Power pressure cooker XL. Season with the salt and pepper.
- Place the lid on the Power pressure cooker XL, lock the lid and switch the pressure release valve to closed.
- Choose the SOUP/STEW function; then, cook for 30 minutes. Ladle your soup into serving dishes and garnish with Smetana (sour cream). Enjoy!

204. Creamy Savoy Cabbage Soup

Ready in about 15 minutes
Servings 6

In addition to giving a mild and earthy flavor, Savoy cabbage adds a nutritional value to your soup. Savoy cabbage is a powerhouse of precious vitamins, minerals and fibers.

Per serving: 183 Calories; 8g Fat; 14.9g Carbs; 12.3g Protein; 9.7g Sugars

Ingredients

1 pound savoy cabbage, shredded
3/4 cup Swiss cheese, shredded
1 cup yellow onions, sliced
1 ½ cups carrots, trimmed and chopped
1 ½ cups yogurt
1 teaspoon cayenne pepper
1/2 teaspoon ground bay leaf
3 teaspoons olive oil
Salt and freshly cracked black pepper, to taste
1/2 teaspoon granulated garlic
4 ½ cups vegetable broth

Directions

- Press the CHICKEN/MEAT key and heat the oil until sizzling. Then, sauté the onions until translucent, about 4 minutes. Choose the CANCEL function.
- Add Savoy cabbage, carrots, broth, ground bay leaf, cayenne pepper and granulated garlic.
- Place the lid on the Power pressure cooker XL, lock the lid and switch the pressure release valve to closed.
- Choose the FISH/VEGETABLE/STEAM function. Cook for 10 minutes. Once the timer reaches 0, the cooker will automatically switch to KEEP WARM/CANCEL. When the steam is completely released, remove the cooker's lid.
- Stir in yogurt and shredded sharp cheese; season with salt and black pepper. Serve warm.

205. Yellow Tomato Chutney

Ready in about 10 minutes
Servings 12

This chutney is a great addition to your burgers, sandwiches and fries as a healthy homemade alternative to a ketchup. You can add less sugar to this recipe as well as mustard powder or red chile flakes, it's just a matter of taste!

Per serving: 81 Calories; 2.8g Fat; 13.4g Carbs; 0.9g Protein; 11.1g Sugars

Ingredients

2 ½ pounds yellow peach tomatoes, diced
1 cup yellow onions, peeled and chopped
2 tablespoons butter
1 ½ cups bell peppers, diced
2 green chile peppers, stemmed, seeded and thinly sliced
1/2 teaspoon sea salt
1 teaspoon curry powder
1/2 cup raw sugar
1/2 cup cider vinegar
1/2 tablespoon fresh ginger, grated
3 garlic cloves, peeled and minced

Directions

- Put all ingredients into the Power pressure cooker XL.
- Place the lid on the Power pressure cooker XL, lock the lid and switch the pressure release valve to closed. Choose the RICE/RISOTTO function. Cook for 9 minutes.
- Afterwards, allow pressure to release naturally and remove the cooker's lid.
- Place in a refrigerator before serving. You can spread your chutney over pizza crust if desired. Keep in your refrigerator for 2 months. Enjoy!

206. Red Potato and Swiss Chard Soup

Ready in about 15 minutes
Servings 6

You can't go wrong with a pressure cooked and well-seasoned potato soup. If you prefer brown rice, feel free to use it in this recipe; just increase the cooking time to 18 minutes. Enjoy!

Per serving: 328 Calories; 11.3g Fat; 45g Carbs; 9.5g Protein; 4.4g Sugars

Ingredients

1 ½ pounds red potatoes, peeled and diced
2 cups frozen Swiss chard, torn into large pieces
3 tablespoons Prosecco
3/4 cup white rice
3 tablespoons canola oil
2 serrano peppers, seeded and chopped
1/2 teaspoon sea salt
1/2 teaspoon ground black pepper
1 tomato, finely chopped
1 ½ cups red onions, white part only, sliced
3/4 cup Swiss cheese, grated
1 cup celery with leaves, chopped
6 cups vegetable stock

Directions

- Choose the CHICKEN/MEAT function and warm the oil. Then, sauté the onions, peppers and celery for about 3 minutes.
- Stir in rice and red potatoes. Continue cooking an additional 2 minutes. Press the CANCEL button.
- Add the stock, salt, black pepper, Prosecco, chopped tomatoes and Swiss chard. Stir well to combine.
- Place the lid on the Power pressure cooker XL, lock the lid and switch the pressure release valve to closed.
- Choose the RICE/RISOTTO function and cook for 6 minutes.
- To serve, divide the soup among individual bowls and garnish with grated Swiss cheese.

207. Cream of Mushroom Soup

Ready in about 25 minutes
Servings 4

This homemade, rustic cream of mushroom soup will win your heart! It is so easy to prepare in your Power pressure cooker XL.

Per serving: 211 Calories; 11.1g Fat; 18.8g Carbs; 8.6g Protein; 10.1g Sugars

Ingredients

2 ½ cups cremini mushrooms, sliced
3/4 cup béchamel sauce
2 tablespoons ghee
2 ½ cups milk
2 sprigs dried rosemary, crushed
3 cloves garlic, minced
1 cup carrots, diced
Salt and ground black pepper, to taste
1 teaspoon dried marjoram
1 cup scallions, diced
3 tablespoons white wine

Directions

- Press the CHICKEN/MEAT key and warm ghee; now, sauté the scallions until translucent, about 3 minutes.
- Add the garlic, mushrooms, carrots; continue sautéing for 4 minutes longer. Press the CANCEL button.
- Stir in the wine, milk, rosemary, marjoram, and béchamel sauce. Season with salt and black pepper.
- Place the lid on the Power pressure cooker XL, lock the lid and switch the pressure release valve to closed. Press the SOUP/STEW key and then, TIME ADJUST-MENT key. Set the time to 10 minutes.
- Lastly, allow pressure to release naturally. Purée the soup with an immersion blender or a regular food processor and serve warm.

208. Vegetable and Garbanzo Bean Stew

Ready in about 25 minutes
Servings 4

Here's a perfect vegan stew for a cozy winter dinner at home. Make something extraordinary and amaze your family!

Per serving: 410 Calories; 24.1g Fat; 42.4g Carbs; 11.4g Protein; 11.2g Sugars

Ingredients

1/3 cup nut butter
1 cup garbanzo beans, soaked overnight
1 cup almond milk
1 cup scallions, chopped
1 tablespoon fresh ginger, minced
1/2 pound red potatoes, peeled and cubed
1 ½ cups tomato puree
1 ½ cups vegetable broth
2 teaspoons sesame oil
2 bell peppers, chopped
Kosher salt and ground black pepper, to taste
1 teaspoon garlic, finely minced
1 ½ cups water

Directions

- Press the BEANS/LENTILS key. Set time to 15 minutes. Warm sesame oil and sauté the scallions, garlic and peppers for 4 minutes. Add the ginger, and sauté for an additional minute.
- Add the remaining ingredients, except for the almond milk, to the Power pressure cooker XL.
- Place the lid on the cooker, lock the lid and switch the pressure release valve to closed.
- Once the timer reaches 0, the cooker will automatically switch to KEEP WARM/CANCEL. When the steam is completely released, remove the cooker's lid.
- Ladle the soup into individual bowls and serve. Enjoy!

209. Creamed Pumpkin Soup

Ready in about 25 minutes
Servings 6

The Power pressure cooker XL is the perfect tool to achieve a velvety texture of pumpkin soup. Sautéing gives the veggies a slightly "caramelized" flavor.

Per serving: 189 Calories; 12.8g Fat; 19.2g Carbs; 3.8g Protein; 6g Sugars

Ingredients

1 ½ pounds pumpkin, cut into small pieces
2 teaspoons lime juice
5 ½ cups stock
2 shallots, diced
1 cup coconut milk
3 teaspoons olive oil
2 garlic cloves, finely minced
1/4 teaspoon black pepper
1/2 teaspoon salt
1/3 teaspoon smoked cayenne pepper

Directions

- Press the BEANS/LENTILS key. Set time to 15 minutes and warm the oil. Now, sauté the shallots until tender and translucent, about 3 minutes.
- Add the pumpkin, garlic, salt, black pepper, and cayenne pepper; sauté for 4 minutes.
- Pour in the stock. Place the lid on the cooker, lock the lid and switch the pressure release valve to closed.
- Once the timer reaches 0, the cooker will automatically switch to KEEP WARM/CANCEL. When the steam is completely released, remove the cooker's lid.
- Allow pressure to release on its own. Add the milk and lime juice; purée your soup using a food processor and serve warm.

210. Cheese and Onion Soup

Ready in about 25 minutes
Servings 6

Here's a classic soup inspired by French cuisine! To serve, you can use Provolone cheese as well. You will need a crusty bread or biscuits for dunking too.

Per serving: 144 Calories; 10.3g Fat; 4.8g Carbs; 7.9g Protein; 3g Sugars

Ingredients

1 cup Swiss cheese, thinly sliced
1 cup spring onions, thinly sliced
Sea salt and freshly ground black pepper, to taste
1/2 teaspoon dried thyme
1/2 teaspoon ground bay leaf
1 tablespoon muscovado sugar
2 tablespoons coconut oil, at room temperature
1 tablespoon wine
6 cups roasted vegetable broth

Directions

- Press the CHICKEN/MEAT key and warm coconut oil; cook spring onions and sugar until they are caramelized, for about 9 minutes. Press the CANCEL key.
- Add the broth, wine, ground bay leaf, dried thyme, salt, and ground black pepper; stir to combine.
- Place the lid on the cooker, lock the lid and switch the pressure release valve to closed. Press the SOUP/STEW key and set time to 10 minutes.
- Once the timer reaches 0, the cooker will automatically switch to KEEP WARM/CANCEL. When the steam is completely released, remove the cooker's lid.
- Ladle the soup into individual bowls and top with Swiss cheese. Serve and enjoy!

211. Herbed Broccoli Braised in Frascati

Ready in about 15 minutes
Servings 6

Power pressure cooker XL cooks your broccoli in no time. If you don't have Frascati on hand, any type of dry white wine will work.

Per serving: 113 Calories; 5.5g Fat; 11.7g Carbs; 3.7g Protein; 3.6g Sugars

Ingredients

1 ½ pounds broccoli, cut into florets
1/3 cup Frascati
2 sweet onions, thinly sliced
2 teaspoons dried sage
Salt and ground black pepper, to your taste
1/2 teaspoon dried thyme
3 teaspoons grape seed oil
1 teaspoon garlic paste

Directions

- Press the FISH/VEGETABLES/STEAM key. Now, set time to 10 minutes.
- Heat the oil and sweat sweet onions, stirring periodically, until they have softened, about 3 minutes.
- Stir in garlic paste, broccoli, Frascati and the remaining seasonings. Place the lid on the cooker, lock the lid and switch the pressure release valve to closed.
- Once the timer reaches 0, the cooker will automatically switch to KEEP WARM/CANCEL. When the steam is completely released, remove the cooker's lid.
- Serve warm and enjoy!

212. Herby Mashed Sweet Potatoes

Ready in about 20 minutes
Servings 6

Relax and look forward to the incredible side dish ahead! Sweet potatoes cook perfectly in the Power pressure cooker XL so that all you need is a tablespoon of freshly grated sharp cheese to makes it magnificent.

Per serving: 264 Calories; 8.9g Fat; 43.5g Carbs; 3.4g Protein; 2.4g Sugars

Ingredients

1/2 stick cold butter, cut into pieces
3/4 cup whole milk
2 pounds sweet potatoes, peeled and cut into chunks
1 sprig dried thyme, crushed
3/4 teaspoon red pepper flakes, crushed
1/4 teaspoon ground black pepper
1 teaspoon dried marjoram
2 sprigs dried rosemary, crushed
1/2 teaspoon seasoned salt

Directions

- Simply drop the potatoes in your Power pressure cooker XL; then, fill the cooker with the water to cover the potatoes. Sprinkle with the salt. Close and lock the lid.
- Press the SOUP/STEW button. Set to 10 minutes.
- Once the timer reaches 0, the cooker will automatically switch to KEEP WARM/CANCEL.
- Switch the pressure release valve to open. When the steam is completely released, remove the cooker's lid. Drain your potatoes in a colander.
- Using a potato masher, mash the potatoes. Add ground black pepper, red pepper, rosemary, thyme, marjoram, butter and the whole milk.
- Beat the mixture to the desired consistency. Serve with your favorite sharp cheese.

213. Zucchini and Lima Bean Stew

Ready in about 20 minutes
Servings 4

If you are looking for a vegetarian treat, here's a fragrant and hearty stew that might become your family favorite. Accompany with cornbread and mashed potatoes.

Per serving: 263 Calories; 4.7g Fat; 41.6g Carbs; 16.3g Protein; 11g Sugars

Ingredients

1 cup lima beans, soaked overnight
3 ½ cups broth
2 carrots, diced
1/2 teaspoon cumin
1/2 teaspoon celery seeds
2 ½ cups water
1 teaspoon red pepper flakes, crushed
1/3 teaspoon ground black pepper
1/3 teaspoon salt
1 pound zucchini, diced
1/4 cup fresh parsley, chopped
1/2 cup tomato puree

Directions

- Add all of the above ingredients to your Power pressure cooker XL.
- Place the lid on the cooker, lock the lid and switch the pressure release valve to closed.
- Press the BEANS/LENTILS key; set to 15 minutes.
- Once the timer reaches 0, the cooker will automatically switch to KEEP WARM/CANCEL. Carefully remove the cooker's lid. Serve warm and enjoy!

214. Yam and Green Pea Delight

Ready in about 20 minutes
Servings 6

Cooking vegetables in the Power pressure cooker XL has a number of advantages to the traditional methods of simmering and sautéing. See it for yourself!

Per serving: 155 Calories; 2.6g Fat; 29.2g Carbs; 4.2g Protein; 3.6g Sugars

Ingredients

1 pound yams, peeled and cubed
1/2 teaspoon Garam masala
1 teaspoon garlic, minced
3/4 teaspoon salt
1/4 teaspoon ground black pepper
3/4 pound frozen green peas, broken into florets
3 teaspoons vegetable oil
1 (1-inch) piece fresh ginger, peeled and finely minced

Directions

- Add the yams to the Power pressure cooker XL; cover them with your favorite stock. Add the remaining ingredient, minus green peas.
- Place the lid on the cooker. Choose the FISH/VEGETABLES/STEAM function and set to 10 minutes. Press the CANCEL key.
- When the steam is completely released, remove the cooker's lid.
- Afterwards, add green peas and place the lid on the cooker; choose the FISH/VEGETABLES/STEAM function and set time to 4 minutes.
- Once the timer reaches 0, the cooker will automatically switch to KEEP WARM/CANCEL.
- Switch the pressure release valve to open. When the steam is completely released, remove the cooker's lid. Serve immediately.

215. Creamed Roma Tomato Soup

Ready in about 25 minutes
Servings 6

If you are lucky enough to own the Power pressure cooker XL, you can make the creamiest tomato soup ever. This old-fashion recipe can be served in less than 30 minutes.

Per serving: 123 Calories; 4.9g Fat; 14g Carbs; 6.8g Protein; 8.8g Sugars

Ingredients

1 pound fresh Roma tomatoes, finely chopped
3/4 cup yogurt
2 cups tomato puree
1 teaspoon minced garlic
3 ½ cups vegetable broth
4 spring onions, chopped
1 ½ tablespoons peanut oil
1 teaspoon oregano
Sea salt and ground black pepper, to taste
1 tablespoon fresh chopped basil

Directions

- Press the BEANS/LENTILS key and warm the peanut oil. Use the cook time selector to adjust to 15 minutes.
- Sweat spring onions for about 4 minutes.
- Add the remaining ingredients, except for the yogurt. Place the lid on the cooker, lock the lid and switch the pressure release valve to closed.
- Once the timer reaches 0, the cooker will automatically switch to KEEP WARM/CANCEL. When the steam is completely released, remove the cooker's lid.
- Stir in the yogurt and serve immediately.

FAST SNACKS & APPETIZERS

216. Roasted Fingerling Potatoes

Ready in about 20 minutes
Servings 4

To make these potatoes look great and taste delicious, use grated cheese, instead of chunks. Petite potatoes work well too.

Per serving: 377 Calories; 12.3g Fat; 27.9g Carbs; 10.8g Protein; 1.9g Sugars

Ingredients

1 ½ pounds fingerling potatoes
1 cup blue cheese, grated
1/3 cup broth
4 tablespoons melted ghee
1/2 teaspoon kosher salt
1/2 teaspoon cayenne pepper

Directions

- Combine melted ghee with fingerling potatoes and broth in your Power pressure cooker XL. Press the SOUP/STEW key; set for 10 minutes.
- Place the lid on the Power pressure cooker XL, lock the lid and switch the pressure release valve to closed.
- Once the timer reaches 0, the cooker will automatically switch to KEEP WARM/CANCEL.
- When the steam is completely released, carefully remove the cooker's lid.
- Sprinkle the potatoes with cayenne pepper, salt and grated blue cheese; serve immediately.

217. Candied Beet Chips

Ready in about 1 hour 25 minutes
Servings 6

These melt-in-your-mouth candied bites are a wonderful make-ahead snack for your next party! You can serve it with soups and salads.

Per serving: 243 Calories; 7.8g Fat; 43.5g Carbs; 2g Protein; 40g Sugars

Ingredients

1 ½ pounds baby beets, sliced very thin
1 cup water
1/2 stick butter, unsalted
1/2 teaspoon sea salt
1 cup firmly packed light brown sugar

Directions

- Place the baby beets in your Power pressure cooker XL; add the water.
- Press the BEANS/LENTILS key and use the cook time selector to adjust to 15 minutes. Place the lid on the Power pressure cooker XL, lock the lid and switch the pressure release valve to closed.
- Once the timer reaches 0, the cooker will automatically switch to KEEP WARM/CANCEL.
- When the steam is completely released, carefully remove the cooker's lid.
- Meanwhile, in a saucepan, cook the sugar, salt and butter. Add the beets and gently stir until they're glazed, about 5 minutes. Then, transfer the beets to a baking sheet lined with a parchment paper.
- Bake at 250 degrees F about 1 hour. Allow them to cool completely before serving.

218. Braised Kale with Spring Garlic

Ready in about 15 minutes
Servings 4

Braised kale is always a hit! Besides being delicious, this recipe is easy to make. If you don't have spring garlic on hand, simply use a regular freshly minced garlic.

Per serving: 110 Calories; 7g Fat; 10.5g Carbs; 2.8g Protein; 0.3g Sugars

Ingredients

4 cups kale, torn into pieces
4 spring garlic, chopped
2 tablespoons grapeseed oil
1 cup stock
1 teaspoon paprika
Sea salt and freshly ground black pepper, to your liking

Directions

- Choose the FISH/VEGETABLES/STEAM function and use the cook time selector to adjust to 4 minutes.
- Warm the oil and cook the garlic until it's fragrant and just browned. Add the paprika, stock and kale leaves. Sprinkle with the salt and freshly ground black pepper.
- Place the lid on the Power pressure cooker XL, lock the lid and switch the pressure release valve to closed.
- Once the timer reaches 0, the cooker will automatically switch to KEEP WARM/CANCEL.
- When the steam is completely released, carefully remove the cooker's lid.
- Taste and adjust the seasonings.

219. Corn on the Cob with Butter Cheese

Ready in about 15 minutes
Servings 4

You can easily double the recipe if desired. Corn is an extremely healthy food; it prevents diabetes, heart diseases, obesity, and anemia.

Per serving: 168 Calories; 13.5g Fat; 10.7g Carbs; 1.9g Protein; 1.9g Sugars

Ingredients

4 fresh corn on the cob, husked
1/2 cup butter cheese, softened
Salt and white pepper, to your liking
1/3 teaspoon allspice
1 cup water

Directions

- Prepare your Power pressure cooker XL by adding a rack and water; place the corn on the cob on the rack. Press the BEANS/LENTILS key.
- Then, place the lid on the Power pressure cooker XL, lock the lid and switch the pressure release valve to closed. Cook for 5 minutes.
- Once the timer reaches 0, the cooker will automatically switch to KEEP WARM/CANCEL.
- When the steam is completely released, carefully remove the cooker's lid.
- Spread the butter cheese over each corn on the cob; sprinkle with allspice, salt, and white pepper. Serve.

220. Glazed Carrot Sticks with Walnuts

Ready in about 5 minutes
Servings 6

Carrots are among the world healthiest foods! For your party, make sure to double or triple the recipe because these flavorful sticks will disappear so fast!

Per serving: 157 Calories; 10.7g Fat; 14.5g Carbs; 2.3g Protein; 5.7g Sugars

Ingredients

1 ½ pounds carrots, sliced into sticks
4 tablespoons walnuts, coarsely chopped
1/2 stick butter, at room temperature
3 teaspoons agave syrup
1/2 teaspoon ground cinnamon
1/4 teaspoon kosher salt
1 ½ cups water

Directions

- Add the water, carrots, and walnuts to the Power pressure cooker XL. Choose the FISH/VEGETABLES/STEAM function.
- Place the lid on the Power pressure cooker XL, lock the lid and switch the pressure release valve to closed. Cook for 2 minutes.
- Once the timer reaches 0, the cooker will automatically switch to KEEP WARM/CANCEL.
- When the steam is completely released, carefully remove the cooker's lid.
- Next, add the remaining ingredients to the warm carrots. Give it a good stir. Serve at room temperature.

221. The Best Lima Bean Dip

Ready in about 20 minutes + chilling time
Servings 16

Make this hummus-like dip for your next cocktail party and delight your guests! Serve with raw vegetable sticks and pita chips.

Per serving: 87 Calories; 1.5g Fat; 15g Carbs; 4.5g Protein; 2.6g Sugars

Ingredients

2 pounds lima beans, soaked overnight
2 onions, finely chopped
1 ½ cups tomato puree
1/4 cup loosely packed fresh parsley, minced
Grated zest and juice of 1/2 lemon
3 teaspoons extra-virgin olive oil
4 cups water
1 tablespoon chile pepper, finely minced
Kosher salt and ground black pepper, to taste
1 teaspoon celery seeds

Directions

- Choose the BEANS/LENTILS function and use the cook time selector to adjust to 15 minutes. Add the water and lima beans.
- Place the lid on the Power pressure cooker XL, lock the lid and switch the pressure release valve to closed.
- Once the timer reaches 0, the cooker will automatically switch to KEEP WARM/CANCEL.
- When the steam is completely released, carefully remove the cooker's lid.
- Transfer your lima beans to a food processor. Puree until everything is well incorporated. Serve well chilled.

222. Braised Yellow Wax Beans

Ready in about 20 minutes
Servings 6

This easy and healthy appetizer can be assembled ahead of time. Your family will love its fresh and rich taste. Add a few sprinkles of chile powder just before serving!

Per serving: 101 Calories; 2.5g Fat; 15.5g Carbs; 3.1g Protein; 4.5g Sugars

Ingredients

2 ½ pounds yellow wax beans, ends trimmed
3 cloves garlic, minced
3 teaspoons olive oil
1/4 cup white wine
1 cup scallions, chopped
1 cup tomato puree
3/4 cups water
Sea salt and freshly ground black pepper, to your liking
1 teaspoon smoked paprika

Directions

- Press the FISH/VEGETABLES/STEAM key. Heat the oil and sauté the scallions and garlic; cook, stirring occasionally for 4 minutes.
- Add the yellow wax beans, tomatoes, water, and wine. Season with salt, pepper, and smoked paprika.
- Place the lid on the Power pressure cooker XL, lock the lid and switch the pressure release valve to closed.
- Then, use the cook time selector to adjust to 4 minutes.
- Once the timer reaches 0, the cooker will automatically switch to KEEP WARM/CANCEL.
- When the steam is completely released, carefully remove the cooker's lid. Serve warm or at room temperature.

223. Fastest-Ever Baba Ghanoush

Ready in about 20 minutes
Servings 16

Eggplant is very versatile food. This time, we use a fabulous tahini-spices-oil combination to make an easy and crowd-pleasing dip.

Per serving: 51 Calories; 3.7g Fat; 4.2g Carbs; 1.2g Protein; 2.1g Sugars

Ingredients

2 eggplants, peeled and diced
1 ½ tablespoons sesame paste
1 tablespoon finely minced garlic
1/4 cup fresh cilantro
2 teaspoons canola oil
2 tablespoons extra-virgin olive oil
3/4 cup water
1/2 teaspoon black pepper, to taste
1 teaspoon salt

Directions

- Press the FISH/VEGETABLES/STEAM key; use the cook time selector to adjust to 10 minutes.
- Now, heat the oil and sauté the eggplant until it is tender, about 3 minutes. Add the garlic and continue sautéing an additional minute.
- Pour in the water. Place the lid on the Power pressure cooker XL, lock the lid and switch the pressure release valve to closed.
- Once the timer reaches 0, the cooker will automatically switch to KEEP WARM/CANCEL. When the steam is completely released, carefully remove the cooker's lid.
- Spoon prepared mixture into a food processor along with the remaining ingredients, minus olive oil. Purée until well combined.
- Transfer to a serving bowl. Drizzle with the olive oil. Serve with pita wedges and enjoy.

224. Party Black Bean Spread

Ready in about 25 minutes
Servings 6

Let's explore new ways to prepare a party menu and give this recipe a try! It's quick and easy to prepare so that you can make more time for yourself.

Per serving: 260 Calories; 3.3g Fat; 44.8g Carbs; 14.6g Protein; 1.4g Sugars

Ingredients

1 cup shallots, thinly sliced
2 cups dry black beans, soaked and rinsed
3 teaspoons canola oil
2 thyme sprigs, chopped
1 teaspoon garlic powder
1/2 teaspoon paprika
2 rosemary sprigs, chopped
Salt and black pepper, to taste
2 tablespoons wine vinegar
3 ½ cups water

Directions

- Press the BEANS/LENTILS key and use the cook time selector to adjust to 15 minutes.
- Heat the oil and sauté the shallots. Stir in the beans and water. Place the lid on the Power pressure cooker XL, lock the lid and switch the pressure release valve to closed.
- Once the timer reaches 0, the cooker will automatically switch to KEEP WARM/CANCEL. When the steam is completely released, carefully remove the cooker's lid.
- Add the remaining ingredients; transfer the mixture to your food processor and purée until it is smooth. Serve with dippers of choice.

225. Sweet Potatoes with Tangerine and Cashews

Ready in about 15 minutes
Servings 6

Tangerines are a great source of vitamin C, vitamin A, minerals and fibers. In this recipe, you can use Clementines or Tangelos; anyway, if you don't have tangerines on hand, simply use oranges.
This appetizer pairs perfectly with light-bodied wines.

Per serving: 451 Calories; 21.9g Fat; 61.4g Carbs; 5.8g Protein; 7.9g Sugars

Ingredients

10 sweet potatoes, peeled and cubed
2 tangerines, peeled and sectioned
3/4 cup cashews, coarsely chopped
1 cup mayonnaise
1/2 teaspoon allspice
1 teaspoon fresh ginger, peeled and grated
1 teaspoon kosher salt
1/4 teaspoon white pepper, ground
1/3 teaspoon ground nutmeg
Juice of 1 lime plus 1 teaspoon of grated lemon peel
1 cup water
2 tablespoons sunflower seeds, for garnish

Directions

- Add the water and trivet to the bottom of your Power pressure cooker XL. Arrange sweet potato cubes in a steamer basket. Sprinkle with the lemon juice.
- Then, lower the steamer basket onto the trivet. Press the SOUP/STEW key. Set to 10 minutes.
- Place the lid on the Power pressure cooker XL, lock the lid and switch the pressure release valve to closed.
- Once the timer reaches 0, the cooker will automatically switch to KEEP WARM/CANCEL. When the steam is completely released, carefully remove the cooker's lid.
- Transfer prepared sweet potatoes to a serving dish.
- In a bowl, whisk together the mayonnaise, lemon zest, ginger, kosher salt, white pepper, allspice, and nutmeg; whisk till everything is well incorporated.
- Add this mixture to the serving dish with potatoes. Add the cashews and tangerines. Toss to combine and sprinkle with sunflower seeds. Serve and enjoy!

226. Sweet Zesty Cauliflower Appetizer

Ready in about 15 minutes
Servings 4

The Power pressure cooker XL transforms "dull" veggies into this super healthy, stunning appetizer. You can substitute sultanas with black raisins or chopped dates.

Per serving: 85 Calories; 1g Fat; 15.3g Carbs; 2.9g Protein; 10.1g Sugars

Ingredients

1 pound cauliflower, broken into small florets
1/2 cup scallions, chopped
1 cup sultanas
2 tablespoons birch sugar
1/2 cup stock
1/4 cup sweet dessert wine
1 tablespoon grape seed oil
2 tablespoons lemon juice
A pinch of sea salt

Directions

- Choose the FISH/VEGETABLES/STEAM function and use the cook time selector to adjust to 4 minutes.
- Then, heat grape seed oil and sauté the scallions until soft, about 4 minutes.
- Add the cauliflower and toss to combine with the scallions and oil. Stir in the stock, wine, sugar and sea salt.
- Place the lid on the Power pressure cooker XL, lock the lid and switch the pressure release valve to closed.
- Once the timer reaches 0, the cooker will automatically switch to KEEP WARM/CANCEL. When the steam is completely released, carefully remove the cooker's lid.
- Add the sultanas and lemon juice. Taste and adjust the seasonings.

227. Asparagus, Cheese and Lentil Dip

Ready in about 25 minutes
Servings 20

If you're hosting a cocktail party, minimize stress by making this amazing dip in advance. Serve in a bread bowl.

Per serving: 143 Calories; 5.1g Fat; 16.1g Carbs; 8.8g Protein; 1.4g Sugars

Ingredients

2 pounds asparagus, trimmed and roughly chopped
3/4 cup cream cheese
3/4 cup Gruyere cheese, grated
1 pound red lentils
2 tablespoons fresh lemon juice
2 tablespoons mayonnaise
3 cloves of garlic, smashed
1 teaspoon Dijon mustard
1 teaspoon salt
1/3 teaspoon ground black pepper
2 cups water

Directions

- Add the lentils, water and asparagus to the Power pressure cooker XL. Press the BEANS/LENTILS key and use the cook time selector to adjust to 15 minutes.
- Place the lid on the Power pressure cooker XL, lock the lid and switch the pressure release valve to closed.
- Once the timer reaches 0, the cooker will automatically switch to KEEP WARM/CANCEL. When the steam is completely released, carefully remove the cooker's lid.
- Add the remaining ingredients. Lastly, mix the ingredients with an immersion blender. Serve at room temperature with dippers of choice.

228. Easy Aromatic Peppers

Ready in about 15 minutes
Servings 6

Make sure to use different colored peppers for a better presentation. Serve with bruschetta and olives.

Per serving: 97 Calories; 8g Fat; 6.6g Carbs; 1.4g Protein; 3.4g Sugars

Ingredients

1 ½ pounds bell peppers, deveined and sliced
3/4 cup tomato puree
1/2 cup stock
1/2 tablespoon miso paste
1 tablespoon garlic, crushed
1/2 cup scallions, chopped
1/2 stick butter, melted
Sea salt and freshly ground black pepper
2 tablespoons champagne vinegar

Directions

● Press the FISH/VEGETABLE/STEAM key use the cook time selector to adjust to 10 minutes.
● Then, warm the butter and sauté the scallions until soft, about 4 minutes.
● Add the crushed garlic and stir for a further minute. Add the peppers, tomato puree, stock, and pesto sauce.
● Place the lid on the Power pressure cooker XL, lock the lid and switch the pressure release valve to closed.
● Once the timer reaches 0, the cooker will automatically switch to KEEP WARM/CANCEL. When the steam is completely released, carefully remove the cooker's lid.
● Season to taste with salt and black pepper. Serve drizzled with champagne vinegar.

229. Pancetta and Adzuki Bean Dip

Ready in about 25 minutes
Servings 12

The trick to making this dip silky and smooth is to serve it in a fondue pot. Chipotle powder and black pepper amp up the heat in this fabulous party dip.

Per serving: 241 Calories; 11.9g Fat; 17.5g Carbs; 15.9g Protein; 0.8g Sugars

Ingredients

1/2 pound pancetta, finely diced
1 ½ cups dry adzuki beans, soaked overnight
1 ½ cups stock
1/2 cup scallions, peeled and diced
2 ripe tomatoes, chopped
3 cloves garlic, peeled and minced
6 ounces Provolone cheese, grated
2 tablespoons fresh chives, chopped
1 teaspoon chipotle powder
1 teaspoon dried basil
Sea salt and black pepper, to taste

Directions

● Press the BEANS/LENTILS key and use the cook time selector to adjust to 15 minutes. Now, sauté pancetta, garlic, and scallions for 5 minutes.
● Add the beans, stock, tomatoes, chipotle powder, basil, salt and black pepper.
● Place the lid on the Power pressure cooker XL, lock the lid and switch the pressure release valve to closed.
● Once the timer reaches 0, the cooker will automatically switch to KEEP WARM/CANCEL. When the steam is completely released, carefully remove the cooker's lid.
● Now, transfer the prepared bean mixture to your food processor. Add fresh chives and blend until smooth.
● Transfer the dip to a fondue pot; add Provolone cheese, stir to combine and serve with your favorite dippers.

230. Cheesy Polenta Bites

Ready in about 15 minutes
Servings 6

Here is an insanely easy, elegant appetizer that is perfect for your holiday party! It is also dinner-worthy.

Per serving: 369 Calories; 18.9g Fat; 42.9g Carbs; 6.8g Protein; 1.7g Sugars

Ingredients

2 cups polenta
1/2 cup cheddar cheese, grated
1 cup onions, chopped
3 cups vegetable stock
1 stick butter, melted
1/2 teaspoon salt
1/4 teaspoon ground black pepper
1 ½ cups water

Directions

- Press the SOUP/STEW key and warm 2 tablespoons of butter; sauté the onions until they're softened and translucent.
- Add the stock, water, cornmeal, salt, and black pepper. Place the lid on the Power pressure cooker XL, lock the lid and switch the pressure release valve to closed. Cook for 10 minutes.
- Once the timer reaches 0, the cooker will automatically switch to KEEP WARM/CANCEL. When the steam is completely released, carefully remove the cooker's lid.
- Stir in cheddar cheese and the remaining butter; give it a good stir. Transfer the polenta to a lightly oiled 13x9-inch baking pan. Chill until cold and set.
- Then, cut out polenta rounds with a cutter. Heat 2 tablespoons of oil in a large nonstick skillet; sauté the polenta bites until they are lightly browned. Serve at room temperature.

231. Pancetta and Swiss Chard Appetizer

Ready in about 15 minutes
Servings 4

This budget-friendly recipe will get everyone excited for a festive meal. You can substitute pancetta for Canadian bacon as well.

Per serving: 324 Calories; 24.1g Fat; 3.6g Carbs; 22.1g Protein; 1.4g Sugars

Ingredients

1/2 pound pancetta, diced
3 cups Swiss chard, chopped
2 ½ cups stock
1/2 cup red onions, chopped
3 cloves garlic, crushed
2 sprigs dry rosemary, crushed
Sea salt and ground black pepper, to taste

Directions

- Press the RICE/RISOTTO key and fry the pancetta for 3 minutes. Now, add the garlic and onions and continue sautéing for 3 more minutes. Press the CANCEL key.
- Add the remaining ingredients. Place the lid on the Power pressure cooker XL, lock the lid and switch the pressure release valve to closed. Cook for 6 minutes.
- Once the timer reaches 0, the cooker will automatically switch to KEEP WARM/CANCEL. When the steam is completely released, carefully remove the cooker's lid. Serve.

232. Amazing Steamed Broccoli

Ready in about 15 minutes
Servings 6

This steamed broccoli is about to be your new favorite appetizer or side dish. Serve with Riesling or Prosecco.

Per serving: 79 Calories; 3.6g Fat; 10.5g Carbs; 3.3g Protein; 2.7g Sugars

Ingredients

1/4 cup mayonnaise
2 tablespoons lime juice
1 ½ pounds broccoli, broken into florets
1 teaspoon cayenne pepper
1/2 teaspoon mustard powder
Salt and ground black pepper, to taste

Directions

- Pour 1 cup of water into the Power pressure cooker XL. Now, add a steamer basket. Add the broccoli to the steamer basket; drizzle with lime juice.
- Press the FISH/VEGETABLES/STEAM key and use the cook time selector to adjust to 4 minutes.
- Place the lid on the Power pressure cooker XL, lock the lid and switch the pressure release valve to closed.
- Once the timer reaches 0, the cooker will automatically switch to KEEP WARM/CANCEL. When the steam is completely released, carefully remove the cooker's lid.
- Then, make the sauce. In a mixing bowl, combine the mustard powder together with mayonnaise, cayenne pepper, salt and black pepper. Serve with prepared broccoli.

233. Black Bean and Mango Salsa

Ready in about 20 minutes
Servings 12

This sour and sweet combination of beans, mango and spices is sinfully delicious! Serve with your favorite dippers.

Per serving: 124 Calories; 2.4g Fat; 21.9g Carbs; 5.2g Protein; 8.1g Sugars

Ingredients

1 1/3 cups black beans, soaked overnight and rinsed
2 ripe mangoes, peeled and chopped
2 tablespoons red wine vinegar
1 ½ tablespoons sesame paste
4 tablespoons fresh lime juice
1 tablespoon grapeseed oil
1 teaspoon chili powder
1/2 teaspoon garlic powder
Salt and ground black pepper, to taste
2 tablespoons fresh cilantro, finely minced
4 cups water

Directions

- Add the water, black beans and oil to the Power pressure cooker XL. Press the BEANS/LENTILS key and use the cook time selector to adjust to 15 minutes.
- Place the lid on the Power pressure cooker XL, lock the lid and switch the pressure release valve to closed.
- Once the timer reaches 0, the cooker will automatically switch to KEEP WARM/CANCEL. When the steam is completely released, carefully remove the cooker's lid.
- Add the cooked beans to the bowl of your blender or food processor. Stir in the rest of the above ingredients and pulse until it is well combined but still a little chunky.
- Place in a refrigerator to chill and serve.

234. Party Mushroom Dip

Ready in about 15 minutes
Servings 12

This is not an average mushroom dip. Pressure cooked and well-seasoned, this dip is your ticket to Flavor Town!

Per serving: 315 Calories; 3.4g Fat; 38.2g Carbs; 19.1g Protein; 0g Sugars

Ingredients

2 pounds porcini mushrooms, sliced
4 cloves garlic, minced
2 teaspoons vegetable oil
1 tablespoon sesame paste
2 tablespoons extra-virgin olive oil
1/2 teaspoon ground black pepper
2 tablespoons fresh parsley
1 teaspoon salt
1 tablespoon fresh lemon juice
1 cup water

Directions

- Press the FISH/VEGETABLES/STEAM key and use the cook time selector to adjust to 4 minutes.
- Then, heat the vegetable oil; sauté the garlic and mushrooms until they begin to get soft. Pour in the water.
- Place the lid on the Power pressure cooker XL, lock the lid and switch the pressure release valve to closed.
- Once the timer reaches 0, the cooker will automatically switch to KEEP WARM/CANCEL. When the steam is completely released, carefully remove the cooker's lid.
- Pulse the mushroom/garlic mixture in your food processor along with the parsley, salt, black pepper, lemon juice, and sesame paste.
- Then, pour in the extra-virgin olive oil and process until the mixture is smooth. Garnish with fresh chopped chives if desired and serve.

235. Spicy Great Northern Bean Dip

Ready in about 35 minutes + chilling time
Servings 16

It's surprisingly easy to whip up the addictive bean dip in your own kitchen. In this recipe, you can use Ancho, Guindilla Verde, Anaheim, Cayenne or any other type of your favorite chile pepper.

Per serving: 138 Calories; 3.6g Fat; 20.8g Carbs; 6.7g Protein; 2g Sugars

Ingredients

2 ½ cups Great Northern beans, soaked overnight
1 tablespoon chile pepper, finely minced
3 cloves garlic, minced
1 cup tomato puree
2 medium-sized onions, chopped
2 tablespoons olives, pitted and chopped
1/4 cup extra-virgin olive oil
2 tablespoons champagne vinegar
1/3 teaspoon sea salt
1/4 teaspoon ground black pepper, or more to taste
1 teaspoon celery seed
1/4 cup fresh cilantro
4 cups water

Directions

- Place the water and beans in your Power pressure cooker XL. Press the BEANS/LENTILS key and use the cook time selector to adjust to 30 minutes.
- Place the lid on the Power pressure cooker XL, lock the lid and switch the pressure release valve to closed.
- Once the timer reaches 0, the cooker will automatically switch to KEEP WARM/CANCEL. When the steam is completely released, carefully remove the cooker's lid.
- Drain your beans and transfer them to a food processor.
- Throw in the remaining ingredients and puree until everything is well incorporated. Refrigerate your dip at least 2 hours before serving.

236. Zesty Cippolini Onions

Ready in about 15 minutes
Servings 6

For this appetizer, you can experiment with ingredients to add a spectrum of flavors to each bite. You can toss the onions with roasted jalapeños and serve topped with crumbled Cabrales.

Per serving: 126 Calories; 0g Fat; 27.5g Carbs; 0.8g Protein; 26g Sugars

Ingredients

1 ½ pounds cippolini onions, outer layer removed
1/4 cup wine vinegar
3 tablespoons sugar
2 teaspoons white flour
2 bay leaves
1 teaspoon salt
1/2 teaspoon black pepper, freshly ground
1 cup water

Directions

- Press the FISH/VEGETABLES/STEAM key and use the cook time selector to adjust to 4 minutes.
- Throw the water and cippolini onions into your Power pressure cooker XL along with the bay leaves, black pepper, and salt.
- Place the lid on the Power pressure cooker XL, lock the lid and switch the pressure release valve to closed.
- Once the timer reaches 0, the cooker will automatically switch to KEEP WARM/CANCEL. When the steam is completely released, carefully remove the cooker's lid.
- Transfer cippolini onions to the bowl.
- In a saucepan, combine the rest of the above ingredients. Cook over low heat about 2 minutes. Pour the sauce over the cippolini onions in the bowl. Serve at room temperature and enjoy.

237. Pickled Chile and Cheese Dip

Ready in about 15 minutes
Servings 12

Cook's note: You can transfer your dip to a bread bowl and place on a baking sheet. Put under the broiler for a few minutes or until your dip is warmed through and bubbling. Serve hot with chips.

Per serving: 146 Calories; 10.8g Fat; 4.6g Carbs; 8g Protein; 2.3g Sugars

Ingredients

1 tablespoon minced pickled chile peppers
12 ounces Colby cheese, shredded
1 ½ tablespoons flour
1 cup tomato puree
3 teaspoons olive oil
1 ¼ cups milk
1/2 teaspoon black pepper
1/2 teaspoon cayenne pepper
1/2 teaspoon basil
1/2 teaspoon sea salt, or more to taste

Directions

- Press the SOUP/STEW key. Heat the oil; slowly stir in the flour; cook, stirring continuously until you have a paste.
- Pour in the milk and stir until the mixture has thickened. Bring it to a boil.
- Add the cheese; vigorously stir until it is smooth. Add the rest of your ingredients. Place the lid on the Power pressure cooker XL, lock the lid and switch the pressure release valve to closed. Cook for 10 minutes.
- Once the timer reaches 0, the cooker will automatically switch to KEEP WARM/CANCEL. When the steam is completely released, carefully remove the cooker's lid.

238. Easiest Salsa Ever

Ready in about 15 minutes
Servings 8

This bright and fresh salsa is sure to WOW your guests. This is a great idea for Super Bowl parties and it also freezes and reheats well.

Per serving: 35 Calories; 0.3g Fat; 7.6g Carbs; 1.4g Protein; 4.6g Sugars

Ingredients

1/4 cup jalapeno peppers, chopped
2 yellow onions, chopped
1 large-sized chili pepper, chopped
8 fresh tomatoes, seeded and chopped
1 cup cold water
2 tablespoons fresh basil, chopped
2 tablespoons fresh cilantro, chopped
2 tablespoons fresh sage, chopped
1/2 teaspoon freshly cracked black pepper, to taste
1/2 teaspoon kosher salt

Directions

- Firstly, place the tomatoes in your Power pressure cooker XL. Pour in enough water to cover them.
- Press the FISH/VEGETABLES/STEAM and cook for 4 minutes. Place the lid on the Power pressure cooker XL, lock the lid and switch the pressure release valve to closed. Cook for 10 minutes.
- Once the timer reaches 0, the cooker will automatically switch to KEEP WARM/CANCEL. When the steam is completely released, carefully remove the cooker's lid. After that, drain the tomatoes and transfer them to your food processor.
- Now, add the peppers, onions, cold water, basil, cilantro, sage, black pepper, and salt to your food processor. Mix until everything is well combined.
- Serve chilled with corn tortilla chips.

239. Savoy Cabbage with Ham

Ready in about 15 minutes
Servings 4

A well-prepared Savoy cabbage is a royal meal. You can make a big batch of this special dish and store them in your refrigerator. Enjoy!

Per serving: 170 Calories; 8.5g Fat; 12.8g Carbs; 12g Protein; 6g Sugars

Ingredients

1 tablespoon lard
1 head Savoy cabbage, shredded
1/2 pound ham, diced
1 ½ cups stock
1/2 tablespoon mustard powder
1/2 teaspoon dry sage
1/2 teaspoon dry basil
Salt and ground black pepper, to taste

Directions

- Press the BEANS/LENTILS key. Warm the lard.
- Fry the ham for 3 minutes, until well browned. Add the remaining ingredients.
- Place the lid on the Power pressure cooker XL, lock the lid and switch the pressure release valve to closed. Cook for 5 minutes.
- Once the timer reaches 0, the cooker will automatically switch to KEEP WARM/CANCEL. When the steam is completely released, carefully remove the cooker's lid.
- Taste, adjust the seasonings and replace to a serving platter. Enjoy!

240. Brussels Sprout and Ground Beef Appetizer

Ready in about 20 minutes
Servings 6

This appetizer is so easy to prepare that you will wonder how you have ever been without it and your Power pressure cooker XL. Brussels sprouts are an excellent source of antioxidants, fiber, folate and Vitamin C.

Per serving: 402 Calories; 26.6g Fat; 11.5g Carbs; 31.3g Protein; 2.6g Sugars

Ingredients

1 ½ pounds Brussels sprouts, ends trimmed and yellow leaves removed
1 tablespoon tallow
1 pound ground beef
1/3 cup Colby cheese, grated
2 tablespoons butter
1 cup cream cheese
Sea salt and freshly ground black pepper, to taste
2 tablespoons fresh cilantro, for garnish
1 ½ cups water

Directions

- Press the CHICKEN/MEAT key and set to 15 minutes. Melt the tallow.
- Sauté the beef until it is browned, about 4 minutes. Crumble the beef and add the remaining ingredients, minus the cilantro.
- Place the lid on the Power pressure cooker XL, lock the lid and switch the pressure release valve to closed. Once the timer reaches 0, the cooker will automatically switch to KEEP WARM/CANCEL. When the steam is completely released, carefully remove the cooker's lid.
- Afterwards, garnish with fresh cilantro and serve.

241. Herbed Bean Spread

Ready in about 35 minutes
Servings 6

Kidney beans work greatest for this recipe but you can freely use Great Northern or Navy beans. Just make sure to consult the cooking chart.

Per serving: 246 Calories; 3g Fat; 42.1g Carbs; 14.5g Protein; 1.3g Sugars

Ingredients

2 cups red kidney beans, soaked overnight and rinsed
1 cup shallots, chopped
1 tablespoon vegetable oil
2 teaspoon wine vinegar
2 rosemary sprigs, chopped
1/2 teaspoon cumin
2 thyme sprigs, chopped
Salt and black pepper, to taste
3 ½ cups water

Directions

- Choose the RICE/RISOTTO function; use the cook time selector to adjust to 25 minutes. Warm the oil and sauté the shallots for 3 minutes.
- Stir in the beans and water. Place the lid on the Power pressure cooker XL, lock the lid and switch the pressure release valve to closed.
- Once the timer reaches 0, the cooker will automatically switch to KEEP WARM/CANCEL. When the steam is completely released, carefully remove the cooker's lid.
- Drain the beans and allow them to cool. Purée them in your food processor. Add the rest of the above ingredients. Purée until it is uniform and smooth.
- Transfer to a serving bowl and drizzle with some extra olive oil if desired.

242. Yummy Paprika Peanuts

Ready in about 55 minutes
Servings 16

You don't have to heat your oven to make the roasted peanuts, you can pressure cook them too. This is a great way to serve a healthy snack. Savory, aromatic and simple, this snack is irresistible.

Per serving: 362 Calories; 31.4g Fat; 10.3g Carbs; 16.5g Protein; 2.5g Sugars

Ingredients

4 quarts water
2 teaspoons paprika
1 cup sea salt
2 ¼ pounds raw peanuts

Directions

- Add the peanuts and water to the Power pressure cooker XL. Press the CHICKEN/MEAT key and use the cook time selector to adjust to 40 minutes.
- Place the lid on the Power pressure cooker XL, lock the lid and switch the pressure release valve to closed.
- Once the timer reaches 0, the cooker will automatically switch to KEEP WARM/CANCEL. When the steam is completely released, carefully remove the cooker's lid.
- Drain and transfer them to a serving bowl. Toss with the paprika and salt, and serve at room temperature.

243. Cold Appetizer with Beets and Walnuts

Ready in about 20 minutes
Servings 8

There's more than one way to cook beetroot. However, when you want to please your family in no time, pressure cooked tender and flavorsome beets are a must. Just like grandma used to make!

Per serving: 144 Calories; 8.9g Fat; 22g Carbs; 3.4g Protein; 11.9g Sugars

Ingredients

1 teaspoon cumin seeds
1/4 cup olive oil
3 teaspoons wine vinegar
1/2 teaspoon brown sugar
3 cups water
2 ½ pounds beets
1/4 teaspoon freshly ground black pepper, or more to taste
1/2 teaspoon sea salt
1/4 cup chopped walnuts

Directions

- Press the "FISH/VEGETABLES/STEAM" key.
- Add the beets and water to the inner pot of the Power Pressure Cooker XL.
- Place the lid on the Power Pressure Cooker XL, lock the lid and switch the pressure release valve to closed.
- Press the "TIME ADJUSTMENT" key until you reach 15 minutes. Press the "CANCEL" key. Switch the pressure release valve to open. When the steam is completely released, remove the cooker's lid.
- Drain and rinse the beets and rub off the skins. Cut the beets into wedges. Transfer to a serving dish.
- In a mixing bowl, combine the vinegar, cumin, brown sugar, salt, ground black pepper, and olive oil. Drizzle the mixture over the prepared beets. Scatter chopped walnuts over the beets and serve well-chilled. Bon appétit!

244. Easy Steamed Potatoes

Ready in about 15 minutes
Servings 8

Steamed potatoes are a cinch to make in the Power Pressure Cooker XL. With an addition of selected seasonings, this is a great, belly filling appetizer.

Per serving: 117 Calories; 0.2g Fat; 26.7g Carbs; 2.9g Protein; 2g Sugars

Ingredients

3/4 cup water
3 pounds potatoes, peeled and quartered
1 teaspoon salt
1/2 teaspoon freshly ground black pepper
1 teaspoon cayenne pepper

Directions

- Press the "FISH/VEGETABLES/STEAM" key.
- Insert the wire rack in the Power Pressure Cooker XL. Add the potatoes and water to the inner pot of the Power Pressure Cooker XL.
- Place the lid on the Power Pressure Cooker XL, lock the lid and switch the pressure release valve to closed. Press the "TIME ADJUSTMENT" key until you reach 8 minutes
- Press the "CANCEL" key. Switch the pressure release valve to open. When the steam is completely released, remove the cooker's lid.
- Season the potatoes and serve immediately. Bon appétit!

245. Carrot Sticks with Pine Nuts

Ready in about 15 minutes
Servings 8

Carrot sticks are a dangerously addictive snack! Pine nuts are a great addition to this healthy, make-ahead dish.

Per serving: 161 Calories; 9.7g Fat; 17.7g Carbs; 2g Protein; 8.8g Sugars

Ingredients

1/4 cup sesame oil
1/4 teaspoon sea salt, or more to taste
1/2 teaspoon brown sugar
3 ½ cups water
3 pounds carrots, cut into matchsticks
2 teaspoons fresh orange juice
1/4 cup balsamic vinegar
1/4 cup pine nuts

Directions

- Press the "FISH/VEGETABLES/STEAM" key. Add the carrot sticks and water to the Power Pressure Cooker XL.
- Place the lid on the Power Pressure Cooker XL, lock the lid and switch the pressure release valve to closed. Press the "TIME ADJUSTMENT" key until you reach 5 minutes.
- Press the "CANCEL" key. Switch the pressure release valve to open. When the steam is completely released, remove the cooker's lid.
- Drain and rinse the carrots.
- Then, make the vinaigrette. Combine the balsamic vinegar, fresh orange juice, sugar, salt, and sesame oil.
- Drizzle the vinaigrette over the prepared carrots. Sprinkle with pine nuts and serve.

246. Winter Beef Dipping Sauce

Ready in about 25 minutes
Servings 10

Need something to pair with your favorite dippers such as pita wedges, veggie sticks, and tortilla chips? This meat dipping sauce will fit the bill!

Per serving: 123 Calories; 5.8g Fat; 3.1g Carbs; 14.3g Protein; 1.2g Sugars

Ingredients

1 pound ground beef
1 cup ripe tomato, chopped
1/2 teaspoon cayenne pepper
1 teaspoon salt
1 teaspoon dried thyme
1/2 teaspoon dried basil
1/4 teaspoon ground black pepper, or more to taste
1 teaspoon dried oregano
2 tablespoons canola oil
4 cloves garlic, sliced
1 ½ tablespoons arrowroot
1 ½ cups white onion, finely chopped

Directions

- Press the "CHICKEN/MEAT" key and heat the oil. Stir in the ground meat and cook for 6 minutes, until the meat is no longer pink.
- Add the other ingredients and stir until everything is well combined.
- Place the lid on the Power Pressure Cooker XL, lock the lid and switch the pressure release valve to closed. Cook for 15 minutes.
- Press the "CANCEL" key. Switch the pressure release valve to open. When the steam is completely released, remove the cooker's lid. Bon appétit!

247. Mediterranean Tomato Dip

Ready in about 20 minutes
Servings 12

One of the best ways to make sure you will enjoy your party is to serve a multitude of make-ahead snacks. You can make this dipping sauce a day ahead. Serve with bread sticks and enjoy!

Per serving: 45 Calories; 1.6g Fat; 6.7g Carbs; 1.7g Protein; 4g Sugars

Ingredients

4 cloves garlic, crushed
1/2 cup fresh basil leaves
1/4 teaspoon ground black pepper, to taste
1/2 teaspoon salt
1 cup carrots, chopped
1/3 cup olives, pitted and sliced
3/4 cup water
1/2 cup onions, peeled and chopped
3 teaspoons olive oil
25 ounces canned crushed tomatoes

Directions

- Press the "SOUP/STEW" key and heat the olive oil. Now, sauté the garlic and onions until they are tender.
- Add the carrots and basil leaves. Pour in the crushed tomatoes, olives, and the water. Season with salt and black pepper.
- Place the lid on the Power Pressure Cooker XL, lock the lid and switch the pressure release valve to closed. Cook for 15 minutes.
- Press the "CANCEL" key. Switch the pressure release valve to open. When the steam is completely released, remove the cooker's lid. Bon appétit!

248, Quick and Easy Potato Appetizer

Ready in about 20 minutes
Servings 6

Need last minute appetizer for your next dinner party? Potatoes are always a good idea! This meal is so simple to make and contains rich flavors of butter and garlic.

Per serving: 175 Calories; 7.8g Fat; 24.4g Carbs; 2.8g Protein; 1.8g Sugars

Ingredients

1/2 stick butter, melted
2 pounds potatoes, peeled and quartered
1 cup water
1 teaspoon salt
1/2 teaspoon paprika
1/4 teaspoon ground black pepper
1 tablespoon garlic, finely minced

Directions

- Press the "SOUP/STEW" key. Place the wire rack on the bottom of the inner pot of the Power Pressure Cooker XL; pour in the water.
- Add the potatoes and the garlic to the Power Pressure Cooker XL. Place the lid on the Power Pressure Cooker XL, lock the lid and switch the pressure release valve to closed. Cook for 10 minutes.
- Press the "CANCEL" key. Switch the pressure release valve to open. When the steam is completely released, remove the cooker's lid; taste the potatoes for doneness.
- Transfer the prepared potatoes to a large-sized serving bowl. Toss them with the butter, paprika, salt, and black pepper. Bon appétit!

249. Buttery Acorn Squash

Ready in about 15 minutes
Servings 6

Did you know that acorn squash may help boost your immune system, improve vision health, and regulate blood pressure?

Per serving: 167 Calories; 15.4g Fat; 8.1g Carbs; 0.8g Protein; 0g Sugars

Ingredients

1 cup water
1 teaspoon baking soda
1/2 teaspoon sea salt
1/4 teaspoon freshly cracked black pepper
1/2 cup butter, melted
1 pound acorn squash, halved
1/4 teaspoon ground cinnamon
2 tablespoons apple cider vinegar

Directions

- Press the "FISH/VEGETABLES/STEAM" key. Add the water and acorn squash to the Power Pressure Cooker XL.
- Drizzle the squash with the apple cider vinegar. Add the remaining ingredients.
- Place the lid on the Power Pressure Cooker XL, lock the lid and switch the pressure release valve to closed. Cook for 10 minutes.
- Press the "CANCEL" key. Switch the pressure release valve to open. When the steam is completely released, remove the cooker's lid
- Arrange the squash on a serving platter and serve.

250. Favorite Artichoke and Spinach Dip

Ready in about 15 minutes
Servings 12

Eating a diet rich in vegetables may help keep your body healthy and strong. Artichokes are an excellent source of dietary fiber, vitamins A and K, magnesium, phosphorus, and calcium.

Per serving: 113 Calories; 8.1g Fat; 8.1g Carbs; 3.7g Protein; 1.1g Sugars

Ingredients

1 ½ cups Mozzarella cheese, shredded
1/2 teaspoon ground black pepper
1 teaspoon kosher salt
1/2 cup light mayonnaise
15 ounces artichoke hearts, roughly chopped
12 ounces frozen spinach, thawed, drained and chopped
1 cup sour cream

Directions

- Press the "FISH/VEGETABLES/STEAM" key.
- Set a wire rack in the Power Pressure Cooker XL. Add all the ingredients to a baking dish; stir to combine well. Then, cover the baking dish with a piece of foil.
- Lower the baking dish onto the wire rack.
- Place the lid on the Power Pressure Cooker XL, lock the lid and switch the pressure release valve to closed. Cook for 11 minutes.
- Press the "CANCEL" key. Switch the pressure release valve to open. When the steam is completely released, remove the cooker's lid
- Serve warm with your favorite crackers. Enjoy!

251. Two-Pepper Tomato Dip

Ready in about 20 minutes
Servings 8

Here's a great addition to your holiday party! This rich, vegan dip is simply delicious; plum tomatoes, Mediterranean herbs and vegetables make a great blend.

Per serving: 84 Calories; 5.4g Fat; 9.3g Carbs; 1.2g Protein; 5.9g Sugars

Ingredients

1 cup carrot, chopped
1/2 teaspoon sea salt
1 pound plum tomatoes, peeled, cored and sliced
2 tablespoons brown sugar
1 teaspoon seeded and chopped Serrano pepper
1/2 cup shallot, diced
1/2 teaspoon dried basil
1 cup red bell pepper, seeded and chopped
1/4 teaspoon ground black pepper, or more to taste
3 tablespoons olive oil
1 sprig dried rosemary
1 cup water

Directions

- Press the "SOUP/STEW" key and heat the olive oil; then, sauté the bell pepper, Serrano pepper, carrot, shallot, and tomatoes. Sauté for about 4 minutes, until the vegetables are softened.
- Stir in the tomatoes, water, brown sugar, salt, black pepper, rosemary, and basil.
- Place the lid on the Power Pressure Cooker XL, lock the lid and switch the pressure release valve to closed. Cook for 10 minutes.
- Press the "CANCEL" key. Switch the pressure release valve to open. When the steam is completely released, remove the cooker's lid. Bon appétit!

252. Green Bean Delight

Ready in about 15 minutes
Servings 6

Green beans can help reduce the risk of diabetes, colon cancer and heart disease. This amazing appetizer tastes best when served right away.

Per serving: 65 Calories; 1.4g Fat; 12.7g Carbs; 3.2g Protein; 2.6g Sugars

Ingredients

1 ½ tablespoons bouillon cube
1/2 cup water
2 pounds green beans
1/2 tablespoon olive oil
4 garlic cloves, minced
1 cup green onions, minced

Directions

- Press the "FISH/VEGETABLES/STEAM" key.
- Add all of the above ingredients to the Power Pressure Cooker XL.
- Place the lid on the Power Pressure Cooker XL, lock the lid and switch the pressure release valve to closed. Cook for 5 minutes.
- Press the "CANCEL" key. Switch the pressure release valve to open. When the steam is completely released, remove the cooker's lid. Transfer to a serving platter and serve.

253. Black Bean Dip

Ready in about 30 minutes
Servings 12

Throw a few ingredients into your Power Pressure Cooker XL and make one of the most popular dipping sauces. What could be simpler?

Per serving: 238 Calories; 5.1g Fat; 37.3g Carbs; 12.6g Protein; 2g Sugars

Ingredients

1/4 cup olive oil
A pinch of black pepper, freshly ground
1/2 teaspoon salt
1 cup tomatoes, chopped
1 ½ teaspoons red chili powder
3 garlic cloves, minced
1 cup red onion, finely chopped
1 sprig coriander leaves, finely minced
1 ½ pounds black beans, soaked overnight
1 ½ tablespoons Garam masala powder

Directions

- Choose the "BEANS/LENTILS" function.
- Add the black beans to the Power Pressure Cooker XL; cook until tender. Place the lid on the Power Pressure Cooker XL, lock the lid and switch the pressure release valve to closed. Cook for 15 minutes.
- In the meantime, heat the olive oil in a nonstick skillet. Then, sauté the onions, garlic, and tomatoes for about 5 minutes. Then, add the red chili powder, Garam masala, coriander, salt, and black pepper; continue sautéing for 5 minutes.
- Press the "CANCEL" key. Switch the pressure release valve to open. When the steam is completely released, remove the cooker's lid.
- Now, transfer the sautéed mixture to the Power Pressure Cooker XL.
- Then, blend the bean mixture in a food processor, working in batches. Serve with your favorite dippers.

254. Cheesy Corn on the Cob

Ready in about 5 minutes
Servings 6

Whether as a great snack or a light dinner, a healthy corn on the cob sprinkled with seasonings and freshly grated Parmesan is very likely to hit the spot.

Per serving: 229 Calories; 5.1g Fat; 38.7g Carbs; 12g Protein; 6.7g Sugars

Ingredients

1 tablespoon sea salt
8 ears of corn, husked, halved crosswise
1 cup freshly grated Parmesan cheese

Directions

- Press the "FISH/VEGETABLES/STEAM" key. Set the wire rack in your Power Pressure Cooker XL.
- Pour 1 cup of water into the base of the Power Pressure Cooker XL. Arrange the ears of corn on the wire rack.
- Place the lid on the Power Pressure Cooker XL, lock the lid and switch the pressure release valve to closed. Cook for 4 minutes.
- Press the "CANCEL" key. Switch the pressure release valve to open. When the steam is completely released, remove the cooker's lid. Sprinkle with salt and Parmesan cheese.

255. Famous Sweet Potato Snack

Ready in about 20 minutes
Servings 6

This is a complete treat for your guests! Sweet potatoes are loaded with antioxidants, anti-inflammatory nutrients and beta-carotene.

Per serving: 219 Calories; 4.8g Fat; 42.3g Carbs; 2.4g Protein; 0.8g Sugars

Ingredients

2 pounds sweet potatoes
1/2 teaspoon ground black pepper
1/2 teaspoon sea salt
1/2 teaspoon dried dill weed
2 tablespoons sesame oil
1/4 teaspoon paprika
1 ½ cups boiling water

Directions

- Press the "SOUP/STEW" key. Place the wire rack on the bottom of the Power Pressure Cooker XL.
- Pour in the boiling water. Next, drizzle the sweet potatoes with the sesame oil; wrap them in a piece of aluminum foil. Arrange the sweet potatoes on the wire rack.
- Place the lid on the Power Pressure Cooker XL, lock the lid and switch the pressure release valve to closed. Cook for 11 minutes.
- Press the "CANCEL" key. Switch the pressure release valve to open. When the steam is completely released, remove the cooker's lid.
- Add the seasonings and serve immediately.

256. Yellow Wax Beans with Sesame Seeds

Ready in about 5 minutes + chilling time
Servings 6

Fresh wax beans are low in calories and high in vitamins and minerals. They taste great mixed with sesame oil, leeks and garlic.

Per serving: 84 Calories; 4.7g Fat; 8.7g Carbs; 2.5g Protein; 3.2g Sugars

Ingredients

3 teaspoons sesame oil
1 ½ cups vegetable stock
1 cup leeks, white parts only, minced
2 pounds yellow wax beans
3 garlic cloves, minced
3 tablespoons toasted sesame seeds

Directions

- Press the "FISH/VEGETABLES/STEAM" key. Add all of the above ingredients, except for the sesame seeds, to the Power Pressure Cooker XL.
- Place the lid on the Power Pressure Cooker XL, lock the lid and switch the pressure release valve to closed. Cook for 3 minutes.
- Press the "CANCEL" key. Switch the pressure release valve to open. When the steam is completely released, remove the cooker's lid.
- Serve chilled and sprinkled with sesame seeds.

257. Roasted Winter Squash with Sage

Ready in about 15 minutes
Servings 8

Here is a simple and nutritious way to prepare and enjoy the super powerful winter squash. You can substitute ground cloves for ground allspice.

Per serving: 47 Calories; 0.3g Fat; 11.9g Carbs; 0.9g Protein; 0g Sugars

Ingredients

2 teaspoons avocado oil
2 pounds winter squash, halved
1/4 teaspoon ground cloves
1/2 cup fresh sage leaves
1/2 teaspoon sea salt
1 cup water

Directions

- Press the "FISH/VEGETABLES/STEAM" key.
- Set the wire rack on the bottom of the Power Pressure Cooker XL. Pour in the water and arrange the squash on the wire rack.
- Place the lid on the Power Pressure Cooker XL, lock the lid and switch the pressure release valve to closed. Cook for 10 minutes.
- Meanwhile, melt the avocado oil in a saucepan over medium heat. Now, add the sage leaves and cook until they're crispy, approximately 1 minute.
- Arrange the squash on a serving platter; sprinkle with crispy sage, sea salt, and ground cloves.

258. Cannellini Bean and Corn Dip

Ready in about 25 minutes
Servings 16

If you are feeling lazy, but still would rather prepare your own party dip instead of purchasing store-bought snacks, this recipe is here to help. Serve with veggie sticks or tortilla chips.

Per serving: 137 Calories; 1.1g Fat; 24.3g Carbs; 9g Protein; 1.6g Sugars

Ingredients

1 cup fresh corn kernels
3 garlic cloves, minced
1/3 cup tomato sauce
2 teaspoons olive oil
1/2 teaspoon cumin seeds
20 ounces canned cannellini beans, rinsed and drained
1/4 teaspoon ground black pepper, or more to taste
1/2 teaspoon paprika
1/2 teaspoon sea salt
1 ½ cups scallions, finely chopped

Directions

- Press the "BEANS/LENTILS" key. Then, pour the can of beans into the Power Pressure Cooker XL.
- Meanwhile, in a pan, cook the rest of the above ingredients until aromatic and tender.
- Place the lid on the Power Pressure Cooker XL, lock the lid and switch the pressure release valve to closed. Cook for 15 minutes.
- Once the timer reaches 0, the cooker will automatically switch to "KEEP WARM/CANCEL". Switch the pressure release valve to open. When the steam is completely released, remove the lid.
- Next, add the sautéed mixture to the beans. Stir until everything is well combined.
- Now, puree the mixture in a food processor or a blender, working in batches. Bon appétit!

259. Cilantro Lime Corn Snack

Ready in about 15 minutes
Servings 6

So quick to throw together, this tasty and corn snack is perfect served with white wine. Corn is a great source of antioxidants, dietary fiber, vitamins and minerals,

Per serving: 216 Calories; 7.1g Fat; 38.8g Carbs; 6.7g Protein; 6.7g Sugars

Ingredients

2 teaspoons lime juice
8 ears of corn, husked and halved crosswise
1/2 teaspoon salt
1/4 cup fresh cilantro, finely chopped
1/4 teaspoon ground black pepper
2 tablespoons melted coconut oil

Directions

- Press the "FISH/VEGETABLES/STEAM" key. Set the wire rack in your Power Pressure Cooker XL; pour in 1 cup water.
- Stack the ears of corn on the wire rack.
- Place the lid on the Power Pressure Cooker XL, lock the lid and switch the pressure release valve to closed. Cook for 5 minutes.
- Once the timer reaches 0, the cooker will automatically switch to "KEEP WARM/CANCEL". Switch the pressure release valve to open. When the steam is completely released, remove the lid.
- Meanwhile, in a mixing dish, combine the remaining ingredients; mix to combine well. Toss the corn with this mixture and serve right away.

260. Vegan Spinach Dip

Ready in about 15 minutes
Servings 12

Here is a healthy and protein-rich vegan dip! You can play around with the amount of mayonnaise to match your preference.

Per serving: 88 Calories; 7.3g Fat; 3.4g Carbs; 3.4g Protein; 0.3g Sugars

Ingredients

1 ½ cups tofu
12 ounces frozen spinach, thawed
1 teaspoon dried dill weed
2 teaspoons fresh lemon juice
1/2 teaspoon ground black pepper
1 teaspoon salt
1 ¼ cups vegan mayonnaise
1 teaspoon grated lemon zest, for garnish

Directions

- Press the "FISH/VEGETABLES/STEAM" key. Set the wire rack in your Power Pressure Cooker XL; pour in 1 cup of water.
- Combine all the ingredients, except for the lemon zest, in a baking dish; give it a good stir. Wrap the baking dish with a piece of foil. Make a foil sling and lower the dish onto the rack.
- Place the lid on the Power Pressure Cooker XL, lock the lid and switch the pressure release valve to closed. Cook for 8 minutes.
- Once the timer reaches 0, the cooker will automatically switch to "KEEP WARM/CANCEL". Switch the pressure release valve to open. When the steam is completely released, remove the lid.
- Sprinkle with lemon zest and serve.

261. Green Garlic Kale Hummus

Ready in about 25 minutes
Servings 12

Make the best hummus ever in a fraction of the time using a revolutionary easy-to-use electric pressure cooker. Serve with dippers of choice, such as crackers or veggie sticks.

Per serving: 169 Calories; 6.3g Fat; 22.2g Carbs; 7.4g Protein; 3.6g Sugars

Ingredients

3 tablespoons tahini
1/4 teaspoon ground black pepper
1/2 teaspoon sea salt
2 cups chickpea
1 cup green garlic, minced
4 ½ cups water
2 tablespoons grapeseed oil
2 cups packed kale leaves

Directions

- Press the "BEANS/LENTILS" key. Add the water and chickpea to the Power Pressure Cooker XL.
- Place the lid on the Power Pressure Cooker XL, lock the lid and switch the pressure release valve to closed. Cook for 20 minutes.
- Once the timer reaches 0, the cooker will automatically switch to "KEEP WARM/CANCEL". Switch the pressure release valve to open. When the steam is completely released, remove the lid.
- Now drain the chickpeas; replace them to a food processor.
- Add the kale, garlic, salt, black pepper, and tahini. Puree until creamy. Then, gradually pour the oil in a thin stream. Mix until everything is well incorporated.

262. Crispy Mustard Polenta Bites

Ready in about 40 minutes
Servings 6

Make these easy and healthy bites in no time. In this recipe, you can freely experiment with seasonings. Red pepper flakes, chipotle powder, dried rosemary and turmeric powder work well, too.

Per serving: 180 Calories; 5g Fat; 30.7g Carbs; 3g Protein; 0.4g Sugars

Ingredients

2 teaspoons Dijon mustard
1 ½ cups dry polenta
1/4 teaspoon ground white pepper, or more to taste
1 teaspoon kosher salt
1 teaspoon cayenne pepper
4 ½ cups water
1/2 teaspoon ground bay leaf
2 tablespoons coconut oil, at room temperature

Directions

- Press the "CHICKEN/MEAT" key. Add the water, mustard, coconut oil, cayenne pepper, salt, and white pepper to the Power Pressure Cooker XL.
- Press the "COOK TIME SELECTOR" key until the time reads 9 minutes. Slowly stir the polenta into the boiling liquid, stirring frequently. Add the ground bay leaf.
- Place the lid on the Power Pressure Cooker XL, lock the lid and switch the pressure release valve to closed.
- Once the timer reaches 0, the Power Pressure Cooker XL will automatically switch to "KEEP WARM/CAN-CEL". Let the steam naturally release. When the steam is completely released, remove the cooker's lid.
- Pour the polenta mixture into a cookie sheet. Refrigerate the polenta for about 30 minutes. Cut into bite-sized cubes and serve.

263. Yummy Healthy Caponata

Ready in about 5 minutes
Servings 8

Hello Skinny! Enjoy this healthy and guilt-free recipe with the Mediterranean aperitif such as Vermouth, Campari or Amaro.

Per serving: 71 Calories; 3.7g Fat; 9.7g Carbs; 1.3g Protein; 5.1g Sugars

Ingredients

1 pound eggplant, cut into thick slices
2 tablespoons extra-virgin olive oil, to taste
2 onions, peeled and chopped
2 bell peppers, seeded and sliced
2 carrots, cut into thick slices
1 tablespoon jalapeno pepper, deveined and sliced
Salt and black pepper, to taste
1/2 teaspoon dried basil
1 teaspoon dried oregano
1 teaspoon garlic powder
1 teaspoon onion powder

Directions

- Press the FISH/VEGETABLES/STEAM key and use the cook time selector to adjust to 4 minutes.
- Add all of the above ingredients to your Power pressure cooker XL, except for olive oil. Place the lid on the Power pressure cooker XL, lock the lid and switch the pressure release valve to closed.
- Once the timer reaches 0, the cooker will automatically switch to KEEP WARM/CANCEL. When the steam is completely released, carefully remove the cooker's lid.
- Transfer to a serving bowl. Drizzle with olive oil and serve. Enjoy!

264. Two-Cheese Veggie Appetizer

Ready in about 25 minutes
Servings 6

Mashed vegetables are always a good idea for any gathering. This is a set-it-and-forget-it, delicious appetizer full of valuable nutrients.

Per serving: 175 Calories; 11.8g Fat; 10.8g Carbs; 7.9g Protein; 0.7g Sugars

Ingredients

1 cup Monterey-Jack cheese, shredded
1/2 cup Ricotta cheese
1 ½ pounds Yukon Gold potatoes, peeled and diced
1 ½ cups broccoli, broken into florets
2 tablespoons olive oil
1 ½ cups water
1 teaspoon sea salt
3/4 teaspoon paprika
1/2 teaspoon ground black pepper, to taste
1/3 teaspoon cumin powder

Directions

- Add the water, potatoes, and broccoli to the Power pressure cooker XL. Press the CHICKEN/MEAT key.
- Place the lid on the Power pressure cooker XL, lock the lid and switch the pressure release valve to closed. Cook for 15 minutes.
- Once the timer reaches 0, the cooker will automatically switch to KEEP WARM/CANCEL. When the steam is completely released, carefully remove the cooker's lid.
- Drain the vegetables using a colander.
- Now, mash your veggies with a potato masher; add the rest of the above ingredients; mash again until smooth. Serve as a cold appetizer.

265. Herby Tomato Sauce

Ready in about 20 minutes
Servings 16

Tomato is an excellent source of vitamin C, vitamin K, and vitamin A and vitamin B6. It contains significant amounts of magnesium, potassium, manganese, thiamin and folate. Did you know that cooked tomatoes contain the larger amount of lycopene and antioxidants than a fresh plant?

Per serving: 50 Calories; 3.6g Fat; 4.5g Carbs; 0.8g Protein; 3g Sugars

Ingredients

3 pounds tomatoes, peeled and diced
1 cup red onions, chopped
1/4 cup canola oil
2 teaspoons granulated sugar
1/2 teaspoon dried basil
1/2 teaspoon dried oregano
4 cloves garlic, peeled and finely minced
1/2 teaspoon dried sage
Salt and freshly ground black pepper, to taste

Directions

- Press the SOUP/STEW key; use the cook time selector to adjust to 15 minutes, Now, heat canola oil until sizzling; then, sauté green onions and garlic until just tender or for 2 minutes.
- Add the tomatoes along with the remaining ingredients.
- Place the lid on the Power pressure cooker XL, lock the lid and switch the pressure release valve to closed.
- Once the timer reaches 0, the cooker will automatically switch to KEEP WARM/CANCEL. When the steam is completely released, carefully remove the cooker's lid.
- Use immediately or refrigerate for up to a week. Enjoy!

266. Cheesy Chickpea Dip

Ready in about 35 minutes
Servings 16

For best results, cook this amazing dip a day ahead to let the flavors blend well. It pairs well with white wine and chapatti.

Per serving: 179 Calories; 9g Fat; 17.3g Carbs; 8.4g Protein; 3.6g Sugars

Ingredients

2 cups chickpea, soaked overnight and rinsed
1 ¼ cups Swiss cheese, shredded
1 cup cream cheese
2 bell peppers, chopped
2 jalapeno peppers, chopped
2 teaspoons mixed peppercorns, crushed
1 teaspoon dried basil
Sea salt and ground black pepper, to taste

Directions

- Add the chickpeas to the Power pressure cooker XL; cover with water by 3 inches. Press the RICE/RISOTTO key and use the cook time selector to adjust to 25 minutes.
- Place the lid on the Power pressure cooker XL, lock the lid and switch the pressure release valve to closed.
- Once the timer reaches 0, the cooker will automatically switch to KEEP WARM/CANCEL. When the steam is completely released, carefully remove the cooker's lid.
- Then, puree the cooked chickpeas in your food processor. Transfer to a lightly oiled baking dish.
- Add the remaining ingredients and stir to combine well. Prepare the Power pressure cooker XL by adding 1 ½ cups of water and a trivet to the bottom.
- Lower the baking dish onto the trivet and choose the RICE/RISOTTO function; cook for 6 minutes more and serve at room temperature.

267. Zesty Parsnips with Walnuts

Ready in about 10 minutes
Servings 4

Pressure cooker transforms regular vegetables into a festive rich appetizer! If your mouths are already watering, give this recipe a try!

Per serving: 276 Calories; 10.3g Fat; 45g Carbs; 4.7g Protein; 13.9g Sugars

Ingredients

2 pounds parsnips, peeled and cut into rounds
1/4 cup walnuts, toasted and chopped
1 tablespoon tallow
1/2 cup Sultanas
1 cup water
1/2 sea salt
1 tablespoon champagne vinegar
Freshly ground black pepper, to taste

Directions

- Choose the FISH/VEGETABLES/STEAM function. Melt the tallow and sauté the parsnips until just tender.
- Add Sultanas, water and salt. Place the lid on the Power pressure cooker XL, lock the lid and switch the pressure release valve to closed. Cook for 2 minutes.
- Once the timer reaches 0, the cooker will automatically switch to KEEP WARM/CANCEL. When the steam is completely released, carefully remove the cooker's lid.
- Stir in the vinegar and ground black pepper. Stir to combine well. Scatter the walnuts over the top. Serve hot and enjoy.

268. The Best Candied Pecans Ever

Ready in about 20 minutes
Servings 6

Make sure to watch your pecans close during baking because they can burn fast. You can add a pinch of smoked paprika for an extra oomph!

Per serving: 172 Calories; 3.8g Fat; 35.9g Carbs; 0.5g Protein; 31.4g Sugars

Ingredients

4 ½ cups raw pecans
1/2 cup water
1 cup maple syrup
1/2 teaspoon ground nutmeg
1/4 teaspoon ground ginger powder
1 teaspoon ground cinnamon
1/4 teaspoon salt

Directions

- Throw all ingredients into your Power pressure cooker XL. Press the SOUP/STEW key.
- Place the lid on the Power pressure cooker XL, lock the lid and switch the pressure release valve to closed. Cook for 10 minutes.
- Once the timer reaches 0, the cooker will automatically switch to KEEP WARM/CANCEL. When the steam is completely released, carefully remove the cooker's lid.
- Next, spread out on a baking sheet.
- Bake in the preheated oven at 350 degrees F for 4 to 5 minutes.

269. Broccoli and Cheese Dipping Sauce

Ready in about 20 minutes
Servings 16

This savory combination of broccoli and cheeses is sinfully delicious. Dip into this quick and easy recipe!

Per serving: 134 Calories; 10.5g Fat; 5.1g Carbs; 5.5g Protein; 1.8g Sugars

Ingredients

1 head broccoli, chopped into small florets
1/3 cup cream cheese
1 ¼ cups goat cheese, shredded
1 cup bell peppers, chopped
3/4 cup mayonnaise
1/2 teaspoon paprika
1/4 teaspoon dried dill weed
Sea salt and ground black pepper, to taste

Directions

- Pour 1 ½ cups of water into your Power pressure cooker XL; place a rack in the bottom.
- Mix all of the above ingredients; transfer them to a baking dish that fits in your cooker. Then, cover the baking dish with a piece of foil. Lower the baking dish onto the rack.
- Press the CHICKEN/MEAT key. Place the lid on the Power pressure cooker XL, lock the lid and switch the pressure release valve to closed. Cook for 15 minutes.
- Once the timer reaches 0, the cooker will automatically switch to KEEP WARM/CANCEL. When the steam is completely released, carefully remove the cooker's lid. Serve with pita wedges of choice. Enjoy!

270. Zesty Appetizer Meatballs

Ready in about 25 minutes
Servings 8

These flavorful and juicy meatballs are absolutely perfect! They are buttery, juicy, and palatable. You can play with the veal-to-pork ratio as well as your favorite spices.

Per serving: 293 Calories; 7.1g Fat; 47.9g Carbs; 12.5g Protein; 17.8g Sugars

Ingredients

1/2 pound veal mince
1/2 pound pork mince
1/2 cup grape jelly
1 ½ tablespoons cornstarch
2/3 cup breadcrumbs
1/4 cup chili sauce
1 cup onions, diced
1 tablespoon mustard
1/4 cup granulated sugar
1 tablespoon minced garlic
1 cup water
Salt and pepper, to taste

Directions

- Add the sugar, grape jelly, water, chili sauce, mustard, and cornstarch to the Power pressure cooker XL.
- Press the BEANS/LENTILS key and stir the mixture continuously until it has thickened; press the CANCEL key.
- In a mixing bowl, combine the meat, garlic, onions and bread crumbs; mix until it is well combined. Season with salt and pepper.
- Roll the mixture into 16 equal meatballs; add meatballs to the sauce in the cooker. Press the CHICKEN/MEAT key.
- Place the lid on the Power pressure cooker XL, lock the lid and switch the pressure release valve to closed. Cook for 15 minutes.
- Transfer to a large serving platter and serve warm.

VEGAN & VEGETARIAN

271. Classic Winter Oatmeal

Ready in about 15 minutes
Servings 4

If you like oatmeal, and you also like savory breakfast, this winter meal may become one of your all-time favorites. As a bonus, oats are extremely healthy food and so easy to make!

Per serving: 160 Calories; 5.5g Fat; 23g Carbs; 5.2g Protein; 0.6g Sugars

Ingredients

1 ½ cups oats
1/2 teaspoon salt
3 cups water
1/2 cup fresh chopped scallions, for garnish
1/2 cup savory cashew cream, for garnish

Directions

- Choose the "RICE/RISOTTO" function and put the inner pot into the Power Pressure Cooker XL.
- Add the wire rack and 1½ cups of warm water to the inner pot.
- Put the oats together with the remaining 1½ cups of water into a heat-proof bowl; sprinkle with salt. Lower the bowl onto the wire rack.
- Place the lid on the Power Pressure Cooker XL, lock the lid and switch the pressure release valve to closed. Press the "TIME ADJUSTMENT" key until you reach 8 minutes.
- Switch the pressure release valve to open. When the steam is completely released, remove the cooker's lid.
- Divide the oatmeal among serving bowls; serve topped with cream and scallions. Enjoy!

272. Lemon and Blackberry Jam

Ready in about 20 minutes
Servings 16

A twist on a childhood favorite, this jam is so quick to prepare. Enjoy with peanut butter and toast.

Per serving: 211 Calories; 0g Fat; 56.3g Carbs; 0g Protein; 56.3g Sugars

Ingredients

4 ½ cups caster sugar
2 tablespoons lemon juice
2 ½ tablespoons pectin powder
2 vanilla beans
3 ½ liquid pints fresh blackberries
1 cinnamon stick

Directions

- Choose the "CHICKEN/MEAT" function.
- Put the blackberries into your Power Pressure Cooker XL along with the pectin powder. Now, add the cinnamon stick, vanilla bean, and 2 cups of sugar; cook until the sugar dissolves.
- Once the sugar has dissolved, allow the mixture to a boil for about 4 minutes. Add the remaining sugar and lemon juice. Then, ladle the jam into the 5 liquid pint jars.
- Next, gently press the jam to release any excess air bubbles with a flexible spatula. Seal the prepared jars.
- Place the jars in the Power Pressure Cooker XL; pour in the water. Put the lid on and press the "CANNING/PRESERVING" key; press the "TIME ADJUST-MENT" key until you reach 10 minutes.
- Switch the pressure release valve to open. When the steam is completely released, remove the cooker's lid; carefully remove the jars with kitchen tongs or a jar lifter.

273. Creamed Green Lentil Soup

Ready in about 20 minutes
Servings 6

Delicious and filling, a hot bowl of soup is sure to warm the soul, no matter what the season. Green lentils have a mild flavor and soft texture and they're perfect for a thick and satisfying soup.

Per serving: 143 Calories; 5.1g Fat; 19.7g Carbs; 7.1g Protein; 6.5g Sugars

Ingredients

2 cups green lentils
1 tablespoon curry paste
1 teaspoon minced garlic
1 cup coconut milk
3 cups vegetable broth
2 medium-sized yellow onions, peeled and diced
1/2 teaspoon ground black pepper, or more to taste
1 teaspoon salt
1 teaspoon dried dill weed
2 green Serrano peppers, thinly sliced

Directions

- Press the "SOUP/STEW" key on your Power Pressure Cooker XL. Sauté the onions and garlic until tender or about 5 minutes.
- You can add a splash of stock to prevent the mixture from sticking.
- Add the curry paste and green Serrano pepper; stir to combine well. Pour in the coconut milk and broth. Now add the lentils, dill weed, salt and black pepper. Stir again.
- Place the lid on the Power Pressure Cooker XL, lock the lid and switch the pressure release valve to closed.
- Press the "TIME ADJUSTMENT" key until you reach 8 minutes. When the steam is completely released, remove the cooker's lid.
- Switch the pressure release valve to open. Serve warm and enjoy!

274. Perfect Three-Bean Chili

Ready in about 30 minutes
Servings 8

It's almost embarrassing how easy this chili is! Beans fight free radicals, lower cholesterol, and prevent diabetes. Enjoy!

Per serving: 122 Calories; 5.6g Fat; 13.6g Carbs; 5.7g Protein; 3.7g Sugars

Ingredients

3 cups hot vegetable stock
1 teaspoon minced chili pepper
1/2 cup red bell pepper, seeded and thinly sliced
1 cup leeks, thinly sliced
1 teaspoon minced garlic
2 tablespoons vegetable oil
1 cup carrots, chopped into sticks
1 cup dried kidney beans, soaked, drained and rinsed
1 cup dried pinto beans, soaked, drained and rinsed
1 cup dried cannellini beans, soaked, drained and rinsed
1/4 teaspoon sea salt, to taste
1/2 teaspoon celery seeds
5-6 black peppercorns
1/2 teaspoon red pepper flakes, crushed
24 ounces canned diced tomatoes

Directions

- Press the "BEANS/LENTILS" key and heat the oil; now, sauté the leeks and garlic for 6 minutes.
- Now, stir in the other ingredients, except for the canned tomatoes. Place the lid on the Power Pressure Cooker XL, lock the lid and switch the pressure release valve to closed.
- Press the "TIME ADJUSTMENT" key until you reach 20 minutes. When the steam is completely released, remove the cooker's lid. Switch the pressure release valve to open.
- Add the tomatoes; stir until they are heated through. Serve topped with nutritional yeast if desired.

275. Oatmeal with Soy Sauce and Fried Eggs

Ready in about 10 minutes
Servings 4

Be inspired by amazing oats that will fuel you through hectic days! In this recipe, use steel-cut oats because they retain much of their shape after pressure cooking.

Per serving: 238 Calories; 13.1g Fat; 29.0g Carbs; 13.9g Protein; 4.7g Sugars

Ingredients

1 ½ cup oats
1/2 teaspoon sea salt
2 ½ cups water
4 fried eggs
1/2 cup fresh chopped cilantro, for garnish
1/3 cup soy sauce

Directions

- Choose the "RICE/RISOTTO" function and put the inner pot into the Power Pressure Cooker XL.
- Add the wire rack and 1 cup of warm water to the inner pot. Drop the oats in a heat-proof bowl; add the remaining 1½ cups of water and sea salt. Lower the bowl onto the wire rack.
- Place the lid on the Power Pressure Cooker XL, lock the lid and switch the pressure release valve to closed. Press the "TIME ADJUSTMENT" key until you reach 8 minutes.
- Switch the pressure release valve to open. When the steam is completely released, remove the cooker's lid.
- Add the soy sauce and give it a good stir.
- Spoon the oatmeal into four serving bowls; top each oatmeal with a fried egg; scatter the chopped cilantro over the top. Enjoy!

276. Indian-Style Red Lentils

Ready in about 25 minutes
Servings 6

Who said lentils have to be boring? Red lentils, also known as masoor, are a staple of Indian cuisine, along with Garam masala, a spice mix that typically includes dalchini (cinnamon), clove, and cardamom.

Per serving: 318 Calories; 8.1g Fat; 51.9g Carbs; 13.3g Protein; 3.3g Sugars

Ingredients

4 ½ cups vegetable broth
1 ½ cups tomatoes, diced
1 ½ cups red lentils, rinsed
1 heaping teaspoon minced garlic
1 cup onions, diced
3 tablespoons grapeseed oil
1/4 teaspoon black pepper, or more to your liking
1 teaspoon cayenne pepper
1 teaspoon salt
2 pounds butternut squash, roughly chopped
2 teaspoons Garam masala
1/2 cup fresh chopped cilantro, for garnish

Directions

- Press the "BEANS/LENTILS" key and heat the oil. Sauté the onions and garlic for 6 minutes.
- Add the butternut squash, Garam masala, salt, black pepper, and cayenne pepper.
- Continue cooking for an additional 4 minutes. Add the broth and lentils. Stir in the tomatoes.
- Place the lid on the Power Pressure Cooker XL, lock the lid and switch the pressure release valve to closed. Press the "TIME ADJUSTMENT" key until you reach 8 minutes.
- Switch the pressure release valve to open. When the steam is completely released, remove the cooker's lid.
- Puree the soup with an immersion blender. Serve topped with fresh cilantro. Serve hot and enjoy!

277. Mushroom and Bean Soup

Ready in about 35 minutes
Servings 4

Delight your tummy with this appetizing and protein-packed soup! This recipe calls for fresh mushrooms such as raw portabella, morel, oysters, enoki, and so forth.

Per serving: 145 Calories; 3.4g Fat; 20.3g Carbs; 12.1g Protein; 9.4g Sugars

Ingredients

5 cups vegetable stock, preferably homemade
1 ¼ cups canned cannellini beans
4 cloves garlic, smashed
1 ½ cups onions, chopped
2 ½ cups canned tomatoes, crushed
1 cup celery stalks, chopped
1 ¼ pounds mushrooms, thinly sliced
1/4 teaspoon ground black pepper
1 teaspoon dried dill weed
1 teaspoon dried basil
1/2 teaspoon sea salt
1/2 cup parsnip, chopped
1 cup carrots, trimmed and thinly sliced

Directions

- Press the "SOUP/STEW" key.
- Simply throw all of the above ingredients into your Power Pressure Cooker XL; stir to combine well.
- Place the lid on the Power Pressure Cooker XL, lock the lid and switch the pressure release valve to closed. Press the "TIME ADJUSTMENT" key until you reach for 30 minutes.
- Press the "CANCEL" key. Switch the pressure release valve to open. When the steam is completely released, remove the cooker's lid. Serve right now!

278. Cauliflower and Broccoli Salad

Ready in about 15 minutes
Servings 6

Redefine your favorite comfort foods and make this crispy salad in no time. Scatter toasted pepitas over the salad.

Per serving: 80 Calories; 4.5g Fat; 8.1g Carbs; 4.1g Protein; 2.8g Sugars

Ingredients

For the Salad:
1 ½ cups water
1 pound broccoli, broken into florets
1 pound cauliflower, broken into florets
1 ½ cups carrots, thinly sliced

For the Vinaigrette:
1/2 tablespoon capers
3 teaspoons fresh orange juice
1/3 teaspoon ground black pepper
1 teaspoon salt
1/4 cup extra-virgin olive oil

Directions

- Press the "FISH/VEGETABLES/STEAM" key.
- Throw the carrots, cauliflower, broccoli and water into the Power Pressure Cooker XL.
- Lock the lid and switch the pressure release valve to closed. Press the "TIME ADJUSTMENT" key until you reach 10 minutes.
- Once the timer reaches 0, the Power Pressure Cooker XL will automatically switch to "KEEP WARM/CANCEL". Switch the pressure release valve to open.
- When the steam is completely released, remove the lid.
- Meanwhile, mix all the ingredients for the vinaigrette. Strain out the vegetables and dress with the vinaigrette. Serve at once.

279. Chipotle Pumpkin Soup with Pecans

Ready in about 30 minutes
Servings 6

Hot, hot, hot! The recipe calls for chipotle pepper, but be sure to use the type of chili peppers that are best suited to the amount of heat you and your family are able to handle.

Per serving: 120 Calories; 6g Fat; 13.8g Carbs; 4.6g Protein; 4.1g Sugars

Ingredients

2 chipotle peppers, seeded and finely minced
2 ¼ cups vegetable stock
1 cup onions, peeled and chopped
2 ¼ cups water
1/3 cup pecans, pulsed
1/2 teaspoon cayenne pepper
1/4 teaspoon black pepper
1/2 teaspoon salt
1/2 pound potatoes, peeled and diced
1 cup apples, peeled, cored and diced
28 ounces canned pumpkin puree
1 heaping teaspoon smashed garlic
1/2 teaspoon ground allspice
2 tablespoons toasted pumpkin seeds, for garnish

Directions

* Press the "SOUP/STEW" key and sauté the garlic and onion until they are browned, about 5 minutes.
* Add the allspice, salt, cayenne pepper, black pepper, and the chipotle; cook for an additional 5 minutes. Add the potatoes, apples, pumpkin puree, ground pecans, water, and the stock.
* Lock the lid and switch the pressure release valve to closed. Press the "TIME ADJUSTMENT" key until you reach 15 minutes.
* Once the timer reaches 0, the Power Pressure Cooker XL will automatically switch to "KEEP WARM/CANCEL". Switch the pressure release valve to open.
* When the steam is completely released, remove the lid.
* Afterwards, transfer the soup to your food processor; pulse until completely smooth and creamy, working in batches. Serve warm, sprinkled with toasted pumpkin seeds.

280. Black Bean Soup

Ready in about 25 minutes
Servings 4

You'll be happy to know that these beans stay perfectly tender, unlike some other bean recipes you might have tried in the past.

Per serving: 151 Calories; 6.6g Fat; 13.5g Carbs; 10.1g Protein; 2.8g Sugars

Ingredients

5 cups vegetable stock
1/3 teaspoon chipotle powder
3 teaspoons vegetable oil
1/2 teaspoon ground black pepper
1/4 teaspoon cayenne pepper, or more to taste
1/2 teaspoon sea salt
3 cloves garlic, minced
2 cups dry black beans, soaked overnight
1 teaspoon dried basil leaves
1 cup onions, chopped
1 bay leaf
1/2 cup fresh chopped cilantro, for garnish

Directions

* Press the "SOUP/STEW" key. Drain the black beans and reserve.
* Next, warm the vegetable oil and sauté the onions and garlic for 3 minutes.
* Add the chipotle powder, reserved beans, vegetable stock, bay leaves, and basil; season with salt, black pepper, and cayenne pepper; stir well.
* Lock the lid and switch the pressure release valve to closed. Press the "TIME ADJUSTMENT" key until you reach 15 minutes.
* Switch the pressure release valve to open. When the steam is completely released, remove the lid. Garnish with cilantro and serve.

281. Creamy Curry Lentil Soup

Ready in about 20 minutes
Servings 6

Curry lentils are comfort food in their purest form. You can use any type of lentils for this one, including brown, green and red.

Per serving: 75 Calories; 1.3g Fat; 12.3g Carbs; 5.7g Protein; 3.5g Sugars

Ingredients

2 cups lentils
16 ounces canned coconut milk
1 heaping teaspoon minced garlic
1 cup red onions, diced
2 ½ cups vegetable stock
1 ½ tablespoons red curry paste
1/4 teaspoon ground black pepper, to taste
1 teaspoon salt
1 cup ripe tomatoes, chopped

Directions

- Press the "SOUP/STEW" key and sauté the onions and garlic until beginning to brown, approximately 4 minutes. You can add a splash of stock to prevent the mixture from sticking.
- Add the curry paste, and stir well. Pour in the coconut milk and stock. Now, add the lentils and tomatoes. Season with salt and black pepper. Stir again to combine well.
- Lock the lid and switch the pressure release valve to closed. Press the "TIME ADJUSTMENT" key until you reach 10 minutes.
- Switch the pressure release valve to open. When the steam is completely released, remove the lid. Bon appétit!

282. Three-Bean Vegan Chili

Ready in about 30 minutes
Servings 8

Whether as a great family lunch or a festive holiday fare, a chili with three types of beans is very likely to hit the spot. Serve with shredded vegan cheese or nutritional yeast if desired.

Per serving: 146 Calories; 1.8g Fat; 25.3g Carbs; 9.2g Protein; 5.4g Sugars

Ingredients

4 cups hot vegetable stock
1/2 teaspoon red pepper flakes, crushed
1 teaspoon minced chili pepper
30 ounces canned tomatoes, diced
1 cup carrots, chopped into sticks
1/2 cup green bell pepper, de-seeded and thinly sliced
3 cloves garlic, minced
1 cup leeks, thinly sliced
1/2 teaspoon coriander
1/2 teaspoon sea salt, to taste
1 teaspoon black peppercorns
1 cup dried pinto beans, soaked, drained and rinsed
1 cup dried cannellini beans, soaked, drained and rinsed
1 cup dried kidney beans, soaked, drained and rinsed
1 cup parsnip, chopped

Directions

- Press the "BEANS/LENTILS" key and sauté the garlic and leeks for 6 minutes, adding a splash of vegetable stock as needed.
- Now, stir in the other ingredients, except for the canned tomatoes. Lock the lid and switch the pressure release valve to closed. Press the "TIME ADJUSTMENT" key until you reach 20 minutes.
- Switch the pressure release valve to open. When the steam is completely released, remove the lid. Add the tomatoes, stir, and cover until heated through. Bon appétit!

283. Potato-Leek Soup with Cremini Mushrooms

Ready in about 25 minutes
Servings 10

Cremini mushrooms, also known as Baby Portobello, have a deep savory flavor. This soup tastes great served with quinoa as a quick and nutritious dinner.

Per serving: 133 Calories; 2.1g Fat; 25.1g Carbs; 4.7g Protein; 5.8g Sugars

Ingredients

6 potatoes, peeled and cubed
2 cups cremini mushrooms, roughly chopped
1 cup leeks, trimmed and sliced
2 cups carrots, peeled and diced
1 cup parsnips, peeled and diced
1 teaspoon minced garlic
1 teaspoon fennel seeds
1/4 teaspoon black pepper, or more to taste
1/2 teaspoon salt
1/2 teaspoon marjoram
8 ½ cups water, boiling
2 ¼ cups coconut milk, unsweetened

Directions

- Press the "SOUP/STEW" key and sauté the leeks and garlic approximately 6 minutes, adding boiling water as needed.
- Add the rest of the above ingredients, except for the coconut milk.
- Place the lid on the Power Pressure Cooker XL, lock the lid and switch the pressure release valve to closed. Cook for 10 minutes.
- Switch the pressure release valve to open. When the steam is completely released, remove the lid. Pour in the coconut milk.
- Mix your soup with an immersion blender for about 3 minutes. Adjust the seasonings, and serve warm, topped with nutritional yeast if desired.

284. Basmati Rice and Orange Salad

Ready in about 15 minutes +
chilling time
Servings 6

Using cooled rice is even better in this light and refreshing salad. You can substitute mint leaves for fresh chives or cilantro.

Per serving: 194 Calories; 3.2g Fat; 35g Carbs; 5.2g Protein; 2.5g Sugars

Ingredients

2 ½ cups water
2 ½ cups basmati rice
2 tablespoons extra-virgin olive oil
1/2 cup orange, chopped
1 large bunch of spring onions, white and green parts, chopped
1/3 cup fresh mint, roughly chopped
1 cup bell peppers, cut into thin strips

Directions

- Press the "RICE/RISOTTO" key. Rinse the basmati rice and add it to the Power Pressure Cooker XL. Pour in the water and place the lid on the Power Pressure Cooker XL.
- Cook for 10 minutes. Switch the pressure release valve to open. When the steam is completely released, remove the lid.
- Let the cooked rice cool completely and fluff with a fork. Transfer the prepared rice to a serving dish.
- Add the remaining ingredients and stir to combine. Bon appétit!

285. Summer Quinoa Salad

Ready in about 10 minutes + chilling time
Servings 4

Here is a simple and refreshing way to prepare and enjoy the super powerful and nutritious quinoa. Quinoa is loaded with vegan protein, manganese, fiber, and iron.

Per serving: 321 Calories; 5.2g Fat; 56.2g Carbs; 12.3g Protein; 1g Sugars

Ingredients

2 cups uncooked quinoa, well rinsed
1/2 teaspoon ground white pepper, to taste
A pinch of sea salt
A pinch of ground cinnamon
3 cups water
1/2 teaspoon dried basil
1 cup thinly sliced cucumber
1 cup diced tomatoes

Directions

- Press the "RICE/RISOTTO" key. Put the quinoa, water, cinnamon, salt, pepper, and basil into the Power Pressure Cooker XL.
- Place the lid on the Power Pressure Cooker XL and set the cooking time to 2 minutes.
- Then, use a Quick pressure release and carefully remove the lid.
- Add the tomatoes and cucumber. Serve well chilled.

286. Winter Sweet Potato Soup

Ready in about 20 minutes
Servings 6

It's easy being vegan with this creamy soup! Sweet potatoes are a great source of fiber, vitamins, and minerals; coconut milk is also high in good-for-you minerals.

Per serving: 168 Calories; 7.2g Fat; 21.5g Carbs; 5.3g Protein; 5.5g Sugars

Ingredients

1 pound sweet potatoes, cubed
2 teaspoons fresh lemon juice
2 tablespoons canola oil
1/2 teaspoon cinnamon powder
1/4 teaspoon freshly grated nutmeg
3 tablespoons peanut butter
1 cup onions, roughly chopped
15 ounces coconut milk
2 ½ cups vegetable stock
3 cloves garlic, finely chopped
1/2 teaspoon black pepper, or more to taste
1 teaspoon sea salt
1 cup tomatoes, peeled, seeded and chopped

Directions

- Press the "SOUP/STEW" key and heat the canola oil; sauté the garlic and onions, stirring frequently, until they are softened, about 5 minutes.
- Throw in the other ingredients; stir to combine well.
- Place the lid on the Power Pressure Cooker XL and set the cooking time to 6 minutes. Switch the pressure release valve to open.
- When the steam is completely released, remove the cooker's lid. Puree the soup to your desired consistency, using an immersion blender. Serve in six individual bowls.

287. British-Style Beans

Ready in about 30 minutes
Servings 8

Rich in flavor and sinfully delicious, these beans could also be made with another type of dry beans. Serve hot, topped with roasted red peppers if desired.

Per serving: 121 Calories; 0.7g Fat; 23.1g Carbs; 6.9g Protein; 4.4g Sugars

Ingredients

2 ripe tomatoes, chopped
1/2 cup bell pepper, seeded and thinly sliced
1 heaping teaspoon minced garlic
1 cup celery stalk, chopped
1 tablespoon chili powder
1/2 teaspoon black pepper, or more to taste
1/2 teaspoon cayenne pepper
1/2 teaspoon coriander
1 teaspoon salt
1/2 teaspoon cumin powder
3 cups boiling water
2 cups dried black beans, soaked
1/2 cup dried red beans, soaked
1 cup carrots, chopped into sticks
2 medium-sized onions, peeled and chopped

Directions

- Press the "BEANS/LENTILS" key. Drain and rinse the soaked beans.
- Now, sauté the onions and garlic for about 6 minutes, adding a splash of boiling water as needed.
- Add the remaining ingredients, except for the tomatoes.
- Place the lid on the Power Pressure Cooker XL and set the cooking time to 15 minutes; lock the lid and switch the pressure release valve to closed.
- Press the "CANCEL" key. Switch the pressure release valve to open.
- When the steam is completely released, remove the cooker's lid. Stir in the tomatoes. Bon appétit!

288. Delectable Ginger Risotto with Almonds

Ready in about 15 minutes
Servings 4

As a common spice in Asian cuisine, ginger is among the healthiest foods in the world. It prevents heart diseases, fights bacterial infections and boosts immunity.

Per serving: 354 Calories; 15.14g Fat; 65.1g Carbs; 9.9g Protein; 29g Sugars

Ingredients

2 cups risotto rice
A pinch of ground cinnamon
A pinch of grated nutmeg
1 cup apples, cored and diced
1/3 cup candied ginger, diced
3 ½ cups almond milk
1/3 cup golden raisins
1/3 cup almonds, toasted and roughly chopped

Directions

- Press the "RICE/RISOTTO" key; simply throw all the components, except the almonds, into the Power Pressure Cooker XL.
- Place the lid on the Power Pressure Cooker XL; lock the lid and switch the pressure release valve to closed. Set the cooking time to 10 minutes
- Press the "CANCEL" key. Switch the pressure release valve to open. When the steam is completely released, remove the cooker's lid.
- Divide the risotto among individual bowls and serve garnished with the chopped and toasted almonds. Enjoy!

289. Refreshing Kidney Bean Salad

Ready in about 20 minutes
Servings 4

This kidney bean salad is amazing on its own, but you can also use it on your favorite tortilla or toss it with greens for a delicious and healthy lunch.

Per serving: 124 Calories; 9.7g Fat; 6.6g Carbs; 2.6g Protein; 1.2g Sugars

Ingredients

2 cups red kidney beans, soaked overnight
1 cup red onions, peeled and coarsely chopped
1 ½ tablespoons wine vinegar
2 bay leaves
5 cups water
1/4 teaspoon freshly cracked black pepper
1 teaspoon salt
1 teaspoon dried dill weed
1 teaspoon smashed garlic
1/4 cup extra-virgin olive oil
1/2 cup fresh cilantro, chopped

Directions

- Press the "BEANS/LENTILS" key.
- Add the water, kidney beans, and bay leaves to the inner pot of your Power Pressure Cooker XL.
- Place the lid on the Power Pressure Cooker XL and lock the lid; switch the pressure release valve to closed. Set the cooking time to 15 minutes
- Press the "CANCEL" key. Switch the pressure release valve to open. When the steam is completely released, remove the cooker's lid.
- Drain the cooked beans and stir in the rest of the above ingredients. Stir to combine and serve chilled. Bon appétit!

290. Sweet Potato and Lentil Soup

Ready in about 25 minutes
Servings 6

Quick and tasty, this dish is perfect for your next family lunch. The combo of sweet potatoes, lentils, and canned beans has never tasted better!

Per serving: 259 Calories; 6.1g Fat; 48.4g Carbs; 5.9g Protein; 13.8g Sugars

Ingredients

2 pounds sweet potatoes, diced
20 ounces canned beans, drained and rinsed
3 ½ cups vegetable broth
1 can tomatoes, diced
2 tablespoons olive oil
2 tablespoons apple cider vinegar
1/2 teaspoon celery seeds
1 ¼ cups dried lentils
1/2 teaspoon ground black pepper
1/2 teaspoon sea salt
1 tablespoon chili powder
1/2 teaspoon cumin powder
1 cup onions, diced
1/2 tablespoon curry paste
1/4 cup fresh cilantro, roughly chopped
2 tablespoons parsley, roughly chopped
1 teaspoon minced garlic
10 ounces almond milk

Directions

- Press the "SOUP/STEW" key and heat the olive oil; sauté the onions and garlic until tender, about 5 minutes.
- Add the sweet potatoes and cook for a further 3 minutes. Throw all the remaining ingredients, minus the almond milk, into the Power Pressure Cooker XL.
- Place the lid on the Power Pressure Cooker XL, lock the lid and switch the pressure release valve to closed.
- Press the "TIME ADJUSTMENT" key until you reach 12 minutes. Switch the pressure release valve to open. When the steam is completely released, remove the cooker's lid.
- Pour in the almond milk and stir well. Bon appétit!

291. Barley with Strawberries and Cashews

Ready in about 30 minutes
Servings 8

Barley is among healthiest foods in the world and a versatile cereal grain with pasta-like texture. Power pressure cooker XL cooks your barley to perfection, it is wonderfully tender and chewy.

Per serving: 301 Calories; 10.3g Fat; 47.2g Carbs; 7.8g Protein; 3g Sugars

Ingredients

2 cups pot barley, rinsed and drained
2 cups fresh strawberries
1 cup cashews, chopped
Juice of 1/2 fresh lime
3 teaspoons vegetable oil
1/2 teaspoon kosher salt
6 cups water

Directions

- Combine the barley, oil, salt, and water in your Power pressure cooker XL that has been oiled with a non-stick cooking spray.
- Press the RICE/RISOTTO key and use the cook time selector to adjust to 25 minutes. Place the lid on the Power pressure cooker XL, lock the lid and switch the pressure release valve to closed.
- Once the timer reaches 0, the cooker will automatically switch to KEEP WARM/CANCEL. When the steam is completely released, carefully remove the cooker's lid.
- Add the remaining ingredients and stir to combine. To serve, divide prepared barley salad among individual bowls. Enjoy!

292. Wild Rice with Acorn Squash

Ready in about 30 minutes
Servings 6

This main-course-worthy dish is easy to make in your Power pressure cooker XL. You can sprinkle it with some nutritional yeast just before serving. Enjoy!

Per serving: 311 Calories; 3.8g Fat; 62g Carbs; 10.8g Protein; 3.4g Sugars

Ingredients

2 ½ cups wild rice, rinsed and drained
1 pound Acorn squash, cubed
1 tablespoon minced chile pepper
1/2 cup carrots, chopped
1/2 cup parsnip, chopped
1 turnip, chopped
3 teaspoons olive oil
1 ½ teaspoons salt
6 cups water

For the Dressing:
1/4 cup extra-virgin olive oil
Freshly squeezed juice of 1/2 lemon
Sea salt and freshly ground black pepper, to taste
1/2 teaspoon cayenne pepper

Directions

- Combine the rice, salt, olive oil, and water in your Power pressure cooker XL. Press the RICE/RISOTTO key and use the cook time selector to adjust to 25 minutes.
- Place the lid on the Power pressure cooker XL, lock the lid and switch the pressure release valve to closed.
- Once the timer reaches 0, the cooker will automatically switch to KEEP WARM/CANCEL. When the steam is completely released, carefully remove the cooker's lid.
- Drain the rice; then, fluff it with a fork. Allow it to cool completely.
- Now, add the squash, carrots, parsnip, chile pepper and turnip. Give it a good stir.
- In a mixing bowl, combine all the dressing ingredients; whisk until everything is well incorporated. Drizzle the dressing over your salad. Serve well-chilled.

293. Breakfast Quinoa with Veggies

Ready in about 20 minutes
Servings 6

This impressive vegan breakfast is bursting with flavor. Quick pressure cooking also ensures that your veggies retain their valuable nutrients.

Per serving: 381 Calories; 6.5g Fat; 46.4g Carbs; 11g Protein; 4.2g Sugars

Ingredients

2 cups quinoa
2 onions, chopped
1 head broccoli, chopped into small-sized florets
4 cups stock
2 ripe tomatoes, chopped
3 cloves garlic, finely minced
3 teaspoons canola oil
1/2 teaspoon ground black pepper
1 teaspoon dried basil
1 teaspoon kosher salt
1/4 cup chopped fresh chives, for garnish

Directions

- Press the RICE/RISOTTO key and warm the oil. Now, sauté the onions until translucent, about 2 minutes. Then, add the broccoli and garlic; continue sautéing for 4 minutes more.
- Add the rest of the above ingredients, except for the chives.
- Place the lid on the Power pressure cooker XL, lock the lid and switch the pressure release valve to closed. Cook for 6 minutes.
- Once the timer reaches 0, the cooker will automatically switch to KEEP WARM/CANCEL. When the steam is completely released, carefully remove the cooker's lid.
- Taste and adjust the seasonings. Sprinkle with fresh chives and serve.

294. Zesty Orange Marmalade

Ready in about 20 minutes
Servings 18

Eating a plant-based diet can be incredibly tasty and easy with the Power pressure cooker XL. This marmalade is a great idea for breakfast for the whole family.

Per serving: 302 Calories; 0.1g Fat; 79.7g Carbs; 0.6g Protein; 78g Sugars

Ingredients

6 navel oranges, halved
3 ¼ pounds granulated sugar
1 tablespoon Scotch
1 lemon, zest finely grated and juiced

Directions

- Squeeze the juice from the oranges. Chop the orange peel; place the pith and pips in a muslin bag. Soak the peel together with muslin bag in 1-pint water overnight.
- Next, squeeze the juice from the muslin bag; discard the bag. Transfer to the Power pressure cooker XL; add the lemon juice and lemon zest.
- Press the RICE/RISOTTO key. Place the lid on the Power pressure cooker XL, lock the lid and switch the pressure release valve to closed. Cook for 18 minutes.
- Once the timer reaches 0, the cooker will automatically switch to KEEP WARM/CANCEL. When the steam is completely released, carefully remove the cooker's lid.
- Add the sugar and Scotch. Choose the FISH/VEGE-TABLES/STEAM function and cook, stirring often, until the sugar is dissolved.
- Cool your marmalade slightly and spoon into sterilized jars.

295. Millet with Dates and Pears

Ready in about 20 minutes
Servings 6

Fresh and dry fruits provide flavor and texture to this sweet vegan breakfast. Millet prevents cardiovascular disease, diabetes and childhood asthma.

Per serving: 321 Calories; 3.2g Fat; 65.8g Carbs; 7.9g Protein; 10.5g Sugars

Ingredients

2 cups millet
1/3 cup dried dates, pitted and chopped
1/2 pound pears, cored and diced
3/4 cup rice milk
1/3 cup dried currants
1/3 teaspoon ground nutmeg
1/2 teaspoon cinnamon powder
4 cups water

Directions

● Add all of the above ingredients to the Power pressure cooker XL.
● Press the CHICKEN/MEAT key. Place the lid on the Power pressure cooker XL, lock the lid and switch the pressure release valve to closed. Cook for 15 minutes.
● Once the timer reaches 0, the cooker will automatically switch to KEEP WARM/CANCEL. When the steam is completely released, carefully remove the cooker's lid.
● Sweeten with maple syrup or honey if desired. Serve.

296. Risotto with Veggies and Corn

Ready in about 40 minutes
Servings 6

To remove the pits from your olives, simply press down on the olives with the flat side of a large knife.

Per serving: 300 Calories; 4.6g Fat; 58.4g Carbs; 10.4g Protein; 6.9g Sugars

Ingredients

2 cups wild rice
2 small-sized white onions, chopped
1 cup carrots, chopped
1 cup bell peppers, stemmed, cored, and chopped
2 cups frozen corn kernels, thawed
5 cups vegetable stock
1 tablespoon olive oil
1/2 cup Kalamata olives, pitted and sliced
1/3 teaspoon saffron

Directions

● Press the RICE/RISOTTO key and warm the oil. Then, sauté the onions, carrots and bell peppers, stirring frequently, until they have softened, for 5 minutes.
● Add the saffron, rice, stock and olives.
● Place the lid on the Power pressure cooker XL, lock the lid and switch the pressure release valve to closed. Cook for 25 minutes.
● Once the timer reaches 0, the cooker will automatically switch to KEEP WARM/CANCEL. When the steam is completely released, carefully remove the cooker's lid.
● Add the corn kernels, place the lid on the Power pressure cooker XL and let it stand for 6 to 7 minutes. Serve immediately.

297. Cocoa Oatmeal with Walnuts

Ready in about 20 minutes
Servings 2

This fantastic vegan staple does double duty as breakfast or dinner. You can use any other type of non-dairy milk.

Per serving: 340 Calories; 12.5g Fat; 49.7g Carbs; 13.2g Protein; 10g Sugars

Ingredients

2 tablespoons cocoa powder
1 ¼ cups steel-cut oats
1/2 cup walnut milk
3 tablespoons walnuts, toasted and roughly chopped
1 cup apricots, pitted and diced
1 teaspoon vanilla essence
1/2 teaspoon ground cinnamon
1/3 teaspoon pure hazelnut extract
1 1/3 cup water

Directions

- Throw all of the above ingredients, except for the cocoa and walnuts, into to your Power pressure cooker XL.
- Press the SOUP/STEW key. Place the lid on the Power pressure cooker XL, lock the lid and switch the pressure release valve to closed. Cook for 10 minutes.
- Once the timer reaches 0, the cooker will automatically switch to KEEP WARM/CANCEL. When the steam is completely released, carefully remove the cooker's lid.
- Add the cocoa powder and gently stir to combine. Divide the oatmeal among serving bowls and scatter chopped walnuts over the top. Serve right now!

298. Protein Adzuki Bean Salad

Ready in about 15 minutes
Servings 6

Adzuki beans are an excellent source of antioxidants, fiber and minerals. They can help you fight diabetes, heart diseases and obesity.

Per serving: 166 Calories; 7.1g Fat; 23.1g Carbs; 3.8g Protein; 1.6g Sugars

Ingredients

2 cups Adzuki, soaked overnight and rinsed
1 tablespoon canola oil
2 carrots, diced
1 cup leeks, finely chopped
2 cloves garlic, finely minced
1/4 cup fresh parsley, chopped
1/3 teaspoon ground black pepper
1 teaspoon dried basil
1/3 teaspoon salt
1/2 teaspoon ground bay leaf
3 tablespoons red wine vinegar
3 ½ cups water

Directions

- Add the beans and water to the Power pressure cooker XL.
- Press the SOUP/STEW key. Place the lid on the Power pressure cooker XL, lock the lid and switch the pressure release valve to closed. Cook for 10 minutes.
- Once the timer reaches 0, the cooker will automatically switch to KEEP WARM/CANCEL. When the steam is completely released, carefully remove the cooker's lid.
- Then, drain the beans and add the remaining ingredients. Serve warm or at room temperature.

299. Apples in Berry Sauce

Ready in about 20 minutes
Servings 4

Give a regular compote a makeover with fragrant spices and mixed berries. Serve with chopped pistachios and whipped cream.

Per serving: 142 Calories; 0.4g Fat; 35.2g Carbs; 0.8g Protein; 28.7g Sugars

Ingredients

1 pound apples, peeled, cored, and halved
2 ½ cups mixed berries
1 teaspoon vanilla paste
1/3 cup granulated sugar
2 teaspoons arrowroot
1/4 teaspoon grated nutmeg
1/2 teaspoon ground cardamom
1 ½ cups water

Directions

- Throw all ingredients, except for the sugar and arrowroot, into your Power pressure cooker XL.
- Press the RICE/RISOTTO key. Place the lid on the Power pressure cooker XL, lock the lid and switch the pressure release valve to closed. Cook for 10 minutes.
- Once the timer reaches 0, the cooker will automatically switch to KEEP WARM/CANCEL. When the steam is completely released, carefully remove the cooker's lid. Remove the apples with a slotted spoon.
- Next, mash the berries with a heavy spoon. Combine the sugar and arrowroot with 1 ½ tablespoons of water.
- Press the FISH/VEGETABLE/STEAM key; allow it to simmer for 4 minutes, until the sauce has thickened.
- Divide the apples among serving plates. Top with the berry sauce, serve and enjoy.

300. Country Black-Eyed Peas

Ready in about 25 minutes
Servings 8

Ladle these amazing black-eyed peas over hot cooked rice and sprinkle with roasted almonds. So glam!

Per serving: 103 Calories; 4.8g Fat; 13.6g Carbs; 4.6g Protein; 7g Sugars

Ingredients

3 cups black-eyed peas, soaked overnight
1/2 teaspoon salt
2 tablespoons vegetable oil
2 red onions, peeled and chopped
3 cloves garlic, finely minced
2 Roma tomatoes, chopped
Salt and ground black pepper, to taste
1/2 teaspoon ground cumin
2 quarts water

Directions

- Add the water, black-eyed peas, 1 tablespoon of oil and salt to your Power pressure cooker XL.
- Press the BEANS/LENTILS key and use the cook time selector to adjust to 15 minutes. Place the lid on the Power pressure cooker XL, lock the lid and switch the pressure release valve to closed.
- Once the timer reaches 0, the cooker will automatically switch to KEEP WARM/CANCEL.
- When the steam is completely released, carefully remove the cooker's lid.
- In a saucepan, warm the remaining 1 tablespoon of oil; sauté the onions until they are caramelized.
- Add the remaining ingredients; cook for 5 minutes longer, stirring often. Next, add the onion mixture to the black-eyed peas; mix to combine well. Serve warm.

301. Mushroom, Pepper and Rice Soup

Ready in about 20 minutes
Servings 8

Mushrooms and peppers give this soup unexpected brightness and creaminess. You can use the combination of bell peppers and chile peppers to spice up your soup!

Per serving: 243 Calories; 5.3g Fat; 47.5g Carbs; 5.8g Protein; 3.6g Sugars

Ingredients

2 tablespoons vegetable oil
1 pound porcini mushrooms, chopped
1 cup bell peppers, deveined and chopped
2 cups white rice, rinsed and drained
1 cup onions, finely chopped
3 cloves garlic, minced
1 cup stock
2 tablespoons wine vinegar
1 cup celery with leaves, chopped
1 cup tomatoes, seeded and diced
2 sprigs fresh rosemary
2 bay leaves
2 sprigs fresh thyme
Sea salt and freshly ground black pepper
3 ½ cups water

Directions

- Press the RICE/RISOTTO key and warm the oil; now, sauté the onions, mushrooms and garlic until fragrant, about 4 minutes. Add a splash of stock to deglaze the bottom.
- Add the remaining ingredients, minus wine vinegar. Press the RICE/RISOTTO key and then, press the TIME ADJUSTMENT key until you reach 10 minutes.
- Place the lid on the Power pressure cooker XL, lock the lid and switch the pressure release valve to closed.
- Once the timer reaches 0, the cooker will automatically switch to KEEP WARM/CANCEL.
- When the steam is completely released, carefully remove the cooker's lid. Add the vinegar, stir and serve hot.

302. Wheat Berries with Fruits

Ready in about 30 minutes
Servings 6

Pumpkin pie spice and dried fruits are key to providing flavor and depth to this amazing dish. Keep in mind that wheat berries do not require an overnight soak.

Per serving: 200 Calories; 0.7g Fat; 46.1g Carbs; 5.2g Protein; 19.9g Sugars

Ingredients

2 cups wheat berries
2 pears, cored and diced
1/3 cup dried cherries
1/3 cup dried figs, chopped
1/2 teaspoon pumpkin pie spice
1/2 cup nondairy milk
6 ½ cups water

Directions

- Add all of the above ingredients to the Power pressure cooker XL. Press the RICE/RISOTTO key and use the cook time selector to adjust to 25 minutes.
- Place the lid on the Power pressure cooker XL, lock the lid and switch the pressure release valve to closed.
- Once the timer reaches 0, the cooker will automatically switch to KEEP WARM/CANCEL.
- When the steam is completely released, carefully remove the cooker's lid.
- Sweeten with some agave nectar if desired. Enjoy!

303. Quick and Easy Moong Dal

Ready in about 20 minutes
Servings 4

Moong dal is packed with protein, antioxidants and phytonutrients. It can help lower high blood pressure and high cholesterol levels.

Per serving: 165 Calories; 3.8g Fat; 23.3g Carbs; 9.8g Protein; 0.8g Sugars

Ingredients

1 ½ cups moong dal
3 teaspoons grapeseed oil
1/2 teaspoon salt
1/2 teaspoon cayenne pepper
1/2 teaspoon ground bay leaves
1/4 teaspoon black pepper, ground
3 ½ cups water

Directions

- Add all of the above ingredients to the Power pressure cooker XL.
- Choose the RICE/RISOTO function. Now, use the cook time selector to adjust to 18 minutes.
- Place the lid on the Power pressure cooker XL, lock the lid and switch the pressure release valve to closed.
- Once the timer reaches 0, the cooker will automatically switch to KEEP WARM/CANCEL.
- When the steam is completely released, carefully remove the cooker's lid. Ladle into individual bowls and serve warm.

304. French Green Lentils with Collard Greens

Ready in about 35 minutes
Servings 4

Lentils are wonderfully easy to cook in the Power pressure cooker XL. We encourage you to experiment with this recipe. Try "the rainbow of vegetables" like carrots, peppers or celery. Throw in sliced Greek olives or chiffonade fresh basil. Think outside the box and find your favorite combination!

Per serving: 251 Calories; 4.1g Fat; 43.8g Carbs; 13.7g Protein; 7.6g Sugars

Ingredients

2 cups dry French green lentils
1 (1-pound) package fresh collard greens, trimmed
2 teaspoons olive oil
2 medium-sized onions, peeled and chopped
1 ½ cups tomato puree
4 cups water
1/3 teaspoon cumin
1/2 teaspoon coriander
1 teaspoon thyme

Directions

- Choose the BEANS/LENTILS function and use the cook time selector to adjust to 15 minutes.
- Heat the oil and sauté the onions along with the coriander, thyme, and cumin for about 4 minutes.
- Then, add lentils, tomato puree and water; stir to combine well. Place the lid on the Power pressure cooker XL, lock the lid and switch the pressure release valve to closed.
- Once the timer reaches 0, the cooker will automatically switch to KEEP WARM/CANCEL.
- Mix in the collard greens and stir until they're wilted; serve.

305. Easy Curried Beans

Ready in about 40 minutes
Servings 8

Kidney beans are inexpensive, nutritious and delicious. Serve with a homemade cornbread.

Per serving: 286 Calories; 4.2g Fat; 48.2g Carbs; 16.3g Protein; 9.4g Sugars

Ingredients

2 tablespoons curry powder
2 ½ cups dark red kidney beans
1 teaspoon salt
2 tablespoons olive oil
2 red onions, peeled and chopped
1 tablespoon minced garlic
4 cups crushed tomatoes
Salt and ground black pepper, to taste
2 teaspoons chili powder
1/2 teaspoon cumin
3 cups water

Directions

- Add the water, beans, 1 teaspoon of salt and 1 tablespoon of olive oil to your Power pressure cooker XL. Then, press the BEANS/LENTILS key and use the cook time selector to adjust to 30 minutes.
- Place the lid on the Power pressure cooker XL, lock the lid and switch the pressure release valve to closed.
- Once the timer reaches 0, the cooker will automatically switch to KEEP WARM/CANCEL.
- When the steam is completely released, carefully remove the cooker's lid. Drain the beans and reserve.
- To prepare curry mixture, in a saucepan, warm the remaining 1 tablespoon of oil; sauté the onions until they are tender.
- Add the rest of the above ingredients and cook for about 5 minutes, stirring frequently.
- Stir the curry mixture into the prepared beans; mix to combine well. Serve warm and enjoy!

306. Navy Beans and Tomato Delight

Ready in about 40 minutes
Servings 6

Every home cook has their own secret ingredient to the bean dishes. What is your secret recipe ingredient for this amazing food?

Per serving: 399 Calories; 3.3g Fat; 74.2g Carbs; 22.1g Protein; 10.7g Sugars

Ingredients

2 ½ cups navy beans, soaked overnight
4 tomatoes, chopped
1 teaspoon minced chile pepper
2 shallots, chopped
2 bell peppers, chopped
1 cup turnips, chopped
1/2 cup celery with leaves, chopped
2 parsnips, chopped
2 teaspoons grapeseed oil
1 ½ teaspoons red pepper, flakes, crushed
Kosher salt and ground black pepper, to taste
3 cups water

Directions

- Press the BEANS/LENTILS key and use the cook time selector to adjust to 30 minutes.
- Heat grapeseed oil and sauté the parsnip, turnips, celery, peppers, and shallots. Sauté until the vegetables have softened, about 6 minutes.
- Then add the remaining ingredients and stir well. Place the lid on the Power pressure cooker XL, lock the lid and switch the pressure release valve to closed.
- Once the timer reaches 0, the cooker will automatically switch to KEEP WARM/CANCEL.
- When the steam is completely released, carefully remove the cooker's lid. Enjoy!

307. Hot-and-Sour Pepper and Chickpea Soup

Ready in about 20 minutes
Servings 4

This silky and satisfying soup includes vegan essentials like chickpeas, yams and tamari sauce. Keep in mind that chickpeas double in volume after soaking.

Per serving: 317 Calories; 7g Fat; 54.1g Carbs; 12.9g Protein; 9.5g Sugars

Ingredients

2 bell peppers, divined and chopped
6 ounces chickpeas, soaked overnight
4 ½ cups vegetable stock, preferably homemade
2 shallots, thinly sliced
1 cup fresh chives, thinly sliced
1 cup yams, peeled and diced
3 teaspoons olive oil
1/2 teaspoon white pepper
2 tablespoons tamari sauce
2 tablespoons cider vinegar

Directions

- Press the BEANS/LENTILS key and use the cook time selector to adjust to 15 minutes.
- Then, heat the oil and sauté the shallots until it's translucent, for 3 minutes.
- Add the remaining ingredients, minus fresh chives.
- Place the lid on the Power pressure cooker XL, lock the lid and switch the pressure release valve to closed.
- Once the timer reaches 0, the cooker will automatically switch to KEEP WARM/CANCEL.
- When the steam is completely released, carefully remove the cooker's lid. Serve warm topped with fresh chopped chives.

308. Easy Lemony Brussels Sprouts

Ready in about 15 minutes
Servings 4

There are so many reasons to eat more Brussels sprouts; they lower cholesterol, fight free radicals, help improve energy levels, etc. And they are super yummy when cooked in the Power pressure cooker XL.

Per serving: 168 Calories; 10.8g Fat; 16.8g Carbs; 6g Protein; 4g Sugars

Ingredients

1 lemon, grated peel and juiced
1 ½ pounds Brussels sprouts
3 tablespoons grapeseed oil
Sea salt and ground black pepper, to taste
1 ½ cups water

Directions

- Place the water and a rack in the Power pressure cooker XL; add a steamer basket.
- Arrange the Brussels sprouts in the steamer basket. Choose the FISH/VEGETABLES/STEAM and use the cook time selector to adjust to 4 minutes.
- Place the lid on the Power pressure cooker XL, lock the lid and switch the pressure release valve to closed.
- Once the timer reaches 0, the cooker will automatically switch to KEEP WARM/CANCEL.
- Sprinkle with salt and black pepper; drizzle with olive oil and serve.

309. Breakfast Dessert Quinoa

Ready in about 10 minutes
Servings 2

Ta-da! A flavorful dessert breakfast with a vegan flair. Adjust it to suit your taste by increasing or decreasing the spices or adding a sweetener.

Per serving: 574 Calories; 13.3g Fat; 98.4g Carbs; 18.8g Protein; 17.2g Sugars

Ingredients

1 ¼ cups quinoa
3 nectarines, peeled, cored, and diced
1/2 cup rice milk
1/4 cup hazelnuts, chopped
1/4 teaspoon cardamom
1/3 teaspoon vanilla essence
1/4 teaspoon ground cinnamon
2 cups water

Directions

- Put all of the above ingredients into your Power pressure cooker XL. Press the RICE/RISOTTO key once to select 6 minutes.
- Place the lid on the Power pressure cooker XL, lock the lid and switch the pressure release valve to closed.
- Once the timer reaches 0, the cooker will automatically switch to KEEP WARM/CANCEL.
- When the steam is completely released, carefully remove the cooker's lid. Serve with some extra non-dairy milk if desired.

310. Spicy Couscous Chowder

Ready in about 15 minutes
Servings 8

This healthy soup goes beautifully with garlic croutons and roasted nuts. Would you rather have a chunky chowder? For that matter, don't blend it too much.

Per serving: 256 Calories; 4.5g Fat; 45.6g Carbs; 7.6g Protein; 1.5g Sugars

Ingredients

1 teaspoons chile powder
2 ½ cups dried couscous
1 ½ cups unsweetened almond milk
2 tablespoons grapeseed oil
2 onions, thinly sliced
1 tablespoon minced garlic
3 ½ cups vegetable stock
1/2 teaspoon garam masala
Salt and ground black pepper, to taste

Directions

- Press the RICE/RISOTTO key. Heat the oil and sauté the onions until tender and translucent, about 3 minutes. Add the garlic, garam masala, and chile powder; then, sauté for 30 seconds more.
- Pour in the stock and almond milk. Place the lid on the Power pressure cooker XL, lock the lid and switch the pressure release valve to closed. Cook for 6 minutes.
- Once the timer reaches 0, the cooker will automatically switch to KEEP WARM/CANCEL.
- When the steam is completely released, carefully remove the cooker's lid.
- Season with salt and pepper according to your taste. Add the soup to a food processor and purée until smooth; work in batches. Divide puréed soup among soup bowls and serve warm.

311. The Best Vegan Stew Ever

Ready in about 20 minutes
Servings 4

This hearty and colorful stew is inexpensive, healthy and filling - great for the main course to impress your vegan mates.

Per serving: 365 Calories; 4.4g Fat; 77.6g Carbs; 6.8g Protein; 20g Sugars

Ingredients

1 teaspoon habanero pepper, minced
2 bell peppers, diced
2 ripe tomatoes, finely chopped
2 white onions, chopped
1 cup parsnips, chopped
1 cup green peas
1/3 cup barbecue sauce
2 carrots, chopped
4 sweet potatoes, peeled and diced
1 tablespoon olive oil
2 tablespoons ketchup
1/3 teaspoon cayenne pepper
1/2 teaspoon salt
1/3 teaspoon black pepper

Directions

- Press the SOUP/STEW key. Heat olive oil and sauté the onions, carrots, parsnip, and peppers until all the vegetables are soft, about 6 minutes.
- Add the remaining ingredients. Add the water to cover the ingredients.
- Place the lid on the Power pressure cooker XL, lock the lid and switch the pressure release valve to closed. Cook for 10 minutes.
- Once the timer reaches 0, the cooker will automatically switch to KEEP WARM/CANCEL. When the steam is completely released, carefully remove the cooker's lid. Serve right away.

312. Vegan Sausage and Potato Stew

Ready in about 20 minutes
Servings 6

This satisfying yet super healthy stew is all cooked in the Power pressure cooker XL for minimum washing up!

Per serving: 358 Calories; 4.8g Fat; 66.4g Carbs; 14.1g Protein; 5.5g Sugars

Ingredients

6 vegan sausages, thinly sliced
9 russet potatoes, diced
3 cloves garlic, peeled
2 cups corn kernels, frozen
1/2 teaspoon dried basil
1/2 teaspoon cayenne pepper
Salt and black pepper, to taste
8 cups water

Directions

- Add the water and potatoes to your Power pressure cooker XL.
- Press the SOUP/STEW key. Place the lid on the Power pressure cooker XL, lock the lid and switch the pressure release valve to closed. Cook for 10 minutes.
- Once the timer reaches 0, the cooker will automatically switch to KEEP WARM/CANCEL. When the steam is completely released, carefully remove the cooker's lid.
- Add the remaining ingredients and press the FISH/VEGETABLES/STEAM key. Cook for 2 minutes; let the pressure drop on its own.
- Remove the ingredients from the cooker with a slotted spoon. Serve and enjoy!

313. Vegan Oats with Dried Figs

Ready in about 20 minutes
Servings 2

Whip up this vegan breakfast in less than 20 minutes and amaze your beloved one. This recipe is easily doubled as well.

Per serving: 409 Calories; 10.1g Fat; 78.5g Carbs; 6.7g Protein; 47.1g Sugars

Ingredients

1 ½ cups steel-cut oats
1/2 cup dried figs, roughly chopped
2 tablespoons agave nectar
1 tablespoon coconut oil
3/4 cup fresh orange juice
A pinch of freshly grated nutmeg
1/3 teaspoon ground cinnamon
4 cups water

Directions

- Add a metal rack and 1 cup of water to the bottom of your Power pressure cooker XL.
- Add all of the above ingredients to a baking bowl that fits inside the cooker. Stir to combine well.
- Press the SOUP/STEW key. Place the lid on the Power pressure cooker XL, lock the lid and switch the pressure release valve to closed. Cook for 10 minutes.
- Once the timer reaches 0, the cooker will automatically switch to KEEP WARM/CANCEL.
- When the steam is completely released, carefully remove the cooker's lid. Serve right away!

314. Aromatic Zucchini Stew

Ready in about 20 minutes
Servings 4

This vegan dish is bountiful and nutritious and it is ready to eat in under 20 minutes. Serve with lots of homemade bread and it is guaranteed to be a hit with your guests.

Per serving: 216 Calories; 1.7g Fat; 36.1g Carbs; 15.7g Protein; 5.1g Sugars

Ingredients

1 pound zucchini, cut into cubes
3 cups vegetable broth
2 carrots, chopped
1 can kidney beans, drained
1/2 cup celery, chopped
1 tomato, chopped
1 teaspoon fennel seeds
1/2 teaspoon cayenne pepper
1/2 teaspoon cumin
1/3 teaspoon ground black pepper
1/2 teaspoon salt
1/2 teaspoon celery seeds
1 ½ cups water

Directions

- Add all of the above ingredients to your Power pressure cooker XL.
- Press the SOUP/STEW key. Place the lid on the Power pressure cooker XL, lock the lid and switch the pressure release valve to closed. Cook for 10 minutes.
- Once the timer reaches 0, the cooker will automatically switch to KEEP WARM/CANCEL.
- When the steam is completely released, carefully remove the cooker's lid. Next, ladle the stew into individual serving dishes.
- Serve warm topped with grated vegan cheese if desired.

315. Broccoli and Pepper Stew

Ready in about 25 minutes
Servings 4

Is there anything better than rich warm stew during winter weekdays? Serve warm over rice or pasta.

Per serving: 296 Calories; 17.3g Fat; 28.1g Carbs; 11.9g Protein; 6.9g Sugars

Ingredients

1 head broccoli, chopped into small florets
2 bell peppers, thinly sliced
1 (14-ounce) can full-fat coconut milk
1 teaspoon minced garlic
3 teaspoons canola oil
2 shallots, chopped
4 cups vegetable broth
1 bunch lacinato kale, roughly chopped
2 teaspoons fresh lime juice

Directions

- Press the FISH/VEGETABLES/STEAM key. Warm the oil and sauté the shallots and garlic until they become tender.
- Add the remaining ingredients, except for the kale, to the Power pressure cooker XL.
- Place the lid on the Power pressure cooker XL, lock the lid and switch the pressure release valve to closed. Cook for 10 minutes.
- Once the timer reaches 0, the cooker will automatically switch to KEEP WARM/CANCEL.
- When the steam is completely released, carefully remove the cooker's lid.
- Stir in the kale, place the lid on the cooker and let it stand for 10 minutes. Enjoy!

316. Delicious Cabbage with Peppers and Walnuts

Ready in about 20 minutes
Servings 8

Cabbage, peppers and spices are all cooked together in this flavorful vegetable dish for an appetizing lunch. You can use almonds instead of walnuts.

Per serving: 107 Calories; 6.5g Fat; 9.6g Carbs; 3.7g Protein; 4.8g Sugars

Ingredients

2 pounds cabbage, shredded
1 cup bell peppers, peeled, cored, and sliced
1/2 cup coarsely chopped walnuts, for garnish
1 cup scallions, chopped
1 tablespoon olive oil
1/4 cup dry wine
1/2 teaspoon salt
1/4 teaspoon freshly ground black pepper
1 teaspoon cayenne pepper

Directions

- Press the FISH/VEGETABLES/STEAM key. Warm the oil and sauté the scallions until soft. Stir in the peppers and dry wine.
- Stir the cabbage into the Power pressure cooker XL. Add the remaining ingredients. Place the lid on the Power pressure cooker XL, lock the lid and switch the pressure release valve to closed. Cook for 10 minutes.
- Once the timer reaches 0, the cooker will automatically switch to KEEP WARM/CANCEL.
- When the steam is completely released, carefully remove the cooker's lid.
- Season with salt, black pepper, and cayenne pepper. Sprinkle with toasted walnuts and serve.

317. Easy Saucy Parsnips

Ready in about 5 minutes
Servings 4

You don't have to heat up your whole stove just for cooking your favorite parsnip appetizer. You can get even better parsnips in your Power pressure cooker XL.

Per serving: 92 Calories; 3.8g Fat; 15g Carbs; 1g Protein; 4g Sugars

Ingredients

6 parsnips, cut into halves lengthwise
1/4 teaspoon allspice
1/2 teaspoon harissa powder
3/4 cup water
3 teaspoons olive oil
1 teaspoon garlic powder
Kosher salt and ground black pepper, to your liking

Directions

- Add all of the above ingredients to the Power pressure cooker XL. Now, stir to combine well. Press the FISH/VEGETABLES/STEAM key.
- Place the lid on the Power pressure cooker XL, lock the lid and switch the pressure release valve to closed. Cook for 2 minutes.
- Once the timer reaches 0, the cooker will automatically switch to KEEP WARM/CANCEL.
- When the steam is completely released, carefully remove the cooker's lid. Serve at room temperature.

318. Colorful Wild Rice Salad

Ready in about 30 minutes
Servings 8

The combination of the creamy rice and fresh veggies is fitting for brunch, dinner or light spring lunch. Serve with enough tortillas or homemade bread.

Per serving: 258 Calories; 6.1g Fat; 46g Carbs; 8.1g Protein; 6.7g Sugars

Ingredients

2 tablespoons tomato ketchup
2 cups wild rice
2 carrots, chopped
1 serrano pepper, deveined and chopped
1/3 cup balsamic vinegar
2 tablespoons extra-virgin olive oil
2 white onions, peeled and chopped
2 cups frozen corn kernels, thawed
1/2 head cabbage, shredded
3 teaspoons canola oil
1 cup celery, finely diced
2 tablespoons fresh cilantro, roughly chopped
1/4 teaspoon freshly ground black pepper
1/2 teaspoon sea salt
6 cups water

Directions

- Press the RICE/RISOTTO key. Then, use the cook time selector to adjust to 25 minutes
- Add the canola oil, water and rice to your Power pressure cooker XL. Place the lid on the Power pressure cooker XL, lock the lid and switch the pressure release valve to closed.
- Cook for 2 minutes.
- Once the timer reaches 0, the cooker will automatically switch to KEEP WARM/CANCEL.
- When the steam is completely released, carefully remove the cooker's lid.
- Make the dressing by processing salt, black pepper, cilantro, balsamic vinegar, extra-virgin olive oil, and onions in your blender.
- Toss the cooked rice with the remaining ingredients. Dress the salad and serve well-chilled.

319. Spicy Lentil Salad with Currants

Ready in about 25 minutes +
chilling time
Servings 12

Lentils are a tasty staple in a vegan diet! They protect your heart and digestive system, lower cholesterol, and regulate diabetes.

Per serving: 216 Calories; 1.9g Fat; 35.9g Carbs; 14.5g Protein; 4g Sugars

Ingredients

3 cups dry green lentils
1 cup currants
2 ½ cups frozen green peas, thawed
1 cup scallions, chopped
1 cup Roma tomatoes, thinly sliced
3 cloves garlic, minced
1 tablespoon extra-virgin olive oil
1/4 cup champagne vinegar
1/4 cup tamari sauce
2 teaspoons chili paste
Salt and freshly cracked black pepper, to taste
1/2 teaspoon red pepper flakes, for garnish

Directions

- Add the lentils to the Power pressure cooker XL. Add the water to cover your lentils. Press the BEANS/LENTILS key and use the cook time selector to adjust to 15 minutes.
- Next, prepare the dressing by whisking tamari sauce, chili paste, garlic, extra-virgin olive oil, and vinegar. Refrigerate this dressing overnight.
- Place the lid on the Power pressure cooker XL, lock the lid and switch the pressure release valve to closed.
- Once the timer reaches 0, the cooker will automatically switch to KEEP WARM/CANCEL.
- When the steam is completely released, carefully remove the cooker's lid.
- Drain the lentils and transfer them to a salad bowl. Add the remaining ingredients. Drizzle with reserved dressing and serve.

320. Aromatic Tomato with Garbanzo Beans

Ready in about 30 minutes
Servings 6

Garbanzo beans, along with fragrant seasonings, go well with tomatoes in every recipe, whatever cooking method you prefer to use. But these garbanzo beans are made saucy and delicious in no time.

Per serving: 292 Calories; 5.8g Fat; 48.8g Carbs; 14.1g Protein; 11.2g Sugars

Ingredients

2 ripe tomatoes, chopped
2 cups garbanzo beans, soaked overnight
1 cup celery with leaves, peeled and chopped
1 cup bell peppers, deveined and chopped
4 spring onions, chopped
1/2 cup parsnip, chopped
1 cup carrots, peeled and chopped
2 teaspoons coconut oil
1 teaspoon fresh rosemary, minced
1/2 teaspoon cayenne pepper
Kosher salt and ground black pepper, to taste
2 ½ cups water

Directions

- Press the RICE/RISOTTO key and use the cook time selector to adjust to 25 minutes.
- Heat coconut oil and sauté the carrots, celery, parsnip, bell peppers, and spring onions. Sauté until they have softened.
- Then add garbanzo beans, tomatoes and water; give it a good stir. Place the lid on the Power pressure cooker XL, lock the lid and switch the pressure release valve to closed.
- Once the timer reaches 0, the cooker will automatically switch to KEEP WARM/CANCEL.
- When the steam is completely released, carefully remove the cooker's lid. Season with cayenne pepper, kosher salt, and ground black pepper. Enjoy!

321. The Best Vegan Gumbo Ever

Ready in about 1 hour 30 minutes
Servings 6

When it comes to a roux, the basic ingredient of the traditional gumbo, the longer it cooks the darker it gets. Anyway, don't cook it more than 30 minutes.

Per serving: 548 Calories; 28.1g Fat; 64.5g Carbs; 10.4g Protein; 7.7g Sugars

Ingredients

1 ½ pounds vegan sausage, sliced
2 cups frozen or fresh okra, cut into rings
1 cup parsnips, chopped
2 cloves garlic, minced
2 carrots, diced
1/2 cup brown rice flour
2 onions, chopped
1 teaspoon habanero pepper, chopped
2 bell peppers, diced
1 cup turnips, diced
2/3 cup vegetable shortening
3 ½ cups vegetable stock
2 teaspoons soy sauce
3 cups cooked white rice
1/2 teaspoon cayenne pepper
Sea salt and black pepper, to taste
1/2 cup fresh cilantro, chopped
1 bay leaf
2 tablespoons fresh parsley, chopped
2 ½ cups water

Directions

- Press the SOUP/STEW key. To make the roux: Warm the vegetable shortening; add the flour and cook, stirring often, until the roux gets a brown rich color, approximately 20 minutes.
- Add the onions, peppers, carrots, turnip, parsnips, and garlic to the roux; sauté for 6 minutes. Press the CANCEL key.
- Add the remaining ingredients, except for the cooked rice. Press the SOUP/STEW key and use the cook time selector to adjust to 60 minutes. Place the lid on the Power pressure cooker XL, lock the lid and switch the pressure release valve to closed.
- Once the timer reaches 0, the cooker will automatically switch to KEEP WARM/CANCEL.
- When the steam is completely released, carefully remove the cooker's lid. Serve over cooked rice.

322. Garbanzo Bean Stew

Ready in about 35 minutes
Servings 4

The Power pressure cooker XL turns vegetables, garbanzo beans and spices into a fresh and aromatic vegan dish.

Per serving: 432 Calories; 5.9g Fat; 79.2g Carbs; 21.1g Protein; 21.1g Sugars

Ingredients

12 ounces garbanzo beans, drained and soaked
1/2 head red cabbage, shredded
1 pound zucchini, diced
2 carrots, diced
2 parsnips, chopped
2 tablespoons fresh parsley, roughly chopped
2 tomatoes, chopped
5 cups vegetable stock
1 teaspoon fennel seeds
1/2 teaspoon salt
1/2 teaspoon ground black pepper
1/2 teaspoon celery seeds

Directions

- Press the RICE/RISOTTO key and use the cook time selector to adjust to 25 minutes.
- Add all of the above ingredients to your Power pressure cooker XL.
- Place the lid on the Power pressure cooker XL, lock the lid and switch the pressure release valve to closed.
- Once the timer reaches 0, the cooker will automatically switch to KEEP WARM/CANCEL.
- When the steam is completely released, carefully remove the cooker's lid.
- To serve, ladle the stew into individual bowls. Enjoy!

323. Aromatic Braised Broccoli

Ready in about 20 minutes
Servings 6

Broccoli with its mild flavor pairs well with onions and garlic. For an extra dose of flavor, drizzle with truffle oil and serve.

Per serving: 75 Calories; 2.7g Fat; 11.1g Carbs; 4g Protein; 3.1g Sugars

Ingredients

1 large-sized head broccoli, cut into small florets
1 cup white onions, peeled and finely chopped
3 teaspoons coconut oil
1 tablespoon finely minced garlic
1/3 teaspoon dried basil
1/3 teaspoon salt
1/2 teaspoon cayenne pepper
1/3 teaspoon ground black pepper
1 cup water

Directions

- Press the FISH/VEGETABLES/STEAM key and use the cook time selector to adjust to 4 minutes.
- Heat coconut oil and sauté the onions and garlic, stirring frequently, about 3 minutes. Add the broccoli florets and continue sautéing an additional 4 minutes.
- Sprinkle with salt, ground black pepper, cayenne pepper and dried basil; pour in the water.
- Place the lid on the Power pressure cooker XL, lock the lid and switch the pressure release valve to closed.
- Once the timer reaches 0, the cooker will automatically switch to KEEP WARM/CANCEL.
- When the steam is completely released, carefully remove the cooker's lid. Serve over cooked pasta.

324. Saucy Brussels Sprouts with Tahini Sauce

Ready in about 15 minutes
Servings 4

This light and bountiful Brussels sprout salad goes well with herbed croutons and sparkling wine.

Per serving: 197 Calories; 11.5g Fat; 23g Carbs; 5.6g Protein; 12.1g Sugars

Ingredients

1 pound Brussels sprouts, halved
1 cup vegetable stock
1 carrot, chopped
1 tablespoon minced garlic
1 teaspoon chipotle pepper, finely minced
1 teaspoon shallot powder

For the Sauce:
2 tablespoons tahini
1/4 cup sherry vinegar
2 tablespoons honey
2 tablespoons extra-virgin olive oil
1/2 teaspoon saffron
Salt and black pepper, to taste

Directions

- Add Brussels sprouts, carrot, garlic, shallot powder and chipotle pepper to the Power pressure cooker XL. Then, pour in the vegetable stock and give it a good stir.
- Press the FISH/VEGETABLES/STEAM key and use the cook time selector to adjust to 4 minutes.
- Place the lid on the Power pressure cooker XL, lock the lid and switch the pressure release valve to closed.
- Once the timer reaches 0, the cooker will automatically switch to KEEP WARM/CANCEL.
- When the steam is completely released, carefully remove the cooker's lid. Meanwhile, make the sauce by mixing all the sauce ingredients in your blender or food processor.
- Toss the vegetables with tahini sauce and transfer to a large-sized bowl; serve.

325. Penne Pasta with Green Peas

Ready in about 20 minutes
Servings 8

Don't settle for ordinary, boring pasta bowl. Use your Power pressure cooker XL and make one of the best pasta dishes you've ever eaten. Chipotle peppers add a touch of heat to the pasta while nutritional yeast gives a cheesy flavor and nutritional value.

Per serving: 464 Calories; 6.8g Fat; 82.3g Carbs; 17.5g Protein; 6.2g Sugars

Ingredients

2 box dry penne pasta
2 cups frozen green peas, thawed
1/4 cup white wine
1 cup celery with leaves, finely chopped
2 tablespoons extra-virgin olive oil
2 white onions, peeled and chopped
1 teaspoon chipotle pepper, seeded and minced
2 bell peppers, seeded and chopped
2 plum tomatoes, chopped
2 tablespoons fresh parsley, chopped
2 tablespoons ketchup
2 tablespoons nutritional yeast
1/2 teaspoon sea salt
1/4 teaspoon freshly ground black pepper
3 cups water

Directions

- Press the SOUP/STEW key to set for 10 minutes. Heat the oil and cook the onions, peppers and celery until just tender and fragrant, about 3 minutes.
- Add the remaining ingredients, minus green peas and nutritional yeast.
- Place the lid on the Power pressure cooker XL, lock the lid and switch the pressure release valve to closed.
- Once the timer reaches 0, the cooker will automatically switch to KEEP WARM/CANCEL. When the steam is completely released, carefully remove the cooker's lid.
- Add green peas and place the lid on the cooker. Divide among serving plates and sprinkle with nutritional yeast.

BEANS & GRAINS

326. Salsa and Cannellini Bean Dip

Ready in about 35 minutes
Servings 12

Homemade salsa with beans goes well with corn chips and veggie sticks. Make this dip today for a hearty and healthy appetizer!

Per serving: 85 Calories; 2.6g Fat; 12.5g Carbs; 3.8g Protein; 2.5g Sugars

Ingredients

1/4 cup seeded and chopped jalapenos
3 cups cannellini beans, soaked and rinsed
2 red onions, peeled and chopped
2 ripe tomatoes, chopped
2 tablespoons cilantro, chopped
2 tablespoons olive oil
2 tablespoons lime juice
Salt and black pepper, to taste

Directions

- Press the BEANS/LENTILS key; use the cook time selector to adjust to 30 minutes.
- Add the beans along with 6 cups water. Place the lid on the Power pressure cooker XL, lock the lid and switch the pressure release valve to closed.
- Once the timer reaches 0, the cooker will automatically switch to KEEP WARM/CANCEL. When the steam is completely released, carefully remove the cooker's lid.
- Add the remaining ingredients.
- Lastly, puree the mixture in a food processor, working in batches. Serve with tortilla chips and enjoy!

327. Pinto Bean and Walnut Salad

Ready in about 40 minutes +
chilling time
Servings 12

Pinto beans, colorful vegetables and carefully selected spices are magically transformed into a refreshing and satisfying salad. In this recipe, you can experiment and substitute the other kind of beans for Pinto beans.

Per serving: 265 Calories; 5.3g Fat; 46.8g Carbs; 12.7g Protein; 4.9g Sugars

Ingredients

3 cups pinto beans, soaked and rinsed
1/2 cup coarsely chopped walnuts
2 red onions, peeled and chopped
2 bell peppers, chopped
2 cups frozen corn kernels, thawed
2 tablespoons wine vinegar
2 shallots, chopped
2 carrots, thinly sliced
1 ½ teaspoons white sugar
1 tablespoon olive oil
1 dash hot pepper sauce
2 teaspoons lime juice
1 tablespoon garlic, crushed
1/2 teaspoon chili powder
Salt and freshly cracked black pepper, to taste

Directions

- Press the BEANS/LENTILS key; use the cook time selector to adjust to 30 minutes.
- Place the lid on the Power pressure cooker XL, lock the lid and switch the pressure release valve to closed.
- Once the timer reaches 0, the cooker will automatically switch to KEEP WARM/CANCEL. When the steam is completely released, carefully remove the cooker's lid.
- Now, prepare the vinaigrette by whisking the lime juice, vinegar, hot pepper sauce, sugar, chili powder, garlic, and olive oil. Place the dressing in the refrigerator.
- Next, drain cooked beans and transfer them to a bowl. Toss the beans with the rest of the above ingredients. Drizzle with the well-chilled vinaigrette. Taste and adjust the seasonings. Serve.

328. Lentil and Pea Dip

Ready in about 20 minutes
Servings 12

A creamy and bountiful lentil dip packed full of flavor. Inspired by French lentils and green peas, you can come up with this appetizer recipe that is just scrumptious!

Per serving: 229 Calories; 4.3g Fat; 34.4g Carbs; 14g Protein; 3.3g Sugars

Ingredients

3 cups lentils, French green
2 cups green peas, cooked
2 teaspoons chili paste
1 tablespoon crushed garlic
2 red onions, finely chopped
3 tablespoons extra-virgin olive oil
1 tablespoon wholegrain mustard
Sea salt and ground black pepper, to your liking

Directions

- Place the lentils in your Power pressure cooker XL. Cover with the water. Press the BEANS/LENTIL key and use the cook time selector to adjust to 15 minutes.
- Place the lid on the Power pressure cooker XL, lock the lid and switch the pressure release valve to closed.
- Once the timer reaches 0, the cooker will automatically switch to KEEP WARM/CANCEL. When the steam is completely released, carefully remove the cooker's lid. Transfer to a food processor.
- Add all ingredients, except for the oil, to a bowl of your food processor. Now, gradually and slowly pour the oil in a thin stream. Blend until everything is well incorporated.
- Sprinkle pepper flakes over everything and serve.

329. Lentil and Sweet Potato Stew

Ready in about 20 minutes
Servings 4

This simple but endlessly crave-worthy stew is both delicious and rustic. Try sprinkling in a pinch of paprika or chili powder to spice it up.

Per serving: 494 Calories; 12g Fat; 80.1g Carbs; 16.3g Protein; 6.4g Sugars

Ingredients

1 cup red lentils, drained and rinsed
4 sweet potatoes, peeled and cubed
1 tablespoon crushed garlic
2 yellow onions, chopped
1 cup celery, chopped
2 carrots, chopped
3 cups stock
1/2 stick butter
1/2 teaspoon dried sage
Kosher salt and ground black pepper, to taste
2 sprigs dried thyme

Directions

- Press the RICE/RISOTTO key and use the cook time selector to adjust to 6 minutes.
- Melt the butter and sauté the onions, celery, and carrots; cook, stirring often, until the vegetables have softened, approximately 5 minutes.
- Stir in the garlic and continue cooking for 1 more minutes.
- Add the sweet potatoes, stock, lentils, thyme, sage, salt, and ground black pepper; stir well.
- Place the lid on the Power pressure cooker XL, lock the lid and switch the pressure release valve to closed.
- Once the timer reaches 0, the cooker will automatically switch to KEEP WARM/CANCEL. When the steam is completely released, carefully remove the cooker's lid. Stir just before serving and enjoy!

330. Cannellini Bean and Zucchini Salad

Ready in about 2 hours 10 minutes
Servings 6

Seriously, cannellini beans are weeknight dinner saviors. They have got a nice serving of protein, soluble fiber and carbs. They are delicious and inexpensive!

Per serving: 383 Calories; 10.1g Fat; 62.1g Carbs; 20.3g Protein; 4.4g Sugars

Ingredients

2 ½ cups cannellini beans, soaked overnight
2 zucchinis, diced
2 cloves garlic, peeled and smashed
2 tablespoons canola oil
2 shallots, chopped
1 can crushed tomatoes
2 teaspoons wine vinegar
2 tablespoons extra-virgin olive oil
1/4 teaspoon ground black pepper
2 sprigs fresh rosemary, finely chopped
2 sprigs fresh thyme, finely chopped
1 teaspoon salt
4 ½ cups water

Directions

- Add the beans, water, canola oil, shallots, and garlic to the Power pressure cooker XL.
- Choose the SLOW COOK function. Cook for 2 hours.
- Place the lid on the Power pressure cooker XL, lock the lid and switch the pressure release valve to closed.
- Once the timer reaches 0, the cooker will automatically switch to KEEP WARM/CANCEL. When the steam is completely released, carefully remove the cooker's lid.
- Next step, strain the beans; now transfer the beans to a refrigerator. Transfer to a serving bowl and add the remaining ingredients. Serve well-chilled.

331. Chunky Red Lentil and Fennel Soup

Ready in about 20 minutes
Servings 6

Firstly, bear in mind that red lentils don't require soaking but you can do it and reduce cooking time. Secondly, use a natural pressure release. Enjoy!

Per serving: 439 Calories; 7.3g Fat; 69.6g Carbs; 24g Protein; 7.7g Sugars

Ingredients

2 cups red lentils, soaked and rinsed
1 pound fennel bulb, diced
6 cups broth
1 cup yellow onions, finely chopped
1 cup carrots, chopped
1 rutabaga, chopped
1/3 cup sour cream
3 teaspoons vegetable oil
Sea salt and black pepper, to taste
1/3 teaspoon dried dill weed
2 sprigs fresh thyme
1/3 teaspoon dried rosemary, chopped

Directions

- Press the RICE/RISOTTO key and warm the oil; sauté the onions, carrots, and rutabaga until they are softened.
- Add the thyme, lentils, broth, salt, and black pepper. Place the lid on the Power pressure cooker XL, lock the lid and switch the pressure release valve to closed. Cook for 6 minutes.
- Once the timer reaches 0, the cooker will automatically switch to KEEP WARM/CANCEL. Let the pressure drop on its own. When the steam is completely released, carefully remove the cooker's lid.
- Next, stir in dried dill weed, rosemary, and fennel bulb. Press the SOUP/STEW key and cook for 10 minutes.
- Serve with a dollop of sour cream.

332. Garbanzo Beans and Sausage Soup

Ready in about 35 minutes
Servings 8

Never underestimate the power of garbanzo beans – they're filling, healthy and easy to cook, as this dish proves.

Per serving: 439 Calories; 14.2g Fat; 62.2g Carbs; 19.6g Protein; 14.5g Sugars

Ingredients

3 cups garbanzo beans, soaked overnight
4 beef sausages, thinly sliced
2 bell peppers, chopped
1 teaspoon crushed garlic
2 tablespoons ketchup
2 small-sized red onions, finely chopped
1 cup carrots, peeled and finely chopped
1 can tomatoes, crushed
2 ears of corn, cut into 1-inch wheels
3 teaspoons grapeseed oil
1/2 teaspoon turmeric
1/2 cup fresh parsley, minced
Sea salt and ground black pepper, to taste

Directions

- Add all of the above ingredients to the Power pressure cooker XL. Press the SOUP/STEW key, then, the cook time selector to adjust to 30 minutes.
- Place the lid on the Power pressure cooker XL, lock the lid and switch the pressure release valve to closed. Once the timer reaches 0, the cooker will automatically switch to KEEP WARM/CANCEL.
- When the steam is completely released, carefully remove the cooker's lid.
- Ladle into eight soup bowls and serve warm.

333. Easy Moong Dal with Prawns

Ready in about 25 minutes
Servings 6

This healthy one-pot recipe combines amazing lentils with seafood and peppers. It is healthy, filling and easy to prepare.

Per serving: 288 Calories; 3.5g Fat; 35.8g Carbs; 29g Protein; 6.1g Sugars

Ingredients

2 ½ cups moong dal
1 pound tiger prawns, frozen
1 cup leeks, chopped
2 ½ tablespoons miso paste
2 bell peppers, stemmed, cored, and chopped
3 ½ cups vegetable stock
2 teaspoons grapeseed oil
2 ripe plum tomatoes, chopped
1 teaspoon molasses
1 teaspoon sea salt
1/4 teaspoon ground black pepper
1/3 teaspoon cumin powder

Directions

- Press the BEANS/LENTILS key and warm the oil; now, sauté the prawns along with leeks and peppers for 5 minutes. Press the CANCEL key and reserve the prawns.
- Next, add the remaining ingredients to the Power pressure cooker XL. Press the BEANS/LENTILS key; use the cook time selector to adjust to 15 minutes.
- Place the lid on the Power pressure cooker XL, lock the lid and switch the pressure release valve to closed. Once the timer reaches 0, the cooker will automatically switch to KEEP WARM/CANCEL.
- When the steam is completely released, carefully remove the cooker's lid. Add the reserved prawns and serve. Stir and serve.

334. Kidney Beans with Tomato and Bacon

Ready in about 35 minutes
Servings 4

Pressure cooked kidney beans are tender and flavorsome. This versatile food goes well with your favorite vegetables and meat. In this recipe, the secret lies in the simple approach – fry the bacon to enhance the flavor.

Per serving: 416 Calories; 7.4g Fat; 64.3g Carbs; 25.5g Protein; 6g Sugars

Ingredients

2 cups kidney beans, soaked overnight and rinsed
1 ½ cups ripe tomatoes, chopped
2 slices bacon, diced
2 onions, thinly sliced
2 teaspoons vegetable oil
4 cups water
1/2 teaspoon cumin
1 sprig rosemary
2 sprigs thyme
1/4 cup fresh parsley, chopped

Directions

- Press the BEANS/LENTILS key and warm the oil; then, fry the bacon for 3 minutes, stirring frequently; reserve.
- Add the onions, thyme and rosemary; cook for 2 minutes longer or until fragrant. Press the CANCEL key. Add the remaining ingredients.
- Press the RICE/RISOTTO key and use the cook time selector to adjust to 25 minutes.
- Place the lid on the Power pressure cooker XL, lock the lid and switch the pressure release valve to closed. Once the timer reaches 0, the cooker will automatically switch to KEEP WARM/CANCEL.
- When the steam is completely released, carefully remove the cooker's lid. Add the reserved bacon, stir and serve in individual bowls.

335. Mom's Curried Chickpeas

Ready in about 40 minutes
Servings 8

Whether served as a lunch or a side dish, this recipe will be sure to impress. Consider adding a pinch of ground coriander, a splash of coconut milk, or a small pinch of ground ginger. Enjoy!

Per serving: 326 Calories; 8.3g Fat; 50.6g Carbs; 15.3g Protein; 10.1g Sugars

Ingredients

3 cups chickpeas, soaked and rinsed
2 tablespoons curry powder
2 tablespoons vegetable oil
2 Roma tomatoes, chopped
3 cloves garlic, minced
2 yellow onions, chopped
1/2 teaspoon ground black pepper
1/2 teaspoon cumin
1/2 teaspoon sea salt
2 teaspoons chipotle powder
6 cups water

Directions

- Add the chickpeas, water, 1 tablespoon of vegetable oil, salt, and black pepper to your Power pressure cooker XL.
- Press the BEANS/LENTILS key and use the cook time selector to adjust to 30 minutes.
- Place the lid on the Power pressure cooker XL, lock the lid and switch the pressure release valve to closed. Once the timer reaches 0, the cooker will automatically switch to KEEP WARM/CANCEL.
- When the steam is completely released, carefully remove the cooker's lid.
- To prepare the curry mixture: warm the remaining 1 tablespoon of the oil in a saucepan; sauté the garlic and onions until they have softened.
- Add the remaining ingredients; cook an additional 5 minutes, stirring continuously.
- Stir the curried mixture into the prepared chickpeas; mix to combine well. Serve warm and enjoy!

336. Summer Two-Bean Salad

Ready in about 20 minutes +
chilling time
Servings 6

This flavorful and refreshing salad is brimming with colorful vegetables, a Dijon vinaigrette, and aromatic garlic paste.

Per serving: 473 Calories; 14.1g Fat; 69g Carbs; 21.4g Protein; 5.2g Sugars

Ingredients

1 ½ cups Adzuki beans, soaked overnight
1 ½ cups black beans, soaked overnight
2 bell peppers, deveined and chopped
2 tablespoons grapeseed oil
2 small-sized onions, chopped
1 can tomatoes, crushed
1 tablespoon garlic paste
1/4 cup extra-virgin olive oil
2 teaspoons wine vinegar
2 teaspoons Dijon mustard
2 sprigs fresh thyme, finely chopped
Sea salt and freshly ground black pepper, to your liking
6 cups water

Directions

- Add the water, beans, grapeseed oil, and onions to the Power pressure cooker XL. Press the BEANS/LENTILS key and use the cook time selector to adjust to 15 minutes.
- Place the lid on the Power pressure cooker XL, lock the lid and switch the pressure release valve to closed. Once the timer reaches 0, the cooker will automatically switch to KEEP WARM/CANCEL.
- When the steam is completely released, carefully remove the cooker's lid.
- Strain the beans and transfer them to a refrigerator in order to cool completely. Transfer to a serving bowl and add the rest of the above ingredients. Gently stir to combine and serve.

337. The Easiest Lima Beans Ever

Ready in about 20 minutes
Servings 6

Is there anything better than a simple bowl of tender, buttery beans? Serve as a side dish with your favorite meatballs.

Per serving: 79 Calories; 2.8g Fat; 10.5g Carbs; 3.6g Protein; 0.8g Sugars

Ingredients

3 teaspoons olive oil
2 cups lima beans, soaked and rinsed
2 gloves garlic, finely minced
1/2 teaspoon ground black pepper
1/2 teaspoon ground bay leaf
1/2 teaspoon salt
4 cups water

Directions

- Add all of the above ingredients to the Power pressure cooker XL. Press the BEANS/LENTILS key and use the cook time selector to adjust to 15 minutes.
- Place the lid on the Power pressure cooker XL, lock the lid and switch the pressure release valve to closed. Once the timer reaches 0, the cooker will automatically switch to KEEP WARM/CANCEL.
- When the steam is completely released, carefully remove the cooker's lid. Serve hot.

338. Yellow Split Lentil with Beef

Ready in about 30 minutes
Servings 4

This bountiful and yummy dish combines lentils, stew meat and potatoes for an amazing family lunch. Try adding another combination of spices to satisfy your senses.

Per serving: 372 Calories; 7.4g Fat; 50.9g Carbs; 26.6g Protein; 6.2g Sugars

Ingredients

1 ½ cups yellow split lentils, rinsed
1/2 pound beef stew meat, cubed
1 cup scallions, chopped
2 garlic cloves, minced
4 potatoes, peeled and diced
1 cup carrots, chopped
3 teaspoons vegetable oil
1 cup celery, chopped
5 cups stock
Sea salt and freshly cracked black pepper
1 teaspoon saffron

Directions

- Press the CHICKEN/MEAT key and heat the oil; sweat the scallions and garlic for 3 minutes. Add the meat and cook for 6 minutes more or until they're no longer pink.
- Add the remaining ingredients. Place the lid on the Power pressure cooker XL, lock the lid and switch the pressure release valve to closed.
- Press the TIME ADJUSTMENT key until you reach 20 minutes.
- When the steam is completely released, carefully remove the cooker's lid. Serve.

339. Navy Bean Chili

Ready in about 25 minutes
Servings 8

What's the fastest and easiest way to get dinner on the table? The Power pressure cooker XL, of course!

Per serving: 387 Calories; 7.8g Fat; 46g Carbs; 33.8g Protein; 3g Sugars

Ingredients

1/2 (48-ounces) jar Navy beans
1 pound mixed ground meat
1 tablespoon vegetable oil
1 teaspoon minced garlic
1/2 cup Swiss cheese, freshly grated
Kosher salt and ground black pepper
3 cups water

Directions

- Press the SOUP/STEW key and warm the oil. Now, cook the ground meat until no longer pink, about 4 minutes.
- Add the remaining ingredients. Place the lid on the Power pressure cooker XL, lock the lid and switch the pressure release valve to closed. Cook for 10 minutes.
- Once the timer reaches 0, the cooker will automatically switch to KEEP WARM/CANCEL.
- When the steam is completely released, carefully remove the cooker's lid.
- Ladle the stew into serving dishes; top each serving with grated cheese. Serve.

340. Two-Bean Christmas Relish

Ready in about 35 minutes
Servings 12

Let this relish sit in your refrigerator at least 3 hours to allow the flavors to blend nicely. In this recipe, you can freely omit the sesame paste (tahini).

Per serving: 299 Calories; 7.3g Fat; 44.2g Carbs; 15.8g Protein; 2.2g Sugars

Ingredients

15 ounces pinto beans, rinsed
15 ounces navy beans, rinsed
1/3 cup extra-virgin olive oil
1/3 cup fresh scallions, finely minced
1 tablespoon sesame paste
1/3 cup red wine vinegar
1 teaspoon garlic powder
1 teaspoon onion powder
Salt and ground black pepper, to taste
8 cups water

Directions

- Add the water and beans to the Power pressure cooker XL. Sprinkle with sea salt. Place the lid on the Power pressure cooker XL, lock the lid and switch the pressure release valve to closed.
- Press the BEANS/LENTILS key and use the cook time selector to adjust to 30 minutes.
- Once the timer reaches 0, the cooker will automatically switch to KEEP WARM/CANCEL. When the steam is completely released, carefully remove the cooker's lid.
- Transfer to a nice serving dish. Stir in the remaining ingredients; serve well-chilled with your favorite dippers.

341. Favorite Pinto Beans Appetizer

Ready in about 25 minutes
Servings 4

There're so many delicious ways to eat pinto beans. This one can be served as a side dish to complement the main roast dish or as an appetizer for a special dinner party!

Per serving: 417 Calories; 12.8g Fat; 53.8g Carbs; 22.1g Protein; 2.2g Sugars

Ingredients

12 ounces pinto beans, soaked
2 cups stock, preferably homemade
2 tablespoons grapeseed oil
1/2 cup grated cheddar cheese
1 teaspoon crushed garlic
1 tablespoon fresh parsley, chopped
1 teaspoon sea salt
1/2 teaspoon freshly cracked black pepper

Directions

- Place the beans, parsley, garlic, and salt in your Power pressure cooker XL. Add black pepper, stock and oil.
- Press the SOUP/STEW key and, then, press the TIME ADJUSTMENT key until you reach 20 minutes.
- Place the lid on the Power pressure cooker XL, lock the lid and switch the pressure release valve to closed.
- Once the timer reaches 0, the cooker will automatically switch to KEEP WARM/CANCEL. When the steam is completely released, carefully remove the cooker's lid.
- Taste and adjust the seasonings; serve immediately topped with cheese. Bon appétit!

342. Herbed Black Bean and Mushroom Spread

Ready in about 25 minutes
Servings 6

Black beans are packed with good fiber and protein as well as unique phytonutrients. They are certain to warm you up during windy and cold days.

Per serving: 287 Calories; 3.4g Fat; 47.2g Carbs; 17.9g Protein; 2.5g Sugars

Ingredients

2 cups black beans, soaked and rinsed
1 cup porcini mushrooms, thinly sliced
1 cup red onions, chopped
2 cups beef bone broth
2 tablespoons red wine vinegar
1 tablespoon lard, melted
1 ½ teaspoons paprika
2 rosemary sprigs, finely chopped
1/2 teaspoon ground cumin
1 teaspoon fennel seeds
1 teaspoon garlic powder
Salt and black pepper, to taste
2 ½ cups water

Directions

- Press the CHICKEN/MEAT key and warm the lard; now, sweat the onions until just tender, about 3 minutes, stirring periodically.
- Add the mushrooms and continue cooking an additional 3 minutes. Press the CANCEL key and reserve the mushroom mixture.
- Add your beans to the Power pressure cooker XL. Choose the BEANS/LENTILS function and use the cook time selector to adjust to 15 minutes.
- Drain the beans; allow the beans to cool. Purée the beans in a food processor. Add the remaining ingredients along with the reserved mushroom mixture.
- Purée until smooth. Transfer to a serving dish; serve well-chilled or at room temperature.

343. Bean and Pork Stew

Ready in about 35 minutes
Servings 8

These Brazilian-inspired beans cook perfectly in your Power pressure cooker XL. Pressure cooking is one of the best ways to enjoy their nurturing essence.

Per serving: 281 Calories; 4.7g Fat; 33.3g Carbs; 25.9g Protein; 2.6g Sugars

Ingredients

2 cups pinto beans, soaked overnight
1 pound boneless pork shoulder, cut into 1 inch chunks
4 ½ cups chicken stock
2 onions, finely chopped
1 teaspoon minced garlic
3 teaspoons olive oil
1 ½ teaspoons paprika
1 bay leaf
2 tablespoons parsley, chopped
Kosher salt and ground black pepper, to taste

Directions

- Press the CHICKEN/MEAT key and heat olive oil until sizzling; now, brown the meat for 4 to 5 minutes, stirring occasionally. Press the CANCEL key.
- Pour in a splash of chicken stock in order to scrape up any browned bits.
- Next, choose the SOUP/STEW function and then, press the TIME ADJUSTMENT key until you reach 20 minutes.
- Place the lid on the Power pressure cooker XL, lock the lid and switch the pressure release valve to closed.
- Once the timer reaches 0, the cooker will automatically switch to KEEP WARM/CANCEL. When the steam is completely released, carefully remove the cooker's lid. Serve warm and enjoy

344. Artichoke and Bean Dipping Sauce

Ready in about 30 minutes
Servings 20

Here's an amazing party dip, Ready in about 30 minutes thanks to the Power pressure cooker XL. If you like spicy food, you can add a chile powder or hot paprika according to your taste.

Per serving: 136 Calories; 5g Fat; 17.2g Carbs; 7.1g Protein; 1g Sugars

Ingredients

2 pounds artichokes, outer leaves removed
2 cups Great Northern beans, soaked overnight and rinsed
Juice of 1 fresh lime
1 teaspoon granulated garlic
3/4 cup Swiss cheese, grated
1 ½ cups sour cream
1/2 teaspoon salt, or more to taste
1 teaspoon red pepper flakes, crushed
4 cups water

Directions

- Throw the beans and water into your Power pressure cooker XL.
- Then, cut off the top about 1/3 of each artichoke. Slice your artichokes in half lengthwise; remove the "choke". Drizzle with fresh lime juice and put into the cooker cut-side up.
- Press the CHICKEN/MEAT key and press the TIME ADJUSTMENT key until you reach 25 minutes.
- Place the lid on the Power pressure cooker XL, lock the lid and switch the pressure release valve to closed.
- Once the timer reaches 0, the cooker will automatically switch to KEEP WARM/CANCEL. When the steam is completely released, carefully remove the cooker's lid.
- Add the rest of the above ingredients, minus Swiss cheese. Lastly, puree the content by using an immersion blender. Fold in the cheese; stir to combine well.
- Serve warm or at room temperature with dippers of choice.

345. Spring Garbanzo Bean Stew

Ready in about 25 minutes
Servings 4

This vegan protein stew is perfect for warming up on cold weeknights. Consider adding another combo of seasonings such as turmeric, cumin or chili powder.

Per serving: 478 Calories; 7.7g Fat; 81.1g Carbs; 25.8g Protein; 20.6g Sugars

Ingredients

4 spring onions, chopped
1 (15 1/2-ounce) can garbanzo beans, rinsed and drained
2 carrots, diced
1 (14-ounce) can organic vegetable broth
1 cup bell peppers, chopped
1 (28-ounce) can diced tomatoes, undrained
1/2 teaspoon ground black pepper
2 tablespoons fresh basil, chopped
1/2 teaspoon salt
2 sprigs dried thyme
2 cups water

Directions

- Add all of the above ingredients to the Power pressure cooker XL.
- Choose the SOUP/STEW function and then, press the TIME ADJUSTMENT key until you reach 20 minutes.
- Place the lid on the Power pressure cooker XL, lock the lid and switch the pressure release valve to closed.
- Once the timer reaches 0, the cooker will automatically switch to KEEP WARM/CANCEL. When the steam is completely released, carefully remove the cooker's lid.
- Taste and adjust the seasonings. Serve warm.

346. Banana and Apple Rice Pudding

Ready in about 20 minutes
Servings 6

Light and delicious, this pudding is an ideal breakfast to munch on when you're on the go! If an apple and banana combo isn't your cup of tea, try adding your favorite fruits.

Per serving: 519 Calories; 12.8g Fat; 88.4g Carbs; 13.2g Protein; 35.6g Sugars

Ingredients

3 eggs
1 cup brown sugar
2 cups jasmine rice
1 ¼ cups half-and-half
1/3 cup apples, dried
1 cup bananas, dried
1/2 teaspoon ground cloves
1/2 teaspoon almond extract
1 teaspoon ground cinnamon
3 ½ cups whole milk
2 ¼ cups water

Directions

- Press the "RICE/RISOTTO" key. Then, combine the jasmine rice, sugar, milk, and water in the inner pot of the Power Pressure Cooker XL.
- Bring to a boil, stirring often, until the sugar is dissolved.
- Place the lid on the Power Pressure Cooker XL, lock the lid and switch the pressure release valve to closed. Cook for 8 minutes.
- Meanwhile, in a mixing bowl, whisk the eggs, half-and-half, cinnamon, cloves, almond extract.
- Once the timer reaches 0, the cooker will automatically switch to "KEEP WARM/CANCEL". Switch the pressure release valve to open. When the steam is completely released, remove the lid.
- Then, stir in the egg mixture, dried banana and dried apples. Serve warm or at room temperature.

347. Kidney Bean and Rice Salad

Ready in about 25 minutes
Servings 4

This is great, refreshing salad you can eat as a complete meal or as a side dish, no matter what the time of day. You can substitute kidney beans for black beans.

Per serving: 441 Calories; 1.5g Fat; 88.5g Carbs; 17.9g Protein; 2.6g Sugars

Ingredients

3 teaspoons avocado oil
1 ¼ cups kidney beans, soaked overnight
1 1/3 cups white rice, cooked
1/2 cup fresh cilantro, chopped
1 cup red onions, peeled and coarsely chopped
3 teaspoons balsamic vinegar
4 garlic cloves, smashed
1 tablespoon fresh orange juice
1 teaspoon orange zest, grated
1 teaspoon salt
1 teaspoon dried dill weed
1/2 teaspoon freshly cracked black pepper, to your liking
3 bay leaves
4 ¼ cups water

Directions

- Press the "BEANS/LENTILS" key.
- Add the water, kidney beans, and bay leaves to the inner pot of the Power Pressure Cooker XL. Place the lid on the Power Pressure Cooker XL, lock the lid and switch the pressure release valve to closed; cook for 20 minutes.
- Press the "CANCEL" key. Switch the pressure release valve to open. When the steam is completely released, remove the cooker's lid.
- Drain the cooked beans and stir in the other ingredients. Stir to combine and serve well chilled.

348. Friday Night Lasagna

Ready in about 1 hour
Servings 6

This lasagna is perfectly suited for special occasions, giving your favorite family dish a chance to shine! Pick your favorite lasagna noodles, a pasta sauce and a combo of the best seasonings, arrange all ingredients in the inner pot, set back and enjoy!

Per serving: 351 Calories; 21g Fat; 31.8g Carbs; 9.5g Protein; 3.6g Sugars

Ingredients

1 ¼ cups mushrooms, thinly sliced
1 ½ jars pasta sauce
1 teaspoon cayenne pepper
2 teaspoons dried basil
1 teaspoon dried rosemary
1 teaspoon red pepper flakes
1/2 teaspoon dried oregano
1/2 teaspoon sea salt
1 1/3 cups cream cheese
1/2 teaspoon ground black pepper
1 ½ packages prebaked lasagna noodles

Directions

- Place two lasagna shells on the bottom of the inner pot of the Power Pressure Cooker XL.
- Then, spread the pasta sauce. Place the layer of the cream cheese on it.
- Top with the sliced fresh mushrooms. Sprinkle with some spices and herbs. Repeat the layers until you run out of ingredients.
- Place the lid on the Power Pressure Cooker XL, lock the lid and switch the pressure release valve to closed.
- Press the function key until you reach the bake setting; then press the "COOK TIME SELECTOR" key until you reach 50 minutes.
- Press the "CANCEL" key. Switch the pressure release valve to open. When the steam is completely released, remove the cooker's lid. Bon appétit!

349. Cilantro Bean Purée

Ready in about 25 minutes
Servings 6

This recipe opens the door to endless possibilities. Serve this healthy, flavorful purée with pork chops, beef ribs or chicken wings.

Per serving: 282 Calories; 3.2g Fat; 47.8g Carbs; 15.9g Protein; 2.5g Sugars

Ingredients

2 ½ cups water
1 ½ teaspoons garlic powder
1 cup red onions, peeled and chopped
2 ¼ cups dry pinto beans, soaked
3 teaspoons vegetable oil
1/4 teaspoon black pepper
1 teaspoon chipotle powder
1/2 teaspoon red pepper flakes, crushed
1/2 teaspoon sea salt
1/2 cup fresh cilantro, roughly chopped

Directions

- Press the "BEANS/LENTILS" key and heat the oil. Now, sauté the onions, cilantro, garlic powder, and chipotle powder.
- Stir in the beans and the water. Season with black pepper, red pepper, and salt.
- Place the lid on the Power Pressure Cooker XL, lock the lid and switch the pressure release valve to closed; cook for 20 minutes.
- Press the "CANCEL" key. Switch the pressure release valve to open. When the steam is completely released, remove the cooker's lid.
- Next, reserve two spoonfuls of beans. Puree the remaining beans using a potato masher. Season with black pepper, red pepper, and salt. Garnish with the reserved beans.

350. Pear and Coconut Dessert Risotto

Ready in about 15 minutes
Servings 6

This is a filling and comforting one-pot dish that is chock-full of wonderful aromas. Add 1-2 tablespoons of maple syrup if you want to satisfy your sweet tooth!

Per serving: 544 Calories; 28.8g Fat; 67.8g Carbs; 7.4g Protein; 11.1g Sugars

Ingredients

2 pears, cored and diced
1/2 teaspoon cardamom
1 cup coconut
2 ½ cups coconut milk
2 ½ cups water
2 tablespoons candied ginger, diced
2 cups white rice
A pinch of ground cinnamon

Directions

- Press the "RICE/RISOTTO" key. Throw all of the above ingredients into the Power Pressure Cooker XL.
- Place the lid on the Power Pressure Cooker XL, lock the lid and switch the pressure release valve to closed; cook for 10 minutes.
- Press the "CANCEL" key. Switch the pressure release valve to open. When the steam is completely released, remove the cooker's lid.
- Serve at room temperature or well-chilled. Bon appétit!

351. Dates and Apricots Oatmeal Dessert

Ready in about 15 minutes
Servings 4

There are numerous benefits of eating oats. Oats are a whole-grain food with well-balanced nutrient composition. They are packed with antioxidants, soluble fiber, and minerals.

Per serving: 456 Calories; 23.3g Fat; 62.5g Carbs; 6g Protein; 43.8g Sugars

Ingredients

1 ½ cups steel-cut oats
2 ¼ cups water
1 ½ cups almond milk
3/4 cup brown sugar
6 fresh dates, pitted and sliced
8 apricots, pitted and halved
1 teaspoon vanilla paste
1/4 teaspoon ground cloves

Directions

- Press the "RICE/RISOTTO" key.
- Stir everything into the Power Pressure Cooker XL.
- Place the lid on the Power Pressure Cooker XL, lock the lid and switch the pressure release valve to closed; cook for 8 minutes.
- Press the "CANCEL" key. Switch the pressure release valve to open. When the steam is completely released, remove the cooker's lid. Serve well-chilled.

352. Beans with Mushrooms and Farro

Ready in about 25 minutes
Servings 4

Need something to go with your main course? Look no further! This bean and farro side dish is the perfect companion to stews, meat dishes and salads.

Per serving: 251 Calories; 1.3g Fat; 46g Carbs; 17.1g Protein; 5.1g Sugars

Ingredients

1/2 tablespoon shallot powder
1 teaspoon finely minced jalapeno pepper
1 tablespoon smashed garlic
3/4 cup farro
1 ¼ cups dried navy beans
4 green onions, chopped
1 cup tomatoes, diced
2 ½ cups mushrooms, thinly sliced

Directions

- Press the "BEANS/LENTILS" key. Throw all of the above ingredients, except for the tomatoes, into the Power Pressure Cooker XL.
- Place the lid on the Power Pressure Cooker XL, lock the lid and switch the pressure release valve to closed. Set the cooking time to 20 minutes.
- Once the timer reaches 0, the cooker will automatically switch to "KEEP WARM". Press the "CANCEL" key and switch the pressure release valve to open.
- When the steam is completely released, remove the cooker's lid. Add the diced tomatoes. Stir to combine well. Bon appétit!

353. Mexican-Style Bean and Corn Salad

Ready in about 25 minutes + chilling time
Servings 4

Whether as a great starter or a light dinner, a healthy salad tossed with a flavorful vinaigrette is very likely to hit the spot. Enjoy this nutritious and delicious salad!

Per serving: 544 Calories; 26.4g Fat; 68.4g Carbs; 22.4g Protein; 3.8g Sugars

Ingredients

1 teaspoon smashed garlic
1/2 teaspoon freshly cracked black pepper
1 teaspoon salt
2 tablespoons wine vinegar
1/2 cup fresh cilantro, chopped
1 teaspoon dried dill weed
1/4 teaspoon hot pepper sauce
1/4 teaspoon chili powder
1 tablespoon ground cumin
1/2 cup extra-virgin olive oil
2 cups cannellini beans, soaked overnight
4 ½ cups water
1 cup red onions, peeled and coarsely chopped

Directions

- Press the "BEANS/LENTILS" key. Simply pour the water and cannellini beans in the inner pot of the Power Pressure Cooker XL.
- Place the lid on the Power Pressure Cooker XL, lock the lid and switch the pressure release valve to closed. Set the cooking time to 20 minutes.
- Once the timer reaches 0, the cooker will automatically switch to "KEEP WARM". Press the "CANCEL" key and switch the pressure release valve to open.
- When the steam is completely released, remove the lid. Drain the cannellini beans; stir in the other ingredients. Serve well-chilled. Bon appétit!

354. Buttery Parmesan Risotto

Ready in about 20 minutes
Servings 4

Carnaroli is a short-grain rice that is perfect for any kind of risotto. Everybody will love this yummy and creamy dish!

Per serving: 493 Calories; 13.2g Fat; 64.6g Carbs; 18g Protein; 3.5g Sugars

Ingredients

1 ½ cups Carnaroli rice, uncooked
1 teaspoon grated lemon rind
2 ½ cups chicken broth
1 ½ cups sparkling white wine
2 tablespoons butter
1/2 teaspoon fresh thyme leaves
1 teaspoon sea salt
1/2 teaspoon freshly ground black pepper
2 garlic cloves, minced
2 onions, finely chopped
4 ounces Parmesan cheese, divided

Directions

- Press the "RICE/RISOTTO" key and melt the butter. Now, sauté the onions for 3 minutes.
- Add the garlic and sauté for 1 more minute, stirring frequently.
- Stir in the rice and cook for a further 2 minutes. Pour in the sparkling white wine and the chicken broth and cook for 2 minutes longer.
- Place the lid on the Power Pressure Cooker XL, lock the lid and switch the pressure release valve to closed; cook for 10 minutes.
- Press the "CANCEL" key. Switch the pressure release valve to open. When the steam is completely released, remove the cooker's lid.
- Sprinkle everything with the cheese, thyme, and lemon rind. Season with salt and black pepper and serve.

355. Super Creamy Rice Pudding

Ready in about 15 minutes
Servings 6

A creamy, fragrant and tender rice . . . Arborio rice is a short-grained, high-starch rice that cooks quick and easy in your Power Pressure Cooker XL. It takes over 30 minutes to make it in a traditional way, at the stove. Need we say more?

Per serving: 322 Calories; 13.2g Fat; 40.4g Carbs; 8.8g Protein; 15.5g Sugars

Ingredients

2 tablespoons butter
1/2 cup heavy cream
2 eggs plus 2 egg yolks, lightly beaten
1 tablespoon pure vanilla extract
1/4 teaspoon ground cinnamon
1 teaspoon almond extract
1/8 teaspoon salt
1 ¼ cups water
1/3 cup sugar
1 cup Arborio rice
1/8 teaspoon grated nutmeg
1 ¾ cups whole milk

Directions

- Press the "RICE/RISOTTO" key and melt the butter.
- Toast the rice for 2 minutes, stirring frequently. Next, add the milk, sugar, vanilla extract, almond extract, salt, nutmeg, ground cinnamon, and water. Cook the mixture for 2 minutes more or until heated through, stirring constantly.
- Place the lid on the Power Pressure Cooker XL, lock the lid and switch the pressure release valve to closed; cook for 10 minutes.
- Press the "CANCEL" key. Switch the pressure release valve to open. When the steam is completely released, remove the cooker's lid.
- In a mixing dish, whisk the eggs, egg yolks, and heavy cream until smooth and frothy. Add about 2 cups of the hot pudding mixture to the egg mixture; add the mixture to the Power Pressure Cooker XL.
- Afterwards, stir the pudding until it has thickened. Serve warm.

356. Mashed Garbanzo Beans

Ready in about 20 minutes
Servings 6

This is a delicious, high-protein dish that can be eaten as an appetizer or a side dish. Serve with a sparkling wine as an aperitif. In addition, garbanzo beans are loaded with antioxidants.

Per serving: 247 Calories; 6.2g Fat; 37g Carbs; 12.8g Protein; 6.3g Sugars

Ingredients

1/2 tablespoon stone ground mustard
1 bay leaf
1 ¾ cups dried garbanzo beans
3 garlic cloves, finely minced
1/4 cup toasted pumpkin seeds, for garnish
1/2 cup cilantro
Salt and pepper, to your liking

Directions

- Press the "BEANS/LENTILS" key. Place the garbanzo beans and bay leaf in your Power Pressure Cooker XL.
- Add the water to cover the beans.
- Place the lid on the Power Pressure Cooker XL, lock the lid and switch the pressure release valve to closed; cook for 10 minutes.
- Press the "CANCEL" key. Switch the pressure release valve to open. When the steam is completely released, remove the cooker's lid.
- Drain and rinse the garbanzo beans; discard the bay leaf. Then, mash them with a fork, potato masher or pastry blender.
- Add the minced garlic, cilantro, and mustard, salt and pepper. Adjust the seasonings. Serve sprinkled with the toasted pumpkin seeds. Enjoy!

357. Indian-Style Bean Dip

Ready in about 25 minutes
Servings 12

An easy to make dipping sauce that goes best with Indian starters and naan. You can add some extra Indian spices like turmeric, tejpat, tamarind, saffron, kokam and so forth.

Per serving: 238 Calories; 4.9g Fat; 37.1g Carbs; 13.2g Protein; 2.2g Sugars

Ingredients

1 heaping tablespoon coriander leaves, finely minced
1/2 tablespoon Garam masala powder
1 cup onions, finely chopped
1 ½ cups tomatoes, chopped
1/2 teaspoon cumin seeds
1/4 cup olive oil
1 ½ pounds kidney beans, soaked overnight
1 teaspoon fresh ginger, grated
1/4 teaspoon salt
1/2 teaspoon red chili powder
4 garlic cloves, minced

Directions

- Press the "BEANS/LENTILS" key. Add the kidney beans to the Power Pressure Cooker XL. Add the water to cover the beans. Place the lid on the Power Pressure Cooker XL, lock the lid and switch the pressure release valve to closed; cook for 20 minutes.
- Meanwhile, in a saucepan, heat the olive oil. Then, sauté the onions with the garlic, ginger, tomatoes, Garam masala, red chili powder, and the cumin seeds.
- Press the "CANCEL" key. Switch the pressure release valve to open. When the steam is completely released, remove the cooker's lid.
- Next, stir the sautéed mixture into your Power Pressure Cooker XL. Add the coriander leaves and salt.
- Next, blend the bean mixture in a food processor; work with batches. Serve and enjoy!

358. Bread Pudding with Dried Apricots

Ready in about 25 minutes
Servings 6

Bread pudding is a comfort food that truly satisfies. Don't throw stale bread away because you can make a sophisticated, no-fuss family meal in no time!

Per serving: 416 Calories; 19.9g Fat; 47.4g Carbs; 15g Protein; 18.8g Sugars

Ingredients

4 eggs
1 ½ cups almond milk
1/2 teaspoon vanilla extract
8 slices stale bread, torn into bite-sized pieces
1/3 teaspoon grated nutmeg
1/3 cup sugar
1 ½ cups water
1 teaspoon almond extract
1/4 teaspoon salt
1/2 cup chopped dried apricot, for garnish

Directions

- Press the "RICE/RISOTTO" key.
- Lightly butter a baking dish. Throw the bread pieces into the bowl.
- To make the custard, combine the almond milk, water, eggs, vanilla extract, almond extract, salt, sugar, and the nutmeg.
- Pour the custard mixture over the bread pieces. Scatter the chopped apricots over the top. Cover tightly with a piece of foil that has been greased.
- Place the wire rack in the inner pot of the Power Pressure Cooker XL. Pour in 2 cups of water. Secure the lid on your Power Pressure Cooker XL.
- Press the "COOK TIME SELECTOR" to set for 18 minutes. Press the "CANCEL" key. Switch the pressure release valve to open. When the steam is completely released, remove the cooker's lid. Bon appétit!

359. Italian-Style Penne Pasta with Sausage

Ready in about 15 minutes
Servings 4

If you want meaty pasta dish with less fat but that is entirely delicious, use low-fat Italian sausage and avoid adding any extra oil. Seasonings will enhance the flavor, so be generous with them.

Per serving: 648 Calories; 16.9g Fat; 87g Carbs; 36.8g Protein; 13.1g Sugars

Ingredients

1 ¼ pounds Italian sausage
1 teaspoon minced garlic
1 cup onion, diced
1 ½ cups Porcini mushrooms, thinly sliced
1 pound penne pasta
2 cups pasta sauce
3 cups water
1 cup Mozzarella cheese, shredded

Directions

- Choose the "RICE/RISOTTO" function. Set the cooking time to 8 minutes.
- Then, brown the Italian sausage along with the garlic, onions, and mushrooms. Cook until the vegetables are tender.
- Add the penne pasta, pasta sauce, and water. Stir well with a large-sized spatula.
- Place the lid on the Power Pressure Cooker XL, lock the lid and switch the pressure release valve to closed.
- Once the timer reaches 0, the cooker will automatically switch to "KEEP WARM/CANCEL". When the steam is completely released, remove the lid.
- Stir in the mozzarella cheese and serve.

360. Banana Cranberry Oatmeal

Ready in about 15 minutes
Servings 4

Thanks to its amazing technology, The Power Pressure Cooker XL will take your oatmeal from "blah" to "yippee"! In this recipe, you can substitute the cranberries for dried cherries.

Per serving: 290 Calories; 5.4g Fat; 53.9g Carbs; 6.6g Protein; 21.9g Sugars

Ingredients

1/3 cup sugar
1 teaspoon vanilla extract
1/4 teaspoon ground cloves
1/2 cup dried cranberries
1 cup ripe banana, chopped
1/8 teaspoon salt
1 cup steel-cut oats
1/4 cup whipped cream
2 ½ cups water

Directions

- Choose the "RICE/RISOTTO" function.
- Press the "TIME ADJUSTMENT" key and set the timer for 10 minutes.
- Mix all of the above ingredients, except for the heavy cream, in your Power Pressure Cooker XL. Stir to combine well.
- Place the lid on the Power Pressure Cooker XL, lock the lid and switch the pressure release valve to closed.
- Once the timer reaches 0, the cooker will automatically switch to "KEEP WARM/CANCEL". When the steam is completely released, remove the lid.
- Serve with the whipped cream.

361. Bulgur and Almond Porridge

Ready in about 15 minutes
Servings 8

Bulgur is a kind of wheat that is good for your digestion. It may protect your heart, fight diabetes, and help with weight loss. Bulgur wheat pairs deliciously with cardamom, anise star, and vanilla.

Per serving: 177 Calories; 1.7g Fat; 38.9g Carbs; 4.8g Protein; 11.9g Sugars

Ingredients

2 cups bulgur wheat
1/4 teaspoon freshly grated nutmeg
1/2 teaspoon ground cloves
1/2 teaspoon ground cinnamon
3 tablespoons toasted almonds, chopped
1/3 cup honey
6 cups water

Directions

- Choose the "BEANS/LENTILS" function. Mix all the ingredients, the minus honey, in your Power Pressure Cooker XL.
- Place the lid on the Power Pressure Cooker XL, lock the lid and switch the pressure release valve to closed. Cook for 10 minutes.
- Once the timer reaches 0, the cooker will automatically switch to "KEEP WARM/CANCEL". When the steam is completely released, remove the lid.
- Add the honey and stir well before serving. Bon appétit!

362. Smoky Winter Grits

Ready in about 30 minutes
Servings 6

Here's one of the easiest ways to cook perfect grits. So quick to throw together, grits go well with ham, shallots, and Parmesan cheese.

Per serving: 296 Calories; 19.2g Fat; 12.7g Carbs; 19.5g Protein; 0.7g Sugars

Ingredients

1 cup quick-cooking grits
1/2 stick butter
3 eggs, whisked
1/2 teaspoon ground black pepper, to your liking
1 teaspoon sea salt
1 teaspoon smoked paprika
2 medium-sized shallots, chopped
10 ounces ham, chopped
1 cup Parmesan cheese, grated

Directions

- Choose the "RICE/RISOTTO" function and warm the butter.
- Now, brown the ham for 2 minutes and crumble it. Add the shallots, salt, black pepper, and the smoked paprika; cook for 3 more minutes, stirring frequently. Reserve the mixture.
- In a saucepan, bring 3 cups of water to a boil. Whisk in the grits and cook, until thickened, about 6 minutes. Stir into the bowl with the ham mixture.
- Stir in the eggs and the Parmesan cheese.
- Place the wire rack in the Power Pressure Cooker XL; pour in 2 cups of water. Make the foil sling and butter the bottom and sides of a baking dish. Spread the mixture in the baking dish.
- Place the lid on the Power Pressure Cooker XL, lock the lid and switch the pressure release valve to closed. Cook for 10 minutes.
- Afterwards, press the "CANCEL" key. When the steam is completely released, remove the cooker's lid. Serve warm.

363. Honey Pecan Oatmeal

Ready in about 15 minutes
Servings 4

There is absolutely nothing a good oatmeal won't cure. Add amazingly healthy pecans and honey, and delight your family with something special!

Per serving: 321 Calories; 22.8g Fat; 29.6g Carbs; 5.3g Protein; 18.7g Sugars

Ingredients

1 ¼ cups steel-cut oats
1/4 cup honey
2 cups water
1/4 cup pecans, chopped
1/4 teaspoon kosher salt

Directions

- Choose the "RICE/RISOTTO" function. Press the "TIME ADJUSTMENT" key and set the time to 10 minutes.
- Add the water, oats, and salt to your Power Pressure Cooker XL. Stir to combine well.
- Place the lid on the Power Pressure Cooker XL, lock the lid and switch the pressure release valve to closed.
- While the oats are cooking, toast the pecans in a small-sized skillet.
- Once the timer reaches 0, the cooker will automatically switch to "KEEP WARM/CANCEL".
- When the steam is completely released, remove the lid. Afterwards, add honey and stir to combine well. Serve sprinkled with chopped pecans. Bon appétit!

364. Ham Bread Pudding with Swiss Cheese

Ready in about 35 minutes
Servings 6

This bread pudding will wow your guests! Serve with a spoonful of Greek-style yogurt for an extra special treat!

Per serving: 499 Calories; 15.7g Fat; 64.6g Carbs; 24.1g Protein; 9.5g Sugars

Ingredients

1 ½ pounds Hawaiian bread rolls, torn into pieces
Nonstick cooking spray
2 cups milk
1/4 teaspoon ground black pepper, or more to taste
1/2 teaspoon salt
1 cup ham, chopped
1/2 tablespoon Dijon mustard
1/2 teaspoon brown sugar
4 eggs, at room temperature
4 green onions, chopped
4 ounces Swiss cheese, shredded

Directions

● Choose the "CHICKEN/MEAT" function. Coat the inside of a soufflé dish with a nonstick cooking spray; set aside. Place the wire rack in your Power Pressure Cooker XL; pour in 2 cups of warm water.
● Heat a cast-iron skillet over medium heat and cook the ham and green onions for 5 minutes. Transfer the ham-onion mixture to the soufflé dish; add the bread pieces.
● In another bowl, whisk the eggs, Dijon mustard, milk, brown sugar, salt, and black pepper. Pour the egg mixture over the bread pieces; press with a spatula to submerge the bread pieces. Allow it to stand for 5 minutes.
● Cover the baking dish with a piece of parchment paper; then seal with a piece of aluminum foil. Make the foil sling and lower the sealed dish onto the rack.
● Press the "TIME ADJUSTMENT" key and set time to 20 minutes. Place the lid on the Power Pressure Cooker XL, lock the lid and switch the pressure release valve to closed.
● Once the timer reaches 0, the cooker will automatically switch to "KEEP WARM/CANCEL".
● When the steam is completely released, remove the lid. Serve at room temperature topped with shredded Swiss cheese.

365. Black Bean and Corn Dip

Ready in about 25 minutes
Servings 16

A combo of corn kernels and black beans is always a good idea. Serve with potato chips or veggie sticks for a memorable Super Bowl feast.

Per serving: 139 Calories; 3.4g Fat; 21.4g Carbs; 6.9g Protein; 1.5g Sugars

Ingredients

1 cup fresh corn kernels
5 cups water
1 pound black beans, rinsed and drained
1 cup onion, finely chopped
1/2 teaspoon celery seeds
4 garlic cloves, minced
2 tablespoons canola oil
1/2 teaspoon sea salt
1/4 teaspoon ground black pepper, or more to your liking
1/2 teaspoon cumin seeds
1 cup mild picante sauce

Directions

● Press the "BEANS/LENTILS" key. Then, empty the can of beans into your Power Pressure Cooker XL. Add the water.
● Place the lid on the Power Pressure Cooker XL, lock the lid and switch the pressure release valve to closed. Cook your beans for 10 minutes.
● Meanwhile, in a saucepan, cook the remaining ingredients for 5 minutes or until tender.
● Once the timer reaches 0, the Power Pressure Cooker XL will automatically switch to "KEEP WARM/CANCEL". Switch the pressure release valve to open.
● When the steam is completely released, remove the cooker's lid. Throw in the sautéed mixture; stir to combine.
● Now, pulse the mixture in your blender or a food processor, working in batches. Bon appétit!

366. Ground Beef and Lentil Soup

Ready in about 30 minutes
Servings 4

Preparing lentils in the Power pressure cooker XL is not only fun, it's also very simple. Lentils are a quite versatile food so let your imagination run wild!

Per serving: 498 Calories; 8.8g Fat; 66.5g Carbs; 39.2g Protein; 9.3g Sugars

Ingredients

1/2 pound ground beef
2 cups red lentils
4 Yukon gold potatoes, peeled and diced
1 teaspoon minced garlic
2 yellow onions, peeled and chopped
1/2 pound carrots, chopped
1/4 cup sour cream
2 ripe tomatoes, chopped
4 cups broth
1 teaspoon sea salt
1/4 teaspoon ground black pepper
1/3 teaspoon dried dill weed
1 teaspoon cayenne pepper

Directions

- Press the CHICKEN/MEAT key and cook the beef and onions for 5 minutes. Press the CANCEL key.
- Add all of the above ingredients, except the sour cream, to your Power pressure cooker XL; give it a good stir.
- Press the CHICKEN/MEAT key. Place the lid on the Power pressure cooker XL, lock the lid and switch the pressure release valve to closed. Cook for 15 minutes.
- Once the timer reaches 0, the cooker will automatically switch to KEEP WARM/CANCEL. When the steam is completely released, carefully remove the cooker's lid.
- Serve warm, topped with the sour cream. Serve at once and enjoy!

367. Two-Bean Sausage Chili

Ready in about 35 minutes
Servings 8

Here's a nice, traditional sausage chili with old-fashioned goodness. You can pair it with crusty rolls topped with melted mozzarella cheese.

Per serving: 353 Calories; 8.3g Fat; 50.8g Carbs; 20.4g Protein; 5.8g Sugars

Ingredients

4 beef sausages, sliced
1 ½ cups black beans, soaked overnight, drained and rinsed
1 ½ cups dried Great Northern beans, soaked overnight, drained and rinsed
2 red bell peppers, deveined and thinly sliced
4 cups broth, preferably homemade
2 tomatoes, chopped
2 tablespoons ketchup
3 teaspoons vegetable oil
2 carrots, chopped into sticks
1 teaspoon minced chipotle pepper
1/3 teaspoon ground black pepper
1/2 teaspoon fennel seeds
1/2 teaspoon sea salt, to taste
1/2 teaspoon celery seeds
1 cup scallions, chopped
3 cloves garlic, minced
1 bay leaf

Directions

- Press the CHICKEN/MEAT key. Heat the oil and brown the sausage for 3 to 4 minutes. Now, add the scallions and garlic; sauté for a further 3 minutes or until just tender. Press the CANCEL key.
- Add the remaining ingredients and press the SOUP/STEW key. Then, press the TIME ADJUSTMENT key until you reach 20 minutes.
- Once the timer reaches 0, the cooker will automatically switch to KEEP WARM/CANCEL. When the steam is completely released, carefully remove the cooker's lid.
- Serve warm, topped with the sour cream and enjoy!

368. Lima Bean and Bacon Dip

Ready in about 20 minutes
Servings 12

Frozen lima beans give an amazing bright green color to this tasty dip. Serve with favorite crackers and enjoy.

Per serving: 88 Calories; 3.4g Fat; 9.6g Carbs; 5g Protein; 0.7g Sugars

Ingredients

2 (10-ounce) boxes frozen lima beans
3 slices bacon, cooked and crumbled
3 teaspoons butter, melted
1/2 teaspoon cayenne pepper
Seasoned salt and freshly ground pepper, to taste

Directions

- Add the beans to the Power pressure cooker XL. Press the BEANS/LENTILS key and use the cook time selector to adjust to 15 minutes.
- Place the lid on the Power pressure cooker XL, lock the lid and switch the pressure release valve to closed.
- Once the timer reaches 0, the cooker will automatically switch to KEEP WARM/CANCEL. When the steam is completely released, carefully remove the cooker's lid.
- Afterwards, remove the beans to a bowl of the food processor; add the butter, salt, black pepper and cayenne pepper; puree until smooth and uniform. Top with the bacon and serve.

369. Cheese and Adzuki Bean Dip

Ready in about 25 minutes
Servings 16

Preparing cheesy bean dip in the Power pressure cooker XL is not only fun, it's also very simple. Let your imagination run wild!

Per serving: 77 Calories; 3.1g Fat; 8.4g Carbs; 4.4g Protein; 0.7g Sugars

Ingredients

1/4 cup cream cheese
1/2 cup goat cheese, grated
1/2 pound adzuki beans, soaked overnight
1 tablespoon minced garlic
2 bell peppers, deveined and chopped
1/2 teaspoon dried dill weed
Sea salt and ground black pepper, to your liking
2 ½ cups water

Directions

- Place the beans in the Power pressure cooker XL.
- Press the SOUP/STEW key and, then, press the TIME ADJUSTMENT key until you reach 20 minutes.
- Once the timer reaches 0, the cooker will automatically switch to KEEP WARM/CANCEL. When the steam is completely released, carefully remove the cooker's lid.
- Add the remaining ingredients and stir to combine well. Bon appétit!

370. Chickpea Stew with Fennel and Cheese

Ready in about 30 minutes
Servings 4

Here's a rich stew with amazing colorful veggies. You can combine the vegetables to use what you've got. Carrots, celery and sweet potatoes work well too.

Per serving: 374 Calories; 11.2g Fat; 51.9g Carbs; 20.1g Protein; 8.3g Sugars

Ingredients

2 cups chickpeas, soaked
1 fennel bulb, chopped
1/2 cup finely grated Parmigiano-Reggiano cheese
1/2 cup scallions, chopped
3 teaspoons canola oil
3 cloves garlic, minced
Salt and ground black pepper
4 ½ cups water

Directions

● Press the RICE/RISOTTO key and use the cook time selector to adjust to 20 minutes. Heat the oil and cook the fennel, garlic and scallions until just tender.
● Add the remaining ingredients, except for the cheese, to the Power pressure cooker XL. Place the lid on the Power pressure cooker XL, lock the lid and switch the pressure release valve to closed.
● Once the timer reaches 0, the cooker will automatically switch to KEEP WARM/CANCEL. When the steam is completely released, carefully remove the cooker's lid.
● Ladle the stew into individual dishes; top each serving with grated Parmigiano-Reggiano cheese.

371. Pepper and Kidney Bean Soup

Ready in about 30 minutes
Servings 4

Serrano pepper adds a spicy heat to this amazing soup, making beans less boring and more appealing! One tablespoon of balsamic vinegar works well with this soup, too.

Per serving: 386 Calories; 2.1g Fat; 72.3g Carbs; 24.1g Protein; 8.5g Sugars

Ingredients

2 bell peppers, thinly sliced
1 serrano pepper, thinly sliced
2 cups kidney beans, soaked overnight
1 cup scallions, chopped
3 cloves garlic, minced
1/2 cup celery, finely chopped
1 carrot, trimmed and thinly sliced
1 large can crushed tomatoes
1 fennel bulb, chopped
4 ½ cups stock, preferably homemade
1/3 teaspoon cayenne pepper
2 sprigs dried rosemary
2 sprigs dried thyme
1/4 teaspoon freshly cracked black pepper
1/2 teaspoon kosher salt

Directions

● Press the CHICKEN/MEAT key and spray the bottom of the Power pressure cooker XL with a nonstick cooking spray. Then, sauté the scallions, garlic and peppers until just tender and fragrant, for 4 to 5 minutes. Pres the CANCEL key.
● Throw the remaining ingredients into your Power pressure cooker XL; stir until everything is well incorporated.
● Press the SOUP/STEW key and then, press the TIME ADJUSTMENT key until you reach 20 minutes.
● Place the lid on the Power pressure cooker XL, lock the lid and switch the pressure release valve to closed.
● Once the timer reaches 0, the cooker will automatically switch to KEEP WARM/CANCEL. When the steam is completely released, carefully remove the cooker's lid. Bon appétit!

372. Avocado Hummus with Paprika

Ready in about 30 minutes
Servings 16

Here's an excellent dip, something between a traditional hummus and guacamole! Try it on your favorite tacos.

Per serving: 176 Calories; 9.6g Fat; 18.8g Carbs; 5.7g Protein; 2.9g Sugars

Ingredients

2 ripe avocados, peeled and mashed
2 cups chickpeas, soaked, drained and rinsed
2 teaspoons paprika
1/2 cup shallots, chopped
3 garlic cloves, minced
3 tablespoons extra-virgin olive oil, plus more for serving
3 teaspoons tahini
2 tablespoons white miso paste
2 teaspoons lime juice
1/2 tablespoon coriander seeds
1/2 teaspoon sea salt
4 ½ cups water

Directions

- Add the chickpeas and water to the Power pressure cooker XL. Press the SOUP/STEW key and then, press the TIME ADJUSTMENT key until you reach 20 minutes.
- Place the lid on the Power pressure cooker XL, lock the lid and switch the pressure release valve to closed.
- Once the timer reaches 0, the cooker will automatically switch to KEEP WARM/CANCEL. When the steam is completely released, carefully remove the cooker's lid. Drain the chickpeas and transfer them to a food processor.
- Throw in the shallots, garlic, avocado, paprika, salt, and coriander seeds. Puree until everything is well combined.
- Next, add miso paste, lime juice, and tahini; puree again. Gradually pour in olive oil. Continue blending until everything is well incorporated. Add a few drizzles of olive and serve!

373. Old-Fashioned Minestrone

Ready in about 30 minutes
Servings 6

The Power pressure cooker XL cooks this Italian classic perfectly and effortlessly. Just sauté your veggies to enhance the flavor, throw in the remaining ingredients and enjoy!

Per serving: 480 Calories; 7.1g Fat; 85.7g Carbs; 20.4g Protein; 6.1g Sugars

Ingredients

2 shallots, chopped
1 tablespoon dried Italian herb blend
1/2 cup pearl barley, rinsed and drained
1 cup celery, finely chopped
1 cup broken pieces spaghetti
1 carrot, diced
1 tablespoon garlic paste
2 cups croutons
6 beef bouillon cubes
1 pound potatoes, peeled and cut into bite-size chunks
1 cup rutabaga, peeled and diced
2 tablespoons olive oil
1 can tomatoes, crushed
2 cups white beans
1/4 teaspoon freshly ground black pepper
1/4 teaspoon salt
6 cups water

Directions

- Press the SOUP/STEW key and heat the oil until sizzling. Sauté the shallots, celery and carrot until just tender, about 4 minutes. Press the CANCEL key.
- Add the garlic paste, Italian herb blend, barley, potatoes, rutabaga, water, bouillon cubes, and canned tomatoes.
- Add the remaining ingredients. Press the SOUP/STEW key and then, press the TIME ADJUSTMENT key until you reach 20 minutes.
- Place the lid on the Power pressure cooker XL, lock the lid and switch the pressure release valve to closed.
- Once the timer reaches 0, the cooker will automatically switch to KEEP WARM/CANCEL. When the steam is completely released, carefully remove the cooker's lid.
- Serve hot with the croutons on the side. Enjoy!

374. Lentil and Dukkah Dip

Ready in about 15 minutes
Servings 12

Although you can eat this great snack dip with pita chips, crackers or veggie sticks, you can serve it over roasted vegetables for dinner.

Per serving: 155 Calories; 4g Fat; 21.4g Carbs; 9g Protein; 1.7g Sugars

Ingredients

2 cups dry green lentils, rinsed
1/2 teaspoon dukkah
3 garlic cloves, minced
1/4 cup tomato paste
2 tablespoons tahini
2 tablespoons vegetable oil
1 teaspoon maple syrup
1/2 teaspoon ground black pepper
1 teaspoon salt
1 teaspoon dry thyme, minced
1/4 teaspoon cardamom

Directions

- Throw the lentils and 4 cups water into the Power pressure cooker XL. Press the RICE/RISOTTO key; place the lid on the Power pressure cooker XL, lock the lid and switch the pressure release valve to closed. Cook for 6 minutes.
- Once the timer reaches 0, the cooker will automatically switch to KEEP WARM/CANCEL. When the steam is completely released, carefully remove the cooker's lid.
- Stir in the remaining ingredients. Enjoy!

375. Mediterranean Red Bean Salad

Ready in about 25 minutes
Servings 4

This light and refreshing salad is perfect for potlucks! Consider adding spiralized zucchini or cucumbers to impress your family!

Per serving: 233 Calories; 5.8g Fat; 33.4g Carbs; 11.2g Protein; 3.3g Sugars

Ingredients

1 cup dry red beans, soaked overnight and rinsed
1/2 cup onions, chopped
1/2 teaspoon maple syrup
1/2 cup olives, pitted and sliced
1 cup grape tomatoes, sliced
2 cloves garlic, minced
3 teaspoons grapeseed oil
1 teaspoon chili powder
2 tablespoons wine vinegar
2 bay leaves
2 sprigs dried thyme
1/2 teaspoon dried basil leaves
2 sprigs dried rosemary
1/2 teaspoon smoked paprika
1/2 teaspoon red pepper flakes, crushed
1/2 teaspoon ground black pepper
1/2 teaspoon seasoned salt
1/4 cup fresh mint, roughly chopped
3 cups water

Directions

- Add the beans and water to the Power pressure cooker XL.
- Press the SOUP/STEW key and then, press the TIME ADJUSTMENT key until you reach 20 minutes.
- Place the lid on the Power pressure cooker XL, lock the lid and switch the pressure release valve to closed.
- Once the timer reaches 0, the cooker will automatically switch to KEEP WARM/CANCEL. When the steam is completely released, carefully remove the cooker's lid.
- Allow the beans to chill in your refrigerator. Toss with the remaining ingredients and serve well-chilled.

376. Lemony Garbanzo Bean Dip

Ready in about 25 minutes
Servings 16

This is an elegant and flavorsome dip for the perfect dinner party. You should cook your own garbanzo beans because they cost less than canned beans and they don't contain preservatives and too much salt.

Per serving: 127 Calories; 4.8g Fat; 16.8g Carbs; 5.3g Protein; 3.5g Sugars

Ingredients

2 tablespoons lemon juice
2 cups garbanzo beans
2 bell peppers, deveined and chopped
2 cloves garlic, minced
1/2 cup low-fat sour cream
2 tablespoons olive oil, preferably extra-virgin
1 teaspoon hot sauce
1/3 tablespoon fresh dill, chopped
1/2 tablespoon salt
4 ½ cups water

Directions

- Add the chickpeas and water to the Power pressure cooker XL. Press the SOUP/STEW key and then, press the TIME ADJUSTMENT key until you reach 20 minutes.
- Place the lid on the Power pressure cooker XL, lock the lid and switch the pressure release valve to closed.
- Once the timer reaches 0, the cooker will automatically switch to KEEP WARM/CANCEL. When the steam is completely released, carefully remove the cooker's lid.
- Switch the chickpeas to a food processor; add the remaining ingredients, except the oil; blitz the mixture into a smooth purée.
- While the machine is still running, gradually add olive oil. Process until your dip is uniform, creamy and smooth. Enjoy!

377. Tangy White Bean and Rice Salad

Ready in about 25 minutes+ chilling time
Servings 6

Healthy food is fast, tasty and fits your budget! Beans pair well with rice in this fresh mixed salad.

Per serving: 531 Calories; 9.5g Fat; 92g Carbs; 20.6g Protein; 2g Sugars

Ingredients

2 cups dried white beans, soaked overnight and rinsed
2 cups white rice
1/4 cup olive oil
2 cups iceberg lettuce
6 spring onions, chopped
3 garlic cloves, smashed
Fresh juice of 1/2 lime
1/3 teaspoon dried marjoram
1/2 teaspoon cayenne pepper
1 teaspoon sea salt
1/3 cup fresh cilantro, chopped
1 teaspoon mixed peppercorns
1 bay leaf
4 ½ cups water

Directions

- Add the water and beans to the Power pressure cooker XL. Press the SOUP/STEW key and then, press the TIME ADJUSTMENT key until you reach 20 minutes.
- Place the lid on the Power pressure cooker XL, lock the lid and switch the pressure release valve to closed.
- Once the timer reaches 0, the cooker will automatically switch to KEEP WARM/CANCEL. When the steam is completely released, carefully remove the cooker's lid. Transfer the beans to the serving bowl.
- Add white rice to the Power pressure cooker XL. Press the RICE/RISOTTO key. Place the lid on the Power pressure cooker XL, lock the lid and switch the pressure release valve to closed. Cook for 6 minutes.
- Add chilled rice to the beans; toss with the remaining ingredients. Serve well-chilled and enjoy!

378. Chunky Bean and Turkey Soup

Ready in about 30 minutes
Servings 6

This hearty soup recipe comes together in 30 minutes or less, but it is packed full of vegetables and flavor!

Per serving: 465 Calories; 11.7g Fat; 57.8g Carbs; 35.2g Protein; 6.3g Sugars

Ingredients

1 pound white kidney beans, soaked, drained and rinsed
1/2 pound extra lean ground turkey
1 parsnip, trimmed and chopped
2 yellow onions, chopped
1 cup Parmigiano-Reggiano cheese, freshly grated
1 cup carrots, trimmed and chopped
8 ounces baby spinach
8 cups stock
1 tablespoon olive oil
1 teaspoon dried thyme, finely chopped
2 sprigs dried rosemary, finely chopped
Sea salt and ground black pepper, to taste

Directions

- Choose the CHICKEN/MEAT function; warm the oil until sizzling and brown ground turkey along with the onions for 3 to 4 minutes. Add the carrots and parsnip and continue sautéing until everything is cooked through, or 3 more minutes. Press the CANCEL key.
- Stir in the remaining ingredients, except for Parmigiano-Reggiano cheese. Press the SOUP/STEW key and then, press the TIME ADJUSTMENT key until you reach 20 minutes.
- Place the lid on the Power pressure cooker XL, lock the lid and switch the pressure release valve to closed.
- Once the timer reaches 0, the cooker will automatically switch to KEEP WARM/CANCEL. When the steam is completely released, carefully remove the cooker's lid. Stir in Parmigiano-Reggiano cheese; gently stir to combine. Enjoy!

379. Creamiest Pumpkin Hummus Ever

Ready in about 25 minutes
Servings 12

Every home cook likes set-it-and-forget-it recipes! Serve with veggie sticks or potato chips.

Per serving: 166 Calories; 5.1g Fat; 24.6g Carbs; 7.2g Protein; 5.3g Sugars

Ingredients

2 tablespoons olive oil
2 cups chickpeas
2 cups pumpkin puree
1 tablespoon tahini
1 onion, peeled and chopped
1/2 teaspoon garlic powder
1/2 teaspoon shallot powder
Sea salt and ground black pepper, to your liking
4 ½ cups water

Directions

- Add the chickpeas and water to the Power pressure cooker XL. Press the SOUP/STEW key and then, press the TIME ADJUSTMENT key until you reach 20 minutes.
- Place the lid on the Power pressure cooker XL, lock the lid and switch the pressure release valve to closed.
- Once the timer reaches 0, the cooker will automatically switch to KEEP WARM/CANCEL. When the steam is completely released, carefully remove the cooker's lid.
- Transfer the chickpeas to your food processor. Add the remaining ingredients, except the oil, to the food processor. Blend until uniform and creamy.
- Next, gradually pour the oil in a thin stream and blend again. Bon appétit!

380. Bean and Potato Soup

Ready in about 25 minutes
Servings 6

This soup is a great choice when you're short on time. Serve with Mexican-style sour cream and diced avocado.

Per serving: 399 Calories; 3g Fat; 78.4g Carbs; 18.6g Protein; 5.8g Sugars

Ingredients

2 cups red kidney beans, drained and rinsed
6 Yukon Gold potatoes, diced
1 chipotle chili packed in adobo, finely chopped
1/2 cup celery, chopped
2 teaspoons canola oil
2 tomatoes, diced
1 tablespoon apple cider vinegar
2 onions, peeled and chopped
2 cloves garlic, peeled and minced
4 ½ cups vegetable stock
1 cup rice milk
1/2 teaspoon freshly cracked black pepper
1/2 teaspoon sea salt
2 tablespoons fresh parsley, roughly chopped

Directions

- Add all ingredients, minus apple cider vinegar, to the Power pressure cooker XL. Press the SOUP/STEW key and then, press the TIME ADJUSTMENT key until you reach 20 minutes.
- Place the lid on the Power pressure cooker XL, lock the lid and switch the pressure release valve to closed.
- Once the timer reaches 0, the cooker will automatically switch to KEEP WARM/CANCEL. When the steam is completely released, carefully remove the cooker's lid.
- Add the vinegar and ladle the soup into individual bowls. Bon appétit!

RICE & GRAINS

381. Creamy and Rich Rice Pudding

Ready in about 20 minutes
Servings 6

Although the recipe calls for whole milk, feel free to add a nondairy milk if you prefer. Serve with an oatmeal crumble topping.

Per serving: 345 Calories; 6.2g Fat; 64.7g Carbs; 7.1g Protein; 15.1g Sugars

Ingredients

2 cups white rice
1/2 cup Sultanas
2 eggs plus 1 egg yolk, at room temperature
8 ounces whole milk
1/3 cup sugar
3 teaspoons coconut oil
1/4 teaspoon ground cinnamon
1/2 tablespoon vanilla extract
1/4 teaspoon kosher salt
1/4 teaspoon ground cardamom
8 ounces water

Directions

* Add the oil, rice, water and milk to the Power pressure cooker XL.
* Now, add the sugar, cinnamon, vanilla, salt and cardamom. Press the RICE/RISOTTO key once and select 6 minutes.
* Place the lid on the Power pressure cooker XL, lock the lid and switch the pressure release valve to closed.
* Once the timer reaches 0, the cooker will automatically switch to KEEP WARM/CANCEL. When the steam is completely released, carefully remove the cooker's lid.
* Then, add the whisked eggs to the cooker, along with Sultanas. Choose the RICE/RISOTTO function. Cook uncovered until the mixture begins to boil. Serve at room temperature. Bon appétit!

382. Aromatic Bread Pudding with Cranberries

Ready in about 35 minutes
Servings 6

A yummy, creamy bread pudding loaded with the finest ingredients. How could it be any better than this?

Per serving: 313 Calories; 7.4g Fat; 55.7g Carbs; 7.3g Protein; 36.7g Sugars

Ingredients

3 cups stale cinnamon raisin bread, cubed
1 cup dried cranberries
2 cups whole milk
3 egg yolks, at room temperature
3/4 cup sugar
1/2 teaspoon kosher salt
1/3 teaspoon anise seeds
1/2 tablespoon vanilla extract

Directions

* In a mixing bowl, whisk the milk, eggs, sugar, vanilla, salt, and anise seeds. Soak the bread cubes in this mixture about 15 minutes.
* Pour the mixture into a baking dish; add the cranberries and stir to combine; cover with a piece of foil.
* Set the wire rack in your Power pressure cooker XL. Add 2 cups of warm water. Place the baking dish on the wire rack.
* Choose the CHICKEN/MEAT function. Set time to 15 minutes. Once the timer reaches 0, the cooker will automatically switch to KEEP WARM/CANCEL.
* When the steam is completely released, carefully remove the cooker's lid. Allow your pudding to cool before serving and enjoy!

383. Dad's Creamy Oatmeal with Walnuts

Ready in about 15 minutes
Servings 4

Here's an old-fashioned, deliciously creamy oatmeal. But that's only the beginning for this versatile food. You can come up with your own oatmeal recipe and cook it easily in the Power pressure cooker XL. Almonds, maple syrup, fresh berries and apricot jam work well too.

Per serving: 356 Calories; 23.8g Fat; 29g Carbs; 11.2g Protein; 13g Sugars

Ingredients

2 cups steel-cut oats
3/4 cup walnuts, toasted and roughly chopped
2 tablespoons honey
1 ½ cups milk
2 tablespoons coconut oil
1/4 teaspoon kosher salt
1/2 teaspoon grated nutmeg
1/3 teaspoon ground cinnamon
2 ½ cups water

Directions

- Add the oats, water, spices, and milk to the Power pressure cooker XL. Press the RICE/RISOTTO key.
- Use the TIME ADJUSTMENT key to set time to 8 minutes.
- Place the lid on the Power pressure cooker XL, lock the lid and switch the pressure release valve to closed.
- Once the timer reaches 0, the cooker will automatically switch to KEEP WARM/CANCEL. When the steam is completely released, carefully remove the cooker's lid.
- Divide among individual bowls and drizzle the coconut oil and honey over the top; serve topped with walnuts.

384. Honey Apricot Oatmeal

Ready in about 10 minutes
Servings 2

Cooking the oatmeal with fruits in the Power pressure cooker XL gives this bowl an extra-creamy texture. Enjoy every bite!

Per serving: 471 Calories; 10.8g Fat; 85.6g Carbs; 13.1g Protein; 43.9g Sugars

Ingredients

1 ¼ cups quick cooking oats, toasted
1/2 cup apricots, sliced
1/4 cup honey
3/4 cup milk
1/2 cup dried cherries
4 teaspoons peanut butter, chopped
1 cup water

Directions

- Simply throw all of the above ingredients, minus peanut butter, into your Power pressure cooker XL. Press the RICE/RISOTTO key.
- Place the lid on the Power pressure cooker XL, lock the lid and switch the pressure release valve to closed. Cook for 6 minutes.
- Once the timer reaches 0, the cooker will automatically switch to KEEP WARM/CANCEL. When the steam is completely released, carefully remove the cooker's lid.
- Serve right now topped with peanut butter.

385. Tropical Rice Pudding

Ready in about 10 minutes
Servings 6

Pressure cooking is one of the easiest cooking methods to cook white rice. Topped with pineapple and coconut, each bite gets you to the Tropical Paradise.

Per serving: 438 Calories; 10.4g Fat; 83.1g Carbs; 5.2g Protein; 30.8g Sugars

Ingredients

2 cups white rice
1/2 cup toasted coconut flakes
1 (15.25-ounce) can pineapple slices
1/2 stick butter
1/2 cup honey
1 teaspoon rum extract
1 teaspoon vanilla extract
1/3 teaspoon ground nutmeg
1/3 teaspoon ground cinnamon
16 ounces water

Directions

- Add all ingredients, except the pineapple, coconut and honey, to the Power pressure cooker XL.
- Press the RICE/RISOTTO key once and select 6 minutes. Place the lid on the Power pressure cooker XL, lock the lid and switch the pressure release valve to closed.
- Once the timer reaches 0, the cooker will automatically switch to KEEP WARM/CANCEL. When the steam is completely released, carefully remove the cooker's lid.
- Afterwards, divide among individual bowls and top with the pineapple and coconut flakes. Drizzle the honey over the top. Enjoy!

386. Old-Fashioned Polenta with Honey

Ready in about 15 minutes
Servings 6

Feel free to add Greek-style yogurt just before serving. Cleaning tip: Wash the inner pot right after you're done using it.

Per serving: 338 Calories; 8.1g Fat; 63.9g Carbs; 4g Protein; 23.7g Sugars

Ingredients

2 cups polenta
1/2 cup honey
1/2 stick butter
1 teaspoon salt
2 quarts water

Directions

- In a mixing bowl, whisk the polenta, 2 cups water and salt.
- Pour the remaining water into the bottom of your Power pressure cooker XL. Press the RICE/RISOTTO key. Use the TIME ADJUSTMENT key to set time to 8 minutes.
- Place the lid on the Power pressure cooker XL, lock the lid and switch the pressure release valve to closed.
- Once the timer reaches 0, the cooker will automatically switch to KEEP WARM/CANCEL. Allow the pressure to drop on its own; carefully remove the cooker's lid.
- Stir in the butter and honey. Serve and enjoy!

387. Cinnamon Pumpkin Oatmeal

Ready in about 15 minutes
Servings 4

Oatmeal is a staple food among people who tend to eat healthily. If you have never made oatmeal in your Power pressure cooker XL, here's a chance to amaze your family for breakfast!

Per serving: 264 Calories; 17.6g Fat; 23.6g Carbs; 6g Protein; 3.2g Sugars

Ingredients

1 ½ cups pumpkin puree
2 cups steel-cut oats
1 ½ teaspoons cinnamon
3/4 cup unsweetened almond milk
1/2 stick butter
1/4 cup pepitas
2 tablespoons agave syrup
1/2 teaspoon salt
1/2 teaspoon grated nutmeg
3 cups water

Directions

- Simply throw all of the above ingredients, minus pepitas, into your Power pressure cooker XL.
- Press the RICE/RISOTTO key. Place the lid on the Power pressure cooker XL, lock the lid and switch the pressure release valve to closed. Cook for 6 minutes.
- Once the timer reaches 0, the cooker will automatically switch to KEEP WARM/CANCEL. When the steam is completely released, carefully remove the cooker's lid.
- Sprinkle toasted pepitas over the top and serve right away!

388. Millet and Sweet Potato Soup

Ready in about 15 minutes
Servings 4

With a mild and delicate flavor, millet pairs perfectly with sweet potatoes. This gorgeous ancient grain couldn't be easier to prepare!

Per serving: 374 Calories; 6g Fat; 73.3g Carbs; 7.6g Protein; 3.1g Sugars

Ingredients

3/4 cup millet
4 sweet potatoes, peeled and diced
1 carrot, diced
1 teaspoon garlic paste
1 celery stalk, chopped
1/2 cup white onions, chopped
3 teaspoons coconut oil
5 cups stock
1/2 teaspoon dried thyme
1/4 teaspoon ground black pepper
1 teaspoon red pepper, flakes
1/2 teaspoon sea salt

Directions

- Add all of the above ingredients to your Power pressure cooker XL. Press the SOUP/STEW key.
- Place the lid on the Power pressure cooker XL, lock the lid and switch the pressure release valve to closed. Cook for 10 minutes.
- Once the timer reaches 0, the cooker will automatically switch to KEEP WARM/CANCEL. When the steam is completely released, carefully remove the cooker's lid.
- Taste and adjust the seasonings; serve right away!

389. Barley with Goat Cheese

Ready in about 30 minutes
Servings 6

Barley is an amazingly nutritious grain that can help lower cholesterol and high blood pressure. Eat this dish as a hot breakfast during winter or an appetizer.

Per serving: 425 Calories; 19.1g Fat; 54.3g Carbs; 9.8g Protein; 1.6g Sugars

Ingredients

2 cups pot barley
1/2 cup goat cheese, crumbled
1 stick butter, melted
6 cups stock
1 cup spring onions, finely chopped
1 teaspoon cayenne pepper
1/4 teaspoon ground black pepper
1/2 teaspoon kosher salt

Directions

- Press the RICE/RISOTTO key and use the cook time selector to adjust to 25 minutes. Then, warm the butter; sauté spring onions until just tender, about 3 minutes.
- Add the stock, barley and spices. Place the lid on the Power pressure cooker XL, lock the lid and switch the pressure release valve to closed.
- Once the timer reaches 0, the cooker will automatically switch to KEEP WARM/CANCEL. When the steam is completely released, carefully remove the cooker's lid.
- Add the goat cheese just before serving.

390. Chia and Orange Oatmeal

Ready in about 15 minutes
Servings 4

Don't skip the last step and soak chia seeds at least 15 minutes. You will have a gel consistency like pudding; in addition, it makes this oatmeal much more nutritious to your body.

Per serving: 238 Calories; 7g Fat; 40.1g Carbs; 6.2g Protein; 14.7g Sugars

Ingredients

1 ½ cups orange juice
1 ½ cups steel cut oats
1/3 cup chia seeds
3 tablespoons brown sugar
2 teaspoons coconut oil
1/2 teaspoon kosher salt
1/2 teaspoon grated orange peel
1 ½ cups water

Directions

- Press the RICE/RISOTTO key. Warm coconut oil and toast the steel-cut oats until they smell nutty, about 3 minutes. Press the CANCEL key.
- Add the remaining ingredients, minus chia seeds.
- Press the RICE/RISOTTO key. Place the lid on the Power pressure cooker XL, lock the lid and switch the pressure release valve to closed. Cook for 6 minutes.
- Once the timer reaches 0, the cooker will automatically switch to KEEP WARM/CANCEL. When the steam is completely released, carefully remove the cooker's lid.
- Stir in chia seeds. Then, let it sit about 15 minutes. Serve with a splash of milk if desired.

391. Chicken and Kamut Soup

Ready in about 15 minutes
Servings 4

Kamut is an ancient grain that is loaded with manganese, fiber and protein. This is a must-try recipe for a family dinner.

Per serving: 247 Calories; 9g Fat; 18.8g Carbs; 23.4g Protein; 4.6g Sugars

Ingredients

4 chicken thighs
1/2 cup kamut
1 cup celery, diced
3 cloves garlic, pressed
2 onions, chopped
1 cup carrots, diced
1 tablespoon vegetable oil
1 cup fennel bulb, chopped
1 cup cauliflower, cut into florets
1 teaspoon cayenne pepper
1/2 teaspoon sea salt
1/4 teaspoon ground black pepper
4 ½ cups water

Directions

- Press the CHICKEN/MEAT key and warm the oil; then, brown the chicken thighs for 3 to 4 minutes per side. Press the CANCEL key.
- Add the remaining ingredients. Press the SOUP/STEW key; place the lid on the Power pressure cooker XL, lock the lid and switch the pressure release valve to closed. Cook for 10 minutes.
- Once the timer reaches 0, the cooker will automatically switch to KEEP WARM/CANCEL. When the steam is completely released, carefully remove the cooker's lid.
- Season to taste and serve right away!

392. Tropical Quinoa Salad

Ready in about 15 minutes
Servings 8

Here's a great summertime recipe your family will love. With a nutty flavor and amazing health benefits, quinoa is a king in the grain family!

Per serving: 378 Calories; 23.6g Fat; 35.8g Carbs; 8.8g Protein; 2.5g Sugars

Ingredients

For the Salad:
2 cups quinoa, rinsed and drained
4 cups water
1 cup grapefruit, peeled and broken into sections
3 teaspoons vegetable oil
2 avocados, peeled and sliced
1/2 cup slivered almond
1/2 teaspoon kosher salt

For the Dressing:
2 tablespoons olive oil
1/2 cup sour cream
2 teaspoons lemon juice
2 tablespoons fresh mint leaves, chopped

Directions

- Add quinoa and water to the Power pressure cooker XL. Press the RICE/RISOTTO key. Use the TIME ADJUSTMENT key to set time to 8 minutes.
- Place the lid on the Power pressure cooker XL, lock the lid and switch the pressure release valve to closed.
- Once the timer reaches 0, the cooker will automatically switch to KEEP WARM/CANCEL. After that, carefully remove the cooker's lid. Allow your quinoa to cool completely.
- Add the remaining ingredients for the salad and stir to combine.
- Then, whisk the ingredients for the dressing. Dress the salad and serve.

393. Wheat Berry Salad with Walnuts

Ready in about 35 minutes
Servings 6

You can't go wrong with a healthy wheat berry salad. Serve with Comté cheese, strong-flavored Swiss cheese like Gruyere or smooth Beaufort if desired.

Per serving: 138 Calories; 6.8g Fat; 17.9g Carbs; 3.9g Protein; 1.3g Sugars

Ingredients

2 cups wheat berries
2 tablespoons walnuts, toasted and roughly chopped
2 tomatoes, chopped
2 tablespoons extra-virgin olive oil
4 scallions, white and green parts, chopped
1/4 cup parsley leaves, finely chopped
1/2 teaspoon salt
6 cups water

Directions

- Place the water and wheat berries in the Power pressure cooker XL. Press the RICE/RISOTTO key and use the cook time selector to adjust to 25 minutes.
- Place the lid on the Power pressure cooker XL, lock the lid and switch the pressure release valve to closed. Cook for 6 minutes.
- Once the timer reaches 0, the cooker will automatically switch to KEEP WARM/CANCEL. When the steam is completely released, carefully remove the cooker's lid.
- Toss with the remaining ingredients and serve well-chilled.

394. Breakfast Risotto with Bacon

Ready in about 30 minutes
Servings 6

Combat windy and cold mornings with this rich and satisfying breakfast. Regardless of whether you are a very beginner or an old hand at pressure cooking, you must try this recipe.

Per serving: 306 Calories; 8.5g Fat; 42.1g Carbs; 15.8g Protein; 2.1g Sugars

Ingredients

2 cups wild rice
6 strips bacon, diced
1 teaspoon minced garlic
4 cups roasted vegetable stock
1 yellow onion, peeled and chopped
1/2 teaspoon ground black pepper
1 teaspoon salt
1 tablespoon fresh sage leaves, chopped

Directions

- Press the CHICKEN/MEAT key and brown the bacon for 4 minutes. Add the onions and garlic and sauté them until just tender. Press the CANCEL key and reserve.
- Now, add the rice and stock to the Power pressure cooker XL. Press the RICE/RISOTTO key and use the cook time selector to adjust to 25 minutes.
- Place the lid on the Power pressure cooker XL, lock the lid and switch the pressure release valve to closed.
- Once the timer reaches 0, the cooker will automatically switch to KEEP WARM/CANCEL. When the steam is completely released, carefully remove the cooker's lid.
- Add the reserved bacon mixture; stir in sage, salt and black pepper. Give it a good stir before serving. Top with poached egg and serve.

395. Polenta Squares with Gorgonzola and Pancetta

Ready in about 1 hour 20 minutes
Servings 6

Looking for a stress-free festive appetizer? A rich and flavorsome, these polenta squares are guaranteed to make your holidays so much better.

Per serving: 349 Calories; 14.1g Fat; 43.9g Carbs; 12.1g Protein; 1.8g Sugars

Ingredients

2 cups polenta
6 strips pancetta, diced and fried
1 ½ ounces Gorgonzola cheese, crumbled
1 teaspoon garlic, finely minced
1 onion, chopped
1 tablespoon vegetable oil
4 cups stock
2 sprigs dried rosemary
2 sprigs dried thyme
Sea salt and black pepper, to taste

Directions

- Press the SOUP/STEW key and warm the oil; sauté the garlic and onions until they're softened and translucent.
- Add the stock, polenta, salt, black pepper, rosemary and thyme. Place the lid on the Power pressure cooker XL, lock the lid and switch the pressure release valve to closed. Cook for 10 minutes.
- Once the timer reaches 0, the cooker will automatically switch to KEEP WARM/CANCEL. When the steam is completely released, carefully remove the cooker's lid.
- Spoon polenta into a baking pan coated with a non-stick cooking spray. Place in your refrigerator for 1 hour; after that, cut the firm polenta into squares.
- Heat a nonstick skillet over medium-high flame. Coat the pan with a nonstick cooking spray. Fry polenta squares for 6 minutes on each side or until golden.
- Top each square with pancetta and cheese. Serve and enjoy!

396. Family Colorful Risotto

Ready in about 40 minutes
Servings 6

This nice and easy family dish features brown rice cooked with a variety of vegetables and basic spices. For an extra flavor, add a few pinches of Mediterranean herbs.

Per serving: 315 Calories; 4.4g Fat; 61.8g Carbs; 7.8g Protein; 7g Sugars

Ingredients

2 cups brown rice
1 red onion, peeled and chopped
2 ripe Roma tomatoes, chopped
1/2 teaspoon brown sugar
1/2 cup carrots, chopped
3 teaspoons canola oil
4 cups roasted vegetable broth
2 bell peppers, stemmed, cored, and chopped
1 ½ teaspoons finely minced garlic
1 ½ cups frozen green peas, thawed
Salt and ground black pepper, to your liking

Directions

- Press the RICE/RISOTTO key and heat canola oil until sizzling. Now, sauté the onions and garlic until tender and aromatic.
- Now, add the carrots and bell peppers; cook, stirring continuously, for 5 more minutes. Press the CANCEL key.
- Add the rice, salt, black pepper, broth, chopped tomatoes and brown sugar to the Power pressure cooker XL.
- Now, choose the RICE/RISOTTO function and use the cook time selector to adjust to 18 minutes.
- Place the lid on the Power pressure cooker XL, lock the lid and switch the pressure release valve to closed.
- Once the timer reaches 0, the cooker will automatically switch to KEEP WARM/CANCEL. When the steam is completely released, carefully remove the cooker's lid.
- Throw in the thawed green peas; place the lid on the cooker and allow it to sit approximately 15 minutes. Serve warm.

397. Millet Breakfast Porridge

Ready in about 20 minutes
Servings 6

You can experiment with this breakfast porridge and add sweetener of choice, nuts, toasted coconut flakes and another combo of fruits.

Per serving: 439 Calories; 17.1g Fat; 65.1g Carbs; 9g Protein; 7g Sugars

Ingredients

2 cups millet, rinsed and drained in a fine mesh strainer
1/4 cup dried figs, roughly chopped
2 bananas, sliced
1 cup almond milk
2 tablespoons coconut oil
1/2 teaspoon vanilla
1/2 teaspoon cinnamon
1/4 teaspoon nutmeg
1/2 teaspoon kosher salt
2 cups water

Directions

- Add all ingredients, except for bananas, to your Power pressure cooker XL. Press the SOUP/STEW key.
- Place the lid on the Power pressure cooker XL, lock the lid and switch the pressure release valve to closed. Cook for 10 minutes.
- Once the timer reaches 0, the cooker will automatically switch to KEEP WARM/CANCEL. When the steam is completely released, carefully remove the cooker's lid.
- Serve in individual bowls topped with sliced bananas.

398. Wild Rice Pilaf with Chicken

Ready in about 30 minutes
Servings 6

Make the most of your Power pressure cooker XL and prepare a big batch for easy meals throughout the week.

Per serving: 328 Calories; 6.5g Fat; 46.7g Carbs; 22.2g Protein; 5g Sugars

Ingredients

2 cups wild rice, rinsed and drained
2 chicken breasts, cut into bite-sized chunks
1 tablespoon habanero pepper, seeded and chopped
2 bell peppers, seeded and chopped
2 yellow onions, chopped
1 teaspoon finely minced garlic
1 tablespoon vegetable oil
1 teaspoon cayenne pepper
2 sprigs dry rosemary
1/4 teaspoon ground black pepper
4 cups water

Directions

- Press the RICE/RISOTTO key and warm the oil. Then, sauté the onions and garlic until just tender and fragrant.
- Then, stir in the chicken; cook until no longer pink.
- Add the remaining ingredients. Place the lid on the Power pressure cooker XL, lock the lid and switch the pressure release valve to closed. Use the cook time selector to adjust to 25 minutes.
- Once the timer reaches 0, the cooker will automatically switch to KEEP WARM/CANCEL. When the steam is completely released, carefully remove the cooker's lid.
- Give it a good stir and serve.

399. Tangy Barley with Goat Cheese

Ready in about 30 minutes
Servings 4

Here's a rich and refreshing salad you will crave during summer days! This recipe calls for pearl barley but pot barley would work just as well.

Per serving: 294 Calories; 9.7g Fat; 42.2g Carbs; 11g Protein; 2.2g Sugars

Ingredients

1 ½ cups pearl barley
1/2 cup goat cheese
1 tablespoon canola oil
1/2 celery, chopped
1 carrot, thinly sliced
1 cup onions, peeled and chopped
1 teaspoon basil
1 teaspoon sea salt
1/2 teaspoon ground black pepper

Directions

- Press the RICE/RISOTTO key and warm the oil; now, sauté the onions, celery and carrot until tender, about 4 minutes.
- Add the remaining ingredients, minus goat cheese. Pour in 6 cups of water.
- Place the lid on the Power pressure cooker XL, lock the lid and switch the pressure release valve to closed. Use the cook time selector to adjust to 25 minutes.
- Once the timer reaches 0, the cooker will automatically switch to KEEP WARM/CANCEL. When the steam is completely released, carefully remove the cooker's lid.
- Serve topped with goat cheese. Enjoy!

400. Red Quinoa Pudding with Banana

Ready in about 10 minutes
Servings 4

If you are not in a hurry, soak the quinoa for 30 minutes before adding to the cooker. If you want to indulge your sweet tooth, drizzle honey or maple syrup over the pudding.

Per serving: 417 Calories; 31.8g Fat; 32.7g Carbs; 5.5g Protein; 13.9g Sugars

Ingredients

2 cups red quinoa
2 bananas, sliced
2 cups almond milk
2 tablespoons golden raisins
2 teaspoons peanut oil
1/2 teaspoon ground cardamom
1 teaspoon pure vanilla extract
1/4 teaspoon nutmeg
1/4 teaspoon ground anise star
1/4 teaspoon salt
2 cups water

Directions

- Press the RICE/RISOTTO key. Add all ingredients, except for sliced banana.
- Place the lid on the Power pressure cooker XL, lock the lid and switch the pressure release valve to closed.
- Once the timer reaches 0, the cooker will automatically switch to KEEP WARM/CANCEL.
- When the steam is completely released, carefully remove the cooker's lid. Serve topped with sliced banana. Bon appétit!

401. Indian-Style Rice Pudding

Ready in about 10 minutes
Servings 8

This Indian-inspired recipe has a rich taste thanks to the carefully selected seasonings. If you don't have jaggery on hand, use regular brown sugar.

Per serving: 309 Calories; 8.2g Fat; 52.5g Carbs; 6.8g Protein; 5.6g Sugars

Ingredients

2 ½ cups jasmine rice
1/2 cup slivered almonds, toasted
1/2 cup pistachios, thinly sliced
1 ½ ounces jaggery
2 tablespoons unsalted butter
1 cup milk
1 teaspoon vanilla extract
1 teaspoon lightly crushed saffron
3/4 teaspoon cardamom seeds
1/4 teaspoon salt
3 cups water

Directions

- Add the rice, butter, water, salt, milk, jaggary, saffron, cardamom seeds, and vanilla extract to the Power pressure cooker XL.
- Press the RICE/RISOTTO key. Place the lid on the Power pressure cooker XL, lock the lid and switch the pressure release valve to closed. Cook for 6 minutes.
- Once the timer reaches 0, the cooker will automatically switch to KEEP WARM/CANCEL.
- When the steam is completely released, carefully remove the cooker's lid. Stir in the almonds and place the lid on the cooker.
- Serve in individual bowls, topped with pistachios.

402. Homemade Sweet Cornbread

Ready in about 35 minutes
Servings 4

The Power pressure cooker XL keeps the cornbread plump and moist, a good match for honey. Serve with Greek-style yogurt.

Per serving: 332 Calories; 14.6g Fat; 41.7g Carbs; 8.5g Protein; 3.6g Sugars

Ingredients

1 ¼ cups cornmeal
1 teaspoon baking powder
1/2 stick butter, melted but at room temperature
1 cup buttermilk
2 eggs, whisked
1/2 teaspoon salt
1/2 cup water
Honey, to drizzle

Directions

- Combine the polenta, baking powder and salt in a mixing bowl. In another bowl, mix the butter, buttermilk, water and eggs. Then, stir the wet ingredients into the dry ingredients.
- Pour the batter into a well-greased baking pan. Add 1 ½ cups of water and a metal rack to the Power pressure cooker XL.
- Press the SOUP/STEW key. Place the lid on the Power pressure cooker XL, lock the lid and switch the pressure release valve to closed. Use the cook time selector to adjust to 30 minutes.
- Once the timer reaches 0, the cooker will automatically switch to KEEP WARM/CANCEL. When the steam is completely released, carefully remove the cooker's lid.
- Serve warm drizzled with honey. Enjoy!

403. Autumn Porridge with Pumpkin

Ready in about 15 minutes
Servings 8

Himalayan salt regulates water levels in your body and promotes vascular health. It is definitely the cleanest salt available on the Earth.

Per serving: 332 Calories; 14.6g Fat; 41.7g Carbs; 8.5g Protein; 3.6g Sugars

Ingredients

2 ½ cups basmati rice
2 cups pumpkin purée
1/2 cup butter
1/2 cup walnuts, roasted and coarsely chopped
1/4 teaspoon Himalayan salt
1/3 teaspoon cardamom
1/8 teaspoon freshly grated nutmeg
1/2 teaspoon crystallized ginger
1/4 teaspoon cinnamon
3 2/3 cups water

Directions

- Add the rice and water to the Power pressure cooker XL. In a bowl, combine the remaining ingredients, except for the walnuts. Add this mixture to the cooker and stir to combine.
- Press the RICE/RISOTO key once to select 6 minutes.
- Place the lid on the Power pressure cooker XL, lock the lid and switch the pressure release valve to closed.
- Once the timer reaches 0, the cooker will automatically switch to KEEP WARM/CANCEL. When the steam is completely released, carefully remove the cooker's lid.
- Scatter chopped walnuts over the top. Serve and enjoy!

404. Aromatic and Sweet Wild Rice

Ready in about 30 minutes
Servings 8

This dessert risotto is as delicious as it looks. You can use another combo of dried fruits; to serve, feel free to add your favorite fresh fruits or nuts.

Per serving: 258 Calories; 5.9g Fat; 46.1g Carbs; 7.4g Protein; 14.7g Sugars

Ingredients

2 cups wild rice
1/2 cup dried apricot, roughly chopped
1/3 cup maple syrup
1 ½ cups apple juice
3 egg yolks
1/2 cup almond milk
1/2 teaspoon ground cinnamon
1 teaspoon vanilla extract
1/2 teaspoon candied ginger
1/4 teaspoon salt
4 cups water

Directions

- Add all of the above ingredients, except dried apricots, to the Power pressure cooker XL. Press the RICE/RISOTO key; use the cook time selector to adjust to 25 minutes.
- Place the lid on the Power pressure cooker XL, lock the lid and switch the pressure release valve to closed.
- Once the timer reaches 0, the cooker will automatically switch to KEEP WARM/CANCEL. When the steam is completely released, carefully remove the cooker's lid.
- Stir in the chopped apricots. Served dolloped with whipped cream if desired. Enjoy!

405. Saucy Jasmine Rice

Ready in about 15 minutes
Servings 4

So healthy, so tasty, this risotto-like dish makes a complete meal for your family. When it comes to a carb intake in your diet, you should give up white bread but you don't have to give up amazing jasmine rice.

Per serving: 324 Calories; 4.1g Fat; 65.1g Carbs; 5.9g Protein; 2.6g Sugars

Ingredients

1 ½ cups jasmine rice
1 cup fennel bulb, chopped
1 cup parsnip, trimmed and chopped
2 spring onions, sliced
1 carrot, trimmed and chopped
3 teaspoons olive oil
1 teaspoon dried sage
1/4 teaspoon ground black pepper
1 teaspoon salt
2 cups stock
1 cup water

Directions

- Press the RICE/RISOTTO key and heat olive oil until sizzling; now, sauté the onions until translucent. Add the carrots, parsnip and fennel and continue sautéing another 3 minutes.
- Press the KEEP/WARM/CANCEL key. Add the remaining ingredients.
- Press the RICE/RISOTTO key and then, press the TIME ADJUSTMENT key until you reach 10 minutes.
- Place the lid on the Power pressure cooker XL, lock the lid and switch the pressure release valve to closed.
- Once the timer reaches 0, the cooker will automatically switch to KEEP WARM/CANCEL. When the steam is completely released, carefully remove the cooker's lid. Serve right away.

406. Chocolate and Berry Oatmeal

Ready in about 15 minutes
Servings 4

Oatmeal with a twist! The combination of berries and oats is incredibly delicious whilst the cocoa powder completes the whole dish. Dark chocolate sprinkles work well as a garnish.

Per serving: 310 Calories; 14g Fat; 43.4g Carbs; 4.9g Protein; 17.8g Sugars

Ingredients

2 tablespoons cocoa powder
1 cup mixed berries, for garnish
1 ½ cups quick cooking oats
1/2 cup apple juice
1/2 stick butter
4 tablespoons maple syrup
1/2 teaspoon grated nutmeg
1/2 teaspoon cinnamon
1/4 teaspoon kosher salt
2 ½ cups water

Directions

- Firstly, press the RICE/RISOTTO key and melt the butter; next, toast the oats until they have a nutty aroma, about 4 minutes. Press the CANCEL key.
- Add the remaining ingredients, except for mixed berries. Press the RICE/RISOTTO key once to select 6 minutes.
- Place the lid on the Power pressure cooker XL, lock the lid and switch the pressure release valve to closed.
- Once the timer reaches 0, the cooker will automatically switch to KEEP WARM/CANCEL. When the steam is completely released, carefully remove the cooker's lid.
- Serve topped with mixed berries. Enjoy!

407. Garbanzo Bean and Rice Salad

Ready in about 25 minutes
Servings 8

If you are looking for a healthy lunch option during long summer days, this salad is sure to please! Add a few Kalamata olives to awaken all the senses.

Per serving: 444 Calories; 10.6g Fat; 73.6g Carbs; 15.3g Protein; 7.9g Sugars

Ingredients

1 (15-ounce) can garbanzo beans
2 cups brown rice
2 carrots, grated
2 Roma tomatoes, diced
1 cup sour cream
1 red onion, peeled and thinly sliced
1 teaspoon saffron
1 teaspoon crushed red pepper flakes
1/2 teaspoon dried marjoram
1/2 teaspoon salt
3 ½ cups water

Directions

- Add the water and rice to the Power pressure cooker XL. Press the RICE/RISOTTO key and use the cook time selector to adjust to 18 minutes.
- Place the lid on the Power pressure cooker XL, lock the lid and switch the pressure release valve to closed.
- Once the timer reaches 0, the cooker will automatically switch to KEEP WARM/CANCEL. When the steam is completely released, carefully remove the cooker's lid. Fluff your rice using a fork; let it cool completely.
- Toss with the remaining ingredients, minus sour cream. Serve well chilled and dolloped with sour cream.

408. Hazelnut Rice Custard with Sultanas

Ready in about 30 minutes
Servings 2

Here's a great idea to impress your Valentine! This restaurant-style custard is easier to make than it looks thanks to your Power pressure cooker XL!

Per serving: 378 Calories; 12.4g Fat; 57.2g Carbs; 12.4g Protein; 36.6g Sugars

Ingredients

4 tablespoons hazelnuts, chopped
1 cup jasmine rice, cooked
1/2 cup sultanas
1 egg plus 1 egg yolk, at room temperature
1/4 cup sugar
8 ounces milk
1/3 teaspoon anise seed
1 teaspoon vanilla paste
A pinch of kosher salt
1/3 teaspoon hazelnut extract

Directions

- Treat the inside of a baking dish with a butter-flavored non-stick cooking spray. Set a metal rack inside the Power pressure cooker XL; pour in 1 ½ cups of water.
- In a bowl, combine the milk, eggs and egg yolks until frothy. Stir in the remaining ingredients; pour the mixture into the prepared baking dish. Cover tightly with a piece of aluminum foil.
- Make an aluminum foil sling and lower the dish onto the rack in the Power pressure cooker XL. Choose the RICE/RISOTTO function and use the cook time selector to adjust to 25 minutes.
- Place the lid on the Power pressure cooker XL, lock the lid and switch the pressure release valve to closed.
- Once the timer reaches 0, the cooker will automatically switch to KEEP WARM/CANCEL. When the steam is completely released, carefully remove the cooker's lid.
- Allow the pressure to release naturally. Serve and enjoy!

409. Barley Salad with Mint and Nuts

Ready in about 30 minutes +
chilling time
Servings 6

Light and vibrantly flavored, this barley salad makes a fine addition to your summer lunch. Whip up the salad ahead of time so the flavors can blend.

Per serving: 370 Calories; 14.4g Fat; 53.9g Carbs; 7.9g Protein; 1g Sugars

Ingredients

2 cups pot barley
1/4 cup chopped fresh mint
1/3 cup pine nuts, chopped
1/4 cup extra-virgin olive oil
3 spring onions, chopped
1/2 cup sparkling wine
2 teaspoons lemon zest
1/2 teaspoon sea salt
1 teaspoon red pepper flakes, crushed
1/2 teaspoon shallot powder
6 cups water

Directions

- Add the water and barley to the Power pressure cooker XL. Press the RICE/RISOTTO key. Use the cook time selector to adjust to 25 minutes.
- Place the lid on the Power pressure cooker XL, lock the lid and switch the pressure release valve to closed.
- Once the timer reaches 0, the cooker will automatically switch to KEEP WARM/CANCEL. When the steam is completely released, carefully remove the cooker's lid.
- Add the remaining ingredients. Then, place your salad in the refrigerator at least 3 hours. Eat well-chilled and enjoy!

410. Quinoa Salad with Yogurt and Herbs

Ready in about 15 minutes
Servings 2

This refreshing, herby salad features quinoa, a high-protein grain with lots of health benefits. Add cucumber and baby spinach if desired.

Per serving: 382 Calories; 18.3g Fat; 44.5g Carbs; 11g Protein; 2.4g Sugars

Ingredients

3/4 cup quinoa
1/2 (6-ounce) carton plain low-fat yogurt
2 teaspoons chopped fresh mint leaves
3 tablespoons chopped fresh cilantro
2 green onions, thinly sliced
1 garlic clove, crushed
2 tablespoons olive oil
2 ½ cups water

Directions

- Place the water and quinoa in the Power pressure cooker XL. Press the RICE/RISOTTO key. Use the TIME ADJUSTMENT key to set time to 8 minutes.
- Place the lid on the Power pressure cooker XL, lock the lid and switch the pressure release valve to closed.
- Once the timer reaches 0, the cooker will automatically switch to KEEP WARM/CANCEL. After that, carefully remove the cooker's lid. Allow your quinoa to cool completely.
- Add the remaining ingredients and stir to combine well. Serve well-chilled and enjoy!

411. Easy Quinoa Pilaf

Ready in about 20 minutes
Servings 6

This quinoa dish makes a light and easy dinner or a healthy side dish. Pressure cooking is one of the best methods to cook smooth and flavorsome quinoa.

Per serving: 314 Calories; 6.7g Fat; 52.7g Carbs; 11.3g Protein; 3.7g Sugars

Ingredients

2 ½ cups quinoa
3 teaspoons butter, milted
5 cups stock
2 small-sized white onions, finely chopped
2 carrots, trimmed and chopped
1 teaspoon sea salt
1/2 teaspoon ground black pepper

Directions

- Choose the RICE/RISOTTO function. Now, melt the butter and sauté the onions until tender, about 5 minutes. Add the carrots and continue sautéing for 5 minutes more. Press the CANCEL key.
- Add the remaining ingredients to the Power pressure cooker XL. Press the RICE/RISOTTO key. Use the TIME ADJUSTMENT key to set time to 8 minutes.
- Place the lid on the Power pressure cooker XL, lock the lid and switch the pressure release valve to closed.
- Once the timer reaches 0, the cooker will automatically switch to KEEP WARM/CANCEL. After that, carefully remove the cooker's lid. Serve and enjoy!

412. Kamut Salad with Cheese

Ready in about 20 minutes
Servings 6

Kamut, also known as Khorasan wheat and Oriental wheat, protects your bones, digestive system and brain. This salad is packed with protein, fiber and vitamins. If you don't have halloumi cheese on hand, feel free to use feta cheese or a dollop of mascarpone.

Per serving: 264 Calories; 12.6g Fat; 28.6g Carbs; 10.6g Protein; 4.2g Sugars

Ingredients

For the Salad:
2 cups kamut
2 teaspoons coconut oil, at room temperature
1/2 cup halloumi cheese, for garnish
2 bell peppers, deveined and chopped
2 garlic cloves, chopped
1 cup cherry tomatoes, halved
2 sprigs dried rosemary, crushed
1 teaspoon salt
1/2 teaspoon black pepper
1 teaspoon smoked paprika
5 cups water

For the Vinaigrette:
2 tablespoons olive oil
2 teaspoons lemon juice
1 teaspoon honey
Salt and ground black pepper, to taste

Directions

- Add the water, oil, salt, black pepper, paprika, and rosemary to the Power pressure cooker XL. Choose the SOUP/STEW function.
- Place the lid on the Power pressure cooker XL, lock the lid and switch the pressure release valve to closed. Cook for 10 minutes.
- Once the timer reaches 0, the cooker will automatically switch to KEEP WARM/CANCEL. When the steam is completely released, carefully remove the cooker's lid. Allow your kamut to cool completely.
- Toss kamut with remaining ingredients for the salad. Then, make the vinaigrette by whisking olive oil, lemon juice, honey, salt and pepper. Dress the salad and serve well chilled.

413. Refreshing Tomato and Barley Soup

Ready in about 35 minutes
Servings 4

You will love this "no-stirring" way to cook barley soup. Vegetables and barley make this soup flavorful and filling.

Per serving: 276 Calories; 7.7g Fat; 48g Carbs; 6.5g Protein; 2g Sugars

Ingredients

1 cup pot barley
2 ripe tomatoes, chopped
1 cup shallots, chopped
2 tablespoons olive oil
1 teaspoon smoked paprika
1/2 teaspoon celery seeds
Salt and ground black pepper, to taste
3 ½ cups water

Directions

- Place all of the above ingredient in your Power pressure cooker XL.
- Press the SOUP/STEW key and use the cook time selector to adjust to 30 minutes.
- Place the lid on the Power pressure cooker XL, lock the lid and switch the pressure release valve to closed.
- Once the timer reaches 0, the cooker will automatically switch to KEEP WARM/CANCEL. When the steam is completely released, carefully remove the cooker's lid. Serve hot.

414. Parmesan Polenta Bolognese

Ready in about 45 minutes
Servings 4

This Italian-inspired dish is a nice change from pasta Bolognese. Mixed ground meat works well too.

Per serving: 330 Calories; 8.3g Fat; 39.3g Carbs; 25.4g Protein; 1.7g Sugars

Ingredients

1 ½ cups cornmeal
2 ounces grated Parmigiano-Reggiano cheese, divided
1/2 pound lean ground beef
1 yellow onion, finely chopped
1 tablespoon vegetable oil
1 ½ cups beef bone broth
1 tablespoon garlic, crushed
1/2 teaspoon salt
1 teaspoon dried basil
1 teaspoon dried rosemary, crushed
1/2 tablespoon fresh coriander, chopped
2 tablespoons fresh parsley, chopped
1 ½ cups water

Directions

- Press the MEAT/CHICKEN key; heat the vegetable oil. Now, sauté the onions and garlic until just tender and aromatic, about 3 minutes.
- Now, add the beef along with the spices and herbs; cook until browned, about 6 minutes, stirring frequently. Press the CANCEL key; reserve.
- Add the cornmeal, beef broth and water to the Power pressure cooker XL. Now, press the SOUP/STEW key and use the cook time selector to adjust to 30 minutes.
- Place the lid on the Power pressure cooker XL, lock the lid and switch the pressure release valve to closed.
- Once the timer reaches 0, the cooker will automatically switch to KEEP WARM/CANCEL.
- Divide polenta evenly among four serving bowls. Top each serving with Bolognese sauce; garnish with freshly grated cheese and serve immediately. Bon appétit!

415. Pecan Oatmeal with Pears

Ready in about 20 minutes
Servings 4

Cooking grains in the Power pressure cooker XL might become your favorite, hands-off prep method to getting breakfast on the table with no fuss.

Per serving: 403 Calories; 24.6g Fat; 44g Carbs; 6.9g Protein; 15g Sugars

Ingredients

1/2 cup pecans
1 ½ cups steel cut oats
2 pears, cored and sliced
1/3 cup almond milk
1 tablespoon maple syrup
2 teaspoons butter
1 teaspoon vanilla paste
1/4 teaspoon kosher salt
2 ½ cups water

Directions

- Add all of the above ingredients, except the pears, to the Power pressure cooker XL. Press the RICE/ RISOTTO key once to select 6 minutes.
- Place the lid on the Power pressure cooker XL, lock the lid and switch the pressure release valve to closed.
- Once the timer reaches 0, the cooker will automatically switch to KEEP WARM/CANCEL. When the steam is completely released, carefully remove the cooker's lid.
- Then, allow the oatmeal to rest until it reaches desired thickness. Serve with sliced pears and enjoy.

DESSERTS

416. Sweet Chocolate Dream

Ready in about 35 minutes
Servings 8

Here's a charming one-bowl chocolate dessert that is easy and delicious! Let your imagination run wild and make the chocolate cupcakes following this recipe.

Per serving: 177 Calories; 4.5g Fat; 34.9g Carbs; 5.8g Protein; 28.9g Sugars

Ingredients

1 cup cocoa powder
1 cup sugar
4 egg yolks
1/2 cups milk
2 cups buttermilk
1 teaspoon vanilla paste
1 teaspoon espresso powder
2 cups water

Directions

- In a saucepan, cook buttermilk, milk, sugar, espresso powder and vanilla paste over a medium heat.
- Turn off the heat and add the cocoa powder. Whisk in the egg yolks.
- Prepare the cooker by adding 2 cups of water. Pour the mixture into a baking dish; place the dish on a trivet in your Power pressure cooker XL.
- Press the RICE/RISOTTO key; use the cook time selector to adjust to 25 minutes. Place the lid on the Power pressure cooker XL, lock the lid and switch the pressure release valve to closed.
- Once the timer reaches 0, the cooker will automatically switch to KEEP WARM/CANCEL. When the steam is completely released, carefully remove the cooker's lid.
- Afterwards, allow the cake to cool before serving. Bon appétit!

417. Homemade Orange and Chocolate Pudding

Ready in about 20 minutes
Servings 4

This easy pudding recipe comes together quickly and bakes in your Power pressure cooker perfectly in no time.

Per serving: 407 Calories; 27.6g Fat; 36.4g Carbs; 6.7g Protein; 26.6g Sugars

Ingredients

1 tablespoon fresh orange juice
1 teaspoon grated rind of orange
2 ounces chocolate, coarsely chopped
1/3 cup sugar
2 tablespoons butter, softened
3 eggs, separated into whites and yolks
1/4 cup cornstarch
1 cup almond milk
1/8 teaspoon kosher salt
1/2 teaspoon caramelized ginger

Directions

- In a bowl, combine together the sugar, cornstarch, kosher salt, and softened butter. Stir in fresh orange juice and grated orange rind.
- Now, fold in the egg yolks, ginger, almond milk; whisk to combine well.
- Fold in well-beaten egg whites. Pour the mixture into individual custard cups. Cover each cup with a piece of an aluminum foil.
- Pour 1 ½ cups of water into the base of your Power pressure cooker XL. Place a metal rack in the Power pressure cooker XL; now, lower the cups onto the rack.
- Press the SOUP/STEW key once and place the lid on the Power pressure cooker XL; lock the lid and switch the pressure release valve to closed.
- Once the timer reaches 0, the cooker will automatically switch to KEEP WARM/CANCEL.
- When the steam is completely released, carefully remove the cooker's lid. Add the chocolate and stir to combine. Serve dolloped with whipped cream if desired.

418. Nana's Easy Caramel Flan

Ready in about 25 minutes + chilling time
Servings 4

This traditional recipe doesn't get any easier than this. A real feast for everyone who has a sweet tooth!

Per serving: 257 Calories; 13.2g Fat; 26.1g Carbs; 9.8g Protein; 25.4g Sugars

Ingredients

1/3 cup white sugar
1 (12-ounce) can evaporated milk
6 egg yolks
1/2 teaspoon vanilla paste
1/2 teaspoon cardamom seeds
1/2 teaspoon cinnamon powder
1/3 cup hot water

Directions

- In a medium saucepan, melt the sugar, stirring continuously. Add hot water and keep stirring. Pour the caramel mixture into a well-greased cookie tin.
- Pour the water into the base of the Power pressure cook XL (2 inches). Place the cookie tin in the Power pressure cooker XL. Pour the remaining ingredients into your cookie tin.
- Press the RICE/RISOTTO key and use the cook time selector to adjust to 18 minutes. Place the lid on the Power pressure cooker XL, lock the lid and switch the pressure release valve to closed.
- Once the timer reaches 0, the cooker will automatically switch to KEEP WARM/CANCEL. When the steam is completely released, carefully remove the cooker's lid.
- Let it cool completely. To serve, carefully invert it onto a serving plate when completely cool.

419. Strawberry and Tangerine Sauce

Ready in about 15 minutes + chilling time| Servings 6

Make this sauce ahead of time and impress your family for breakfast or an afternoon dessert. Serve on pikelets or waffles.

Per serving: 181 Calories; 9.9g Fat; 23.2g Carbs; 2.8g Protein; 19.6g Sugars

Ingredients

10 ounces strawberries
6 tangerines, rind and pith removed and segments cut into 1/2-inch pieces
1/2 cup almonds, slivered
1/4 cup brown sugar
3 tablespoons unsalted butter
1/3 cup water
1/2 teaspoon cloves
1 teaspoon vanilla paste
2 teaspoons fresh ginger

Directions

- Press the FISH/VEGETABLES/STEAM key. Melt the butter and add the strawberries, tangerines, ginger, cloves, sugar and water; bring it to a boil. Press the CANCEL key.
- Press the FISH/VEGETABLES/STEAM key; use the cook time selector to adjust to 4 minutes.
- Place the lid on the Power pressure cooker XL, lock the lid and switch the pressure release valve to closed.
- Once the timer reaches 0, the cooker will automatically switch to KEEP WARM/CANCEL. When the steam is completely released, carefully remove the cooker's lid.
- Allow this sauce to cool slightly; stir in vanilla and almonds. You can keep it in a fridge for up to 1 week.

420. Blood Orange and Crystallized Ginger Compote

Ready in about 10 minutes
Servings 6

You can use navel oranges instead of blood oranges; their subtle and aromatic flavor is simply irresistible. Serve over vanilla ice cream or ricotta; it is also great topped with warm custard.

Per serving: 128 Calories; 0.3g Fat; 30.8g Carbs; 1.8g Protein; 26.4g Sugars

Ingredients

6 blood oranges, cut into small pieces
3 tablespoons crystallized ginger, chopped
1/4 cup maple syrup
2 teaspoons Triple Sec
1/2 teaspoon freshly grated nutmeg
1/2 teaspoon cinnamon powder
2 cups water

Directions

- Firstly, squeeze the juice from 3 oranges; strain and reserve. Now, peel the remaining oranges. Cut the oranges into sections. Add the oranges to the Power pressure cooker XL; pour in the water.
- Press the FISH/VEGETABLES/STEAM key once to select 2 minutes. Add the nutmeg, cinnamon, crystallized ginger and reserved juice. Pour in the water.
- Place the lid on the Power pressure cooker XL, lock the lid and switch the pressure release valve to closed.
- Once the timer reaches 0, the cooker will automatically switch to KEEP WARM/CANCEL. Allow the pressure to release naturally.
- While the compote is still warm, stir in the maple syrup and Triple Sec. Allow the compote to cool completely.
- Keep refrigerated in jars for up to 10 days. Enjoy!

421. Two-Chocolate Pudding

Ready in about 20 minutes +
chilling time
Servings 6

Here is an easy version of a favorite chocolate dessert that can be enjoyed all year round! Serve topped with fresh berries, sliced banana or juicy pears.

Per serving: 373 Calories; 25.5g Fat; 28.4g Carbs; 4g Protein; 27.7g Sugars

Ingredients

1 ounce dark chocolate, shaved
5 ounces milk chocolate, chopped
2 cups buttermilk
3 egg yolks, whisked
1/2 cup sugar
1/8 teaspoon grated nutmeg
1/2 tablespoon vanilla essence
1/2 teaspoon pure rum extract

Directions

- Place the chocolate and the sugar in a mixing bowl. Press the BEANS/LENTILS key and heat the buttermilk until it is thoroughly warmed. Press the CANCEL key.
- Pour the warmed buttermilk over the chocolate; whisk until the chocolate has melted.
- Then, whisk in the egg yolks, rum extract, vanilla extract, and grated nutmeg. Pour the mixture into six heat-safe ramekins; fill each ramekin. Cover each ramekin with a piece of foil.
- Set the rack in your Power pressure cooker XL; pour in 1 ½ cups water. Place the ramekins on the rack.
- Press the BEANS/LENTILS key and then, press the COOK TIME SELECTOR key until you reach 15 minutes.
- Place the lid on the Power pressure cooker XL, lock the lid and switch the pressure release valve to closed.
- Once the timer reaches 0, the cooker will automatically switch to KEEP WARM/CANCEL.
- When the steam is completely released, remove the lid. Carefully remove the ramekins and refrigerate for 2 hours. Bon appétit!

422. Mom's Festive Fruit Dessert

Ready in about 45 minutes
Servings 10

You can add a tablespoon or two of fresh orange juice such as Seville. Feel free to decrease the amount of sugar because dried fruits provide enough sweetness.

Per serving: 432 Calories; 11.7g Fat; 73g Carbs; 7g Protein; 34.9g Sugars

Ingredients

1 cup dried figs, roughly chopped
6 ounces dried currants
2 ounces dried dates, pitted and roughly chopped
2 pears, peeled, cored and sliced
2 cups Arborio rice
4 ounces ruby port
2 tablespoons brandy
6 ounces golden caster sugar
4 cups 2% milk
4 ounces unsalted butter
1/2 teaspoon fresh ginger, peeled and grated
1/2 teaspoon ground cinnamon
1/4 teaspoon salt
1/4 teaspoon ground cloves

Directions

- In your Power pressure cooker XL, combine rice, sugar, and milk. Press the BEANS/LENTILS key and stir, bringing to a boil. Stir constantly to dissolve the sugar; press the CANCEL key.
- Then, press the RICE/RISOTTO key; use the cook time selector to adjust to 25 minutes.
- Place the lid on the Power pressure cooker XL, lock the lid and switch the pressure release valve to closed.
- Once the timer reaches 0, the cooker will automatically switch to KEEP WARM/CANCEL. When the steam is completely released, remove the lid.
- While the rice is cooking, whisk ruby port, brandy, butter and spices in a mixing bowl. Stir the spiced wine mixture into the cooker.
- Fold in the fruits and gently stir to combine. Place the lid on the Power pressure cooker XL; let it sit about 15 minutes to allow flavors to blend.

423. Raspberry and Orange Cheesecake

Ready in about 30 minutes
Servings 6

Have you ever made a cheesecake in your pressure cooker? Check out this amazing dessert that is ready in less than 30 minutes.

Per serving: 526 Calories; 33.5g Fat; 51.9g Carbs; 7.8g Protein; 39.8g Sugars

Ingredients

1 ½ cups graham cracker crust
1 cup raspberries
3 cups cream cheese
1 tablespoon fresh orange juice
3 eggs
1/2 stick butter, melted
3/4 cup sugar
1 teaspoon vanilla paste
1 teaspoon finely grated orange zest

Directions

- Set the rack inside a pressure cooker; pour in 1 ½ cups of water. Generously grease the inside of a springform baking pan.
- In a mixing bowl, combine graham cracker crust with sugar and butter. Now, press the mixture to form a crust on the bottom of the baking pan.
- Mix the raspberries and cream cheese using an electric mixer. Fold in the eggs and continue mixing until well combined. Mix in the remaining ingredients.
- Pour the mixture into the pan. Wrap the pan with a piece of foil. Make an aluminum foil sling and lower the baking pan onto the rack in the Power pressure cooker XL.
- Press the CHICKEN/MEAT key; now, use the TIME ADJUSTMENT key until you reach 20 minutes.
- Once the timer reaches 0, the cooker will automatically switch to KEEP WARM/CANCEL. When the steam is completely released, remove the cooker's lid. Allow your cheesecake to cool in the refrigerator for 3 hours. Enjoy!

424. Espresso Sunday Pudding

Ready in about 20 minutes
Servings 6

Here's an idea for a no-fuss espresso pudding for the next brunch! Transform a standard pudding into a dessert masterpiece in your Power pressure cooker XL.

Per serving: 571 Calories; 29.8g Fat; 70.5g Carbs; 7.9g Protein; 45.2g Sugars

Ingredients

For the Pudding:
1 stick butter
3/4 cup sugar
4 eggs
1 ½ cups all-purpose flour
1 teaspoon baking powder
1 ½ cups heavy cream
1/2 tablespoon espresso instant powder
3/4 teaspoon rum extract

For the Glaze:
2 tablespoons whole milk
1 cup confectioners' sugar

Directions

- In a mixing bowl, mix the butter and sugar until well blended. Add the eggs, one at a time. Next, stir in the flour; stir until everything is well incorporated.
- Mix in the remaining ingredients for the pudding. Set a wire rack in the Power pressure cooker XL. Pour 2 cups of warm water into the cooker.
- Lightly grease six ramekins. Divide the mixture among the ramekins. Lower the ramekins onto the rack.
- Choose the BEANS/LENTILS function. Set time to 15 minutes. Once the timer reaches 0, the cooker will automatically switch to KEEP WARM/CANCEL.
- When the steam is completely released, remove the cooker's lid. Invert your pudding onto the plate.
- Choose the CHICKEN/MEAT function. Add the milk and bring to a boil. Press the CANCEL key; stir in the confectioners' sugar; stir until smooth.
- Pour the glaze over the pudding and let it cool completely. Serve and enjoy!

425. Dried Fruit Compote with Ginger

Ready in about 15 minutes
Servings 4

Serve this lavish, aromatic compote and conquer your next family lunch! The best part? Thanks to the Power pressure cooker XL, it will be ready in less than 15 minutes!

Per serving: 122 Calories; 0.4g Fat; 23.8g Carbs; 1.2g Protein; 17.1g Sugars

Ingredients

1 (12-ounce) bottle strong ginger beer
1/3 cup sliced candied ginger
1 1/3 cups dried apricots
1/3 cup dried cherries
1/2 teaspoon ground cinnamon
1 teaspoon vanilla paste
1/2 teaspoon freshly grated nutmeg
4 tablespoons caster sugar
2 cups water

Directions

- Add all ingredients to the Power pressure cooker XL. Press the RICE/RISOTTO key once to select 6 minutes.
- Place the lid on the Power pressure cooker XL, lock the lid and switch the pressure release valve to closed.
- Once the timer reaches 0, the cooker will automatically switch to KEEP WARM/CANCEL. When the steam is completely released, remove the cooker's lid.
- Lastly, serve over vanilla ice cream and enjoy!

426. Cookie-Stuffed Peaches

Ready in about 20 minutes
Servings 4

The Power pressure cooker XL turns an average dessert into an extraordinary, restaurant-style treat! Make this rich-tasting favorite in your own kitchen and enjoy it to the fullest!

Per serving: 292 Calories; 13.1g Fat; 43.7g Carbs; 5.3g Protein; 24.6g Sugars

Ingredients

4 firm-ripe small peaches, halved lengthwise and pitted
8 dried dates, chopped
4 tablespoons walnuts, chopped
3/4 cup coarsely crumbled cookies
1 teaspoon cinnamon powder
1/3 teaspoon grated nutmeg
1/4 teaspoon ground cloves

Directions

- Place the peaches in an ovenproof baking dish. Then, make the filling by mixing the remaining ingredients. Then, stuff the peaches with this filling.
- Next, pour 1 ½ cups of water into your Power pressure cooker XL. Add a wire rack to the Power pressure cooker XL. Cover the ovenproof dish with a piece of foil and lower it onto the rack.
- Press the MEAT/CHICKEN key once to select 15 minutes. Place the lid on the Power pressure cooker XL, lock the lid and switch the pressure release valve to closed.
- Once the timer reaches 0, the cooker will automatically switch to KEEP WARM/CANCEL. When the steam is completely released, remove the cooker's lid. Serve at room temperature.

427. Double-Chocolate Holiday Treat

Ready in about 20 minutes + chilling time
Servings 6

Make a room for a saucy and elegant chocolate dessert! Chocolate and cocoa powder pair with a silky cream and aromatic spices for melt-in-your-mouth dessert that is perfect for a holiday table.

Per serving: 396 Calories; 28.6g Fat; 31.3g Carbs; 5.6g Protein; 25.5g Sugars

Ingredients

8 ounces bittersweet chocolate, finely chopped
3 tablespoons cocoa powder, unsweetened
1/4 cup brown sugar
2 cups heavy cream
3 egg yolks, whisked
1/2 teaspoon cardamom
1/2 tablespoon ginger, finely grated
2 teaspoons finely shredded orange peel
1 teaspoon vanilla extract

Directions

- Place the chocolate, cocoa powder and brown sugar in a mixing bowl. Press the BEANS/LENTILS key and heat the heavy cream until it is thoroughly warmed. Press the CANCEL key.
- Pour the warmed cream over the chocolate; whisk until the chocolate has melted.
- Then, whisk in the remaining ingredients. Pour the mixture into a soufflé dish. Cover the dish with a piece of foil.
- Set the rack in your Power pressure cooker XL; pour in 1 ½ cups water. Place the dish on the rack.
- Press the BEANS/LENTILS key and then press the COOK TIME SELECTOR key until you reach 15 minutes.
- Place the lid on the Power pressure cooker XL, lock the lid and switch the pressure release valve to closed.
- Once the timer reaches 0, the cooker will automatically switch to KEEP WARM/CANCEL.
- When the steam is completely released, remove the lid. Carefully remove the soufflé dish from the cooker and refrigerate for 2 hours. Bon appétit!

428. Chocolate and Macadamia Nut Delight

Ready in about 35 minutes
Servings 16

Mix 1 tablespoon of vinegar with water in the Power pressure cooker XL; it will prevent the inside of your cooker from developing a white residue.

Per serving: 311 Calories; 22.2g Fat; 27.5g Carbs; 3.4g Protein; 22g Sugars

Ingredients

6 ounces chocolate chips
2 cups macadamia nuts, peeled and halved
1 stick butter
1 ¼ cups caster sugar
1/2 teaspoon cinnamon powder
1/2 cup unbleached white flour
1 teaspoon baking powder
1 teaspoon vanilla essence
2 large eggs

Directions

- Melt the butter in a saucepan. Remove from heat and mix in chocolate.
- In a mixing bowl, combine the sugar, cinnamon, flour and baking powder. Now, add the vanilla and eggs; stir in the cooled butter/chocolate mixture. Fold in macadamia nuts.
- Lightly grease a casserole dish with a nonstick cooking spray. Pour in the batter; cover the dish with two to three pieces of foil.
- Add 2 cups of water and a metal trivet to the bottom of the Power pressure cooker XL. Lower the dish onto the trivet.
- Press the BEANS/LENTILS key and use the cook time selector to adjust to 30 minutes. Place the lid on the Power pressure cooker XL, lock the lid and switch the pressure release valve to closed.
- Once the timer reaches 0, the cooker will automatically switch to KEEP WARM/CANCEL.
- When the steam is completely released, remove the lid. Carefully remove the casserole dish from the cooker. It can be served warm or cold. Enjoy!

429. Upside-Down Plum Cake

Ready in about 35 minutes
Servings 8

It's plum season! This sticky cake is perfect for a dinner party dessert. Serve with vanilla frozen yogurt.

Per serving: 324 Calories; 19.5g Fat; 32.2g Carbs; 6.1g Protein; 14.7g Sugars

Ingredients

2 cups firm plums, pitted and sliced
1/2 tablespoon fresh orange juice
1 ½ teaspoons vanilla essence
16 ounces sour cream, room temperature
1/2 cup caster sugar
1/2 stick butter, softened
3 eggs
1 ¼ cups all-purpose flour
1/2 teaspoon baking soda
1 teaspoon baking powder
1/2 teaspoon cinnamon powder
1 teaspoon anise seeds
3/4 cup granulated white sugar

Directions

- Add 1 ½ cups water and a metal rack to the base of your Power pressure cooker XL.
- Coat a shallow heat-proof baking dish with vegetable oil and dust it with flour. Then, place a disk of wax paper at the bottom of the baking dish.
- Sprinkle the bottom of the bowl with granulated sugar; arrange the plums artistically. Drizzle with fresh orange juice.
- In a bowl, whisk together the eggs, sour cream, caster sugar, butter, and vanilla essence. Then, add the flour, cinnamon powder, anise seeds, baking powder, and baking soda. Blend to combine well; pour the mixture over the apples.
- Press the RICE/RISOTTO key and use the cook time selector to adjust to 25 minutes.
- Place the lid on the Power pressure cooker XL, lock the lid and switch the pressure release valve to closed.
- Once the timer reaches 0, the cooker will automatically switch to KEEP WARM/CANCEL. When the steam is completely released, remove the lid.
- To serve: invert your cake onto a serving platter. Bon appétit!

430. Favorite Carrot Coconut Cake

Ready in about 1 hour 5 minutes
Servings 8

This carrot cake turns out great in the Power pressure cooker XL! You can make your own cream cheese frosting ahead of time and refrigerate for three to four days.

Per serving: 320 Calories; 17.5g Fat; 39.4g Carbs; 3.7g Protein; 26.1g Sugars

Ingredients

3/4 cup carrots, shredded
1/2 cup coconut flakes
1 egg plus 1 egg yolk
1 cup sugar
1 stick butter, at room temperature
4 tablespoons macadamia nuts, chopped
1/4 teaspoon kosher salt
1 cup all-purpose flour
1 teaspoon baking powder
1/4 teaspoon baking soda
1/3 teaspoon cinnamon powder
1/2 teaspoon nutmeg
1/3 teaspoon cardamom

Directions

- In a mixing bowl, whisk together the sugar and eggs. Stir in the flour along with all spices; add the baking powder, baking soda and salt; stir until everything is well-blended.
- Fold in the butter, carrots, macadamia nuts, and coconut flakes.
- Spoon prepared batter into a baking pan oiled with a non-stick cooking spray. Cover with a piece of foil; now poke a hole in the middle of that foil.
- Pour 1 ½ cups of water into the Power pressure cooker XL; add the trivet to the bottom. Now, lower the pan onto the trivet.
- Press the SOUP/STEW key and use the cook time selector to adjust to 1 hour. Place the lid on the Power pressure cooker XL, lock the lid and switch the pressure release valve to closed.
- Once the timer reaches 0, the cooker will automatically switch to KEEP WARM/CANCEL. When the steam is completely released, remove the lid. Lastly, spread the cream cheese frosting on the sides and top of your carrot cake.

431. Easy Egg Custard

Ready in about 20 minutes
Servings 4

Top with berries and enjoy! If you have leftover custard, you can serve it with strudel, ice cream or chocolate sauce.

Per serving: 441 Calories; 27.4g Fat; 43.9g Carbs; 8.4g Protein; 41.9g Sugars

Ingredients

1 egg plus 2 egg yolks
3/4 cup sugar
1 ½ cups milk
2 cups heavy cream
1/2 teaspoon pure rum extract
1 teaspoon anise seed

Directions

- In a bowl, beat the egg and egg yolks together; add pure rum extract. Whisk in the milk and heavy cream, stirring constantly.
- Add the sugar and anise seed; pour the mixture into 4 ramekins.
- Add 1-2 cups water to the Power pressure cooker XL. Add the trivet to the cooker. Lower the ramekins onto the trivet.
- Press the SOUP/STEW key once to select 10 minutes. Place the lid on the Power pressure cooker XL, lock the lid and switch the pressure release valve to closed.
- Once the timer reaches 0, the cooker will automatically switch to KEEP WARM/CANCEL. When the steam is completely released, remove the lid. Enjoy!

432. Amazing Pumpkin Pie

Ready in about 55 minutes
Servings 6

Pumpkin pie reminds us of autumn but we can enjoy this silky and luscious dessert all year long. It is very customizable dessert especially if you cook it in your Power pressure cooker XL!

Per serving: 498 Calories; 18.7g Fat; 75.3g Carbs; 9.3g Protein; 51.6g Sugars

Ingredients

For the Filling:
2 cups pumpkin, sliced
3 eggs
3/4 cup sugar
1 1/3 cups evaporated milk
1/3 cup heavy cream
1/8 teaspoon salt
1/4 teaspoon grated nutmeg
1/2 teaspoon ground cloves
1 teaspoon cinnamon
1 teaspoon ground ginger

For the Crust:
16 ginger snaps, crushed
2 tablespoons butter, melted

Directions

- Place the water, trivet, and a steamer basket in your Power pressure cooker XL. To make the pumpkin puree: Place the pumpkin slices in the steamer basket.
- Press the BEANS/LENSTILS key once to select 5 minutes.
- Place the lid on the Power pressure cooker XL, lock the lid and switch the pressure release valve to closed.
- Once the timer reaches 0, the cooker will automatically switch to KEEP WARM/CANCEL. When the steam is completely released, remove the cooker's lid.
- Mash the pumpkin and transfer it to a large-sized bowl. Add the remaining ingredients for the filling; beat until the mixture is uniform and smooth.
- Prepare the crust by mixing crushed ginger snaps and butter. Press the crust into a lined pie pan. Place in the freezer for 15 minutes.
- Pour the filling over the prepared cookie crust. Add 1 ½ cups of water to the Power pressure cooker XL. Put the trivet into the cooker; lower the pan onto the trivet, using the foil sling. Afterwards, cover the top with a sheet of foil.
- Press the SOUP/STEW key and use the cook time selector to adjust to 30 minutes. Place the lid on the Power pressure cooker XL, lock the lid and switch the pressure release valve to closed.
- Once the timer reaches 0, the cooker will automatically switch to KEEP WARM/CANCEL. Afterwards, allow the pressure to release naturally. Chill completely in your refrigerator.

433. Coconut Quinoa Pudding

Ready in about 15 minutes
Servings 6

Quinoa is among the healthiest foods in the world. It is high in protein, fiber, minerals, and antioxidants. Serve with a dollop of whipped cream and a few tablespoons of fresh blueberries.

Per serving: 372 Calories; 16.9g Fat; 50.4g Carbs; 7.4g Protein; 19.6g Sugars

Ingredients

2 cups quinoa
3/4 cup maple syrup
2 cups unsweetened coconut milk
1 teaspoon vanilla essence
1/3 teaspoon ground cinnamon
1/2 teaspoon nutmeg, preferably freshly grated
2 cups water

Directions

- Add the water, milk, quinoa, maple syrup, vanilla, nutmeg and cinnamon powder to the Power pressure cooker XL.
- Press the RICE/RISOTTO key. Use the TIME ADJUSTMENT key to set time to 8 minutes.
- Place the lid on the Power pressure cooker XL, lock the lid and switch the pressure release valve to closed.
- Once the timer reaches 0, the cooker will automatically switch to KEEP WARM/CANCEL. When the steam is completely released, carefully remove the cooker's lid. Bon appétit!

434. Everyday Caramel Flan

Ready in about 20 minutes +
chilling time
Servings 4

If you thought it's difficult to make a caramel, think twice! As a matter of fact, it takes just a few minutes and a little bit of attention.

Per serving: 401 Calories; 10.1g Fat; 69.8g Carbs; 10.8g Protein; 69.5g Sugars

Ingredients

1/2 cup white sugar
1 cup milk
1 cup condensed milk, sweetened
2 eggs, well beaten
1/2 teaspoon ground anise
1 teaspoon vanilla paste

Directions

- Add the sugar to a sauce pan; cook the sugar over a moderate heat for 10 minutes or until the amber color has been reached. Don't forget to keep a very close eye on it!
- Slowly pour your caramel into a round oven-safe dish, tilting to coat the bottom and sides of the dish.
- In a bowl, whisk the remaining ingredients. Add the mixture to the oven-safe dish.
- Add 1-2 cups water to the Power pressure cooker XL. Add the trivet to the cooker. Lower the dish onto the trivet.
- Press the BEANS/LENTILS key once to select 5 minutes. Place the lid on the Power pressure cooker XL, lock the lid and switch the pressure release valve to closed.
- Once the timer reaches 0, the cooker will automatically switch to KEEP WARM/CANCEL. When the steam is completely released, remove the lid.
- Chill your flan overnight or for 3 hours. Unmold the flan by inserting a spatula along the sides of the dish and invert it onto a serving plate. Enjoy!

435. Stewed Fruits in Spiced Wine Syrup

Ready in about 15 minutes
Servings 6

There are a couple of things to remember and your stewed fruits will turn out perfect every time. Cover dried figs with water and microwave until they become plump but not mushy; in the meantime, soak the apricots in a cup of herbal tea.
If you prefer a thinner consistency, add in a few splashes of orange juice. And last but not least, if you want to achieve a smoky flavor, you can add green tea or jasmine tea.

Per serving: 327 Calories; 0.4g Fat; 79.3g Carbs; 1.4g Protein; 61g Sugars

Ingredients

3/4 cup sugar
2 quince, peeled, cored and cut into eighths
4 slices of candied orange
1/2 cup dried apricots
6 sun dried Black Mission figs, stemmed
3/4 cup ruby port
1 cinnamon stick
1 vanilla bean, split lengthwise
1 teaspoon whole cloves
2 cups water

Directions

- Mix all of the above ingredients in your Power pressure cooker XL.
- Press the BEANS/LENTILS key once to select 5 minutes. Place the lid on the Power pressure cooker XL, lock the lid and switch the pressure release valve to closed.
- Once the timer reaches 0, the cooker will automatically switch to KEEP WARM/CANCEL.
- When the steam is completely released, remove the cooker's lid. Enjoy!

436. Orange and Pumpkin Cheesecake

Ready in about 30 minutes
Servings 8

This lavish cheesecake is an impressive dessert that is extra easy to make in your Power pressure cooker XL. Once you taste how good this dessert is, it will become a staple for your holiday menu.

Per serving: 565 Calories; 34.6g Fat; 58.9g Carbs; 58.9g Protein; 44g Sugars

Ingredients

Zest and juice of 1 orange
1 ½ cups cooked pumpkin
2 cups butter cookie crumbs
1/2 stick butter
1/4 cup golden caster sugar
1 cup white sugar
4 eggs
1 pound cream cheese, softened
1/3 teaspoon cardamom seeds
1 teaspoon vanilla extract

Directions

- In a bowl, combine the cookie crumbs, butter and golden caster sugar to make the crust. Now, press the mixture on the bottom of the pie pan.
- Mix the cream cheese with white sugar using an electric mixer. Fold in the eggs, one at a time. Add the other ingredients and mix until everything's well incorporated.
- Pour the mixture over the crust into the pie pan. Cover with a sheet of foil.
- Add 1 ½ cups of warm water and the steaming rack to the Power pressure cooker XL. Lower the pan onto the rack.
- Now, choose the CHICKEN/MEAT function. Press the TIME ADJUSTMENT key until you reach 20 minutes.
- Place the lid on the Power Pressure Cooker XL, lock the lid and switch the pressure release valve to closed.
- Once the timer reaches 0, the cooker will automatically switch to KEEP WARM/CANCEL. When the steam is completely released, remove the cooker's lid.
- Allow it to cool completely in your refrigerator. Bon appétit!

437. Key Lime Pie

Ready in about 20 minutes
Servings 10

It's hard to imagine a festive table without a fruit pie! After cooking, you will notice that the center of the pie is a bit jiggly. Don't worry, it sets as it cools.

Per serving: 347 Calories; 16.4g Fat; 44.9g Carbs; 5.9g Protein; 27.2g Sugars

Ingredients

1 ¼ cups graham-cracker crumbs
2 tablespoons caster sugar
4 tablespoons unsalted butter, at room temperature
1 cup sour cream
4 egg yolks
1 teaspoon vanilla extract
1 (14 ounces) can sweetened condensed milk
1/3 cup white sugar
1/4 cup fresh key lime juice

Directions

- Prepare your Power pressure cooker XL by adding 1 ½ cups of water and the metal trivet to the bottom.
- Next, combine graham-cracker crumbs with butter and 2 tablespoons caster sugar. Press the crust mixture into a spring-form pan and set it aside.
- Then, in a medium-sized bowl, combine sour cream, milk, and white sugar. Beat until smooth and uniform using an electric mixer. Add the egg yolks, key lime juice, and vanilla extract.
- Pour this filling mixture over the crust in the spring-form pan.
- Next, lower the foil-wrapped pan onto the trivet in the Power pressure cooker XL. Press the CHICKEN/ MEAT once to select 15 minutes.
- When the steam is completely released, remove the lid. Carefully remove the cheesecake from the cooker.
- Remove the pan from the Power pressure cooker XL with the foil handle. Serve well-chilled and enjoy!

438. Peach and Dried Cranberry Delight

Ready in about 25 minutes
Servings 2

Make your dessert a little more excessive by adding a tablespoon or two of chopped walnuts. This is one of those desserts that taste better the second day.

Per serving: 538 Calories; 17.3g Fat; 89.7g Carbs; 9.6g Protein; 55.8g Sugars

Ingredients

4 medium-sized firm peaches, pitted and sliced
1/3 cup dried cranberries
1 tablespoon cranberry juice
1/3 stick butter, melted
1 tablespoon melted butter, unsalted
4 tablespoons white sugar
3/4 cup sweet bread crumbs
1/4 teaspoon ground cardamom
1/2 teaspoon pure vanilla extract
1 teaspoon rum extract
1/2 teaspoon ground cinnamon
1/4 teaspoon grated nutmeg

Directions

- Lightly grease a baking dish with 1 tablespoon of melted butter and set it aside. Combine the sugar, sweet bread crumbs, dried cranberries, spices, cranberry juice, vanilla, and rum extract in a mixing dish.
- In the baking dish, alternate layers of peaches and cranberry/crumb mixture.
- Pour 1/2 stick of melted butter over the layers in the baking dish; cover the dish with a piece of foil.
- Prepare the Power pressure cooker XL by adding 1- 1 ½ cups of water to the cooker's base; add a metal rack too. Lower the baking dish onto the metal rack.
- Press the RICE/RISOTTO key and use the cook time selector to adjust to 18 minutes. Place the lid on the Power pressure cooker XL, lock the lid and switch the pressure release valve to closed.
- Once the timer reaches 0, the cooker will automatically switch to KEEP WARM/CANCEL. When the steam is completely released, remove the cooker's lid. Bon appétit!

439. Easy Yummy Pear Crunch

Ready in about 25 minutes
Servings 2

Here's a great recipe for busy holidays like Christmas because you can prepare this dessert up to one day in advance.

Per serving: 426 Calories; 13.1g Fat; 78.9g Carbs; 3.3g Protein; 54.9g Sugars

Ingredients

2 pears, cored, chopped and sliced
1 ¼ cups old-fashioned oats
1/3 cup sugar
2 tablespoons melted butter
1 tablespoon orange juice
1/2 teaspoon freshly grated nutmeg
1/3 teaspoon cinnamon, ground
1/2 teaspoon vanilla essence
1 ½ cups water

Directions

- Lightly grease a baking dish with a nonstick cooking spray. Combine old fashioned oats with sugar, nutmeg, cinnamon, orange juice and vanilla essence.
- Then, alternate layers of pears and crumbs in the baking dish.
- Pour melted butter over the layers; cover baking dish with a piece of aluminum foil.
- Pour the water into the cooker; then, place a metal trivet at the base. Place the baking dish in the prepared Power pressure cooker XL.
- Press the RICE/RISOTTO key and use the cook time selector to adjust to 18 minutes. Place the lid on the Power pressure cooker XL, lock the lid and switch the pressure release valve to closed.
- Once the timer reaches 0, the cooker will automatically switch to KEEP WARM/CANCEL.
- Allow pressure to drop naturally. Afterwards, loosen the foil. Serve in individual serving dishes and enjoy!

440. Berry Tapioca Pudding

Ready in about 20 minutes
Servings 4

Perhaps one of the easiest recipes ever! This recipe brings us back to childhood by using gorgeous tapioca pearls, fragrant coconut milk, one fresh egg and a maple syrup. Lovely!

Per serving: 407 Calories; 15.7g Fat; 66.5g Carbs; 3.3g Protein; 28.7g Sugars

Ingredients

1 cup tapioca pearls
1 handful mixed berries
1/2 cup maple syrup
1 (13.5-ounce) can full fat coconut milk
1 large egg, well beaten
1/2 teaspoon 100% vanilla extract
1/4 teaspoon kosher salt
3 cups water

Directions

- Pour 1 ½ cups of water into the base of your Power pressure cooker Xl and lower in the steaming rack.
- Combine all of the above ingredients, except for berries, in an oven-proof glass bowl. Lower the bowl onto the steaming rack.
- Press the SOUP/STEW key once to select 10 minutes. Place the lid on the Power pressure cooker XL, lock the lid and switch the pressure release valve to closed.
- Once the timer reaches 0, the cooker will automatically switch to KEEP WARM/CANCEL.
- Divide among 4 individual bowls and scatter mixed berries over the top. Serve well-chilled.

441. Peanut Butter Lava Cake

Ready in about 15 minutes
Servings 10

Step into magical chocolate heaven! From now onwards, you can make your favorite cake in no time, without any hassle. And the best part is: it turns out great every time!

Per serving: 289 Calories; 19.6g Fat; 27.7g Carbs; 3.7g Protein; 23.4g Sugars

Ingredients

1 cup semi-sweet chocolate chunks
4 tablespoons peanut butter
1 cup + 2 tablespoons powdered sugar
3 eggs
1 stick butter
1/4 cup self-raising flour
1 tablespoon coconut oil
1 teaspoon pure hazelnut extract
1 teaspoon pure vanilla extract

Directions

- Firstly, microwave the butter and chocolate for 2 minutes. Mix in 1 cup of powdered sugar; mix until uniform and smooth.
- Fold in the eggs and mix again; add the flour and vanilla extract. Spray a cake mold with pam cooking spray.
- In another bowl, mix the peanut butter with coconut oil, remaining 1 tablespoon of powdered sugar and hazelnut extract.
- Pour 1/2 of the batter into the cake mold. Pour the peanut butter mixture over it. Top with the remaining batter.
- Place a metal trivet and 1 ½ cups of water in your Power pressure cooker XL. Lower the cake mold onto the trivet.
- Press the RICE/RISOTTO key. Place the lid on the cooker and cook for 8 minutes. Once the timer reaches 0, the Power pressure cooker XL will automatically switch to KEEP WARM/CANCEL. Bon appétit!

442. Peach and Ginger Cheesecake

Ready in about 25 minutes +
chilling time
Servings 8

This dessert looks fancy and tastes delectable! Decorate your cheesecake with cream swirls.

Per serving: 404 Calories; 23.4g Fat; 43.8g Carbs; 6.5g Protein; 30.9g Sugars

Ingredients

3 peaches, peeled, pitted and sliced
16 gingersnap cookies, coarsely broken
1 (8-ounce) package cream cheese, room temperature
1 tablespoon granulated sugar
3 tablespoons unsalted butter, melted
2 eggs plus 1 egg yolk
1 cup powdered sugar
1 cup sour cream
1/2 teaspoon rum extract
1/2 teaspoon grated ginger

For the Glaze:
1/3 cup peach preserves
1 teaspoon fresh lime juice

Directions

- Set the rack inside a pressure cooker; pour in 1 ½ cups of water. Generously grease the inside of a springform baking pan.
- In a mixing bowl, combine broken gingersnap cookies with granulated sugar and butter. Now, press the mixture to form a crust on the bottom of the baking pan.
- Combine the peaches, powdered sugar, cream cheese and sour cream using an electric mixer. Fold in the eggs, rum extract and ginger, and continue mixing until well combined.
- Pour the mixture into the pan. Wrap the pan with a piece of foil. Make an aluminum foil sling and lower the baking pan onto the rack in the Power pressure cooker XL.
- Press the CHICKEN/MEAT key; now, use the TIME ADJUSTMENT key until you reach 20 minutes.
- Once the timer reaches 0, the cooker will automatically switch to KEEP WARM/CANCEL. When the steam is completely released, remove the cooker's lid. Allow your cheesecake to cool in the refrigerator for 3 hours.
- To make the glaze: Combine peach preserves and lime juice in a heavy saucepan. Stir over medium heat until it comes to simmer. Spread prepared glaze over top of your cheesecake.

443. Hot Chocolate Fondue

Ready in about 5 minutes
Servings 12

There are a zillion variations of this classic chocolate fondue. You can use a tablespoon or two of coffee liqueur, a pinch of ground ancho chili peppers, a pinch of espresso powder, etc.

Per serving: 209 Calories; 14.8g Fat; 15.6g Carbs; 2.4g Protein; 13.2g Sugars

Ingredients

10 ounces milk chocolate, chopped into small pieces
2 teaspoons coconut liqueur
8 ounces heavy whipping cream
1/4 teaspoon cinnamon powder
1/8 teaspoon grated nutmeg
A pinch of salt

Directions

- Prepare your Power pressure cooker XL by adding 1 ½ cups of lukewarm water into the base; place a metal trivet in the cooker.
- In a heat-proof container, such as a mug, melt your chocolate. Add the rest of the above ingredients, except for liqueur. Transfer this container to the metal trivet.
- Choose the FISH/VEGETABLES/STEAM function and use the cook time selector to adjust to 4 minutes.
- Place the lid on the cooker. Once the timer reaches 0, the Power pressure cooker XL will automatically switch to KEEP WARM/CANCEL.
- Then, pull out the container with tongs. Mix in the coconut liqueur and serve right now with fresh fruits. Enjoy!

444. Classic Stuffed Apples

Ready in about 20 minutes
Servings 6

The only thing better than a fresh and juicy apple is the apple stuffed with nuts and dried fruits. Additionally, they are spiced perfectly and cooked in red wine.

Per serving: 127 Calories; 4.2g Fat; 23.8g Carbs; 1g Protein; 18.9g Sugars

Ingredients

1 ½ pounds apples, cored
1/2 cup dried apricots, chopped
1/3 cup sugar
1/3 cup pecans, chopped
1/4 cup graham cracker crumbs
1/3 teaspoon cardamom
1/2 teaspoon grated nutmeg
1/2 teaspoon ground cinnamon
1 ¼ cups red wine

Directions

- Arrange the apples at the bottom of your Power pressure cooker XL. Pour in red wine.
- Thoroughly combine the other ingredients, except for graham cracker crumbs. Press the MEAT/CHICKEN key once to select 15 minutes.
- Place the lid on the Power pressure cooker XL, lock the lid and switch the pressure release valve to closed.
- Once the timer reaches 0, the cooker will automatically switch to KEEP WARM/CANCEL. When the steam is completely released, remove the cooker's lid. Serve warm or at room temperature topped with graham cracker crumbs. Bon appétit!

445. Pineapple Poached in Wine Syrup

Ready in about 15 minutes
Servings 6

Here is a light, tropical-flavored finish to your holiday meal. Garnish with a dollop of whipped cream or strawberry ice cream, if desired.

Per serving: 157 Calories; 0.2g Fat; 28.5g Carbs; 0.8g Protein; 22.8g Sugars

Ingredients

2 pineapples, peeled and sliced
1 bottle fruity dry white wine
3 tablespoons honey
1/2 tablespoon candied ginger, minced
1/2 cinnamon stick
1/2 vanilla bean
1 teaspoon whole cloves
A few strips of orange rind

Directions

- Add all of the above ingredients, except for the orange rind, to your Power pressure cooker XL. Stir to combine well.
- Press the SOUP/STEW key once to select 10 minutes. Place the lid on the Power pressure cooker XL, lock the lid and switch the pressure release valve to closed.
- Once the timer reaches 0, the cooker will automatically switch to KEEP WARM/CANCEL. When the steam is completely released, remove the cooker's lid.
- Serve garnished with the orange rind.

446. Tropical Rice Pudding

Ready in about 15 minutes +
chilling time
Servings 8

Here's one of the simplest and most delicious desserts to make in the Power pressure cooker XL. Garnish your pudding with maraschino cherries, coconut flakes or ground cinnamon if desired.

Per serving: 347 Calories; 6.2g Fat; 68.9g Carbs; 4.8g Protein; 30.6g Sugars

Ingredients

1 cup wedges of papaya
2 cups Arborio rice
2 ½ tablespoons coconut oil
1/2 cups condensed milk
3/4 cup sugar
1/2 teaspoon lime zest
1 teaspoon coconut extract
1/4 teaspoon allspice
1 teaspoon vanilla extract
1/2 teaspoon salt
3 ½ cups water

Directions

- Add all ingredients, minus papaya, to the Power pressure cooker XL.
- Press the SOUP/STEW key once to select 6 minutes. Place the lid on the Power pressure cooker XL, lock the lid and switch the pressure release valve to closed.
- Once the timer reaches 0, the cooker will automatically switch to KEEP WARM/CANCEL. When the steam is completely released, remove the cooker's lid.
- Rice pudding will thicken as it cools. Top with papaya and serve chilled.

447. Dark Chocolate Tapioca Pudding

Ready in about 20 minutes + chilling time
Servings 4

This rich, creamy chocolate dessert goes well with fresh fruits. Feel free to use a coffee liqueur instead of rum and maple syrup instead of honey.

Per serving: 555 Calories; 28g Fat; 75g Carbs; 3.9g Protein; 38.8g Sugars

Ingredients

4 ounces dark chocolate, cut into chunks
1 cup tapioca pearls (not instant)
1 ½ cups almond milk
1/3 cup honey
1 tablespoon rum
1/3 teaspoon cinnamon powder
1 teaspoon vanilla extract
1/4 teaspoon kosher salt
2 cups water

Directions

- Pour 1 ½ cups of water into the base of your Power pressure cooker XL and lower in the steaming rack.
- Combine all of the above ingredients, except for chocolate, in an oven-proof glass bowl. Lower the bowl onto the steaming rack.
- Press the SOUP/STEW key once to select 10 minutes. Place the lid on the Power pressure cooker XL, lock the lid and switch the pressure release valve to closed.
- Once the timer reaches 0, the cooker will automatically switch to KEEP WARM/CANCEL.
- Divide among 4 individual bowls and scatter chocolate chunks over the top. Serve well-chilled.

448. A-Number-1 Banana Bread

Ready in about 45 minutes
Servings 12

Thanks to the Power pressure cooker XL, you can have a freshly made banana bread in 45 minutes or less.

Per serving: 283 Calories; 11.5g Fat; 44.6g Carbs; 2.9g Protein; 25.1g Sugars

Ingredients

3 ripe bananas, mashed
1 ¼ cups white sugar
3/4 cup almond milk
2 cups all-purpose flour
2/3 teaspoon baking soda
2/3 teaspoon baking powder
1 tablespoon orange juice
1 stick butter, room temperature
1/8 teaspoon salt
1/4 teaspoon cinnamon
1/2 teaspoon pure vanilla extract

Directions

- In a medium-sized bowl, combine together the flour, baking soda, baking powder, vanilla, sugar, and salt.
- Add the cinnamon, orange juice and mashed bananas. Slowly stir in the butter and almond milk. Gently stir until everything is well incorporated.
- Pour the batter into a round pan. Next, place the trivet in the bottom of the Power pressure cooker XL and fill with 1 ½ cups of water. Lower the pan onto the trivet.
- Press the CHICKEN/MEAT key and use the cook time selector to adjust to 40 minutes.
- Place the lid on the Power pressure cooker XL, lock the lid and switch the pressure release valve to closed.
- Once the timer reaches 0, the cooker will automatically switch to KEEP WARM/CANCEL. Serve at room temperature.

449. Bread Pudding with Strawberry Sauce

Ready in about 35 minutes
Servings 6

This pudding is chock-full of dried fruits, chocolate and milk and topped with amazing strawberry syrup. Yummy!

Per serving: 543 Calories; 11.1g Fat; 101.8g Carbs; 7.6g Protein; 72.3g Sugars

Ingredients

5 cups dry 3/4-inch Italian bread cubes
1 (16-ounce) container frozen sliced strawberries in syrup, thawed
1/4 cup strawberry preserves
2 cups condensed milk
1 cup semisweet chocolate pieces
1/3 cup sour cream
3/4 cup white sugar
1/4 cup sultanas
1/4 cup dried apricots, chopped
1/4 cup rum
2 eggs plus an egg yolk
1/2 teaspoon ground cinnamon
1/2 teaspoon vanilla extract

Directions

- Prepare the Power pressure cooker XL by adding the water to its base. Place a metal trivet in the Power pressure cooker XL.
- Butter a soufflé dish and set it aside.
- In a small bowl, combine the sultanas, chopped apricots and rum. Let them soak at least 15 minutes. In a separate bowl, microwave the chocolate pieces until they are completely melted.
- In a large-sized mixing bowl, whisk the sour cream, milk, sugar, eggs, cinnamon and vanilla extract.
- Whisk in the warm chocolate. Add the bread cubes and soaked fruits. Pour the mixture into the prepared soufflé dish. Cover the dish with a sheet of foil. Lower the dish onto the metal trivet.
- Press the RICE/RISOTTO key and use the cook time selector to adjust to 18 minutes.
- Place the lid on the Power pressure cooker XL, lock the lid and switch the pressure release valve to closed.
- Once the timer reaches 0, the cooker will automatically switch to KEEP WARM/CANCEL.
- In the meantime, make the strawberry sauce. Add your strawberries with their syrup and the strawberry preserves to a food processor; puree until uniform and smooth. Refrigerate until serving.
- To serve, spoon warm pudding into individual bowls; serve with the strawberry sauce.

450. Macadamia Chocolate Spread

Ready in about 25 minutes
Servings 16

Whip up this kid-friendly nutty spread from scratch – it is a great match for cookies, pikelets, waffles and crumpets.

Per serving: 154 Calories; 8.3g Fat; 21.7g Carbs; 1.2g Protein; 18.8g Sugars

Ingredients

1 1/3 pounds macadamia halves
1/2 cup Dutch cocoa powder
2 ½ cups icing sugar, sifted
1 teaspoon vanilla extract
1/3 teaspoon cardamom, grated
1/3 teaspoon cinnamon powder
1/2 teaspoon grated nutmeg
10 ounces water

Directions

- Process macadamias in a blender until you have a paste. Transfer to the Power pressure cooker XL. Add the remaining ingredients.
- Press the RICE/RISOTTO key and use the cook time selector to adjust to 18 minutes.
- Place the lid on the Power pressure cooker XL, lock the lid and switch the pressure release valve to closed.
- Once the timer reaches 0, the cooker will automatically switch to KEEP WARM/CANCEL. Allow the pressure to release naturally. Enjoy!

451. Classic Chocolate Pudding

Ready in about 20 minutes
Servings 6

When you're looking for just the right thing to serve for dessert, this chocolate pudding will fit the bill. You might need to make a double batch because it disappears almost as fast as you can make it!

Per serving: 502 Calories; 32.7g Fat; 52.2g Carbs; 5.9g Protein; 45.4g Sugars

Ingredients

7 tablespoons brown sugar
1 teaspoon almond extract
8 ounces semisweet chocolate, chopped
10 ounces dark chocolate, chopped
1/2 tablespoon vanilla extract
3 large-sized egg yolks, whisked
1 ¾ cups light cream
1/8 teaspoon salt

Directions

- Press the "SOUP/STEW" key.
- Place the chocolate and the sugar in a mixing dish. Warm the light cream in a pan over low heat.
- Pour the warmed cream over the chocolate; whisk until the chocolate has melted. Add the yolks, almond extract, vanilla extract, and salt.
- Pour the mixture into six heat-safe ramekins. Cover each ramekin with foil.
- Set the wire rack in your Power Pressure Cooker XL; pour in 2 cups of water. Lower the ramekins onto the rack. Place the lid on the Power Pressure Cooker XL, lock the lid and switch the pressure release valve to closed.
- Cook for 12 minutes. Once the timer reaches 0, the cooker will automatically switch to "KEEP WARM/ CANCEL". Switch the pressure release valve to open.
- When the steam is completely released, remove the lid. Serve well chilled.

452. Dark Chocolate Cake

Ready in about 20 minutes
Servings 6

This comforting childhood classic is super-simple and perfect for any occasion. Many studies have proven that dark chocolate can positively affect your health.

Per serving: 464 Calories; 27.1g Fat; 50.3g Carbs; 6.3g Protein; 40.4g Sugars

Ingredients

1/3 cup white flour
1 cup sugar
2 cups dark chocolate
1/2 cup butter, softened
1/2 teaspoon hazelnut extract
1/2 teaspoon cinnamon powder
1 teaspoon vanilla extract
4 small-sized eggs

Directions

- Press the "CHICKEN/MEAT" key. Press the "TIME ADJUSTMENT" key and set the timer for 10 minutes.
- Prepare the Power Pressure Cooker XL by adding 1 cup of water and a wire rack to the inner pot.
- Microwave the chocolate with the butter for 1 to 2 minutes. Add the other ingredients and beat with an electric mixer.
- Divide the prepared batter among six ramekins; lower the ramekins onto the rack.
- Place the lid on the Power Pressure Cooker XL, lock the lid and switch the pressure release valve to closed.
- Press the "CANCEL" key. Switch the pressure release valve to open. When the steam is completely released, remove the cooker's lid.
- Let them cool on a rack before serving. Bon appétit!

453. Coconut-Vanilla Custard

Ready in about 25 minutes
Servings 8

When you find yourself wanting to reach for something sweet, try this flavorful custard that will please everyone. Rediscover the pleasure of making homemade desserts!

Per serving: 252 Calories; 22.7g Fat; 6.8g Carbs; 8.1g Protein; 4.9g Sugars

Ingredients

1 ½ cups water
2 ½ cups canned coconut milk
1 ½ cups milk
1 teaspoon coconut extract
1/2 teaspoon pure vanilla extract
4 whole eggs plus 4 egg yolks, lightly beaten

Directions

- Press the "SOUP/STEW" key.
- Pour the regular milk and coconut milk into a sauté pan; bring to a boil over a medium-high flame.
- In a separate bowl, mix the egg and egg yolks. Next, add 2 tablespoons of the warm milk mixture to the whisked egg mixture.
- Then, add the vanilla extract and coconut extract; mix until everything is well combined.
- Transfer the mixture to the simmering milk and stir to combine. Continue simmering for about 4 minutes, stirring continuously to prevent burning.
- Next, lightly grease a 6-cup soufflé pan; pour the mixture into the soufflé pan. Cover with foil.
- Add the water and wire rack to the Power Pressure Cooker XL; place the soufflé dish on the wire rack.
- Place the lid on the Power Pressure Cooker XL, lock the lid and switch the pressure release valve to closed.
- Cook for 20 minutes. Once the timer reaches 0, the cooker will automatically switch to "KEEP WARM/ CANCEL". Switch the pressure release valve to open. When the steam is completely released, remove the lid.
- Garnish with coconut flakes. Bon appétit!

454. Apple and Fig Oatmeal Crisp

Ready in about 20 minutes
Servings 6

Looking for an easy dessert to seal the end of a meal? An oatmeal crisp is a great choice! Did you know that dried figs improve reproductive health and digestion?

Per serving: 305 Calories; 16.5g Fat; 38.4g Carbs; 3.4g Protein; 19.9g Sugars

Ingredients

1 stick butter
1/2 cup dried figs, chopped
1/3 cup flour
1/2 teaspoon ground cloves
1/2 teaspoon pure vanilla extract
1/3 cup brown sugar
1/4 teaspoon cinnamon powder
1/4 teaspoon grated nutmeg
1 cup old-fashioned oats
1 pound apples, cored, peeled and sliced
1 ½ cups warm water

Directions

- Choose the "RICE/RISOTTO" function. Press the "TIME ADJUSTMENT" key and set the time to 12 minutes.
- Combine the oats, flour, brown sugar, vanilla, nutmeg, ground cloves, cinnamon powder, and the butter. Arrange the sliced apples on the bottom of a lightly-buttered baking dish.
- Spread the oat crisp mixture over the apples. Top with chopped figs. Cover the baking dish with foil. Add the warm water to the inner pot of your Power Pressure Cooker XL.
- Place the wire rack in the Power Pressure Cooker XL. Lower the baking dish onto the wire rack.
- Place the lid on the Power Pressure Cooker XL, lock the lid and switch the pressure release valve to closed.
- Once the timer reaches 0, the cooker will automatically switch to "KEEP WARM/CANCEL". Switch the pressure release valve to open. When the steam is completely released, remove the lid. Enjoy!

455. Pecan and Pumpkin Pie Pudding

Ready in about 30 minutes
Servings 4

Pumpkin is fall's unavoidable ingredient. Apart from being rich in fiber, pumpkin is vitamin-packed food. Enjoy!

Per serving: 470 Calories; 34.8g Fat; 34.4g Carbs; 9.4g Protein; 21.3g Sugars

Ingredients

Nonstick cooking spray
1 tablespoon flour
1/2 teaspoon vanilla essence
1/2 teaspoon ground cloves
3 eggs, at room temperature
1/2 teaspoon ground cinnamon
1/3 cup dark brown sugar
1/2 cup toasted pecans, for garnish
1 cup heavy cream
2 cups canned pumpkin
1 ½ tablespoons molasses

Directions

- Press the "CHICKEN/MEAT" key. Lightly grease the bottom and sides of a round soufflé dish with a non-stick cooking spray; set aside.
- Combine the canned pumpkin, brown sugar, heavy cream, eggs, molasses, and vanilla essence in a large bowl. Whisk in the flour, cloves, and cinnamon.
- Pour the mixture into the prepared soufflé dish. Cover with foil.
- Add the wire rack and 2 cups of water to the Power Pressure Cooker XL. Create an aluminum foil sling.
- Place the lid on the Power Pressure Cooker XL, lock the lid and switch the pressure release valve to closed. Cook for 20 minutes.
- Once the timer reaches 0, the cooker will automatically switch to "KEEP WARM/CANCEL". Switch the pressure release valve to open.
- When the steam is completely released, remove the lid. Serve with toasted pecans.

456. Challah Bread Pudding with Nuts

Ready in about 25 minutes
Servings 6

If you're not a fan of nutmeg – just leave it out of this recipe! You can use ground cinnamon, vanilla, anise star and even ground allspice instead.

Per serving: 413 Calories; 24.7g Fat; 36.4g Carbs; 11.5g Protein; 21.5g Sugars

Ingredients

1 stick butter
1/8 teaspoon grated nutmeg
3 tablespoons hazelnuts, chopped
1 tablespoon almonds, chopped
1/2 cup sugar
1 ½ cups water
3 whole eggs plus 3 egg yolks
1 ½ tablespoons rum
1 teaspoon hazelnut extract
1/4 teaspoon salt
1/2 tablespoon honey
3 cups Challah, torn into bite-sized pieces
1 ½ cups milk

Directions

- Press the "RICO/RISOTTO" key. Simply add the Challah to a lightly greased baking dish. Then, make the custard by mixing all the remaining ingredients.
- Pour the custard mixture over the Challah pieces. Cover with an aluminum foil.
- Insert the wire rack in the inner pot of your Power Pressure Cooker XL. Pour in 2 cups of water.
- Place the lid on the Power Pressure Cooker XL, lock the lid and switch the pressure release valve to closed. Cook for 20 minutes.
- Afterwards, perform a Natural pressure release. Serve at room temperature.

457. Cashew Chocolate Cake

Ready in about 50 minutes
Servings 10

You can easily make your own nut meal (nut flour) in a food processor or blender. You can even utilize a coffee grinder just like grandma used to make.

Per serving: 522 Calories; 31.7g Fat; 58.3g Carbs; 6.9g Protein; 47.7g Sugars

Ingredients

For the Crust:
2 cups nut meal
1/3 cup coconut oil, room temperature
1/3 cup brown sugar

For the Filling:
1/4 teaspoon grated nutmeg
1 cup chocolate chips
1/2 teaspoon cinnamon powder
1/2 teaspoon vanilla essence
2 cups cashews, chopped, soaked and drained
1/2 cup sugar
3/4 cup coconut milk

Directions

- Press the "CHICKEN/MEAT" key. Combine all the ingredients for the crust. Press the crust mixture into a silicone cake pan. You can use the back of a spoon; transfer the crust to a refrigerator.
- Then, make the filling by mixing all the filling ingredients. Pour the filling over the crust.
- Put the wire rack into the Power Pressure Cooker XL. Now, lower the cake pan onto the rack.
- Place the lid on the Power Pressure Cooker XL, lock the lid and switch the pressure release valve to closed. Cook for 45 minutes.
- Once the timer reaches 0, the cooker will automatically switch to "KEEP WARM/CANCEL". Switch the pressure release valve to open.
- When the steam is completely released, remove the lid. Serve well chilled.

458. Nana's Walnut Zucchini Bread

Ready in about 35 minutes
Servings 10

Here's an old-fashioned recipe that is actually lip-smacking good! Add a festive look to your dessert table every day with this rich and delectable zucchini bread.

Per serving: 447 Calories; 19.6g Fat; 63.8g Carbs; 8.9g Protein; 36.9g Sugars

Ingredients

1/3 cup walnuts, chopped
1 cup chocolate chips
1 stick butter, at room temperature
1/4 teaspoon cinnamon powder
1 1/3 cups sugar
2 ¼ cups all-purpose flour
1 teaspoon baking soda
1 teaspoon hazelnut extract
1/2 teaspoon vanilla extract
1/3 teaspoon baking powder
1/3 cup applesauce
4 eggs
3/4 cup cocoa powder
1 ½ cups zucchini, peeled and grated

Directions

- Press the "CHICKEN/MEAT" key. In a mixing dish, combine the eggs, butter, applesauce, sugar, hazelnut extract, and vanilla extract. Add in the zucchini and stir to combine.
- In a separate mixing dish, combine the other items. Stir in the egg-zucchini mixture and mix to combine well.
- Put the wire rack into the inner pot of the Power Pressure Cooker XL; pour in 1 ½ cups water. Pour the batter into a lightly greased baking pan that will fit your Power Pressure Cooker XL. Place the baking pan on the wire rack.
- Place the lid on the Power Pressure Cooker XL, lock the lid and switch the pressure release valve to closed. Cook for 30 minutes.
- Once the timer reaches 0, the cooker will automatically switch to "KEEP WARM/CANCEL". Switch the pressure release valve to open.
- When the steam is completely released, remove the lid. Lastly, allow the cake to cool before serving.

459. Delectable Honey and Walnut Dessert

Ready in about 25 minutes
Servings 6

Honey and walnut are paired with rice for a great, light ending to your meal. This pudding tastes absolutely divine!

Per serving: 440 Calories; 5.8g Fat; 90.8g Carbs; 8.8g Protein; 33g Sugars

Ingredients

3 ripe bananas, mashed
1/8 teaspoon ground cloves
2 cups basmati rice
1/3 cup walnuts, ground
1/2 cup honey
1 tablespoon candied ginger, diced
1/4 teaspoon ground cinnamon
2 ½ cups water
1 ½ cups soy milk

Directions

- Press the "RICO/RISOTTO" key. Simply combine all the ingredients in your Power Pressure Cooker XL; stir until everything is well combined.
- Place the lid on the Power Pressure Cooker XL, lock the lid and switch the pressure release valve to closed. Cook for 15 minutes.
- Once the timer reaches 0, the cooker will automatically switch to "KEEP WARM/CANCEL". Switch the pressure release valve to open.
- When the steam is completely released, remove the lid. Serve in individual bowls. Bon appétit!

460. The Best Apple Crisp Ever

Ready in about 25 minutes
Servings 4

Inspired by crispy apples, you can come up with this dessert idea that's so easy and literally scrumptious! Serve with a dollop of vanilla ice cream and enjoy!

Per serving: 429 Calories; 24.8g Fat; 50.5g Carbs; 4.6g Protein; 23.2g Sugars

Ingredients

1 ½ cups warm water
1 cup old-fashioned oats
1/2 teaspoon lemon rind, grated
1/8 teaspoon sea salt
1 teaspoon ground cinnamon
1/3 cup sugar
1/2 teaspoon grated nutmeg
1/2 cup flour
1 stick butter, softened
1/2 tablespoon lemon juice
1 pound Granny Smith apples, cored, peeled and thinly sliced

Directions

- Press the "RICO/RISOTTO" key. Sprinkle the apples with lemon juice.
- In another bowl, mix the lemon rind, oats, flour, sugar, nutmeg, cinnamon, salt, and butter. Next, layer the apples and the crisp mixture in a baking dish, ending with the layer of crisp mixture. Cover the dish with foil.
- Add the wire rack and warm water to the inner pot of the Power Pressure Cooker XL. Place the baking dish on the rack.
- Place the lid on the Power Pressure Cooker XL, lock the lid and switch the pressure release valve to closed. Cook for 20 minutes.
- Once the timer reaches 0, the cooker will automatically switch to "KEEP WARM/CANCEL". Switch the pressure release valve to open.
- When the steam is completely released, remove the lid. Bon appétit!

461. Summer Apricot and Coconut Delight

Ready in about 25 minutes
Servings 6

Looking for an easy and satisfying dessert? This fragrant and nutritious concoction will be the perfect answer to what your tummy desire!

Per serving: 504 Calories; 28.5g Fat; 58.6g Carbs; 7.1g Protein; 6.5g Sugars

Ingredients

2 cups jasmine rice
1 cup ripe apricots, pitted and halved
1 tablespoon candied ginger, diced
1 teaspoon orange zest
1/4 teaspoon vanilla extract
2 ½ cups coconut milk
1 ½ cups water
1 cup shredded coconut

Directions

- Press the "RICO/RISOTTO" key. Simply add all of the above ingredients to your Power Pressure Cooker XL.
- Place the lid on the Power Pressure Cooker XL, lock the lid and switch the pressure release valve to closed. Cook for 18 minutes.
- Once the timer reaches 0, the cooker will automatically switch to "KEEP WARM/CANCEL". Switch the pressure release valve to open.
- When the steam is completely released, remove the lid. Serve well-chilled. Bon appétit!

462. Aromatic Pears in Red Wine Sauce

Ready in about 15 minutes
Servings 6

Want to impress your guests at your next dinner party? Wow them with this classic dessert with a new twist.

Per serving: 317 Calories; 1.3g Fat; 70.9g Carbs; 1.4g Protein; 62.4g Sugars

Ingredients

1 ½ pounds pears, peeled
1 ¼ cups red wine
2 vanilla beans
10 ounces caster sugar
2 cloves
2 cinnamon sticks

Directions

- Press the "SOUP/STEW" key. Add all of the above ingredients to the Power Pressure Cooker XL.
- Place the lid on the Power Pressure Cooker XL, lock the lid and switch the pressure release valve to closed. Cook for 10 minutes.
- Once the timer reaches 0, the cooker will automatically switch to "KEEP WARM/CANCEL". Switch the pressure release valve to open.
- When the steam is completely released, remove the lid. Bon appétit!

463. Quick and Easy Stuffed Apples

Ready in about 20 minutes
Servings 4

These stuffed apples will remind you of your childhood! Serve with a generous portion of vanilla ice cream for a great presentation!

Per serving: 381 Calories; 22.5g Fat; 38.6g Carbs; 6.9g Protein; 0.4g Sugars

Ingredients

1 ½ cups water
1/2 stick butter, softened
1/2 tablespoon lemon zest, grated
1 teaspoon vanilla paste
1/4 cup walnuts, chopped
6 apples, cored and halved
10 cinnamon cookies, crumbled

Directions

- Press the "RICE/RISOTTO" key. Prepare the Power Pressure Cooker XL by adding 1 ½ cups of warm water and the wire rack.
- In a mixing bowl, combine the walnuts, cookie crumbs, lemon zest, and vanilla paste. Stuff the apples; transfer the apples to the wire rack; dot with the softened butter.
- Place the lid on the Power Pressure Cooker XL, lock the lid and switch the pressure release valve to closed. Cook for 15 minutes.
- Once the timer reaches 0, the cooker will automatically switch to "KEEP WARM/CANCEL". Switch the pressure release valve to open.
- When the steam is completely released, remove the lid. Serve at room temperature.

464. Gorgeous Crème Brule

Ready in about 20 minutes +
chilling time
Servings 4

Here's a gorgeous family dessert that is served in individual bowls. It only takes a few minutes to whip up the ingredients and less than 10 minutes to cook everything in the Power Pressure Cooker XL. Lovely!

Per serving: 430 Calories; 11.6g Fat; 64.2g Carbs; 2.9g Protein; 62.6g Sugars

Ingredients

1 ¼ cups warm water
1/2 teaspoon vanilla paste
1 ½ cups warm heavy cream
3 large-sized egg yolks, large
1 cup sugar
1/4 cup granulated sugar

Directions

* Press the "SOUP/STEW" key.
* Mix the heavy cream, sugar, vanilla, and the egg yolks in a bowl. Then, fill four ramekins with this mixture and wrap them with foil.
* Pour the warm water into the inner pot of the Power Pressure Cooker XL. Add the wire rack; arrange the ramekins on the rack.
* Place the lid on the Power Pressure Cooker XL, lock the lid and switch the pressure release valve to closed. Cook for 10 minutes.
* Once the timer reaches 0, the cooker will automatically switch to "KEEP WARM/CANCEL". Switch the pressure release valve to open.
* When the steam is completely released, remove the lid. Next, refrigerate your Crème Brule for at least 3 hours.
* Top with the granulated sugar; to caramelize the sugar, place the ramekins under the broiler. Enjoy!

465. White Chocolate Lemon Pudding

Ready in about 20 minutes
Servings 6

Creamy and delicious, this lemon pudding is a true comfort in a bowl! To serve, you can drizzle individual portions with white chocolate glaze.

Per serving: 399 Calories; 29.5g Fat; 29.9g Carbs; 5.6g Protein; 26.5g Sugars

Ingredients

3 egg yolks, whisked
1 ¼ cups heavy cream
1 ¼ cups half-and-half
1 teaspoon grated ginger
1/2 tablespoon finely grated lemon zest
2 tablespoons sugar
8 ounces white chocolate, chopped
1/2 teaspoon lemon extract

Directions

* Press the "SOUP/STEW" key.
* Put the white chocolate into a large-sized mixing dish. Combine the cream and half-and-half in a saucepan and warm over medium-low heat.
* Pour the warm cream mixture over the white chocolate; whisk until everything is melted. Add the remaining ingredients and whisk to combine.
* Pour the mixture into six heat-safe ramekins; cover each ramekin with foil. Add the wire rack and 2 cups water to the Power Pressure Cooker XL.
* Lower the ramekins onto the rack. Place the lid on the Power Pressure Cooker XL, lock the lid and switch the pressure release valve to closed.
* Cook for 13 minutes. Once the timer reaches 0, the cooker will automatically switch to "KEEP WARM/ CANCEL". Switch the pressure release valve to open. When the steam is completely released, remove the lid. Bon appétit!

OTHER POWER PRESSURE COOKER XL FAVORITES

466. Cold Breakfast Millet Salad

Ready in about 20 minutes
Servings 8

Why settle for an ordinary breakfast when you can get extraordinary millet salad?! This is a must-try recipe for a healthy family breakfast. Enjoy!

Per serving: 303 Calories; 11.2g Fat; 43.3g Carbs; 8g Protein; 4.7g Sugars

Ingredients

For the Salad:
2 cups millet, rinsed and drained
1/2 stick butter, melted
1/2 teaspoon kosher salt
4 1/3 cups water
2 cups fresh blueberries, halved
1/3 cup walnuts, roughly chopped

For the Dressing:
1/2 cup Greek-style yogurt
1/2 tablespoon orange oil
Fresh juice of 1/2 lime
1/2 teaspoon freshly grated ginger

Directions

- Treat the sides and bottom of your Power pressure cooker XL with a nonstick cooking spray. Then, add the millet, butter, kosher salt, and water to your Power pressure cooker XL.
- Press the BEANS/LENTILS key and then press the COOK TIME SELECTOR key until you reach 15 minutes.
- Place the lid on the Power pressure cooker XL, lock the lid and switch the pressure release valve to closed.
- Once the timer reaches 0, the cooker will automatically switch to KEEP WARM/CANCEL. Allow the pressure to release naturally.
- Add blueberries and walnuts. Stir to combine well.
- Meanwhile, in a mixing bowl, whisk together the dressing ingredients. Toss the salad with the dressing. Serve well-chilled and enjoy!

467. Beef and Scallion Frittata

Ready in about 30 minutes
Servings 6

Ground meat and eggs always go well. Serve with a tablespoon of Dijon mustard or a dollop of sour cream.

Per serving: 262 Calories; 21.7g Fat; 2.7g Carbs; 13.8g Protein; 0.8g Sugars

Ingredients

1 tablespoon butter
1 cup scallions, chopped
1 pound ground beef, chopped
8 eggs
Salt and ground black pepper, to taste

Directions

- Firstly, crack the eggs in a bowl and whisk until frothy; mix in the meat and scallions; season with the salt and pepper.
- Grease a casserole dish with 1 tablespoon of melted butter. Pour the egg mixture into the greased casserole dish.
- Prepare your Power pressure cooker XL by adding a metal trivet and 1 cup of water into its base.
- Press the RICE/ROSOTTO key and use the cook time selector to adjust to 25 minutes.
- Place the lid on the Power pressure cooker XL, lock the lid and switch the pressure release valve to closed.
- Once the timer reaches 0, the cooker will automatically switch to KEEP WARM/CANCEL. Serve hot!

468. Cheesy Spoon Bread

Ready in about 25 minutes
Servings 6

Corn and cheese make it easy to give every dish a little something extra. Prepare to become totally addicted to this easy spoon bread!

Per serving: 248 Calories; 14.4g Fat; 20g Carbs; 9.9g Protein; 4g Sugars

Ingredients

Nonstick cooking spray
2 tablespoons ghee, melted
1 ½ cups vegetable broth
3/4 cup Swiss cheese, shredded
3 medium-sized eggs, well beaten
1/2 cup canned cream corn
1 ¼ cups Bisquick baking mix
1 teaspoon shallot powder
1 teaspoon porcini powder
3/4 cup sour cream
1/2 teaspoon cayenne pepper
1/3 teaspoon black pepper
1/2 teaspoon salt

Directions

- Treat the inside of your Power pressure cooker XL with a nonstick cooking spray.
- In a large-sized bowl, combine dry ingredients. In another bowl, combine wet ingredients. Add the dry mixture to the wet mixture, and mix until everything is well incorporated.
- Press the CHICKEN/MEAT key once to select 15 minutes. Place the lid on the Power pressure cooker XL, lock the lid and switch the pressure release valve to closed.
- Once the timer reaches 0, the cooker will automatically switch to KEEP WARM/CANCEL. When the steam is completely released, carefully remove the cooker's lid.
- Serve in individual bowls. Enjoy!

469. Creamy Maple Peaches

Ready in about 15 minutes
Servings 4

Here's a light and delicious way to end a party dinner! Feel free to use Grand Marnier, Calvados or fresh pear juice instead of orange juice.

Per serving: 217 Calories; 9.5g Fat; 32.3g Carbs; 3g Protein; 28.4g Sugars

Ingredients

1/4 cup maple syrup
4 peaches, pitted and quartered
3/4 cup sour cream
1/2 cup orange juice
1/2 teaspoon vanilla extract
1/3 teaspoon ground cinnamon
1/3 cup water

Directions

- Add all of the above ingredients, except for sour cream, to the Power pressure cooker XL.
- Press the RICE/RISOTTO key once to select 6 minutes. Place the lid on the Power pressure cooker XL, lock the lid and switch the pressure release valve to closed.
- Once the timer reaches 0, the cooker will automatically switch to KEEP WARM/CANCEL. When the steam is completely released, carefully remove the cooker's lid.
- To serve, divide the peaches among four serving plate. Serve topped with a dollop of sour cream; add a few drizzles of maple syrup if desired.

470. Cinnamon Bread Pudding with Banana Sauce

Ready in about 1 hour
Servings 8

This decadent bread pudding cooks perfectly in the Power pressure cooker XL. A Maple-banana sauce completes this rich, special-occasion dessert.

Per serving: 462 Calories; 21.3g Fat; 58.2g Carbs; 11.5g Protein; 25.7g Sugars

Ingredients

For the Pudding:
1 pound cinnamon swirl bread, chopped
1/3 cup sugar
1 tablespoon brandy, optional
1/2 cup almonds, toasted and roughly chopped
3 cups half-and-half
4 eggs, lightly whisked
1 teaspoon pure almond extract
1/3 teaspoon ground cinnamon
Nonstick cooking spray

For the Banana Sauce:
2 small-sized firm bananas, sliced
1/2 cup whipping cream
2 tablespoons packed brown sugar
1 tablespoons pure maple syrup

Directions

- Brush your cake pan with a nonstick cooking spray. Then, add the bread and almonds to the pan; toss to combine.
- In a bowl, whisk together the remaining ingredients for the pudding; pour this mixture over the top of the bread mixture in the pan; press the bread mixture down using a wide spatula. Allow it to sit about 30 minutes.
- Add 1 ½ cups of water and a metal rack to the base of the Power pressure cooker XL. Cover the cake pan with a sheet of foil; then, lower it onto the rack.
- Press the RICE/RISOTTO key and use the cook time selector to adjust to 25 minutes.
- Place the lid on the Power pressure cooker XL, lock the lid and switch the pressure release valve to closed.
- Once the timer reaches 0, the cooker will automatically switch to KEEP WARM/CANCEL. When the steam is completely released, carefully remove the cooker's lid.
- Meanwhile, in a sauté pan, combine whipping cream, sugar and maple syrup; cook for 5 to 6 minutes, stirring constantly. Remove from heat. Stir in sliced bananas. Serve warm over prepared bread pudding.

471. Summer Berry Jam

Ready in about 30 minutes
Servings 16

This berry jam makes a wonderful idea for a perfect family breakfast. Store your jam for up to two weeks in your refrigerator.

Per serving: 122 Calories; 0.2g Fat; 31g Carbs; 0.4g Protein; 28.5g Sugars

Ingredients

1 ¾ pounds mixed berries
4 tablespoon spectin powder
3 cups white sugar
1/2 teaspoon whole cloves
1 teaspoon lemon rind
1/2 vanilla paste

Directions

- Add all of the above ingredients to your Power pressure cooker XL. Press the CHICKEN/MEAT key; let it boil for about 3 minutes.
- Next, ladle the jam into the jars; seal the jars. Place the jars in your Power pressure cooker XL and add the water until the jars are covered 1/4 of the way.
- Choose the CANNING/PRESERVING function and then press the TIME ADJUSTMENT key until you reach 20 minutes.
- Place the lid on the Power pressure cooker XL, lock the lid and switch the pressure release valve to closed.
- Once the timer reaches 0, the cooker will automatically switch to KEEP WARM/CANCEL. When the steam is completely released, carefully remove the cooker's lid.
- Afterwards, remove the jars from the cooker. Don't forget to label your jars.

472. Peaches in Raspberry Sauce

Ready in about 15 minutes
Servings 4

You can experiment with this recipe and, if you like, substitute 1 cup of hulled and halved strawberries and 1 cup of blackberries for 2 cups of the raspberries.

Per serving: 188 Calories; 0.8g Fat; 47.4g Carbs; 2.2g Protein; 39.9g Sugars

Ingredients

4 peaches, pitted and halved
2 cups raspberries
1/3 cup honey
1 ½ tablespoons cornstarch
1/2 vanilla bean, sliced lengthwise
1/3 teaspoon ground cardamom
1/2 cinnamon stick
1 ¼ cups water

Directions

- Add all ingredients, except the honey and cornstarch, to the Power pressure cooker XL.
- Press the RICE/RISOTTO key once to select 6 minutes. Place the lid on the Power pressure cooker XL, lock the lid and switch the pressure release valve to closed.
- Once the timer reaches 0, the cooker will automatically switch to KEEP WARM/CANCEL. When the steam is completely released, carefully remove the cooker's lid. Remove the peaches with a slotted spoon.
- Press the BEANS/LENTILS key and add the honey and cornstarch; let it simmer until the sauce has thickened, about 4 minutes.
- Divide the peaches among serving plates. Top with the raspberry sauce, serve and enjoy.

473. Succulent Apricots with Walnuts and Chevre

Ready in about 10 minutes
Servings 4

The sweetness of the stewed apricots goes well with the creaminess and tanginess of the Chevre. It's like getting a light, skinny cheesecake!

Per serving: 284 Calories; 14.5g Fat; 34.2g Carbs; 9.2g Protein; 30.1g Sugars

Ingredients

1 pound apricots, pitted and halved
1/3 cup orange juice
4 tablespoons honey
3/4 cup chevre cheese
1/2 cup walnuts, chopped
1/4 teaspoon grated nutmeg
1/2 teaspoon ground cinnamon
1/2 teaspoon vanilla extract
1/3 cup water

Directions

- Add all the above ingredients, except for the cheese and walnuts, to the Power pressure cooker XL. Press the FISH/VEGETABLES/STEAM key and use the cook time selector to adjust to 4 minutes.
- Place the lid on the Power pressure cooker XL, lock the lid and switch the pressure release valve to closed.
- Once the timer reaches 0, the cooker will automatically switch to KEEP WARM/CANCEL. When the steam is completely released, carefully remove the cooker's lid.
- To serve: place apricot halves on each serving plate. Serve topped with cheese and chopped walnuts. Enjoy!

474. Breakfast Ham Casserole

Ready in about 20 minutes
Servings 4

This Italian-inspired dish combines the best of both worlds: rich, mellowly cheese and a flavorful ham. This is perfect when you're hosting a weekend brunch!

Per serving: 584 Calories; 30.7g Fat; 52.7g Carbs; 25.6g Protein; 5g Sugars

Ingredients

4 slices ham, diced
4 eggs, lightly beaten
1/2 cup scallions, chopped
2 bell peppers, deveined and chopped
4 sweet potatoes, shredded
1 ½ cups Swiss cheese
3/4 cup sour cream
1 tablespoon lard
1 teaspoon salt
1/2 teaspoon ground black pepper

Directions

- Press the CHICKEN/MEAT key and warm the lard; now, sauté the scallions and bell peppers until they are tender, about 4 minutes.
- Add the ham and cook for 4 more minutes. Press the CANCEL key. Stir in the remaining ingredients.
- Press the FISH/VEGETABLES/STEAM key; use the cook time selector to adjust to 10 minutes.
- Place the lid on the Power pressure cooker XL, lock the lid and switch the pressure release valve to closed.
- Once the timer reaches 0, the cooker will automatically switch to KEEP WARM/CANCEL.
- Serve warm and enjoy!

475. Winter Spiced Porridge

Ready in about 25 minutes
Servings 4

If you love cornmeal, the Power pressure cooker XL is a great tool to prepare this all-in-one meal while saving you time. Top this porridge with poached eggs or chopped smoked ham if desired.

Per serving: 245 Calories; 13.2g Fat; 29.8g Carbs; 3.7g Protein; 0.7g Sugars

Ingredients

1 ¼ cups cornmeal
2 ½ cups stock
1/2 stick butter
1 teaspoon dragon cayenne pepper
1/4 teaspoon salt
1 sprig dried thyme
2 ½ cups water

Directions

- Add all ingredients, except for cayenne pepper, to the Power pressure cooker XL.
- Press the RICE/RISOTTO key once to select 18 minutes. Place the lid on the Power pressure cooker XL, lock the lid and switch the pressure release valve to closed.
- Once the timer reaches 0, the cooker will automatically switch to KEEP WARM/CANCEL. When the steam is completely released, carefully remove the cooker's lid.
- Divide the porridge among four serving bowls; sprinkle with cayenne pepper and serve.

476. French-Style Vegetarian Sandwiches

Ready in about 35 minutes
Servings 6

These all-star sandwiches are popular among both vegetarians and meat eaters. Serve with a fresh or pickled salad on the side if desired.

Per serving: 529 Calories; 16.6g Fat; 67.2g Carbs; 25.2g Protein; 8g Sugars

Ingredients

1 tablespoon vegetable oil
6 vegetarian sausages, sliced
1 garlic cloves, crushed
1/2 cup tamari sauce
2 shallots, chopped
2 cups roasted vegetable stock
2 bell peppers, deveined and sliced
6 burger buns
1 cup freshly grated cheddar cheese
Salt and ground black pepper, to taste
2 ½ cups water

Directions

- Press the CHICKEN/MEAT key and heat the vegetable oil until sizzling. Now, sauté the garlic, and shallots until just tender, about 4 minutes.
- Add the sausages and cook for 3 minutes longer. Add the remaining ingredients, except the burger buns and cheddar cheese, to your Power pressure cooker XL.
- Press the RICE/RISOTTO key and use the cook time selector to adjust to 18 minutes.
- Place the lid on the Power pressure cooker XL, lock the lid and switch the pressure release valve to closed.
- Once the timer reaches 0, the cooker will automatically switch to KEEP WARM/CANCEL. When the steam is completely released, carefully remove the cooker's lid.
- Preheat your oven to 450 degrees F. Now, divide prepared mixture among 6 burger buns. Top with grated cheese.
- Bake your sandwiches in the preheated oven for 6 to 7 minutes, or until the cheese has melted. Serve right away and enjoy!

477. Quick and Easy Hard-Boiled Eggs

Ready in about 15 minutes
Servings 6

It's probably the very first recipe you should try in the Power pressure cooker XL. Eggs contain a little bit of almost every nutrient our body needs. That's fascinating!

Per serving: 105 Calories; 7.3g Fat; 0.6g Carbs; 9.2g Protein; 0.6g Sugars

Ingredients

10 eggs
1 ½ cups water
Salt and ground black pepper, to taste

Directions

- Add a wire rack and water to the Power pressure cooker XL.
- Arrange the eggs in the steamer basket. Lower the basket onto the rack.
- Press the RICE/RISOTTO key once to select 6 minutes.
- Place the lid on the Power pressure cooker XL, lock the lid and switch the pressure release valve to closed.
- Once the timer reaches 0, the cooker will automatically switch to KEEP WARM/CANCEL. When the steam is completely released, carefully remove the cooker's lid.
- Replace the hot eggs to the cold water. Allow the eggs to cool completely. Season with salt and pepper; serve.

478. Aromatic Tofu Bowl

Ready in about 10 minutes
Servings 6

These tofu cubes are coated with an intensely flavored paste, then cooked in the Power pressure cooker XL to make an all-in-one supper dish.

Per serving: 404 Calories; 7.6g Fat; 66.5g Carbs; 21.5g Protein; 4.9g Sugars

Ingredients

20 ounces extra firm tofu, pressed and cut into cubes
2 ½ tablespoons oyster sauce
2 tablespoons mirin wine
3 garlic cloves, minced
3 teaspoons canola oil
2 cups vegetable broth
1 medium-sized yellow onion, peeled and chopped
3 cups cooked wild rice
2 tablespoons fresh chives, roughly chopped
Salt and black pepper, to taste
1 (1-inch) piece fresh root ginger, grated

Directions

- Press the CHICKEN/MEAT key and heat canola oil. Now, fry the tofu cubes until they are lightly browned.
- In your food processor, place the remaining ingredients, except the cooked rice; process them until you get a smooth paste.
- Transfer the pureed mixture to the Power pressure cooker XL. Press the FISH/VEGETABLES/STEAM key once to select 2 minutes.
- Place the lid on the Power pressure cooker XL, lock the lid and switch the pressure release valve to closed.
- Once the timer reaches 0, the cooker will automatically switch to KEEP WARM/CANCEL. When the steam is completely released, carefully remove the cooker's lid.
- Serve over hot cooked rice.

479. Smoky Tempeh Sandwiches

Ready in about 10 minutes
Servings 6

Tempeh is loaded with protein, probiotics, vitamin K and vitamin D. Serve with chopped jalapeños, salsa or sliced avocado.

Per serving: 289 Calories; 10.6g Fat; 33.6g Carbs; 16g Protein; 5.9g Sugars

Ingredients

12 ounces tempeh
3 teaspoons peanut oil
2 tablespoons brown mustard
2 teaspoons agave nectar
1/3 cup stock
1/2 cup apple cider vinegar
2 tablespoons tamari sauce
2 garlic cloves, minced
6 brioche buns
1/2 teaspoon grated fresh ginger
3/4 teaspoon smoked paprika
1 teaspoon five-spice powder
1/3 teaspoon salt
1/3 teaspoon black pepper
A few drops of liquid smoke

Directions

- Cut the tempeh crosswise into slices. Add the tempeh to the Power pressure cooker XL.
- Press the CHICKEN/MEAT key and heat the oil; sauté the tempeh for a minute or so.
- Whisk the remaining ingredients, except for brioche buns, in a mixing bowl. Pour this mixture over the tempeh in the Power pressure cooker XL.
- Press the FISH/VEGETABLES/STEAM key once to select 2 minutes.
- Place the lid on the Power pressure cooker XL, lock the lid and switch the pressure release valve to closed.
- Once the timer reaches 0, the cooker will automatically switch to KEEP WARM/CANCEL. When the steam is completely released, carefully remove the cooker's lid.
- Serve tempeh mixture over the brioche buns. Bon appétit!

480. Mediterranean Deviled Eggs

Ready in about 15 minutes
Servings 8

It's hard to imagine a cocktail party without famous deviled eggs. Add some chopped olives and scallions if desired.

Per serving: 147 Calories; 10.3g Fat; 2.7g Carbs; 10.4g Protein; 1.4g Sugars

Ingredients

12 large-sized eggs
1/4 cup Ricotta cheese
1/4 cup mayonnaise
1/4 teaspoon garlic powder
1 teaspoon shallot powder
Sea salt and freshly ground black pepper, to taste

Directions

- Add a wire rack and 1 ½ cups of water to the Power pressure cooker XL. Arrange the eggs in the steamer basket. Lower the basket onto the rack.
- Press the RICE/RISOTTO key once to select 6 minutes.
- Place the lid on the Power pressure cooker XL, lock the lid and switch the pressure release valve to closed.
- Once the timer reaches 0, the cooker will automatically switch to KEEP WARM/CANCEL. When the steam is completely released, carefully remove the cooker's lid.
- Transfer the eggs to ice cold water to cool completely.
- Slice each egg in half; discard the yolks. Mash the yolks using a fork. Add the rest of the above ingredients.
- Divide the yolk mixture among the egg whites. Arrange on a serving platter and serve.

481. Healthy Apricot Jam

Ready in about 30 minutes
Servings 16

Who said that jam can't be healthy?! Make this apricot jam in your Power pressure cooker XL and fight stereotypes!

Per serving: 153 Calories; 0.3g Fat; 40.5g Carbs; 0.8g Protein; 39.3g Sugars

Ingredients

1 3/4 pounds apricots, peeled and halved
4 tablespoons pectin powder
1/2 teaspoon vanilla paste
2 tablespoons lemon
2 cups honey

Directions

- Place the apricots, pectin powder and vanilla paste in your Power pressure cooker XL. Press the CHICKEN/MEAT key; let it boil for about 3 minutes.
- Add the lemon and honey and stir well to combine. Spoon the mixture into the sterilized jars; now, seal the jars.
- Place the jars in your Power pressure cooker XL and add water until the jars are covered 1/4 of the way.
- Use the CANNING/PRESERVING function and then press the TIME ADJUSTMENT key until you reach 20 minutes.
- Place the lid on the Power pressure cooker XL, lock the lid and switch the pressure release valve to closed.
- Once the timer reaches 0, the cooker will automatically switch to KEEP WARM/CANCEL. When the steam is completely released, carefully remove the cooker's lid. Afterwards, remove the jars from the cooker. Don't forget to label your jars.

482. Chorizo and Bean Delight

Ready in about 25 minutes
Servings 4

This one-pot dinner is so simple! It can also be made with Italian sweet or spicy sausage.

Per serving: 538 Calories; 23.6g Fat; 56.1g Carbs; 28.6g Protein; 9.5g Sugars

Ingredients

4 Chorizo sausages, sliced
1 ¼ cups Adzuki beans, soaked and rinsed
2 carrots, trimmed and sliced
2 shallots, peeled and thinly sliced
1 cup tomato paste
1 teaspoon garlic, crushed
Salt and ground black pepper, to taste

Directions

- Choose the CHICKEN/MEAT function and cook the sausages until they're browned, about 4 minutes. Press the CANCEL key.
- Arrange the shallots, garlic, carrots, and beans in the bottom of the Power pressure cooker XL. Place reserved browned sausage on top of the bean layer in the cooker. Season with salt and black pepper to taste.
- Press the BEANS/LENTILS key and use the cook time selector to adjust to 15 minutes.
- Place the lid on the Power pressure cooker XL, lock the lid and switch the pressure release valve to closed.
- Once the timer reaches 0, the cooker will automatically switch to KEEP WARM/CANCEL. When the steam is completely released, carefully remove the cooker's lid. Serve warm.

483. Skinny Vegetable Egg Soup

Ready in about 20 minutes
Servings 6

This one-pot dish is simple: a can of crushed tomatoes, amazingly healthy olive oil, and aromatics. Whisked eggs complete your soup and add nutritional value.

Per serving: 75 Calories; 6.2g Fat; 3g Carbs; 2.6g Protein; 1.9g Sugars

Ingredients

2 tablespoons olive oil
1 (10-ounce) can tomatoes, crushed
3 cups vegetable stock
2 eggs, whisked
1/2 cup spring onions, chopped
1 teaspoon crushed garlic
1/2 teaspoon fresh grated ginger
1/2 teaspoon celery seeds
1/4 teaspoon star anise
1/2 teaspoon fennel seed
Salt and freshly ground black pepper, to taste
3 cups water

Directions

- Put all of the above ingredients, except for eggs and spring onions, into your Power pressure cooker XL.
- Now, press the SOUP/STEW key once to select 10 minutes.
- Place the lid on the Power pressure cooker XL, lock the lid and switch the pressure release valve to closed.
- Once the timer reaches 0, the cooker will automatically switch to KEEP WARM/CANCEL. When the steam is completely released, carefully remove the cooker's lid.
- Add the whisked eggs and press the FISH/VEGETABLES/STEAM key; gently stir to combine.
- Serve in individual soup dishes, sprinkled with chopped spring onions. Enjoy!

484. Baked Eggs with Prosciutto and Cheese

Ready in about 10 minutes
Servings 4

Here's a winter classic breakfast your family will love! Use bacon if you prefer.

Per serving: 466 Calories; 32.8g Fat; 2.8g Carbs; 41.3g Protein; 1.2g Sugars

Ingredients

8 medium-sized eggs
8 slices prosciutto
4 thick slices Swiss cheese
2 tablespoons butter, softened at room temperature
4 tablespoons spring onions, chopped
2 tablespoons fresh parsley, coarsely chopped

Directions

- Prepare your cooker by adding 1 ½ cups of water and the metal trivet to its base.
- Coat the bottom and sides of four ramekins with the softened butter. Then, lay the prosciutto slices at the bottom. Break 2 eggs into each ramekin. Add the chopped onions.
- Top with the slice of cheese. Lower the ramekins into the steamer basket in your Power pressure cooker XL. Cover the ramekins with foil.
- Press the RICE/RISOTTO key once to select 6 minutes.
- Place the lid on the Power Pressure Cooker XL, lock the lid and switch the pressure release valve to closed.
- Once the timer reaches 0, the cooker will automatically switch to KEEP WARM/CANCEL mode.
- Switch the pressure release valve to open. Serve warm garnished with fresh parsley.

485. Mashed Carrots and Parsnips

Ready in about 10 minutes
Servings 6

This vegetable mash is economical, hearty and abundant. Above all, root vegetables are one of the easiest foods to cook in the Power pressure cooker XL. What more could you wish for?

Per serving: 74 Calories; 3.9g Fat; 9.6g Carbs; 0.7g Protein; 3.4g Sugars

Ingredients

1 ½ cups parsnips, peeled and sliced
2 cups carrots, peeled and sliced
2 tablespoons butter, softened
Salt and black pepper, to taste
1 ½ cups water

Directions

- Fill the cooker's base with 1 ½ cups of water; add a metal rack. Place the parsnips and carrots in the steamer basket. Lower the basket onto the rack.
- Press the FISH/VEGETABLES/STEAM key; use the cook time selector to adjust to 4 minutes.
- Place the lid on the Power Pressure Cooker XL, lock the lid and switch the pressure release valve to closed.
- Once the timer reaches 0, the cooker will automatically switch to KEEP WARM/CANCEL mode.
- Switch the pressure release valve to open. Mash the vegetables with butter, and season with salt and pepper. Enjoy!

486. Minimalist Strawberry Jelly

Ready in about 20 minutes
Servings 12

The Power pressure cooker XL has so many practical uses! For example, you can make a homemade jelly for your peanut butter and toast in 10 minutes. Who would have thought it?

Per serving: 83 Calories; 0.2g Fat; 21.5g Carbs; 0.4g Protein; 19.8g Sugars

Ingredients

1 ½ pounds strawberries, hulled and halved
1 cup sugar
1 ½ ounces fresh orange juice

Directions

- Arrange the strawberries in the Power pressure cooker XL.
- Sprinkle the sugar over the top of the strawberries; allow it to stand for 15 minutes. Pour in the fresh orange juice.
- Press the FISH/VEGETABLES/STEAM key once to select 2 minutes. Place the lid on the Power Pressure Cooker XL, lock the lid and switch the pressure release valve to closed.
- Once the timer reaches 0, the cooker will automatically switch to KEEP WARM/CANCEL mode. Switch the pressure release valve to open.
- Mix with an immersion blender to achieve a jelly texture. Store in an airtight container in the refrigerator. Enjoy!

487. Colorful Millet and Vegetable Salad

Ready in about 25 minutes
Servings 4

This is a versatile salad, so you can add your favorite ingredients to boost this basic recipe. Add chopped nuts, shredded cheese or hard-boiled eggs and delight your family.

Per serving: 494 Calories; 21.8g Fat; 65.4g Carbs; 10.4g Protein; 4g Sugars

Ingredients

1 ½ cups millet
1 cup kale, chopped
2 onions, sliced thin
2 carrots, chopped
1/2 cup broth
1 tablespoon cider vinegar
2 tablespoons butter
1 tablespoon minced garlic
2 sprigs dried thyme
1/4 cup olive oil
1/3 teaspoon cayenne pepper
1/2 teaspoon cumin seeds
1/3 teaspoon freshly ground black pepper
1 teaspoon sea salt
3 cups water

Directions

- Stir the millet, water, and vinegar into the Power pressure cooker XL. Press the SOUP/STEW key once to select 10 minutes.
- Place the lid on the Power Pressure Cooker XL, lock the lid and switch the pressure release valve to closed.
- Once the timer reaches 0, the cooker will automatically switch to KEEP WARM/CANCEL mode.
- Rinse the millet, fluff with a fork, and reserve.
- Then, place a nonstick skillet over a moderate heat; warm the butter; sauté the garlic, onions and carrots until just tender, about 4 minutes.
- Now, add the broth, kale, and thyme. Press the BEANS/LENTILS key once to select 5 minutes. Press the CANCEL key.
- Add the sautéed mixture to the reserved millet. Stir to combine and transfer to the refrigerator.
- Dress the salad with the other ingredients. Serve well-chilled and enjoy!

488. Tofu Scramble with Sautéed Veggies

Ready in about 20 minutes
Servings 4

An exceptional, fruity flavor of tomato gives the dish a unique touch, so make sure to choose fresh, ripe tomatoes. Serve with multi-grain bread.

Per serving: 226 Calories; 10.8g Fat; 26.9g Carbs; 9.8g Protein; 9.1g Sugars

Ingredients

12 ounces firm tofu, drained and mashed
3 cloves garlic, minced
2 tablespoons peanut oil
2 shallots, chopped
1 cup parsnips, chopped
1 fresh tomato, diced
1/4 cup fresh parsley, chopped
2 teaspoons dry cherry
1/3 teaspoon black pepper
1/2 teaspoon salt
1 teaspoon red pepper flakes, crushed
3 cups water

Directions

- In a mixing dish, combine the tofu, dry sherry, salt, crushed red pepper flakes and black pepper. Next, press the CHICKEN/MEAT key and bring the peanut oil to medium warmth.
- Sauté the shallots, garlic, parsnips, and tomato until the vegetables are tender, about 5 minutes. Add the water to the Power pressure cooker XL.
- Press the FISH/VEGETABLES/STEAM key and use the cook time selector to adjust to 4 minutes.
- Place the lid on the Power Pressure Cooker XL, lock the lid and switch the pressure release valve to closed.
- Once the timer reaches 0, the cooker will automatically switch to KEEP WARM/CANCEL mode. Afterwards, serve topped with fresh parsley. Enjoy!

489. Delicious Pizza Beans

Ready in about 35 minutes
Servings 6

Pizza in a bowl! Seriously, this is a bowl full of beans, cheese and meat that all together taste like pizza!

Per serving: 397 Calories; 7.3g Fat; 45.4g Carbs; 37.9g Protein; 2.3g Sugars

Ingredients

2 cups kidney beans, soaked overnight
1/2 cup parmesan cheese, freshly grated
1 ½ cups ground beef
4 ounces sliced prosciutto, diced
1/4 cup tomato puree
2 shallots, diced
4 cups broth
1/3 teaspoon dried oregano
1 teaspoon sea salt
1/3 teaspoon ground black pepper, or to taste
1/3 teaspoon cayenne pepper
1 teaspoon dry basil

Directions

- Add all of the above ingredients, except for cheese, to your Power pressure cooker XL.
- Stir to combine and choose the BEANS/LENTILS key. Then, use the cook time selector to adjust to 30 minutes.
- Place the lid on the Power Pressure Cooker XL, lock the lid and switch the pressure release valve to closed.
- Once the timer reaches 0, the cooker will automatically switch to KEEP WARM/CANCEL mode
- Serve warm topped with cheese and enjoy!

490. Pressure Cooked Eggs de Provence

Ready in about 20 minutes
Servings 4

Customize with your favorite toppings like black olives and don't forget to serve lots of crusty bread on the side!

Per serving: 480 Calories; 32.8g Fat; 14.4g Carbs; 31.8g Protein; 2.2g Sugars

Ingredients

8 eggs
1 ¼ cups fried bacon de Provence, chopped
1/2 cup goat cheese, crumbled
1 cup cream
1 ½ cups kale, torn into pieces
2 shallots, chopped
1/2 teaspoon dried oregano
1/2 teaspoon dried savory
1/2 teaspoon dried marjoram
1/2 teaspoon dried thyme
1 teaspoon sea salt
1/3 teaspoon ground black pepper
4 tablespoons water

Directions

- In a mixing bowl, whisk the eggs along with water and cream.
- Add the remaining ingredients and stir until everything is well combined. Spoon the mixture into a heat-proof dish and cover with a sheet of aluminum foil.
- Add 1 ½ cups of water to the bottom of your Power pressure cooker XL. Place the trivet inside. Lower the dish onto the trivet.
- Press the RICE/RISOTTO key and use the cook time selector to adjust to 18 minutes.
- Place the lid on the Power Pressure Cooker XL, lock the lid and switch the pressure release valve to closed.
- Once the timer reaches 0, the cooker will automatically switch to KEEP WARM/CANCEL mode. Serve warm.

491. Cremini Mushroom and Veggie Spread

Ready in about 20 minutes
Servings 4

Looking for an innovative spread recipe? Whether you want an easy, healthy or luxurious option, this spread will fit the bill!

Per serving: 137 Calories; 3.6g Fat; 24.9g Carbs; 4g Protein; 8g Sugars

Ingredients

1 ½ cups cremini mushrooms, chopped
1 tablespoon butter
2 small-sized shallots, chopped
1 carrot, finely chopped
1 1/3 cups stock
2 medium-sized ripe tomatoes, seeded and finely chopped
1 parsnip, finely chopped
1 celery with leaves, chopped
2 bell peppers, finely chopped
1 teaspoon smashed garlic
1/3 teaspoon ground black pepper
1 teaspoon salt

Directions

- Press the CHICKEN/MEAT key and warm the butter; now, sauté the shallots and garlic until fragrant. Add the vegetables and cook, stirring periodically, for an additional 6 minutes.
- Add the remaining ingredients and press the RICE/RISOTTO key once to select 6 minutes.
- Place the lid on the Power Pressure Cooker XL, lock the lid and switch the pressure release valve to closed.
- Once the timer reaches 0, the cooker will automatically switch to KEEP WARM/CANCEL mode. Allow the pressure to release on its own.
- Serve with your favorite crusty bread.

492. Penne with Meat and Mushroom Sauce

Ready in about 15 minutes
Servings 4

If you're out of ideas for lunch or dinner, give this recipe a try! We opted for a classic ground beef but feel free to use ground turkey or chicken sausage as a substitute.

Per serving: 664 Calories; 19.2g Fat; 70.7g Carbs; 59.8g Protein; 6g Sugars

Ingredients

1 pound dry penne
3/4 pound ground beef
1/2 cup button mushrooms, thinly sliced
1 cup scallions, chopped
1 teaspoon minced garlic
8 ounces Parmesan cheese, freshly grated
2 cups tomato sauce
2 ½ cups water

Directions

- Press the RICE/RISOTO key. Set time to 8 minutes.
- Then, cook the beef until browned; add the scallions, garlic, and mushrooms, and continue sautéing until they're aromatic.
- Stir in the penne, tomato sauce, and water; season to taste; stir to combine well.
- Place the lid on the Power pressure cooker XL, lock the lid and switch the pressure release valve to closed.
- Once the timer reaches 0, the cooker will automatically switch to KEEP WARM. When the steam is completely released, remove the lid.
- Top with grated cheese and serve immediately. Bon appétit!

493. Cheese, Mushroom and Pepper Frittata

Ready in about 30 minutes
Servings 4

This frittata cooks up perfectly in no time in the Power pressure cooker XL. Cheddar or any kind of sharp, yellow cheese will work in this recipe.

Per serving: 209 Calories; 13.8g Fat; 9.2g Carbs; 13.4g Protein; 5.1g Sugars

Ingredients

6 eggs, slightly beaten
1/2 cup Cheddar cheese, grated
1 cup mushrooms, sliced
2 bell peppers, deveined and chopped
1 cup onion, peeled and chopped
2 teaspoons corn oil
3 cloves garlic, minced
1 tablespoon fresh chopped parsley, for garnish
1/2 teaspoon ground black pepper, or to your liking
1/3 teaspoon dried dill weed
1 teaspoon sea salt

Directions

- Add 1 ½ cups of water and a metal rack to the base of your Power pressure cooker XL. Brush a baking dish with a nonstick cooking spray.
- In a skillet, warm the oil and sauté the onions and garlic for 3 minutes; add the mushrooms and peppers and continue sautéing for u further 3 minutes.
- In a mixing dish, beat the remaining ingredients. Now, add the sautéed mixture and stir until everything is well combined.
- Pour the mixture into the greased baking dish. Cover with a piece of foil and lower onto the rack.
- Press the RICE/RISOTTO key and use the cook time selector to adjust to 18 minutes.
- Place the lid on the Power pressure cooker XL, lock the lid and switch the pressure release valve to closed.
- Once the timer reaches 0, the cooker will automatically switch to KEEP WARM. When the steam is completely released, remove the lid. Serve warm.

494. Sweet Potato and Ground Turkey Casserole

Ready in about 25 minutes
Servings 6

Here is an easy cheesy casserole that can be served as a delicious lunch or an elegant dinner. You can substitute Fontina or Parmesan cheese for Gruyère.

Per serving: 570 Calories; 25.7g Fat; 51.6g Carbs; 37.2g Protein; 3.2g Sugars

Ingredients

6 sweet potatoes, peeled and sliced
1 pound ground turkey, crumbled
3 teaspoons olive oil
2 shallots, peeled and chopped
3 cloves garlic, minced
2 bell peppers, chopped
5 eggs, whisked
1 ½ cups Gruyère cheese, shredded
Salt and freshly cracked black pepper, to your liking
1 teaspoon dried basil
1 teaspoon smoked paprika

Directions

- Press the CHICKEN/MEAT key and warm the oil. Now, sauté the shallots, garlic, and bell pepper till tender and fragrant, about 5 minutes. Stir in the ground turkey and continue cooking for 4 more minutes. Press the CANCEL key.
- Add the remaining ingredients to your Power pressure cooker XL.
- Then, press the CHICKEN/MEAT key once to select 15 minutes. Place the lid on the Power pressure cooker XL, lock the lid and switch the pressure release valve to closed.
- Once the timer reaches 0, the cooker will automatically switch to KEEP WARM. When the steam is completely released, remove the lid.
- Taste, adjust the seasonings and serve warm.

495. Colorful Barley Salad

Ready in about 25 minutes
Servings 4

Barley is high in fiber, essential amino acids vitamin B1 thiamine, vitamin B3 niacin, magnesium and selenium.

Per serving: 364 Calories; 10.7g Fat; 59.5g Carbs; 11.3g Protein; 5.3g Sugars

Ingredients

1 ¼ cups pot barley, rinsed and drained
1/2 cup purple onion, thinly sliced
1/2 cup Kalamata olives, pitted and sliced
1 tablespoon grapeseed oil
2 bell peppers, thinly sliced
1 cup grape tomatoes, diced
2 tablespoons vinegar
1/2 cup crumbled goat cheese, to serve
1/3 teaspoon sea salt
1 teaspoon dried basil
1/2 teaspoon dried oregano
1/3 teaspoon ground black pepper
4 cups water

Directions

- Add the barley, water and salt to the Power pressure cooker XL. Press the RICE/RISOTTO key and use the cook time selector to adjust to 18 minutes.
- Place the lid on the Power pressure cooker XL, lock the lid and switch the pressure release valve to closed.
- Once the timer reaches 0, the cooker will automatically switch to KEEP WARM. When the steam is completely released, remove the cooker's lid.
- Transfer the barley to a salad bowl and allow it to cool completely.
- Gently and slowly stir in the rest of the above items. Taste and adjust the seasonings. Bon appétit!

496. Quinoa with Sausage and Vegetables

Ready in about 15 minutes
Servings 6

Quinoa pilaf is an impressive dish that is extra easy to make in the Power pressure cooker XL. Once you taste how good this quinoa is, it will become your family favorite.

Per serving: 316 Calories; 9g Fat; 45.9g Carbs; 13.7g Protein; 3.8g Sugars

Ingredients

2 cups quinoa, rinsed
1 cup parsnips, trimmed and sliced
1 yellow onion, chopped
2 bell peppers, deveined and thinly sliced
3 chicken sausages, sliced
1 teaspoon sea salt
1/3 teaspoon dried basil
1/3 teaspoon ground black pepper, or to taste
1/3 teaspoon cayenne pepper
1 teaspoon dried oregano
2 teaspoons wine vinegar
4 cups water

Directions

- Add all of the above ingredients to the Power pressure cooker XL.
- Choose the RICE/RISOTTO function. Set to 8 minutes. Place the lid on the Power pressure cooker XL, lock the lid and switch the pressure release valve to closed
- Once the timer reaches 0, the cooker will automatically switch to KEEP WARM/CANCEL.
- When the steam is completely released, remove the cooker's lid. Bon appétit!

497. Easy Country Wheat Berries

Ready in about 35 minutes
Servings 4

Ta-da! Your Power pressure cooker XL transforms dull wheat berries into a creamy, family dish with the out-standing flavor of spices and veggies.

Per serving: 170 Calories; 4.7g Fat; 28.2g Carbs; 6.4g Protein; 1.8g Sugars

Ingredients

1 ½ cups wheat berries
1 tablespoon olive oil
1 cup bell peppers, deveined and chopped
1 ½ cups vegetable broth
2 shallots, chopped
3 cups boiling water
1 teaspoon paprika
1/2 teaspoon dried basil
1 teaspoon dried oregano
1 teaspoon paprika

Directions

- Press the SOUP/STEW key and use the cook time selector to adjust to 30 minutes. Warm the oil until sizzling.
- Now, cook the shallots and bell peppers until they are just tender, about 3 minutes.
- Add the remaining ingredients. Place the lid on the Power pressure cooker XL, lock the lid and switch the pressure release valve to closed.
- Once the timer reaches 0, the cooker will automatically switch to KEEP WARM/CANCEL.
- When the steam is completely released, remove the cooker's lid. Bon appétit!

498. Farfalle with Meat and Marinara Sauce

Ready in about 15 minutes
Servings 4

It's easy to cook like an Italian nonna thanks to the Power pressure cooker XL. If you like a rich and spicy flavor, add 1 teaspoon of granulated garlic and 1 dried chile.

Per serving: 411 Calories; 7.4g Fat; 74.8g Carbs; 14.8g Protein; 10.3g Sugars

Ingredients

1 box dry farfalle
1/2 pound ground mixed meat
1 pound tomatoes, finely chopped
2 white onions, peeled and chopped
2 teaspoons white sugar
1 teaspoon garlic, crushed
3 teaspoons grapeseed oil
2 teaspoons dried parsley
1/2 teaspoon salt
1/3 teaspoon freshly ground black pepper, or to taste
1/3 teaspoon dried oregano
1 teaspoon smoked cayenne pepper
1 tablespoon capers

Directions

- Press the RICE/RISOTO key. Set time to 8 minutes. Heat the oil until sizzling.
- Then, cook the onions and garlic until they're aromatic. Add the ground meat and continue cooking until browned.
- Press the CANCEL key. Stir in the remaining ingredients; stir to combine well.
- Place the lid on the Power pressure cooker XL, lock the lid and switch the pressure release valve to closed.
- Once the timer reaches 0, the cooker will automatically switch to KEEP WARM. Press the CANCEL key. When the steam is completely released, remove the lid.
- Top with grated cheese and serve immediately. Bon appétit!

499. Honey and Pineapple Breakfast Risotto

Ready in about 15 minutes
Servings 6

Honey and tropical pineapple make it easy to give every recipe a little something extra. Save your time with this speedy homemade risotto and amaze your family!

Per serving: 381 Calories; 4.8g Fat; 80.5g Carbs; 4.9g Protein; 29.5g Sugars

Ingredients

2 cups white rice
1/2 cup honey
1 cup pineapple, crushed
1 cup orange juice
2 tablespoons ghee
2 cardamom pods
1/2 vanilla bean
1/3 cup water

Directions

- Add all of the above ingredient, except for pineapple and honey, to your Power pressure cooker XL.
- Press the RICE/RISOTTO key once to select 6 minutes.
- Place the lid on the Power pressure cooker XL, lock the lid and switch the pressure release valve to closed.
- Once the timer reaches 0, the cooker will automatically switch to KEEP WARM. Press the CANCEL key. When the steam is completely released, remove the lid.
- Serve topped with pineapple and honey. Bon appétit!

500. Steamed Eggs with Swiss Chard

Ready in about 25 minutes
Servings 4

It's easy to make breakfast for the whole family with the eggs, sour cream and leafy greens. These eggs are a great choice for Sunday breakfast, or even dinner because they reheat well. It is definitely worth trying!

Per serving: 161 Calories; 10.7g Fat; 7.3g Carbs; 9.8g Protein; 3g Sugars

Ingredients

6 eggs
1 cup Swiss chard, torn into pieces
1/3 sour cream
2 white onions, finely chopped
2 cloves garlic, minced
1/3 teaspoon kosher salt
1/3 teaspoon freshly ground black pepper
1 teaspoon cayenne pepper
1/3 teaspoon dried dill weed

Directions

- Start by mixing the eggs and sour cream in a bowl. Now, add the egg/milk mixture to a lightly greased heat-proof bowl
- Stir in the rest of the above ingredients; mix to combine well. Add 1 ½ cups of water and a metal trivet to the base of your Power pressure cooker XL.
- Lower the heat-proof bowl onto the trivet.
- Press the RICE/RISOTTO key and use the cook time selector to adjust to 18 minutes.
- Place the lid on the Power Pressure Cooker XL, lock the lid and switch the pressure release valve to closed.
- Once the timer reaches 0, the cooker will automatically switch to KEEP WARM/CANCEL mode.
- Switch the pressure release valve to open. When the steam is completely released, remove the cooker's lid. Serve warm.

65828159R00153

Made in the USA
San Bernardino, CA
06 January 2018